HEYDAY

Publications by the Author

Dore Schary

HEYDAY

An Autobiography

Little, Brown and Company   Boston — Toronto

Second Printing

The photograph on page 230 is from the MGM release BATAAN © 1943 Loew's
Inc. Copyright renewed 1970 by Metro-Goldwyn-Mayer Inc. The photograph on
page 118 is from the MGM release JOURNEY FOR MARGARET © 1942 Loew's
Inc. Copyright renewed 1969 by Metro-Goldwyn-Mayer Inc.

LIBRARY OF CONGRESS CATALOGING IN PUBLICATION DATA

Schary, Dore.
  Heyday: an autobiography.

  Includes index.
    1. Schary, Dore—Biography. 2. Dramatists,
American—20th century—Biography. 3. Moving-picture
producers and directors—United States—Biography.
I. Title.
PS3537.C253Z523   812'.5'4   79-91255
ISBN 0-316-77270-4

MV
Designed by Susan Windheim

Published simultaneously in Canada
by Little, Brown & Company (Canada) Limited

PRINTED IN THE UNITED STATES OF AMERICA

To
Good Friends
Many Gone
Many Here
With Thanks and Love

heyday: An expression of frolick and exultation, and sometimes of wonder.

From Samuel Johnson's
English Dictionary

Acknowledgments

My thanks are tendered with gratitude to those who helped me fashion this book. It was Robert Emmett Ginna, Jr., who approved the form and suggested the substance. Melissa Clemence, who meticulously edited the script with hundreds of markings and scores of "green flags" that indicated errors and pitfalls, also asked me provocative questions and made me give answers.

At the University of Wisconsin, a magnificent archival building containing state history records and the papers of many politicians also protects and preserves the letters and records and scripts of authors, playwrights, and screenwriters. Mr. Tino Balio long years ago persuaded me to move my scrapbooks, pictures, letters, and even my totally worthless receipted bills to the marbled repository at Madison. More than that, he gave me the opportunity to visit Wisconsin, where I could work quietly and happily. His staff aided me in sorting out needed and sometimes forgotten material. Mr. Balio and his aide, Julie D'Acci, assisted by Christine Rongon, who works directly with the archives, have my profound thanks.

Allen and Laura Rivkin were good enough to read the first few chapters in their raw state and encourage me to press forward.

My dear wife, Miriam, typed a rough copy of the first hundred pages of the manuscript and got me on the way. From there on three ladies labored over the typing and retyping of the script. I am indebted to Cory Shaw, a loyal friend and ally, who got first crack at the manuscript. She was followed by Betty Tash, who in turn was followed by Marcia Hammer. Miss Tash did the cleanup.

To all of them thanks.

Miriam remained patient during the two years it took to finish my labors; my son, Jeb, remained impatient wanting to know if I would include his favorite anecdotes; my daughter Jill refused to read the book "until it's in galleys," arguing that writers can be too picky about other writers' work; and daughter Joy, working for the last two years to get her qualifications for family counseling, did not disturb me except to ask, "When can I read it?"

So I worked to ease Miriam's patience, Jeb's impatience, obtain the galleys for Jill, and provide Joy with an opportunity to get a copy of the script. Now they can all read it.

HEYDAY

O n the nineteenth of November, 1956, the Monday before Thanksgiving, I was in New York on my way to Joe Vogel's office at MGM. He had recently been elevated to the position of president of Loew's, Inc., which was the parent company of MGM films.

There had been seismic rumblings in the trade press and some of the weekly journals indicating that my job as head of the studio and vice-president in charge of production was in jeopardy. Stories about executives who are about to be jettisoned are seldom totally fictitious. Most often they are planted from "a reliable source."

Therefore, on the previous Tuesday I had called Vogel to ask if he intended to issue a statement denying the recurring rumors of my soon-to-be departure. His answer told me all I wanted to know: "I'm not going to make any statements, and I don't want you to make any, and I want you to be in New York by next Monday morning." Joe had been president for only three weeks and his telephone voice had abruptly switched from "Hi, Dore" to "This is your leader!"

My wife, Miriam, and I arrived in New York Sunday morning. When I called Vogel to ask if we could meet that day rather than Monday morning, he said no. He would have his secretary call me and tell me when to come to his office — very likely it would be around eleven o'clock.

I told Miriam to enjoy the day and prophesied it would be her last day as the wife of the head of MGM. "By tomorrow you'll be the wife of an unemployed former writer."

So that Monday morning I was walking from the Sherry-Netherland Hotel west on Central Park South to Seventh Avenue and was strolling toward the Loew building between West Forty-sixth and West Forty-fifth streets. Since I had started early, I was walking slowly, feeling a bit as if I were in a tumbrel, knowing that I was headed for the guillotine but not knowing why.

In times of distress I had always suggested to my kids to tote up lists of good things and bad things — the pluses and minuses — the affirmatives and the negatives. That's what I was doing.

Affirmative, plus, good: I was fifty-one, in good health, and was quite strong. Miriam, whom I adore, and I had been married for over twenty-four years; we had three children, Jill, twenty, Joy, eighteen, Jeb, sixteen. We owned a home free and clear in Brentwood, California, and had between us and the kids six cars, scads of clothing, jewelry, no debts, and about eighty thousand in cash and bonds. We also had a host of good friends and many interests besides film in political, community, and Jewish affairs. Finally, I had a library of about three thousand books that had given me a liberal education.

Negative, minus, bad: My rueful reckoning reminded me that I had made millions in California but had watched them hustle through my fingers for taxes, charities, the care of a number of people, extravagances, and a lack of interest in future security. Also, I knew that in a few days when public announcements were made, I would be identified as the "former head of MGM." Having seen the fate of former studio heads, including the most famous, I knew that in California you could, with such a forlorn identity, disappear without a trace, much as a stone can be slipped into water without leaving a ripple. There was no bitterness in that observation. I simply knew it was true in Hollywood as it was in politics. It is a tribal rite. The chief is dead — long live the chief. Since it had been so for L. B. Mayer, it certainly was going to be so for me. (It occurred to me that the staff always called the new man "Chief," perhaps to avoid forgetting whom they were addressing — it wouldn't have done to call me "L.B.") Also on my minus list was the manner in which I suspected Vogel (this new president of MGM) was going to dump the manure on my head.

Finally, I was in front of the Loew building, and a minute later I was in Vogel's office.

He gave me a pleasant hello, told me to sit down, said I looked in good shape, and wasted no more time in amenities.

"I think we ought to get right to it, Dore. I want you to get out — right away. I want to finish this off. I don't want to put any pressure on you; you're too nice a man for that. I personally have never had anything personal against you. You've been a gentleman — but it's best all around that we wind this up. People are talking."

I asked, "Which people and what are they saying?"

"Lots of people. You've got enemies on the board of directors, among the stockholders, and in the studio. They don't say good things about you. You made enemies — don't work as a team — and your outside activities —" he waved a hand to indicate what they were — "speeches, all the committees and this political stuff with Stevenson — I get a lot of letters complaining."

When I asked to see some of them, he reached into his desk drawer and offered one letter three pages long typed with a blue ribbon on yellow paper. It was signed, "A loyal Studio Employee." It listed among other charges that I had been sleeping with many of our glamorous female stars (it was with some regret that I knew this was not so); that I encouraged male stars to lose to me in gin games in exchange for assigning them juicy roles (that one made me smile as I thought of Tracy, Gable, Gene Kelly, Robert Taylor submitting to such a hustle); that I had commanded studio personnel to work for the Stevenson campaign (the sad fact was that my co-executives and most of the workers were anti-Stevenson and marching in step to Eisenhower's drum).

I looked up at Vogel once or twice as I was reading the list of my malefactions. His tightly skinned skull, always carefully barbered, looked particularly pale. His hair, flesh, eyes, and nails were pale. He was an immaculate dresser who wore starched cuffs and collar. He was wearing his new cloak of El Presidente with enjoyment and snappy authority. After a careful reading of the letter, I asked if there were others — "What about the ones from the stockholders?" Vogel told me they were more or less alike. "The directors?" The same.

He said there was no sense reading any of the others and he added that he didn't want to demean me by taking away my secretaries, offices, phones, and privileges — "You don't deserve *that*." However, it was clear that was exactly what he intended to do if I didn't place my head on the block pronto.

Arthur Loew, former president of Loew's, who had recently returned to his post as head of foreign distribution, entered the office in late response to Vogel's request that he join us to watch my execution. Vogel related what he had said and asked if Arthur had anything to add. He did.

Arthur looked straight at me and said, "I came here to tell you that your record is better than you know it to be. I think it is idiotic that you are being fired. All this is because of Mayer's fight with Schenck [Mayer had resigned in 1951] to regain control." He went on, "You're a victim.

[5]

I'm sorry this had to happen." Arthur turned back to Vogel and added, "If there's nothing else —" There wasn't, and Arthur shook hands with me and left.

Vogel asked me to come in the next day to settle up. "We want to make this quick — confidentially, Sol Siegel is taking over — and David Tannenbaum is trying to work out our deal with Sol."

After a short pause, I told Joe Vogel I'd be back Wednesday with my lawyer and business manager, waved a farewell, and left without a satisfactory punch line. There was no way to top Loew's exit. And no way to recover easily from learning that my attorney, Tannenbaum, had been aware of what was happening and was dealing another deck of cards, cutting me out of the game.

So here it was, Monday, I was walking back to the hotel, and my head was clear but empty; I had no plans — no dreams of reprisal — no anger — just an uneasy sense that I had been bushwhacked and that I had to sit down somewhere and put things together. I got in a cab and went back to Miriam.

Her response to the news was predictable. She was furious at Vogel, and at me for not being in the same state. Why wasn't I preparing a counterattack? I should employ a press agent to tell my side of the story. I had to defend my record. I had to stick their lies down their throats. In those days Miriam threw things when she was storming. Pillows went flying around the room. After a while I tried to answer, but off she went again steaming and cursing. The rest of the scene was equally predictable. I became impatient with her. Instead of unloading on Vogel I turned my bottled-up anger on her. I don't like scenes and she was making one — and — and . . .

Miriam is frightened by my temper, but whether it was fear or temper that quieted her is immaterial. The fact is we quieted down. I suggested we have some lunch. Miriam went in to dry her tears and I resumed my chain-smoking. (Thank God I gave that up years ago.)

Before room service arrived with the food, Miriam and I talked softly. I explained that in show business, statements and counterstatements were useless. In times of failure, you are like a ball player who has just struck out. There is no point in charging that the umpire was blind or the pitcher had used a spitball or the catcher had tipped the bat. There was only one effective way to stop the boos — the next time at bat, get a hit.

We held each other. Miriam murmured, "Joe Vogel is a dirty rat bastard." After we ate our lunch I called Lew Wasserman (at that time

[6]

the head of the MCA talent agency), who suggested I call William Fitelson to act as my attorney. I had met Fitelson in California and remembered him as a direct, tough-minded man. After I sketched out the Vogel scene to Lew, he said, "Just be sure you get all that's due you on the contract."

Then I called Tannenbaum and, never raising my voice, ordered him to return my files, informed him he was no longer my attorney or my friend, and hung up. Miriam got infuriated all over again because I hadn't called David obscene names. She calmed when I reached Bill Fitelson, who said he'd be glad to handle my affairs. Instead of discussing the situation on the phone, he'd come to the hotel the following morning at nine.

One more call to California and I had lined up all the ducks. Morgan Maree, who was my business manager, agreed to be in New York the next night and would meet Fitelson and me early Wednesday before we joined forces to talk with Vogel.

I left a message with Vogel's secretary that we would be in his office Wednesday at three o'clock. Suddenly I was tired. I took a long nap after deciding not to speak to anyone else. We had tickets to *Auntie Mame* for that night. We went — liked it — but both of us were thinking of other things.

We called Jill and her new husband, Jon, then spoke to Joy and Jeb. Miriam and I both played "happy-talk" — the children could wait for a day or two before we hit them with the news.

Miriam drank a glass of sherry and soon fell asleep. I lay in bed looking out at the skyline; as I started to say my nightly prayer my mind wandered. In the spring of that year MGM had copped thirty-one Academy nominations — twice what our nearest competitors had captured. Most lists of ten best pictures had included somewhere in their lineup *Blackboard Jungle*, or *Bad Day at Black Rock*, *Trial*, *Love Me or Leave Me*, or *I'll Cry Tomorrow*, all of which had made money along with *High Society*. *Cat on a Hot Tin Roof*, *Gigi*, and *Ben Hur* were almost ready to go — as a matter of fact *Ben Hur* was doing second-unit work.

I realized I had mouthed my Hebrew prayers without thinking of them. I took a deep breath, cleared my head, recited my prayers aware of what each word meant, then knew that my tranquilizer for the future would be my experiences of the past.

2

*F*ortunately, *my memory* is a long one. I knew from stories told me and from my family and career that most often when a door closes, another one opens. I was accustomed to and knew about success and failure.

Dr. Max Danzis brought me into this world early in the morning of August 31, 1905. I was told I was an exceedingly homely child but that I didn't cry very much.

At my *bris* (circumcision rite) I was given the Hebrew name Yitzhak Ben Herschel — Isaac, Son of Herschel (Herman). Isaac, in turn, became one of the other anglicized forms, Isadore; others are Ike, Irving, Irvin, Erwin. When I was thirteen, a friend of the family, Mrs. Kridel, suggested that my name be circumcised to Dore. My Zayde (Yiddish for Grandfather) approved the change for two reasons. First, I had had a string of illnesses, diphtheria, appendicitis, tonsilitis, and been hit by a truck and badly banged up, so, according to Jewish folklore, a change of name might come in handy by keeping evil spirits away. Second, Dore is Hebrew. *Dor* means "generation." *E* is the personal pronoun singular for "my." Our last name, Schary, means "gate" in Hebrew. Therefore in the Holy Tongue my name suddenly became rather distinctive, "Gate to my Generation." However, to my high-school buddies I remained "Izzy" or "Is" for a few more years, then they accepted the change as did I.

The childhood diseases paid me visitations. I scraped my knees, had street fights, learned to be alternately frightened and brave. My maternal grandmother, Jennie Drachler, taught me my first Hebrew prayer, the Kria'th Shma, the prayer of affirmation, that I've repeated almost every night of my life since I was eleven.

My father, Herman Hugo Schary, gave me a fiery temper but my mother, Belle, helped me to use it sparingly and experience put check-reins on it. Both Mother and Father were extravagant. All the Schary children inherited their disregard for saving; money was made to be spent — for the best medical attention, for charity, clothes, parties, good times, and to help family and friends.

Father was tall, corpulent, and heavily muscled, had a good voice, dressed in custom-made clothes, dreamed beautiful dreams and made some of them come true; others turned into nightmares.

Mother was patient, extremely responsive to people, always punctual, kept promises to herself and others and urged that I do the same. She was beautiful, gracious, and dressed with perfect taste.

Both Mother and Father had energy, humor, liked to dance and sing, and possessed strong opinions, buttressed by stubbornness. They handed these over to me.

Both my parents were emigrants from Russia. Pa was born in Riga in 1873, Ma in Bialystok in 1875. They had traveled different routes to get to Brooklyn — Pa alone by way of Siberia to Vladivostok to Japan to San Francisco to the Empire State of New York; Ma with her sister Bessie, brother Jack, and parents to Hamburg and then to New York in steerage accommodations. My mother and Aunt Bessie worked in shirtwaist factories. My mother's father, Baruch Drachler, worked in hat factories.

Pa was Mother's second choice but after a short engagement they were married, opened a delicatessen store that failed, and moved to Newark because my maternal grandfather, Zayde, had friends from Bialystok who had settled there. Over a period of many years, my parents worked unprofitably in restaurants and peddled decorative holiday and birthday cards. Pa also became a decorator of public buildings but fell off the City Hall while draping the outside in black bunting on the occasion of McKinley's assassination. He broke a leg, thus ending that career. He then went into the business of decorating barroom mirrors for holidays, while Mother drove our horse, Jimmy, and carriage to outlying areas to sell bundles of cards.

For many summers, my family rented and ran boardinghouses in Bradley Beach, Manasquan, and Belmar, all in New Jersey, the summer profits providing funds for winter living. This activity ultimately led them into a kosher catering career in Newark and the business thrived. Pa was an imaginative decorator, Ma a wonderful cook, and between them they fashioned an establishment that gave the family a wide reputation. Even now I meet people who tell me that their parents were married or that they were bar mitzvahed in Schary Manor.

My parents had five children — my brother Sam, ten years older than I; Max, who died of brain fever when he was a year old; Frances, five years older than I; Lillian, born in 1902; and I. Sam and Max were born in Brooklyn; Frances, Lil, and I, in Newark, New Jersey.

An observer could call us a happy family. Pa told stories of his adventures in Russia, China, and Japan. (I believe most of them were mythical.) He had also spent time in England on his first trip away from his native land, where he had sold matches on street corners and had organized a group of even younger boys to peddle the boxes he bought as a wholesaler. With his profits, he bought a fur-collared coat, ivory-handled cane, and spats. He grew a tentative mustache and at eighteen returned to his home in triumph. His father, known to us in later years as Grosspapa, slapped his face and ordered him out for having run away three years before. That's when Pa left Riga and went east to Siberia and Japan.

Pa also sang Russian and German songs, and since all of us could carry a tune with some clarity, we all joined in. Most evenings were happy and melodious, but there were quarrels and debates and angry pinochle games. Occasionally, something important would happen.

I remember Zayde bringing a guest home from the synagogue. His name was Ben Yehudah, the compiler of the first modern Hebrew dictionary. A small man with a Vandyke beard and obvious intensity, he captivated us, and I've never forgotten him even though at the time I understood little or nothing of what was going on. When he left, Zayde recited a prayer of thanks for having been in the company of a great man.

My fingers still feel the touch of our green velour mahogany furniture, which was classy but uncomfortable. (If rubbed one way, it was smooth, the other way it scratched like a cat.) We had a Victrola and later a piano that Lil, my aggressive sister, used to attack with fervor but little skill. Pa filled the house with fancy vases, artificial flowers, and a large figure of a seminude lady with a clock stuck in her belly.

When we moved to High Street, then a fashionable residential street, to establish our first Schary Manor, it was Pa who did the decorating. His taste ran to rococo design and massive chandeliers. Mother had no feeling for furniture or decoration; her interest in the future of Schary Manor was the food, the relationship with the customers, and keeping Pa's explosive and violent temper in check — the one clear failure in Mother's record.

Those young years at home, in the boardinghouses and Schary

Manor, gave me early training and interest in show business. During World War I, I sang on street corners to help sell Thrift Stamps and War Bonds. I also performed in hospitals for sick and wounded dough-boys. I accompanied ditties such as "Long Boy (Good Bye Pa, Good Bye Ma, etc.)," "Keep Your Head Down Fritzie Boy," "There's a Hundred Million Others Like Me," "The Old Fall River Line," "Lena Is the Queen of Palestina," and the like with hand gestures and grimaces that might not have been attractive, but were certainly energetic. Lil worked this gig with me; between us we sold a lot of stamps and bonds.

My repertoire increased during the years with recitals of "Gunga Din," "To Be or Not to Be," "The Road to Mandalay," "Trees," and other conventional shots.

As Schary Manor prospered, charity and political banquets were booked, giving our family eye-to-eye meetings and often handshake introductions to Jewish heroes Samuel Gompers, Louis Brandeis, Louis Marshall, and Benny Leonard, and Gentile celebrities President (then Governor) Woodrow Wilson, President (then Vice-President) Calvin Coolidge, and Eugene V. Debs. Show people who came to entertain included Vincent Lopez, the Ingraham Brothers, and Fannie Brice. It was a busy and lively time that stoked my interests in theater and public life.

The four most active participants of our family in the world of Schary Manor were Mother, Father, my sister Lil, and me. Frances had her own career as a business executive secretary. Sam was forever taking trips on behalf of new associations and wildcat ventures. Mother ruled the kitchen and pantry and the staff in both these areas with authority based on the respect and affection that everyone had for her. She worked laboriously and knew more than anyone under her command. Pa was feared but his Manor was the most handsome, the best run, and the most prestigious in New Jersey. We catered banquets throughout the state.

When I was young, I used to watch closely as Mother's hands stuffed chicken halves (with a special recipe that had the consistency of a pâté) or wait suspensefully as she spread the tissue-thin dough for strudel and then carefully, after showering the dough with raisins, chopped nuts, cinnamon, sugar, and minced orange peel, roll the finished product by pulling the tablecloth without dashing everything to the floor. I saw her chop pike, carp, and whitefish and then form small loaves of gefilte fish; make noodles, farfel, ramekins, matzo balls, and sweet and sour sauce for the smoked hot tongue appetizer. Also, Mother handled most of the arrangements with those who came to contract for family celebrations such as weddings, Bar Mitzvahs, anniversaries, and the like.

Finally, it was Mother with her extraordinary energy reserves who was the supreme hostess; after the meal was served, Mother would, as the speeches were being made, retire to her room, bathe, rest for a few minutes, recoup her strength, then dress in one of her many gowns and make an appearance in time to greet the guests as they exited from the banquet hall. Immediately, she was the main attraction surrounded by admiring men and women who adored her and complimented her on the food and the service and asked, "Belle, how do you do it? You look as though you just came back from a holiday in Atlantic City."

Pa was the gambler, the dreamer, the boss. Schary Manor (over the years there were three of them in different locations) was his creation and each chair, spoon, glass, napkin belonged to him. It was his possessive and paternal view toward his establishment that later aided me in understanding the lords of Hollywood who eyed their studio castles in the same autocratic fashion. Pa's taste was a bit gaudy but he had flair. He also was extremely wary of small expenses; turning off unnecessary lights was a constant preoccupation. However, his clothes were carefully tailored, his cigars were the most expensive, he tipped lavishly, and the china, napery, and crystal in Schary Manor were the best. He disliked people who stood on chairs, tucked napkins into their shirt collars, and hammered silverware on dishes for applause. Since this dislike was coupled with his temper and hamlike fists, he, on a few occasions, had sharp exchanges with guests that ended with Pa flooring the unfortunate celebrants. Once a bootlegger pulled a gun on Pa, holding it tight against his stomach. A silent exchange of looks followed while we held our breath. Then when the bootlegger's eyes told Pa he would not shoot, Pa's right hand smashed the gun away and his left hand knocked the gangster down. Pa then helped the man up, returned the gun to him, and everyone breathed again as the bootlegger and Pa shook hands.

Later, he and Mother talked about this and Pa's predilection for getting into fights with people when he corrected their table manners, and Pa said, "People don't eat with knives at Schary Manor." Mother's answer was charming: "That's right. People at Schary Manor get a punch in the nose from Hugo Schary."

When L. B. Mayer, many years later, began to berate me, I started to walk out of his office and he warned me, "You don't walk out on *me*. I've got a mean temper." I said, "L.B., my father had a temper that makes yours look like a tea party." Then I went back to my office.

Pa was the thunder, Ma the zephyr.

Lil had an exceptionally good contralto voice and wanted to use it

The kid on Zayde's right is my cousin Sam Pocker; that's me with the pacifier and bowlegs on Zayde's left — lost the pacifier, still got the bowlegs

Left to right: Brother Sam, me, Pa (looking like Pancho Villa), sister Frances, sister Lillian, and fake automobile

A high-school play written by our English teacher, B.J.R. Stolper, in the center. I'm next to him in the purple toga. I was playing King Ametus. The fellow fourth from my left is the future director Anthony Mann, who scored a sensational entrance when he came on, bowed to me, and revealed he was not wearing his underpants.

At a YMHA camp bordering on Lake Tiorati near Bear Mountain I had led a squad of campers on a long bike ride. We rested, then marched into camp singing, "A hundred miles to go . . ." We got a rousing welcome, and I remembered it years later for the finish of Battleground.

professionally but never followed up on her impulses. She sang "Oh, Promise Me" at hundreds of weddings and entertained with renditions of "Roses Are Blooming in Picardy" and "Moonlight and Roses." Lil ran the checkroom but as time went by she abdicated, leaving the money-making domain to my care. The typing of contracts, ordering of flowers, booking of orchestras became Lil's obligations, along with acting as hostess at many of the affairs.

I drove the maroon panel truck that picked up and delivered. (It also improved my love life since the blanketed floor of a truck is a lot more comfortable than the backseat of a car.) I also assisted in, then ran, the checkroom, and worked in the pantry making fruit salads and positioning food for the waiter's trays. Later on, I helped as maître d' or porter or waiter. Listening to hundreds of after-dinner speeches, I began to rate them as to content, timing, and delivery. Some men made fools of themselves and others moved me to tears or great laughter. At fund-raising dinners, some donations of a million dollars by Louis Bamberger and Felix Fuld were made simply and briefly and others of a hundred dollars with a lengthy flourish.

Some public figures like Debs and Wilson made unforgettable impressions; others, Coolidge for one, lacked stature and imprint. Brandeis looked like a Supreme Court justice, Gompers like a cigar maker. Both of them spoke like prophets.

My exposure to these disparate experiences and people undoubtedly gave me the confidence to speak to audiences and taught me a few things about how to do it.

My first sorry attempts at original poetry, stories, and plays, written with the encouragement of Kenyon Nicholson, who was directing an amateur group in Newark, moved me into theater as actor and director. In 1925, I became a Young Men's Hebrew Association boys' camp dramatic counselor and spent three pleasurable summers at Lake Tiorati, New York. This activity was followed by work in the Borscht Circuit at Grossinger's with Don Hartman and at the Flagler with Moss Hart.

Those days in the Catskills, if nothing else, endowed me with chutzpah. Fearlessly, I designed scenery, wrote original musical librettos with Moss and Don, acted as Pastor Manders in *Ghosts*, led the orchestra in comedy routines, sang, danced, and played sketches that Eddie Cantor, Frank Fay, and the Avon Comedy Four had made famous. They survived our performances.

With great energy resources plus raw ambition, the twenty-eight members of the staff at the Flagler Hotel performed a "straight play" each Friday night, a musical on Saturday, and a revue on Sunday. We ran Amateur Night for guests on Monday, campfires and ghost stories on Tuesday, a dance contest on Wednesday, and Game Night on Thursday.

Rehearsals were late at night or during the mornings and afternoons. The best ball players played on the softball team that challenged neighborhood rival hotels once a week. I was always put in right field, where I would be least harmful.

We also socialized. Since we were young and aggressive, this fraternizing often took us into rooms with single ladies or with willing wives (whose husbands showed up on Friday nights and left Sunday afternoons) as joyous partners in bed games.

I also had the job of getting out a daily gossip sheet that had to be on the breakfast tables each morning. It was there regularly but often misspelled, dull, and triple-spaced to make up for the lack of information or sleep.

Everyone on the staff earned their keep, including the ancillary benefits of stolen salami, gifts, and sex.

I've written of my young days in *For Special Occasions* and there is little to add to that account, which dealt with Schary Manor and ended with the death of my sister Frances, who in 1926 died of Hodgkin's disease when she was twenty-six.

By then, I had committed myself to working in the theater, a decision deplored by my father but tolerated by my mother.

What Pa wanted was for me to have a diploma that identified me as respectable; a lawyer, doctor, or dentist would have pleased him. He would have settled for my being a CPA — anything but the theater, where he was positive I'd end up as a bum.

For some years I thought he might be right.

3

Before Frances's death, my parents had sold Schary Manor and retired from business affairs. My father was fifty-three, my mother fifty-one. I was told they had a quarter of a million dollars, a sizable sum at that time.

When Frances died, they changed their plans — or rather, my father did. Mother, I believe, would have been content to work on behalf of her various charities, but Pa was restless and ambitious. Overcoming Ma's apprehension, he bought a run-down hotel in Pleasantdale, New Jersey, a small area adjoining Verona. He outlined his plans to the family. The grounds in front of the hotel would be landscaped and covered with tables and umbrellas, chairs and lounges of different colors. (This was pre–Miami Beach.)

Each ballroom would have a separate identity. The main one would be French. A smaller one, a rathskeller. (Shades of Schary Manor, which had a "Beirgarten" that Pa insisted was a rathskeller.) Another ballroom would be Italiano (Pa stretched that one out as he spoke, to Eye-tal-ee-an-ooh). The dining room was to be "elegant" (that was Pa's favorite description) but it turned out to be ersatz English.

The plunge began.

Painters, plasterers, electricians, plumbers, and carpenters flooded the place. Huge iceboxes were built with newly created automatic refrigeration devices. Zayde was still alive and he supervised the rebuilding and cleaning up of the two kosher kitchens — one for meat, the other dairy products.

The furniture flowed in from vans and trucks. Pa stamped through the hotel urging everyone, "Hurry, hurry, we are going to open in March."

March came and hurried away, but nothing else did. Then April,

May — and on Decoration Day, 1927, Schary's Hotel had its opening. It rained buckets. It rained disaster. My mother was distraught and I learned that Pa had poured practically his entire fortune into the Pleasantdale palazzo.

The hotel was "elegant" but it belonged somewhere else. Perhaps Miami — or Lakewood — anywhere but Pleasantdale, where the rates had to be cheap because the prospective clientele was middle-class. It was a seventy-five-dollar-a-week hotel soliciting guests who were willing to pay only twenty-five.

Each weekend the rains came. On Sundays, we loaded the truck and I drove food that could not be preserved to the Hebrew Orphan Asylum, the Old Folks' Home, and a local Montclair hospital.

The summer months and Pa's resources fled by with no change of fortune. It rained on the Fourth of July and on Labor Day. The customers came and each one cost us more than he paid. A brush fire burned down the garage and our truck. We salvaged the Dodge sedan.

Consumed by the flames were two boxes of personal mementos and papers such as newspaper reports of the false armistice in early November, 1918, and the real armistice on November 11. Also destroyed were editions of the *Stars and Stripes* that had been distributed by a boy cadet corps of which I was a member. Those items along with a baseball glove of rich brown leather that I had nurtured with oil and spit into a soft, beautiful, shaped mitt were losses that made me cry. A batch of my early stories and plays were turned into ashes. I remember the glove and the newspapers. Happily I can't remember any of my writing.

Winter marched in on Thanksgiving Day with a snowstorm that cancelled out most of our diners and holiday customers. New Year's also was extremely white and so was Lincoln's Birthday and Washington's Birthday.

It was clear — we were doomed.

In March, 1928, my brother Sam came back after five years in California. He had run out of opportunities and chipped in at the hotel to try to stem the tide. Sam was an attractive man and the ladies hovered about him and none were discouraged — or if they were, Sam recommended me. It was a horny spring. Meanwhile, Pa was getting more frantic. A fruitful weekend would raise his hopes, which would be dashed the following one by the horrendous splash of heavy rainfall.

In June, through my dear and good mentor, Kenyon Nicholson, I received an offer to work in Cincinnati with Stuart Walker's stock company. At the end of June, I departed Pleasantdale and its inevitable catastrophe and went to Cincinnati, where I ran into heavy weather of a different kind.

The stock company in Cincinnati placed me on the professional stage for the first time and I drank the wine of the theater.

During my second week, the company, starring Pauline Lord and George Gaul, were playing *The Road to Romance*. We young fellows, who burst in for a dueling scene late in the show, wore doublets, dolman-sleeved silk shirts, long boots, and, of course, swords. The swords sounded rather like tin — which they were. Following one of the performances a "disciple" (as I learned Stuart Walker's young actors were called) stopped me backstage and tried to kiss me. I was scared, and drew back. When he came after me again, I did a stupid thing — I hit him.

The stage manager straightened the matter out by firing me. There and then. I was an instant villain. I returned to my rented room, which smelled of citronella and furniture polish, where I lay awake all night with anger and the bile of defeat.

After I paid for my room and my laundry, I had little money. I called Mother collect. Pa got on the phone and I said I needed fare home. He told me to go to Western Union. The money would be there.

When I got back to the hotel in Pleasantdale, Pa mocked, "My son, the actor," and knocked me down with a blow to the side of my jaw. When I got up, I said, "If you ever do that again, I'll hit back." He eyed me, then turned to the wall, his favorite conversation companion, and said, "You hear that? My son, the actor, he's a fighter now and he's going to fight his father — do you hear that, wall?"

I anticipated that Pa would now turn and belt me again. Instead, he sat down, turned his back to me, and said, "Get out of here. Go entertain the customers, actor."

The remainder of the summer was more of the same for the Schary Hotel. Business diminished. The weather was better, but we were losing ground each day. It became obvious that Pa was losing heart. His manner was quieter, his temper had lost heat. My brother had gone to New York and been employed as a stock salesman. I was functioning as room clerk and maître d'. Mother looked drawn and was losing weight.

A few nights before the Labor Day weekend, the prognosis for the hotel was "terminal." Bills were piling up and we were stemming the assault of creditors by assuring them that Labor Day would bring a bonanza.

The morning before the holiday weekend, I was awakened by the baker, who asked me to light the stove — a chore my father had reserved for himself from the time there had been an explosion caused by a baker who had turned on the gas jets, gone looking for a match, lit it, and was practically blown to the hospital, where she remained for two weeks. When the stove was warming up, I went to find out why Pa had not responded to the baker's wake-up call. His room was empty. The bed had not been used.

My first grim conclusion was that Pa had committed suicide. My mother dismissed the thought — "Your father wouldn't do that. He ran away."

We discovered that some of his clothes were missing, along with his leather suitcase. The local cab company relayed the news that a cab had called for Pa at three-thirty in the morning and picked him up at the lower end of the driveway. He'd been driven to the Hudson Tube Station in Newark.

The news filtered out and the Newark *Evening News* carried a front-page item headlined H. H. SCHARY NOTED CATERER DISAPPEARS. The phones began to ring. Members of our large family of aunts, uncles, and cousins appeared with theories and advice . . . then rumors.

"He was seen in New York."

"I'll bet he jumped off the Brooklyn Bridge."

"They say he left with over fifteen thousand dollars."

It wasn't possible he left with money because we soon learned that the Schary well was dry as dust. As for jumping into the East River, Mother in her wise and ironic way commented, "Hugo wouldn't jump in the water because he can't swim."

To me, there was only one clear fact. He had run out, leaving Mother and me to wind up the mess. I played my role well; I was the young son left with my brokenhearted mother and now in charge of what had to be done . . . I was acting brave and tough and I swore that one day Pa would pay for his cowardice. Ma disabused me. She took over. No, I was not to put away any of the money that came in on Labor Day weekend . . . those funds would go to pay the employees and the more improvident creditors. After the weekend, we were to invite the creditors in for the scavenger hunt, then lock up the place, let the bank take over, and go to New York, where Lil had rented a small apartment in the Bronx for Mother and me.

Of course, it rained.

On the Tuesday morning after the deluge, we paid off those who were most needy. The Dodge was picked up by the finance company. The locust swarm of creditors stripped the hotel of chandeliers, beds, rugs, dishes, refrigerators, silver, and linen.

It was too painful. We had to get away. We had sent one trunk ahead to New York packed with Mother's most cherished possessions. She had two suitcases and a laundry bag. My luggage consisted of a small bag loaded with one-act playscripts, my pencils, and a few books, including a Roget's (old, torn, and worn — I still have it), a dictionary, and a volume of poems. Two suitcases were loaded with my clothes and my laundry, which I had carefully packed.

I confess — I worry about my laundry. I did not have a room or a dresser of my own until I was eighteen. Some of my shirts were handed down from my brother Sam's wardrobe. Because I was always short of apparel, I worried about losing any of it — so I'd wait for the laundry to get back and I'd put it away to make sure it had all been returned. That concern stuck to me in my travels to boys' camps as counselor, on the Borscht Circuit, on road trips with shows, and in later years, on hundreds of journeys to California and New York, and to scores of other cities in England, France, Italy, and Israel. Laundry must be my security blanket. My care of it is also a hoary family gag.

Mother had paid as many of the hotel help as possible. There had been a total Labor Day cash intake of a little more than four thousand dollars. Ma kept handing out money. When we were down to one hundred, I convinced her to hang on to it.

After fares for the cab to Verona, bus to New York, and cab to Walton Avenue, we arrived with ninety dollars. The apartment was clean and Lil had stocked it with food in the icebox, flowers in some vases, linen on the beds, and hangers in the closets.

We unpacked the bags, opened the trunk, had a bite to eat, and Mother went to her bedroom to take a nap. She was fifty-three, had worked hard all her life, and was left with ninety dollars, a trunk, and two valises. Lil was certain God would punish Pa.

I wasn't waiting for God to pass judgment on my father, I was making my own plans — that is, if I could find Pa.

Sam showed up from a trip to Buffalo with a surprise. He was doing extremely well as a salesman — that was his trade and he was good at it. He could talk fishing, golf, bowling, pool, cards, and women to his prospects and he had a stock of lapel pins — Kiwanis, Rotary, Elks, Masons, and so on — that he would don, chameleonlike, to become whatever he thought his "mark" would want him to be. He gave Mother five hundred dollars and slipped me five tens. He told us not to worry and off he went to sell some more stock.

I went looking for work — any kind. After hours of searching each morning, I'd duck into a movie house, sit there watching the show with feelings of shame, and go home to Walton Avenue and scribble rhymes, stories, and ideas for plays.

One afternoon, after a few weeks of aimless foraging, I came out of the Criterion Theatre, then at Broadway and Forty-fourth Street. Heading toward Times Square, I saw my father walking north past the Astor Hotel on the west side of the street.

He was smoking a cigar, looked quite dapper, and was walking slowly up the Great White Way. Unseen by him, I crossed the street and began trailing him. I bought a newspaper. Playing Jack Holt (that era's hero), I covered the lower part of my face with it as I followed Pa's every move.

At Fiftieth Street and Broadway, he descended into the subway. Guarding myself, I followed. He got on the uptown local. I sneaked into the next car. He got out at Ninety-sixth Street. So did I, but I bent down to fix a shoelace until he had reached the top of the stairs. Then I dashed up and spotted him crossing over to an apartment hotel on the northwest corner of Ninety-sixth and Broadway. After a reasonable time, I entered the hotel and asked for Mr. Schary's apartment. The clerk said there was no such man. Stop kidding — he just came in here. Oh, that was Mr. Sheridan. He lives in Mrs. Krause's apartment.

My stomach turned. I wanted to leave. But I couldn't. Obviously, I had trapped him in his whore's apartment. Up I went to Mrs. Krause's. I rang the bell and after a count of five, Mrs. Krause opened the door. I had expected a redhead, full-bosomed with a bustlelike behind, who would radiate sexuality. Mrs. Krause was well over sixty, drab, arthritic, slovenly, and spoke with a thick German accent. Yes, Mr. Sheridan boarded in her apartment . . . last door down the hall. There was no femme fatale and no fancy apartment. Just an old lady and a rented room in a dingy apartment. My scenario was cockeyed.

Slowly, I walked to Pa's room.

Pa was very deaf so he did not hear me as I came to the half-opened door. His room was about ten feet long and seven feet wide. A cell. A narrow bed on one wall. A small dresser on the opposite wall. An open wardrobe with enough room to hang a few coats and trousers. At the far end there was a large window and facing it a rocking chair in which my Pa was sitting. I saw his profile and the heavy creases in his cheeks. His right hand held his Wilsonian pince-nez. His shock of graying hair was a bit rumpled. He was the saddest-looking man I'd ever seen. I wasn't Jack Holt anymore. I was his son and my eyes tried to squeeze my tears back. I saw the shame he had felt and the indignity of his failure. I saw the broken pride. I called, "Pa." He turned, and when he saw me he looked

[23]

at me in surprise and said, "Sonny," as he burst into tears. I rushed to him and we embraced . . .

Later, I persuaded Pa to come to Walton Avenue. I called Mother and told her I was bringing Pa home. She was noncommittal. When they greeted each other in the apartment, they just shook hands and said hello.

It was easy to guess that Pa would not be staying. Three days later, he was gone. He went to Florida to see if he could find a place for himself in the miniature-golf business. He had an idea he could create a chain of golf courses from Florida to Maine.

Pa was never devoid of a grandiose scheme.

4

*S*am, *now elevated* to a sales manager, was exceptionally successful and offered me a job working for him in Buffalo as a stock sales-man. I shuffled off to Buffalo, where Sam occupied a lavish suite in the Statler Hotel. As an apprentice, I worked in the "boiler room," a crowded area with stalls where thirty men sat at telephones chattering a sales pitch to prospective customers. When one of the prospects bit, a dash to the hopeful's home would, more often than not, bring in a deposit check with a two-dollar commission on each share sold. While I was not adept, the fish were in the sea, and soon I was earning two to three hundred dollars a week. Sam, as sales chief, was earning a fortune of almost two thousand each payday. The living was luxurious. At night Sam hosted poker games or charming and accommodating women. It was Boom Town, U.S.A. I even saved a few dollars each week. Paradise enow.

But it was all tinsel when I heard from Kenyon Nicholson that John Golden was looking for a young actor to go on the road with *Four Walls* starring Muni Weisenfreund, not yet renamed Paul Muni. Sam thought I was stupid to take the job, but off I went to New York, home, and Mother. All Buffalo had to offer was money.

When I arrived for rehearsal in *Four Walls*, I learned I had all of ten lines and some ad-libs in chorus with other "gangsters" in the play. I was to get the blocking from the stage manager, whose role as "Jake" I was to take over. I reported to the theater, which was on the "subway circuit." In those palmy days of 1928, a play would travel from its Broadway run to Brooklyn, the Bronx, and Washington Heights for additional revenue before heading for Chicago, which had a lively and devoted theater audience. Some cast changes would be made to replace those actors either booked for another Broadway play or not interested in road work. The minimum Equity road salary was forty dollars a week. That was me — minimum.

After a Saturday morning understudy run-through, I was told to "go on" that matinee. While appearing to be in command of the situation, I was numb. Once I stepped onto the stage to walk the action with the understudies, I became keyed up and alert. We ran through everything three times and that was it — except for one serious caveat. In a scene where I was supposed to shake Muni's shoulder, "Just pat the back of the chair, not him," George Wright, the stage manager, instructed. "Don't touch him, never."

The members of the company were cordial and pleasant. When Muni arrived, I was taken in to meet him so he would know who I was when I faced him on the stage. Muni waved his hand at me, wished me luck, and I got ready for my first performance. "Jake's" entrance into the play was in the first act — I had to run in, ostensibly breathless, to warn that a rival gang was on the way, looking for trouble. I had to speak a deathless line — "The Rats are coming!"

As the curtain went up, I was in position behind the set, hyperventilating so as to be breathless when I faced Averell Harris, who was the "heavy" in the play. I adjusted my cap, deciding to wear it at a very cocky angle, loosened the knot of my tie, unbuttoned my coat jacket, and when my first cue ever in a Broadway show was given, I burst in and heaved my chest for a few seconds. Jeanne Greene, playing "the moll," whispered, "Your fly's open." That bit of intelligence added to my breathlessness, but I did manage a stammer — "The Rats are coming." In the excitement that followed, I took a quick look. My trousers were buttoned. (No zippers in those days.) After the scene, Jeanne Greene laughed, slapped me on the back, and said, "Good going, good luck."

A few weeks later, we were on our way to Chicago, where we opened to good notices and husky business. Chicago was a wide-open and long-awake city. In 1928, it was, as suggested by William Bolitho in *Twelve Against the Gods*, the biggest threat respectable citizenry had faced since the days of Catiline.

Al Capone had bought judges and justices; the police were in his pocket; the "protection" rackets had reached into the medical and legal professions; elections were a foregone conclusion — they went the way Capone wanted them to go. Booze, "protection," and prostitution were the most profitable professions. Violence was the way of life. Actors were held for ransom. (Muni was threatened, and for two weeks the entire male cast, some eighteen of us, walked him from and to his hotel, the Bismarck, each night.)

Many of us were booked at the Wacker Hotel (a river of easy jokes went along with the name "Wacker"). For bit actors working in a show, life was lazy. You slept late, got up, had breakfast, went to a movie or two, ate a sandwich, got to the theater, did the show, went out with some guys and girls, drank and danced and shacked up for the evening, sometimes at your place, sometimes at hers.

If you were bereft of girls, you went to your room, wrote some letters, washed your socks, handkerchiefs, and underwear, and read a book. The talk was mostly "show biz" adventure stories (half of them lies) about girls, drunks, producers, other actors.

One evening, the stage doorman said that Mr. Weisenfreund wanted to see me. When I went to Muni's room, he, for the first time, addressed me in Yiddish. I answered in kind. He said he heard I was a sometime writer. He told me he had some invitations to speak at various groups such as Hadassah, B'nai B'rith, and the like. Would I help write some speeches for him? In exchange, he offered lessons in makeup, an art of which he was a master. This barter started a friendship that lasted until his death. For a time, it was close and intimate. Later on it became casual but always constant.

During the run of *Four Walls*, I took on some chores of assistant stage manager, a simple task that provided the opportunity of watching Muni from the wings as he performed night after night. He was a highly disciplined actor who never varied his moves or tension on the stage unless the audience was rattled by a "cougher" who would infect others. If that happened, Muni would bring up his voice, sharpen his action, and fight to recapture his customers.

One night, Muni, at the curtain of the first act, blew up with anger. There were two or three people up front who, plagued with colds, had sneezed and coughed a discordant symphony. Muni wanted the manager to give them back their money and invite them to come another time — or, better yet, shoot them. He stormed at his wife, Bella Finkel, who was playing his sweetheart in the play, slammed doors, and cursed in Yiddish. When the second act began, he had regained control but his concentration was ruffled. The first scene in the act was in his mother's home. A few of us, playing his friends, were visiting him, urging him to rejoin the mob after he had pledged to "go straight." (The play, obviously, was no *Moon for the Misbegotten*.) In this scene, I faked slapping Muni on the back and said, "It's better than getting your twenty bucks in a pay

[*27*]

envelope." That night as the scene was played, Muni was distracted. His tension had snapped. When he got his cue, Muni didn't answer. After repeating the line, I realized Muni had gone blank. Placing my job in jeopardy by literally slapping Muni on his shoulder, I said, "Snap out of it, Benny. It's better than getting your twenty bucks in a pay envelope." Muni popped out of his reverie, glared at me, and came back to life.

When the curtain dropped at the first scene of the act, I waited for the ax to fall. Muni came over to me and in Yiddish said that I was right in slapping his back but, and he smiled, "If you ever do it again, I'll give you a *zetz*, your teeth will fall out."

He punched me on the arm, laughed, and went in to change for scene two.

Four Walls closed its Chicago run in April, 1929, and we trained back to New York. There was a boom, but we were all out of work. Show business.

My brother's personal elixir had turned sour, thereby lowering his income and his sparse savings. I had written a draft of a play and was peddling an option on it while I looked for a job. Mother, tired of the Bronx and feeling estranged from roots, decided that we should return to Newark. For the next four months it was an aimless existence. Mother took a job for the summer as a cook in a hotel on the Jersey shore. I worked at the YMHA editing a weekly news sheet and helping Moss Hart, who had been hired to direct the "Y" Players.

Moss even in those early days had a dash about him. His velour hat, worn with one side of the brim turned up, overcame his odd mixture of socks, shirts, ties, and suits.

From the beginning, Moss had an air of confidence, which he used to lift the Y Players into performances that no one else would have tried on their far from proven talents. He dared anything . . . *Ghosts, Redemption, Trial of Mary Dugan, Emperor Jones, Doll's House, The Torchbearers* — an eclectic range of material that he chose, not for the benefit of the players, but, as he confided to me, for his own tempering, schooling, and benefit.

The education I had received from Muni was a valuable gift. On open nights, I gave lectures on makeup to amateur groups or did the makeup on casts for their shows. Moss hired me to go to Brooklyn and Bensonhurst to make up the actors in amateur groups he directed. In addition, I had two amateur groups of my own in Trenton and Plainfield. (One of my actors in Plainfield was the late financier Philip Levin, who in later years claimed I helped make his fortune by urging him not to depend on his acting ability for a living.)

Moss and I worked harder than anyone else we knew. We both were always on the move and there was little recreation time. But the bus, train, and subway travels demanded by our work schedules gave us time to strop our talents and ambition. However, Moss never saw himself as anything but a playwright. He had a single-mindedness that I did not and do not have in my work. Moss's interest in community affairs was limited to the community of the theater. I have been involved, often too involved, in local and national politics, in organization work, and in Jewish affairs.

In 1929, Moss was booked at the Flagler as social director, and he asked me to join as his assistant. It meant room, board, laundry, and four hundred dollars.

When the summer ended, it was back to the Y and little theater groups and writing and whatever work came along. Among the jobs I had in the years from 1925 to 1929 were tie salesman, chinaware salesman, publicity manager in Newark for Admiral Byrd's appearance, and proofreader for a generous employer, Mr. Cozzolino. I also sold printing, wrote features for the Newark *Sunday Call*, the Newark *Ledger*, and Bamberger's magazine, *Charm*. I also kept up my fragmentary connection with the YMHA. Now I had experienced the Borscht Belt.

The point is not how well I did these many jobs, but rather, like a trained dog, that I did them at all.

Pa arrived back from Florida without his chain of miniature golf courses and there was another reconciliation with Ma, but again, even though this time they both tried to make a go of it, it lasted only a couple of months. Pa said good-bye and told us he was going to sell real estate in Elizabeth, New Jersey.

Once, a few years before, when Pa had retired, he owned property in Elizabeth that included a one-block street. He had the right to name it, and he dubbed it Schary Place. He had dismissed "Street," "Avenue," and "Alley" as not being "elegant" enough. Pa thought that Elizabeth would bring him luck.

I prayed it would.

5

*T*he crash banged down on the United States in October. For those of us who had little, it didn't hurt much. Mother thought that a small restaurant serving good home-cooking could be a success. We scraped together enough money to rent a brownstone (actually a red-stone) home on Clinton Avenue, only a block removed from the old Schary Manor. Mother's reputation as a cook was still formidable. We recruited two young men who had worked for us in Pleasantdale, Bill and Clarence, and hung out the shingle. Bill and Clarence lived on the top floor and acted as Mother's assistants, dishwashers, waiters, and housekeepers. Whenever I could, I functioned as captain of the dining room.

The pendulum had swung again for Sam and he was riding it on the upswing. Mother said not to depend on Sam. He would either gamble or blow away his chances. He was too reckless.

Sam had married again — for the third time — and was living in Philadelphia, where his new wife, Fay, had been raised. Sam said he didn't mind Philadelphia — "I spend so little time there." His new job kept him on the road for long stretches and we saw little of him.

Lil still lived on Walton Avenue with her husband, Henry Waldman, and her children, Jane and Edgar. The kids were sweet — the marriage was not, and some years later it fell apart. We had few opportunities to see Lil — she was busy taking care of her home and children and we were working damn hard.

It is obviously true that we are an anthology of our dreams, sins, achievements, our failures, and our interaction with other people. We may, Mother would say, change our manners but never our character, which is fashioned by our aches, our longings, our plans, our genes, our health, and our loves and hates. However, there may be a central core around which all else spins — a centripetal force that holds all else to-gether. My mother was that core in my life.

She was a beautiful woman possessed of splendid posture, an en-dearing smile, china blue eyes, and prematurely gray hair. She had a gift of mimicry, which may have had something to do with her linguistic talents — she spoke English, Yiddish, Russian, Polish, German, and some Hungarian. She would imitate the different handshakes used by the butcher (crushing), the ladies' tailor (limp), the henpeck (just fingers), the politician (two-handed), and the voices, gruff, tinny, wheezy, orotund, or mincing.

My mother was unique. An original. She was no trembling or domi-nating materfamilias. She knew her children, their strengths and weak-nesses. She never complained, but if she believed you behaved badly, she would tell you so and in firm, hard terms. She never slapped any of us — perhaps because Pa took care of the physical harassment. She expected us to do the best we could and was pleased if we did but not heartbroken if we failed. She had patience. People who knew her spoke of her with affection and of the aura about her — the quality of good breeding and dignity. As the youngest child, I was able to see more because the youngest is often left to his own resources and conclusions — the other kids take up so much time. Our entire family worked hard, and as I grew, Mother moved me into the work ethic with little fuss, simply by assuring me I could do what had to be done.

The warehouse of stories that Mother owned never seemed to empty — there always was an apt one for a sad or happy time. Our home was a place where we learned to give to charity. There were tin boxes, pushkes, placed on kitchen shelves, and we were expected to drop extra pennies into the slots. After a while, we were no longer prodded. The plop of copper coins against the tin made us feel pure — assuaging what-ever guilts we might have.

During the rich days and the poor ones, we were aware of Mother's work for the Hebrew Orphan Asylum, the Home for the Aged, and the Beth Israel Hospital. If there was nothing else to do, Mother would be crocheting or knitting a scarf or socks for some old and friendless soul.

It was during the time when we ran the small restaurant that I learned so much more about her. "Grace under pressure" is something Mother never read about, but nevertheless she lived it. Her response to pressure was always a counterpressure, a wry humor, and a determination to schwam daruber — swim over it.

So we swam. We made progress with exceptional Jewish cuisine, excellent service, and a homey ambience that brought in customers in profitable numbers.

During the days, if there were no chores at the Y, or no writing assignments at the Newark newspapers, I'd travel to New York, trying to get my toe in the stage door. Muni was at liberty and was planning to go on a vaudeville tour with one act of *Four Walls*. I was slated to go on the circuit with him, and while waiting, I served as his press agent. Muni was expecting to hear from Jed Harris, who was planning production of a play about Rasputin, Czar Nicholas's mad genius. Muni had met with Harris and, sensing he had scored a strong impression, he was impatiently eager for word. Harris was at the apex of his fame and power, and was pursued by actors.

On the afternoon Muni heard from Jed, I had the good fortune to be in Muni's sitting room, which served also as a rehearsal area. One wall of the room was lined with clothes closets, the doors of which were mirrored from floor to ceiling. In this area, Muni would practice his stances, his moves, his makeup. When the phone rang, we were seated at opposite sides of the room.

As I started toward it, Muni quickly waved me back. He allowed the phone to ring three times, then picked up the receiver and in his rich, deep voice said, "Hello." Then, "Yes, this is he. . . . Oh, fine." He covered the phone speaker and whispered to me, "Harris."

Then he half turned away from me, cleared his throat, and said into the phone, "Hello, Mr. Harris, fine thank you . . . yourself? Good. Yes? . . . Oh, may I ask why? . . . Because I'm too young? . . ."

Muni's voice soared up two notches.

"Mr. Harris, I've been playing old men since I was twelve . . . and damned convincingly. . . . Let me prove it to you. . . . I'll put on makeup and read for . . . Mr. Harris, that's unfair." Muni's voice became sharper and louder. "That's your opinion, but it is a stupid one . . . and you, too." Bang, clatter, went the phone and Muni without looking at me for even an instant moved toward the mirrored wall and addressed his image . . . in Yiddish. (A free translation follows.)

"You hear, I'm too young to play Rasputin — me — I can play any old man — German, Russian, Jew, Pole —"

Muni flung open a closet door and as he dressed in a coat, cane, and hat, he slouched, bent his knees, and became an elderly German who spoke a thick German monologue.

As I watched, not daring to move or talk, Muni donned a different overcoat, hat, and stick, tossing the other props he had used to one side, and he was an old Russian Jew with a quavering voice and a feeble shuffle. Another change and he became a domineering Polish peasant, yelling and storming in a drunken rage. The fourth one I catalogued was a well-groomed landowner with the straight back of a former officer, a haughty manner, and precise and demanding speech.

Suddenly, Muni threw his final character away and quietly mumbled, "Son of a bitch." He turned and saw me. "Please go. Call me in a few days."

I left, the lone member of an audience who would cherish an extraordinary performance by a remarkable actor.

A short time later, Muni went to Hollywood, became Paul Muni and a great star. Years later, when we both were at a dinner party, I reminded Muni of that day in his dressing area. He shook his head, waved his hand in two characteristic moves, and said, "Harris, the schlemiel."

Muni's tour did not take place and I was stranded for the summer. Moss was deep into preparing *Once in a Lifetime* and out of the circuit. I had no opportunity to find a counselor's spot in a boys' camp and since the restaurant was closing down for the summer, Mother was going to work at her sister Bessie's hotel in Bar Harbor, Maine.

For a couple of weeks, I went into business for myself. I bought some lumber and nails and built bookcases and sold them to a few friends. My workshop was the cellar of the home of my friends Ralph and Sylvia Shapiro. However, the volume was small, the profit negligible, so I liquidated my woodworking enterprise. I had a few dollars, a few sore fingers, and an idea for a play. But I needed more money.

The Newark *Sunday Call* arts editor was Edward Sothern Hipp, and I approached him with the idea of traveling to the New England area, stopping in at boys' and girls' camps, and writing a column about Newark-area kids at those camps, thereby spreading sunshine and pride on their families.

Hipp gave me the okay. Fifteen dollars a week for three weeks. I bought a pair of breeches, puttees, a couple of army shirts, and a rucksack and off I went into the wild New England yonder. I hitch-hiked my way, getting free meals and a cot for a night's rest at each camp I visited. On weekends, I stopped at wayside stands or eateries and worked as a dishwasher or a short-order cook. I made sandwiches, salads, hamburgers, and eggs with the worst of them.

I hitched as far north as Bar Harbor and spent a few days with Mother and Aunt Bessie and helped out by entertaining the guests. By now my repertoire included imitations of Groucho Marx, Ed Wynn, and Joe Cook.

By the time I got back to Newark, I had mailed Hipp three long columns, which he cut down to size. With the *Sunday Call*'s forty-five bucks and the money I had earned on the road, I settled down in my room and in a few weeks had written the first draft of a play, *One Every Minute*, which was based on my adventures in Buffalo with Sam, his cronies, and willing ladies.

Moss had directed me to his first agent, Frieda Fishbein, a red-haired darling of a woman with an eternal sad look in her eyes. She wore flowing clothes and jewelry in abundance that tinkled faintly as she talked and walked. Frieda had a stable of young writers, none of whom she could support except with praise and enthusiasm. I handed her the playscript and within two days she called, happy and elated. She loved it and had sent it to George Haight, who was a production assistant to Herman Shumlin, who was a producer of talent challenging Harris's reputation. Haight liked the play and had given it to Shumlin with an A-plus rating.

I had written other plays, and some of them had been optioned to producers. The going rate was two hundred dollars for six months, which in the twenties gave you easy living while you wrote, rewrote, tore up, and rewrote the rewrites. You endured the dropped options with little or no pain because dreams of opening a hit play on Broadway kept morale afloat. Sidney Harmon and James Ramsey Ullman, who produced *Men in White*, had one of my plays for a while; a man named Golden (not John, but Sam) had another; David Boehm kept *Gentlemen of Distinction* in his lap for months — but the news that Herman Shumlin might go for *One Every Minute* was staggering. I passed the word around at the Y — Shumlin was also a Newarker and it was clearly a combination of hometown talent on the verge of a smash success.

The waiting began. There's always waiting. Poor Frieda Fishbein must have had the patience of Job to put up with the calls from her stable of anxious writers with their repeated inquiries: "Did he call?" "What do you think?" "How long does it take?" "Shouldn't you ring him?" "For Christ's sake, doesn't the son of a bitch have a heart?" "Why not call him and tell him to get off the pot?"

This time I wasn't even waiting for the Big Man — but for his assistant. Finally, Frieda called. George Haight, Shumlin's assistant, wanted to see me the next day at two o'clock. Promptly at two, I walked into Haight's office. He was a rangy, lanky man with tousled hair, sleepy eyes, and a perpetual grin. He was also a joker.

To establish his persona, he beckoned me to a chair, called a number, and said, "Listen, lady, you shouldn't be screwing that guy with the shades up." He let me hear the outraged response, then hung up. He told me he liked to call numbers at random. George was a victim, perhaps a beneficiary, of Hecht and MacArthur's *Front Page*, which had done for comedy what *Hair* later did for musicals. The saucy, tough reporters were an inspiration to dozens of playwrights and to the character of Broadway. George dialed another number, got no answer, wagged a finger at me, and got up and walked out of the room with me following. In a moment, I was in Shumlin's office shaking hands with Herman Shumlin. Even in those days, Shumlin was bald, tanned, tough, terse, and looked at you with eyes that made you think, "I'm guilty."

"I was in your folks' place, Schary Manor, years ago," he told me. Getting no response, since none was really called for, Mr. Shumlin told me that he thought *One Every Minute* was a funny idea but not yet a play. Would I be willing to have someone help out — give ideas — not share in it — but advise? I said I welcomed it, assuming it might be George, but it was someone else who worked for Shumlin, Marcel Strauss. I asked if there would be a contract. No, because it wasn't yet a play. But, I had to have some income. Herman had thought of that. There was a small part in his hit play, *The Last Mile*, in the theater just across the street. Thomas Mitchell had just replaced Spencer Tracy, who had gone to Hollywood to make his first film, *Up the River*. The rest of the company were extraordinary — Allen Jenkins, Joe Calleia, Henry O'Neill, Ralph Theodore, and James Bell. I was to be an assistant stage manager and play a reporter who interviews the victim who walks "the Last Mile." Thirty-five dollars per week but a great opportunity to write and act and get paid for it.

It being Wednesday, George walked me across to the theater to meet the company. After the matinee, I walked through my bit with the stage manager, who also briefed me on some of my duties beyond knocking on doors and calling out "Curtain going up." My assignment was to fire shotgun blanks into a garbage can, producing a loud sound backstage that to the audience would be a convincing impression of a large explosion when Killer Mears led the prison break.

After the evening show I was told I would go on the following night. George was leaving town and invited me to use his hotel room at the Chesterfield Hotel, thereby saving the expense of going back to Newark that night. George's room was a small cubicle. It was hot — but the shower was cold. I fell asleep thinking of my name as playwright on a marquee. Of course, Spencer Tracy would have the lead.

When I awoke, the first thought that cropped up was, "Who the hell is Marcel Strauss?"

Later that day in George Haight's office I found out. Marcel was an intense, voluble, scantily blond-haired fellow with sallow skin, lively blue eyes, and an air of attractive intellectuality. He loved *One Every Minute*. So far everyone *loved* the play, but they all wanted to redo it. So did Marcel. I liked him even though some of his references did not seem applicable to my play.

I made some notes, agreed to meet Marcel on Monday, then went to the theater and got ready for my "opening night" in *The Last Mile*. Months before, I had seen the John Wexley play with Spencer Tracy as Killer Mears, and while Thomas Mitchell, who had replaced Tracy, was doing his best, it wasn't good enough. He did not have the raw strength and thrust that was Tracy's. He was simply miscast. All went well my first night, including the precise moment I had to fire those shots into the garbage can. However, the sound, from which I had tried to protect myself by keeping my mouth open, almost stunned me. From that performance on I prepared for the cue by stuffing my ears with cotton.

Four days after my entry into the company, on the Saturday evening performance to be precise, Mr. Mitchell was giving a rousing performance; too rousing. He was yelling, snorting, and giving those magnificent eyebrows a great workout. In the second act, when Killer Mears breaks out of his cell, Mitchell was all muscle and as he slammed out of his cell he swung around in an awkward arabesque and stepped into the footlights, breaking some of them, all of which added to the noise, but he had stepped over the line from drama into broad comedy.

Unknown to us, Chester Erskine, the director, was in the audience. At the end of the act he appeared, his eyes flashing, his mouth clamped in anger. He barked at the stage manager, telling him to hold the company onstage at the end of the play.

When the time came, Erskine whiplashed the company for having allowed their performances to "move out of the frame." He castigated them for being careless, indifferent to the integrity of the play, and for behaving as if they were drunk. During the tirade, Erskine didn't look at Mitchell, but obviously it was intended for him. We were told to be at the theater Monday at twelve o'clock for rehearsals.

Monday's rehearsal went quietly. I watched fascinated as Erskine brought everything "back into the frame." Mitchell, ill, had not reported in. He never returned. Allen Jenkins took over for him as Killer

Mears and finished the run of the play in the role, with the exception of one week when Tracy returned and played it for auld lang syne. Jenkins, who later became a popular "dim-wit" comedian in films, was superb as Mears, but no one ever remembered.

After rehearsal I met with Marcel Strauss and had to listen to a long lecture on the history and art of dramatizing. It was interesting, but added nothing to the practical problem of getting *One Every Minute* ready for production.

When Tracy returned for his week's performance, I got to meet him. Our relationship is best described as skimpy. I addressed him as Mr. Tracy. He called me "kid." After his stint, Tracy returned to Hollywood and I didn't see him again until early 1933.

During this time, I was commuting back and forth from Newark to New York. In New York I was acting and trying to get Marcel off the generalities and onto the specifics. Mother had returned to Newark and we had reopened the restaurant. I had achieved a certain celebrity as an actor, which vanished when friends came to see the play and discovered how little I had to do. The standard joke, which each tormentor assumed was brand-new, was, "Dore's an actor. He's got the title role in *The Last Mile*." The rewriting on *One Every Minute* was beginning to wear me out. Even more enervating were Marcel's lengthy and involved dramaturgical lessons, which kept diverting me from writing. I was no longer patient with him, and when he proposed that I sign over part of my prospective royalties, I shied. So far there had been no structural changes and I didn't feel I owed him anything for lessons. However, Shumlin thought I should divide my prospective royalties, and I signed a contract and got a two-hundred-dollar check. Marcel assured me the omens were good. The only good omen was that the check didn't bounce.

Good went to bad, then to worse. I had a dreadful falling out with Marcel and if he had been bigger, I might have belted him. The loss of temper cost me my job in *Last Mile*, Shumlin's interest in *One Every Minute*, and there I was again between a rock and a hard place.

Back to the restaurant and work at the Y.

After I had returned fifty dollars to Shumlin and reduced Marcel's interest to 25 percent, I started rewriting *One Every Minute*.

Also, I had been asked to stage a show for some friends who had formed a University Club (not *the* University Club). They were all friends — many of them longtime chums. I agreed, and they made me a member — I was to consider this an honor, they told me, because I was the only member not to have gone to college. The dubious distinction did not improve my interest in geometry. We put on shows to raise funds for the club. Dr. Ralph Shapiro, a cherished friend, Marvin Most-will, a boys'-camp buddy, and I did most of the work. We wrote, sang, and acted most of the sketches and I did the staging. My colleagues were friends I'd known for years. We had had joyous times working and wenching together. They were a solid rooting section who had lived through the many rosy announcements of play productions and had not abandoned me when the opening nights never came to be.

Late in the winter of 1930, I finished my final draft of *One Every Minute* and brought it to Frieda Fishbein in a clean and fresh state. She thought it might make a good movie story. That was fine with me.

Frieda submitted the script to Paramount. Merritt Hurlbut, a burly man with an open face and a friendly manner, was a Paramount executive in charge of the story department. Two weeks later, Frieda advised me that Mr. Hurlbut wished to see me. He was interested in buying *One Every Minute*.

Mr. Hurlbut's habitat was the first movie executive's office I'd been in. I liked it and Mr. Hurlbut. I loved him when he said that if Paramount in California agreed with him, they would pay me fifteen thousand dollars for *One Every Minute*. That figure rang in my head like the shotgun blasts in *The Last Mile*. When he asked if I'd be interested in going to the Coast to work, my answer was quick and affirmative. We shook hands and I sped to Frieda's office with the good news. We hugged, kissed, and roared our excitement.

Two weeks went by and the excitement dribbled down to a trickle of expectation.

After another week the trickle ceased with a call from Mr. Hurlbut, who told us that *High Pressure*, a Warner Brothers film starring William Powell about to open on Broadway, had been seen in California by Paramount executives who had sent Hurlbut a report indicating that the film, a breezy and fast-moving story of pressurized stock salesmen, was close in style and story to *One Every Minute;* consequently, "I'm sorry — some other time"; "Let me hear from you" — et cetera.

Foggy gloom settled in, gradually wrapping me in the depressive conviction that I would wind up in the restaurant business. This was a recurrent affliction of mine — a Pavlovian response to disappointment — okay, then I'll be a lecturer, reporter, actor, tie salesman, college professor, agent, makeup artist, china salesman, congressman — something — anything. The therapy for these depressions was and is for me to sit at a desk, take pencil in hand, and begin to write — a letter or free verse, a story or a play idea; it's like mounting a horse after being tossed off.

It was Oscar Serlin who got me back on the horse. Oscar, who had produced a fairly successful play, *Broken Dishes*, was a brawny man with a large head that seemed to weigh heavily on his shoulders; it thrust forward from his short neck and heavy torso. He had a marvelous chuckle, and acid humor coupled with a sense of good theater that was not full-blown until years later when he produced *Life with Father*. That play earned him a fortune, but, as so often happens with people who earn an astounding success, it inhibited his activity, and after the failure of *Life with Mother* Oscar practically went into retirement. Oscar, like all of us in a group that regularly visited Childs, the Tavern, and the Cadillac Cafeteria, was scrabbling for recognition. Archie Leach (Cary Grant), Sam Levene, Moss Hart had broken out of the "Nedick's for lunch" trap and were riding the bright carousel. Oscar, Ira Ashley, Eddie Chodorov, and I were bloody but enrolled for the duration.

Oscar sent for me and suggested we collaborate on a comedy about wrestlers. We started with a title, *The Flying Mare*, then went down into the digs. We were developing a story line when Hollywood reached out and tapped Oscar on the shoulder. He was going to Paramount as a scout for stories and writers. He left me *The Flying Mare* as a good-bye present. It was February, 1931, and damned cold and Oscar was going where it was warm. For me, it was a return to Newark, Clinton Avenue, the Y, and the restaurant.

Some weeks later (by now it was spring), I went to a party given by Mildred Shapiro, the sister of Ralph Shapiro. A record player was in action and the living room was crowded, mostly with people I knew.

As I eyed the possibilities for the latter part of the evening, I noticed a platinum blond girl with round cheeks, a marvelously straight back, and creamy skin. I had seen her once before, in the home of Marion Parsonnet, the night he was celebrating one of his brothers' birthdays. Our family knew the Parsonnets and their friends and relations, the Danzises, Reichs, Svets, Katchens, but I had never met one of Marion's cousins, Miriam Svet, who at eighteen was too young for a sophisticated bachelor of twenty-five like me. At Marion's I had met Miriam but had ignored her as Marion and his brothers, Tom and Gene, were passing the gin that stoned us into grinning, ridiculous gargoyles.

But now Miriam was here at Mildred's party. I crossed to her and asked her to dance. When I took her in my arms and felt her body and smelled the aroma of her skin and hair, I was magnetized. She did not dance divinely — as a matter of fact, she danced awkwardly, but her breath was sweet. I escorted her home. She told me that she had seen me months ago when I strolled through George Bridgman's life class with my cousin Saul, who as an artist was paying a nostalgic call at the Art Students League. I had gone along when he promised a look at the live nude models. Miriam, a student in the class, said she remembered the day and my gray cap and gray belted coat — "You were dashing looking." She could have said anything. I knew I was in love.

Exactly a week later, we decided we were engaged. Miriam's parents, Rose and Mandell Svet, music teachers (she the piano, he, violin and harmony), had once owned a large music studio on High Street, only four blocks from the first Schary Manor. Now they lived on Weequahic Avenue and had fallen on bad times. The depression had lost them students; bad real estate investments had impoverished them. However, they had quality and gentility. Rosalie Svet was a handsome woman and Mandell, who sported a cossack's mustache, was an independent and tough-minded man with humor and talent.

When I spoke to him about our engagement, I admitted I was broke but assured him I was an industrious worker with thirsty ambition. The Svets had heard of me through Miriam's sister and brother-in-law, Lucille and Ira Katchen, who dined almost every Friday night at Mother's restaurant. We discussed theater and they had followed my recommendations with few regrets. Therefore, I had friends in court.

The Svets agreed to my proposal, and much to my surprise, I was engaged to Miriam, the only one of a kind. She has remained that; totally unpredictable in situations in which you *know* she will respond predictably. She is immaculate — always; she is forever young, animates things, invents words like "slired," meaning sleepy and tired; is a good artist; can be as mean as a treed bobcat, as sweet as a toy poodle; trusts men more than she does women; and is a lucky backgammon player. She is jealous of me, her children, her grandchildren, her dog, her possessions. She adjusts and adapts to everything — not easily — but eventually.

She knows where each object in each room belongs and frets if it is out of place or missing. She likes food — almost any kind — has no allergies; loves to travel, and to talk about art and music; hates cocktail parties, but enjoyed herself immensely at dinner parties at the White House with Presidents Truman, Kennedy, and Johnson, all three of whom found her to be good company.

She is given to malaprops, is quickly bored by pedants, is furiously loyal to old friends, and while she forgives slights or oversights she never forgets them.

She adores flying but is terrified of a Ferris wheel or a cable tram. If she is ill she writes out a new will — she must have written dozens of them because she has endured a host of accidents and chronic illnesses.

She is of such concern to me that once, years ago, when I went into shock from food poisoning while in Philadelphia directing a show, Leonard Spigelgass, the author, swears that as I lay alternately fainting and vomiting, I said, "If I die, don't tell Miriam."

It's probably true because I love her very, very much.

Summer was on the way and Moss had called Don Hartman on my behalf to check on whether Don needed someone to help him at Grossinger's, where he was settling in as social director. Don had merry eyes, a shock of brown wavy hair, a sharp sense of humor, but a gritty layer of authority that warned you not to take him lightly. We got along well when we met and he hired me to edit the daily newspaper and aid him in any odd jobs. While I felt it wasn't going to be as much fun as the Flagler, I needed the summer job, which paid fifty a week with the pluses that had been available at the Flagler.

Miriam, whose family had a summer home in Elberon, New Jersey, was distressed that I would be away from her for the summer, but there was nothing we could do about that.

[*41*]

Don greeted me at Grossinger's and took me for a tour and introductions to the staff. He pointed out his Russian male star dancer, who would need a strong hand. He did not need to point out a luscious, sexy, raven-haired performer who stood out from the rest in all the right places.

My hunch was confirmed. I simply was not tuned in to Don as I was to Moss. Don took himself much more seriously, did not have a sense of balance about his work, and was rough on the staff. I loved Jennie Grossinger, whom I would see each day to talk over what went in the newspaper, but I felt separated from the rest of the staff. Trouble developed with the Russian male dancer, and Don, never the physical type, pushed the problem over to me. After a week of patient reasoning, I warned the Russian that if he yelled at the crew one more time, I would toss him off the stage and into the pit, a threat that he assumed, much more surely than I, would be carried out.

The display of bravado brought the raven-haired beauty into my orbit. In a week, I knew there was trouble in River City — more trouble than I felt interested in handling. I did not want to throw the Kazotsky expert off the stage; I did not want to go on with the local Nita Naldi; I missed Miriam; and I wanted to resume writing *The Flying Mare*. I signed off, bade farewell, and fled to Elberon for the remainder of the summer of '31.

I made a short stopover in Newark to check the house, buy some white pants, sneakers, and a couple of sport shirts. Before taking off, I bought Miriam and her family a few inexpensive gifts; another of Mother's instructions as we were growing up was, "Never visit with empty hands." Empty pockets, yes — empty hands, no. When I called Lil to check in and tell her where I'd be, she told me Pa was living with a lady in Elizabeth and that Sam had decided to get the evidence. "What the hell for?" I wanted to know. It seemed silly that Sam, a medal-of-honor womanizer, should righteously hand the black spot to Pa. Lil felt differently and we discussed it vehemently and lengthily in one of the few heated quarrels we ever had. She did not know where I could reach Sam. Angrily, she hung up and I left for Elberon.

Miriam and I had a happy reunion. She always smelled of cologne, gentle perfume, and powder, and the feel of her as we embraced was always new and exciting. Arguments even then — galore — but always reconciliation. And always, morning, night, no matter where or when, Miriam is immaculate. Except for cigarette ashes, which she would distribute generously over everyone and everything. (As with everything

[*42*]

she does, Miriam was an avid smoker. But five years ago, she suddenly said, "That's it!" She threw away the butt she was puffing on, dumped her cigarettes into a wastebasket, and has not touched a cigarette since.)

The summer days were sunny and warm, the nights starry and mild, and the plane tree in the area behind the house was a special spot where we talked and laughed and made love.

Those first few days were a joy. Then Lil called me one morning to tell me that Sam, backed up by a private detective, had broken into Pa's small apartment in Elizabeth and snapped the required pictures. Mother had been told and was going to file for divorce. Sam's behavior outraged me, Lil's compliance annoyed me, and I decided to go to Bar Harbor to see Mother. Not the next day. That very day.

Again a farewell to Miriam and her rather shocked parents. Newark was only an hour and a half away by train; once there, I dressed in my hiking clothes, and that afternoon I was thumbing my way north. By nightfall, I was in Boston. Spotting some trucks near a diner, I went in for a sandwich and coffee and a scouting expedition, which put me in touch with a driver and relief hand heading for Ellsworth, Maine, only a short distance from Bar Harbor. There was no room up front, but if I wanted to ride in back — "There're packing blankets, so hop in." I hopped, and piled some blankets in a space between some well-harnessed pieces of furniture. I slept till dawn, when we stopped for breakfast. It was a beautiful day and the air was full of that special scented Maine pine smell. A couple of hours later, we were in Ellsworth. My thanks were elaborate. My diner friends waved a good-bye.

When I rolled into Bar Harbor in a Packard convertible it was lunchtime. Mother and Aunt Bessie were surprised and delighted to see me, but there was little time to talk. I cleaned up, greeted some of the guests who remembered me from the year before, and walked to a copse of pine trees, where I stretched out on pine-needle-covered earth and suddenly wondered why I had come. My impulsive journey had resulted from a decision with no clear thought behind it. What was I going to suggest to Mother? There was no chance Mother and Pa could repair the wreckage of the thirty-nine-year-old marriage. Nothing was left of that — except three children, and a junkyard of broken schemes and dreams. Why was I here? What was I going to do? Did I have a right to mix in? The troubled thoughts and the fatigue of the long trip put me to sleep.

It was long after lunch when Mother woke me, and we sat on a bench.

Mother asked, "How's Miriam?" I told her. She liked the entire Svet family.

Then Mother said, "Sonny, you came a long way — I think I know why — but there are things you don't know — shouldn't know. I wish Sammy hadn't done what he did — but — the divorce is best for your father and best for me. It's too bad — but that's the way it is." She brushed her hands. "*Schwam daruber.*"

All I could muster was, "You're sure?"

Ma nodded, rose, and said, "Come, have some lunch." She kissed me. "It's good you came. I appreciate." She wiped at her eyes, turned, blew her nose, and walked toward the hotel. Then I knew why I had rushed to Bar Harbor — just to see if Ma was all right. She was.

The next day I strapped up, said good-bye, and headed back home. The weather was balmy and I did some hiking, not only for exercise but to clear my head. *The Flying Mare* wasn't stimulating and I was growing bored with it. I threw it away as I would a wormy apple. I did have another idea for a play, *Man of Ideas*, a satire about advertising.

At home there was a letter from Oscar Serlin wondering if I had any picture ideas, "but not *Flying Mare*." He had reached the same dead end. He didn't know it as yet, but Oscar was going to get an outline of a new play.

Miriam's mother had been raised in Odessa by a girl named Minnie, perhaps four years older than she. Minnie was still with the family, and had helped raise Lucille and Miriam; she also cooked, washed, scrubbed, contributed advice voluntarily on all matters concerning the family, the house, the city, state, and nation. Rosalie Svet, my future mother-in-law, was a handsome woman who viewed the harshness of the world with a myopic stubbornness. People were not bad. Events, if tragic or criminal, in the newspapers were not true; there were no robberies, rapes, or murders, simply stories to sell papers.

However, Minnie was a hard-nosed realist, and she and Rosalie went into war games during breakfast, lunch, tea, dinner, and tea and fruit before bedtime. Mr. Svet would act, most often, as an amused referee, until, weary of the conflict, he would lose his smile and raise his voice, at which point Minnie, with an angry pawing of her hand and a muffled Russian phrase, would retire to the kitchen. Rosalie, unruffled, would shake her head and pass the food.

The Svet homes in Newark and Elberon were lively and loud. During the day, piano and violin students were taking lessons; at night the dinner table was usually crowded with family and guests. Everyone in the family was a talker, Pa Svet, Rosalie, Lucille, Ira, her husband, the cousins, uncles, aunts, nephews, nieces, and in-laws: the chatter was ear-splitting, the food supply unending; through it all, Rosalie Svet moved, her chin raised, her manner imperious — a czarina. Actually, more like Queen Victoria.

The entire family were musicologists: Lucille, a gifted pianist; Miriam, an extraordinary "prima vista" (Rosalie's term) pianist; Pa Svet, composer and violin teacher; Rosalie, famous for her skill as a piano teacher; Ira, a violinist, not exceptional, but a student of opera and music.

The young lion of the pride was Julius Katchen, Lucille and Ira's son, in 1931 a boy of five, who quite obviously was a prodigy. His interest in and talent at the piano were astounding. He was a curly-haired, mischievous kid with a ready smile, and a quick mind and well-coordinated body that in a few years made him a brilliant pianist, an overpowering Ping-Pong player, a blue-ribbon swimmer, and an honor student. His sister, Rita, was another of the unusual Katchen breed, a good violinist and student. All of them talked loudly, hardly listening but catching enough to try to overcome the opposition. Their opinions were never tentative.

When it came to talking, I could make my way through the brambles of the Svets' conversational territory by waiting until someone ran out of breath, affording me the opportunity to challenge them.

For a few weeks, I didn't put pen to paper. Miriam and I swam (in those days she was a better swimmer than I), we went to movies, walked the boardwalk for miles, danced, went to some parties (little or no drinking), listened to music, and laughed a good deal. We argued a bit about her biting her nails, but I persuaded her to give up the habit.

The Svets gave me a party on my birthday, August 31. That ended the summer. Back we went to Newark. Mother returned from Bar Harbor and set up a dinner for the Svets at the restaurant. It became, more or less, a formal acceptance of my engagement to Miriam, and the question was, when do we get married? That had to wait. For money.

Just as I got to outlining *Man of Ideas* a run of parties began for Miriam and me. Miriam, with that unfathomable instinct that true lovers possess, always knew which girls I had previously "dated." Miriam's emotions are as controlled as a hungry tiger's.

At the first party Sylvia and Ralph Shapiro arranged in our honor, Miriam spotted an "enemy." As the party progressed the two women (girls, really) exchanged barked pleasantries, which ended when Miriam reached out and slapped her "opponent." This was followed by Miriam hitting her new acquaintance over the head with her small handbag. By that time, I was able to successfully intervene. The injured party left. The word went out — don't mess with Dore's girl. Later, for the first time, I heard Miriam refer to "the laughing girls" — it was her special phrase, not really for women who laughed, but for women to whom she thought I'd be attracted. The term she used was Freudian and simple to figure out. When she was thirteen, a severe injury to her skull that had occurred when she was a child of two manifested itself in a slight paralysis of left eye and cheek that at first was judged to be Bell's palsy. Time proved it was permanent damage to a facial nerve, which has never been a source of disturbance to me. But it has been to Miriam, though with diminishing intensity. There were combats later with other ladies Miriam viewed as rivals. Miriam won every decision. For years I teased her by calling her "Rocky," as in Marciano.

In quick succession a number of unwanted events slipped into our lives. First in the parade was the draining effect of the depression, which clobbered business at our restaurant. As we were reaching the glum resolution to close down, officials at the YMHA inquired if we would be interested in taking over the concession to run their restaurant and soda fountain. They offered to paint, redecorate, refurnish, and supply the first load of staples for the kitchen. We accepted, closed the Clinton Avenue eatery, and rented an apartment exactly one-half block from the Y. While waiting for all the repairs to be finished, I dug into *Man of Ideas*. That writing was terminated by sensations of dizziness that became extremely uncomfortable.

Our doctor discovered a low-grade fever; a blood study indicated an infection. Further examinations located a large abscess in an antrum. I had had great trouble with my teeth, due partly to neglect, partly to two extra teeth, one practically in the roof of my mouth, and partly to some patchwork dentistry. To clear an antrum in those days (and likely in these days) is a damned painful procedure. The infection prevented complete anesthetization, as a precaution against spreading the mess into my bloodstream.

The operation was done in a dental surgeon's office with another dentist and friend as an aide. Miriam insisted on waiting for me in the outer office. I was strapped into the chair, and given some novocaine to cover the pain of the extraction of a few teeth before they opened up the antrum. Two huge shots of whiskey were poured into me before the troops went into action. Then it was heigh-ho and away we go. The gory details are neither necessary nor rewarding. I moaned a lot and after I don't know how long, my jaw was packed up, covered with a cloth, and I was hustled into a cab with Miriam holding me close.

She had talked me into spending the night in her home because my mother was so busy at the Y. The one night stretched into two weeks when it developed that my infection had spread and that I required a great deal of attention including, for a few days, a trained nurse.

Mother made daily trips and Lil came in from New York. Miriam possessively wanted to care for me by herself and resented the nurse, Mother, Lil, Rosalie, and anyone else who came near me including her uncle, Dr. Aaron Parsonnet, a man with a sure and cheery manner who

[47]

quite bluntly told Miriam that if I didn't get the proper care I might die. That bit of information convinced Miriam that (a) she should set a marriage date before I left her, and (b) that the experienced healers should take over. Well, (a) we agreed on the date of March 5, the following year, for our marriage, and (b) I got well.

By December, I was looking for a job to finance my continued work on *Man of Ideas*. We had been installed in the Y restaurant and soda fountain, where I worked as headwaiter, jerked sodas, and aided Mother in catering numerous luncheons.

Miriam also pinch-hit as cashier; trying desperately to help the cause, she erred by shortchanging a number of customers, not deliberately, but because she did not and still does not add, subtract, or divide very well.

In January, my extensive dental repair was finished and part of the cost of it paid. The wedding date was moving up. The Svets offered us the third-floor suite in their home as our living quarters until we were able to manage our own total living expenses. Mother was going to cater the wedding at the Svets and even Pa was going to attend.

Time came rushing at me at high tide as I scurried for a full-time job. Mr. Sonnenbend, publisher of a neighborhood newspaper, the *Springfield Avenue News*, tendered me the position of advertising solicitor and copywriter. My family and I knew most of the shopkeepers on Springfield Avenue and the response to my pitch was so encouraging that Mr. Sonnenbend raised my salary to forty dollars a week, also adding the duties and title of editor to my labors. I immediately became a runner-up to Hearst, Pulitzer, and Herbert Bayard Swope.

We published once every two weeks. It came as a shock when I was charting ads to realize that an upcoming "pub" date was March 6, one day after my approaching wedding date. A shift in gears was mandatory. I'd have to make up the paper by noon on March 5, and turn it over to the printers for them to run on the morning of the sixth. The forms would have to be locked in time for me to hurry home, bathe, shave, dress in the rented tuxedo, and be ready for the wedding ceremony by six. Paper to bed by afternoon — bride to bed by evening.

Memories of the few days before the deadline are blurred — no, more like a group of strobe camera shots — the images are there but moving too rapidly to see detail.

Buy the bridal flowers, the wedding ring — get the copy for the ads written — attend the stag party given at the University Club — write the filler stories for the paper — be at the Y for the basketball game, which meant busy business at the fountain — buy the shirt and collar for the tux (I kept singing Rogers and Hart, "I've got five dollars; I'm in good condition; and I've got ambition; that belongs to you . . .").

March 5, and at two o'clock in the afternoon I'm covered with sweat, printer's ink, but I'm done. Mr. Sonnenbend has given me my salary and I'm at the barber's — then I'm home — scrubbing like hell to get the ink out of my nails. The damn studs don't fit the shirt — yes they do — the collar digs into my neck — bend the points — Mother and Lil and her husband, Henry, in from New York, escort me, and we're off to see the Wizard, known to one and all as Rabbi Julius Silberfeld, who will run the show at the Svets.

My God, March 5 and I'm to be married. How the hell did I get into this jam? Will the issue of the *Springfield Avenue News* be born alive and kicking? How dare I go to the St. Moritz in New York for a honeymoon with only one hundred and twenty-five dollars in my right-hand pants' pocket? Will they find the Lindbergh baby? Is FDR going to run? Will I ever write *Man of Ideas?*

The landing at Miriam's home on Weequahic Avenue was smooth. The clans were gathering and they oohed and aahed when Miriam appeared and posed for singles, and doubles with me, and triples, quadruples, and full family group shots that Mr. Trubnick, Newark's family photographer, captured for posterity with a camera that might have been used by Mathew Brady. Guests kept arriving. Soon the music heralded the beginning of the wedding. Soon we stood together under the canopy. Soon I was asked the ceremonial "Do you . . ." with the required remuda of words. It occurred to me, "Why the hell would I have gone through a year of commitment without being certain?" So, I answered, "I most certainly do," with an exclamation point in my voice.

The stamping of the glass commemorating the Temple in ancient Israel followed . . . my foot smashed it, and my wife and I kissed amid the chorus of *mazel tovs*, the sound of sobs from members of the families, followed by hugs and kisses in addition to handshakes and the passing of envelopes from friendly hands to mine. Whenever I had a free second, I took a peek at the cash and checks, realizing that we were building a comfortable exchequer. Mr. Svet topped off the celebration with two hundred dollars in cash, which I asked him to hold for us until we returned from our New York honeymoon four days hence.

We taxied to New York with over four hundred dollars and the future looking us smack in the eye. The St. Moritz Hotel had our suite ready, including flowers from Lil. We began our four-day honeymoon.

The following noon, a nagging wish to find out if all had gone well at the *Springfield Avenue News* undid me. I called in to learn that I had locked the forms in wrong order and that the printers hadn't spotted the error. Mr. Sonnenbend had had to reset the issues with consequent extra cost and aggravation. He spoke to me in tired, slow sentences: "So you're fired, don't come back. I owe you three days' salary, where should I send it?"

I hung up without a word.

There was the future, smack in the eye.

We smacked back. We had a fine time in and out of the hotel; went to expensive restaurants, saw *Of Thee I Sing* and *Face the Music*, took long rides in hansoms, drank champagne, and returned to Newark with three one-dollar bills and some coins, but oh, what a lovely beginning.

Mr. Svet's two hundred dollars gave us a running start along with the work at the Y restaurant and soda fountain.

We came back to the bread lines and apple sellers and the empty storefronts that (probably because of my recent mouth surgery) reminded me of gaps in a line of teeth. The Lindbergh tragedy wiped the depression off the right-hand columns for a long time, though unemployment and the rising tide of reaction to it kept their place on the front page. Poor Herbert Hoover, once a national hero, had become a high-stiff-collared figure of derision. Homeless, hungry people raised tin and wooden shacks in empty lots in cities throughout the country; these tiny enclaves took on the generic name of Hoovervilles. Since annual wages were sunk to lows such as coal miner $700, chauffeur $650, college teacher $3,100, doctor $3,400, those of us who scrabbled in free-lance work netting $1,000 to $1,500 a year hardly felt deprived or underprivileged; we even had enough to drop pennies, nickles, or dimes in tin cups or send a dollar to various appeals to help the poor.

Late in March, Don Hartman contacted me. We had not seen each other since the Grossinger episode. Don thought he and I might work together on one or two ideas. We began to see each other frequently and after some preliminary sparring, we both loosened up, finding in each other a compatible sense of humor, a desire for achievement, and a need for recognition. More important, we discovered we liked each other.

Don had no intention of going back to Grossinger's or any other Catskill retreat: "I've had it with the Borscht Belt." One day he told me of a musical concept he had dreamed up designed for the Marx Brothers. After fruitless time spent with the composer Phil Charig, well known for his song "A Sunny Disposish," he had abandoned the idea. I liked Don's notion, which was a satirical view of the journey of the *Mayflower* to

America in 1620. In a few minutes we had a title, *Up Spoke the Captain*, and some visual sketches that I put down on paper. Don called Charig, who was eager to resume work, and we were set: Don and I to do the libretto, Phil the music, and Don the lyrics.

Don's apartment, crowded with him, Chick, his breezy and strong wife, and two daughters, was no place to work. Our blueprint was to work at Phil Charig's place, and at my place in Newark. Our combined energies cascaded a script onto paper in a few short weeks.

Don's agent, Harry Bestry, was a character sired by Damon Runyon. His sharp-featured face was cut in two by a wide, thin slash of a mouth topped by a mustache. His wardrobe was extraordinary. If Harry selected a suit he liked, in fabric and style, he would have duplicates made in his favorite colors — gray, green, light blue, brown, and navy. His closet was lined with racks of twelve different-style suits, each one duplicated exactly in his five favorite colors. "Count them if you want," Harry said, "there's sixty — no more, no less."

Harry smoked, ate pistachio nuts, and radiated overpowering assurance. We had arrived at his apartment to audition our show, but first we had to audition his clothes. Then Bestry stretched out on his divan, nodded his head, and said, "Go to it, good luck."

When after a strenuous workout we had wound up our performance, Harry said, "Great, it's great. I'll get Sam Harris to listen. It's great, just great." This appraisal would have warmed our hearts if Harry knew what we had read and sung to him. But indeed, we were certain he didn't, because he kept telling us, "It's great. A musical about the President's yacht. It's timely. Great." He guaranteed that he would arrange for producer Sam Harris to give us a hearing. We were positive he wouldn't or couldn't, but he did.

The night of the reading for Harris, Don, Phil, and I gathered for a quick rehearsal and review of who was to do what. We arrived promptly at eight-thirty at Sam Harris's apartment. The butler told us to wait. Mr. Harris was at dinner. Phil tested the piano. It was in tune. At nine-thirty, Mr. Harris sauntered in, escorting a young and beautiful woman who Glad-to-meet-ya'ed the three of us and sat down next to Mr. Harris on a high-legged sofa. She toyed with a long string of pearls, which provided an occasional obbligato of clicks. Mr. Harris suggested that, since he was a bit slight of hearing, we keep our voices up. If Mr. Harris, one of the most famous and successful producers on Broadway, wanted us to scream the story, all he had to do was ask. We read and sang like banshees.

The audition lasted an hour and a half. The beautiful young lady thought it was "dreamy." Mr. Harris told us, "I like it. If George Kaufman likes it, I'll do it."

The butler showed us out and we floated down to the street without a word until we were out of earshot of Mr. Harris's apartment house and then we exploded. We were in. Of course Kaufman would like it. It would follow that the Marx Brothers would like it. It was springtime, the auguries were rich in promise. We went to our separate homes in triumph.

I didn't arrive at Weequahic Avenue in Newark until 1:30 A.M. Miriam was waiting, and listened as I outlined the steps we would be taking to fame and fortune; a fieldstone home, Packard roadster — just to begin with. At dawn we fell asleep drunk with fantasies.

But George Kaufman didn't like it.

Don decided to take a summer job — in the Borscht Belt.

Phil had another musical commitment.

Man of Ideas was unfinished so I went back to the drawing board. Summer was coming, the Y restaurant would be closed, and in a few weeks I'd be broke.

*H*enry Stuts, *the athletic director* of the YMHA, owned a boys' camp near Poughkeepsie. He needed a drama counselor; I needed a job. We were well met. He offered me two hundred and fifty dollars, room and board for Miriam and me, plus freedom from routine counselor duties.

The summer months at Camp Stuts were the first time Miriam had been separated from percale sheets, clean tablecloths, and private bath. I "took her away from all that" to a single room attached to the main house. The room (lean-to is a truer identity) had two wooden walls and two walls slatted to waist height with the remaining space screened. Rolled canvas drops protected us from prying eyes, rain, and early morning sun. But nothing protected us from the leaky roof. Miriam didn't miss a beat; she learned to launder, adjusted to the ordinary food, got along well with the kids, and eventually won the affection of Stuts's old grandmother, who was delighted that Miriam could speak a little Yiddish. That proved Miriam was really Jewish, a fact the elderly Mrs. Stuts had not previously believed.

At summer's end, I had a finished draft of *Man of Ideas*. Stuts deducted seventy-five dollars from my summer's pay for "extras." What the "extras" were was never made clear to me but I took the one hundred and seventy-five dollars in cash and we headed for the comfort of a bathtub, running hot water, and Minnie's food at the Svet home in Elberon.

During the summer, Mother had worked as a cook at a hotel on the Jersey shore. She had a few days free and we spent time together before we had to return to open up the Y for the fall and winter season.

Franklin Roosevelt had been nominated to run against Hoover, who had sealed his political execution by burning World War I veterans out of Hooverville in the Anacostia Flats. The presidential campaign was in full bloom with FDR a certain winner.

Don Hartman checked in with Phil Charig and we resumed our re-writes on *Up Spoke the Captain*. Finishing those, we sent the manuscript direct to Groucho Marx in Hollywood.

In October, Frieda Fishbein made a deal with Sidney Harmon for an option on *Man of Ideas* that suddenly poured two hundred dollars into my sock. I gave Mother part of the loot, bought Miriam a few gadgets, brought flowers, candy, cake, and fruit to the Svets, and cut down my debts to the dentists.

That same month Groucho returned our *Captain* script with regrets — but perhaps if we rewrote it into a movie scenario — no promises — but. We didn't wish to do that. Don had an assignment to write lyrics for Vitaphone short subjects and I was starting rewrites for Sidney Harmon on the play he had now retitled *Terrific*, so Don, Phil, and I tabled *Up Spoke the Captain*. It is still there.

FDR's landslide election in November cheered everyone even though his inauguration would not take place until March. But while elation could keep up the spirit it could not warm the windswept shack, feed the belly, or put a chicken in the pot or even one car in the garage.

Moss's success had jetted him into celebrity and moved him into a life-stye he adored. His friends were the elite of the theater, his clothes were tailor-made, and he had begun to collect his assortment of gold bibelots. He had been away for a long time in Hollywood but now he was in New York to work on a new show and we were able to have lengthy talks. As always, Moss was encouraging and kept assuring me, "You'll make it, Butch, you'll see." It was nice to hear but it was a cold winter and I was twenty-seven years old.

During the cold early November, I kept the hope that there would ultimately be enough money to take Miriam to an apartment of our own; my activities included selling Christmas cards with little success, writing sketches with even less success, and working at the Y soda fountain with fair success and a steady diet of ice cream.

Frieda Fishbein had told me that George Givot needed a sketch for *Americana*, a show in which he was starring. His agent had recommended me, setting a date for us to meet at the Lambs Club on a Sunday morning for breakfast at eleven o'clock. A heavy snow blanketed the city on that Sunday, followed by high winds wedded to a bitter cold wave. Getting to New York on schedule was not easy but getting into the Lambs was more difficult — the doorman, knowing of no appointment with Mr. Givot, would not, with justice, allow a stranger to use the warmth of the club as a refuge but did permit me to use the outer lobby, which offered some protection from the wind and cold. Mr. Givot never showed up.

That disappointment left me with another unused manuscript along with a heavy cold that laid me up for a few days. The Givot episode was typical of that November. Business began to fall off in the restaurant, and the script of *Terrific* didn't seem to mesh. On trips to New York to see potential buyers for scripts, Miriam and I ended up with lunches at Nedick's (orange juice and hot dogs) or dinner at Childs (English muffins, one order of French fries and cocoa), while in between my appointments Miriam sat in Frieda's office meeting other writers in the same unfulfilled state as I.

We had been told by Frieda that Jeanne Cohen, the story editor for Columbia Pictures in New York, had been impressed by the work of a few of Frieda's stable of writers and subsequently had informed Frieda that Harry Cohn, the maharaja of Columbia, was coming into New York to search for and sign up writers. Prior to his arrival some scripts were to be sent to the Coast and he would see the authors of those scripts most attractive to him.

Talking motion pictures were now more than the wave of the future — they were a way of life for movies, and every studio was increasing production as the demand for "talkies" increased. Since dialogue had eliminated title cards (though some producers still referred to dialogue as "titles") the search for scenarists was concentrated in New York for established or "promising" playwrights. The established ones had contempt for Hollywood; Broadway was producing two hundred plays or more each season so there was little incentive for successful playwrights to train out to California merely to make a few bucks, perhaps manage a dalliance with a starlet, or get sunburned. There was a lot of money to be made on Broadway. Young ladies were just as avid to make good on the couch before getting to the stage, and you could get sunburned in Florida at the Roney Plaza. The "promising" playwrights had different ideas: many of them liked motion pictures, believed they could write good ones and would not be coerced by the producers.

However, in those early days of the gold rush, the main attraction was the money. Those talents "destroyed" by Hollywood were most often knocked off by self-inflicted wounds. Writers masked their greed or embarrassment by telling their friends they were going to Hollywood only to get some loot and then come home to write the great American novel or play. As a warning to others who were on their way to Hollywood, embittered veterans returning from the Coast would warn the tyros, "Don't buy anything you can't bring home on the Chief." The Chief, of course, was the luxury train to California, later superseded by the (naturally) Super Chief.

Jeanne Cohen had read some of my work and told Frieda she had sent *One Every Minute* to Columbia as being most representative of my writing.

This had happened some weeks before. Since we had heard nothing from Jeanne, Hollywood remained a subject for daydreams and there was "no discharge in the war" between the future and me.

A few days before Thanksgiving, 1932, while I was cleaning up and resupplying the soda bar, Mother said I was wanted on the phone by Frieda Fishbein, who told me that Harry Cohn had come into town and wished to see me that afternoon.

Mother was sure she could manage without me. Then there was a call to Miriam to urge her to think good thoughts. With high hopes and clean fingernails, I was on my way.

When I got to Columbia's headquarters, Jeanne Cohen escorted me into Harry Cohn's office.

My first look at Cohn showed me a tough but rather handsome man with a hard jaw, thinning hair, and a cigar held by thick fingers. When Jeanne introduced us he did not shake my hand but smiled and said, "Fer Chrissakes." He explained his amusement by telling me that Walter Wanger, who was then employed by Cohn, had read *One Every Minute* and had advised that "Dore Schary be signed up because she writes tough like a man." I couldn't think of a clever response so I smiled and shrugged.

The dialogue that follows is an accurate report with the qualification that a few unimportant words may be missing or out of place.

COHN   Would you like to go to work in Hollywood?

ME   Yes, sir.

COHN   When could you go?

ME   Tomorrow.

COHN   I like guys who make up their minds quick.

ME   Thanks.

COHN   Well, that's it. Jeanne will get in touch.

ME   Thank you again.
(I rose and he waved farewell with his cigar.)

COHN   Don't you want to know what you'll get?

ME   I'm sure it's going to be more than I'm making right now.

COHN   It's a hundred a week.

ME   That's a lot more. Thanks.

COHN   See you in California. (He turned to Jeanne.) Who's next?

Walking on air remains the truest metaphor to describe a state of euphoria and that's the state I was in. I wafted into Frieda's office, kissed her, then called Miriam to tell her we were on the road to Hollywood. The psychologists say that daydreaming is good for you — if so, I was healthier than ever. I would write great movies — drive beautiful cars — buy gorgeous clothes and furs for Miriam — live in a home much like Pickfair, where Douglas Fairbanks and Mary Pickford resided. The dreams were in throbbing rosy colors.

That night at the soda fountain each customer got a little extra — not only added syrup and ice cream, but the news that I was going west to write movies for Columbia Pictures.

Word spread rapidly. I have always been blessed with friends, and the line began at the right with congratulations, letters, phone calls, and an item in the Newark *Sunday Call*. My colleagues at the University Club scheduled a farewell bash for me to be catered by Mother at the Y restaurant the following week. Our departure for California was scheduled for December 14.

My father, who was now back in Newark living in his own quarters, was skeptical when I went to see him. He loathed what he called "the show business," believing it to be a refuge for whores and *faygelehs* (homosexuals). Having watched me squander twenty-seven years and perhaps twenty-seven chances for working in "decent" professions, he simply would not believe anyone would pay me one hundred a week to write anything. "Listen, Son, you can tell that to your mother, your wife, and your friends — but don't lie to me. If they only give you fifty a week, consider yourself lucky. Just don't lie to me."

Since in arguing with Pa, incontrovertible truth was no match for mere opinion, I let the matter drop.

The Svets were delighted, partly because Miriam and I might have become a burden to their strained finances. The Katchens were truly pleased. They were willing to write off the three hundred dollars I owed them, but the gift was refused.

Miriam and I began packing a large trunk and a variety of suitcases. Miriam's trousseau had been bought at a shop owned by the couturier Mr. Doop, a genteel, mustachioed man who with Mrs. Svet had selected raiment for a princess but hardly anything for the wife of a junior writer who was going to Hollywood at the far from princely salary of a hundred dollars per week.

The following Monday Mother told me that the University Club had picked the next Thursday, December 1, for my so-long banquet. I went to New York to go over the good news once more with Frieda.

The good news was that Larry Pohle, Edwin Gilbert, and a third writer whom I had not met, Lou Levenson, had also been chosen by Cohn.

The bad news was that the deal had been called off. Cohn had changed his mind.

As in the old joke, I wasn't disappointed or depressed — I simply made plans to kill myself. I called Miriam and told her that. Then I called my sister, Lil, and gave her the unhappy bulletin. Lil, who in many ways was the best battler in the family, said she'd like to know where Harry Cohn was staying and find him and break his nose. In her young days, when we lived on Thirteenth Avenue in Newark, Lil often would join in the ever ongoing gang fights and mete out a lot more than she got, and if I had known where Harry Cohn was that night, Lil and I might have gone scouting for him — after that I would have had time to kill myself.

When I reached home, Miriam had stopped crying but was preparing to call the New York police. Convinced that she would hear tragic news about me, she was also planning to kill herself. But by then I was in no mood for suicide. I had made other less drastic plans.

No one would be told that the job offer had been withdrawn. After previous tales of optioned plays and movie-script sales that never reached fulfillment, the tale of the aborted Columbia contract would simply prove I was a damned liar. I would borrow money, which would be needed in any event; we would go to Chicago via the 20th Century, which was *de rigueur* for travel to Hollywood, and then from Chicago I'd get a job driving a truck or car or bus to California and once there — well, I'd find something to do.

The next few days were agonizing but nothing like the night of the University Club dinner. The boys were in good humor and the booze, smuggled in, heightened the hilarity. When they presented me with a briefcase in which to store "all your rejected scripts," I almost broke down and confessed the entire shabby subterfuge, but I decided the hell with that. Instead I drank a lot of liquor. The evening was a rousing and happy event. I went home singing, "I've got five dollars," plopped into bed and hugged Miriam, and slept the sleep of the innocent drunken bum until Minnie woke me at ten the next morning to inform me that Frieda was on the phone. Again?

I stumbled down and yes, again, it was Frieda. Cohn had changed his mind — again. We were to leave as originally planned on December 14. The terms were all set. One hundred dollars a week for three months.

One twenty-five for three months. One fifty for three months, one seventy-five for three months. Then two hundred dollars for the second year and so on and so on until the seventh year, at which time seven hundred and fifty dollars was the Promised Land.

It was true. We were really going to Hollywood.

M *onday, I was in New York* with Miriam. The contracts were in Frieda's office, signed by Sam Briskin, the executive officer in charge of signing contracts and all manner of other things at Columbia. Two other scribes, Gilbert and Levenson, had already signed up. Larry Pohle and I filled in the blank spaces, shook hands, opened a bottle of champagne Larry had brought for the occasion, and it was "Hallelujah" time.

Then some reckoning was required. The salary was one hundred. Deduct ten for Frieda's commission, ten to help Mother, fifteen for twelve weeks to repay Columbia for Miriam's fare, which they were advancing to me, and other debts to be paid back at a rate of ten per week. That left fifty-five dollars for housing and food. A fortune.

When Miriam and I left Newark for Grand Central Station, we had, counting money still owed my dental surgeon, the Katchens, and friends, a total of eleven hundred and fifty dollars in debts.

Lil, the Katchens, and a galaxy of friends saw us off as we walked down the traditional red carpet the 20th Century spread out for its travelers. There were kisses, hugs, shouts, some good jokes, some bad ones, then waving and more shouting through the car windows, then ultimately tears, a shake and a rattle, and we were on our way.

Gilbert, Levenson, Pohle, Miriam, and I were booked in the same Pullman car.

Gilbert, later a gifted and successful novelist, was then a determined young man who fancied himself as handsome, well-groomed, a shade more intellectual than the other three of us. In fact, he was.

Levenson, a newspaperman and a pulp-magazine writer, worked hard to play a character from *Front Page,* but he was miscast for the role. He wore thick glasses, had some teeth missing from his front lower ridge, and kept leering at Miriam.

The most outgoing and friendliest of the three was Larry. He was a homosexual who made no pretenses. He neither was effeminate nor pretended to be macho. He had indefatigable cheeriness and confidence. While none of us had ever been west of the Mississippi, Larry was the only one who behaved as if he'd made the trip a hundred times. He was a big, blond, red-cheeked man and a delightful companion who became a good friend.

Traveling had always made me uneasy and fretful. The queasiness I felt when making any journey to an unknown (to me) destination was probably based on an experience I had when I was four years old. My mother and father had taken me to Brooklyn to see some of Pa's relatives. I was left alone as the women talked while the men played cards. A bowl of blue grapes attracted my attention and I gorged myself until I became ill with acute indigestion. Mother carried me into a bedroom that was painted a ghastly electric blue. For years after, the sight of that color literally raised the bile. Even now, that shade of blue creates an association that takes me back to that horrid room, the clucking cluster of elders, and the vomiting and cramps.

Whenever I started for a new locale, I anticipated disaster. Once I began going back and forth between New York and California and traveling to many other ports of call, I lost that ailment of anticipating disaster. (Or did I? Recently I read that my habit of always sitting in the first seat on an airplane is a vestigial sign of alarm.)

As we left New York, I got those wang-wang blues. Miriam loved leaving. Now I was hers. She helped me over the bad time. Often, my spells were accompanied by fainting and vomiting. However, Miriam and Larry's unusual excitement and good cheer kept me afloat with no unhappy side effects.

Before we had left, a messenger had arrived with a heavy wooden case wrapped in brown paper. It was, the messenger confided, a case of Scotch. It was to be delivered to Walter Wanger at Columbia. During the trip, I trudged it from the Union Station to the Santa Fe Station, from the Los Angeles Station to the Hollywood Roosevelt Hotel, and ultimately to the Columbia studio.

The trip came alive when word spread through the train that Marie Dressler was a passenger. At each stop, we got off and gawked at the car in which she was riding in drawing-room splendor. (We were in berths — Miriam in a lower, me in the upper.) But it wasn't until

Albuquerque that Marie Dressler appeared on the steps, posed for pictures, waved a royal hand at her fellow passengers, and retreated into her curtained room.

Levenson was a good chess player and toyed with the rest of us as he checkmated us from New York to somewhere past Kansas City. His leers at Miriam became more overt until one evening when I returned from the lavatory and found him trying to paw Miriam as she was pushing him away.

It was not in my nature to suffer maulers gently, so I picked Lou up, slapped his face, hauled him to the end of the car, and threatened, "You touch her again and I'll boot your ass back to New York." The incident inhibited further opportunity for a friendship with Lou.

Larry thought I was silly to bother, Gilbert was contemptuous of my resorting to violence, and Miriam said she had tried to kick Levenson in a vital area but had missed.

As always, I felt guilty that I had lost my temper.

Losing my temper with a resulting welling up of guilt dates back to my father and the beatings he gave Sam, Lillian, and me. He, for some peculiar reason that might have been a rudimentary ESP or perhaps a special affection, never touched Frances in anger. To him, she was "Little Bird." Her death when she was only twenty-six bit into him deeply. Pa made up for harshness never directed at Frances by leveling on us remaining three. His hand was heavy and his temper sudden and frightening, like summer thunder and lightning. Pa was a powerful man. Years later, when he was sixty-four years old, he was held up by two unlucky young men in an antique shop he had acquired. Pa reached behind the counter, ostensibly to give them his money box, but instead came up with a brass candlestick, knocked the man holding the gun to the floor, reached for the other one with his left hand, and brought that unfortunate fellow smashing facedown on the counter. Pa trotted outdoors (West Forty-fourth opposite the Belasco Theatre), blew his police whistle, and presented the thieves to the police, who stared in wonderment at the two unconscious and bloody bandits.

I had been afraid of Pa's temper until I found him in New York after his departure from Pleasantdale, but I remembered the injuries and the indignities he placed on himself, and therefore I have remained embarrassed and guilty each time I have lost my temper.

We arrived in Hollywood on Saturday, December 17, late in the afternoon. Moss was there to meet us. We bade Larry and Gilbert adieu until Monday morning, when we were scheduled to fall in at Columbia at 10:00 A.M. We nodded at Levenson, lifted Wanger's liquor and our suitcases into Moss's car, and set off for the Hollywood hills, where Moss had rented a mansion above what is now the tawdry, cheap, and sometimes violent Sunset Strip.

The view from Moss's front porch was our initiation into the wonder of the movie capital. Stretched out below us and into the beyond lay the carpet of lights that put you up in the universe looking down at the stars. I felt a sense of accomplishment — I was here, paid to write (the amount of money was incidental), and for the first time my name had been listed in *Variety* — "N.Y. to L.A. Dore Schary." It is fulfilling to have identity, but the simple joys of first small rewards are not always matched by subsequent successes. Despite the need for introspection to help keep your head on straight, it is nevertheless true that you begin to accept success and awards as your due, and what you lose are the first career enjoyments — gratefulness that you have made that initial step and a strong confidence that you will keep moving to complete fulfillment.

Moss had a chauffeur-butler who at the end of the evening drove us to the Hollywood Roosevelt Hotel with all our gear. When we opened the window to look out on Vine Street, before us was the storied Brown Derby.

Tomorrow was Sunday. We had calls to make, an apartment to find, and people to see.

It was bedtime and suddenly Hollywood was an aphrodisiac.

In the morning it was sunny and warm. We called Oscar Serlin, who lived only four or five blocks away from Vine on Kingsley Drive. We walked there and met the owners of the apartment house, Mr. and Mrs. Taylor, who informed us they had a one-room apartment available. It was an L-shaped room, furnished quite handsomely. The ell in the room harbored a large closet and an in-a-door bed that pulled down into a commodious and heavily mattressed refuge for the night. Completing the arrangement were a small kitchen area and a tiny dining area separated by a three-quarter-high partition.

The Serlins, Oscar and Jane, came downstairs and approved our selection and were pleased we were to be bivouacked in the same house. Other tenants were Cary Grant, who was moving out in a couple of weeks, and Laird Doyle, an ace writer of screenplays at Warner Brothers. We met Doyle, had coffee with the Serlins, and then went back for our luggage. The rent for the apartment was sixty dollars per month. That sum meant fifteen more off my remaining fifty-five each week, leaving me with forty — still plenty.

Luck was riding at our side: one stop and we had a comfortable apartment with friends as close neighbors and a charming and helpful pair of landlords.

Next was a call to Ruth Tannenbaum, née Katzin, a former Newarker. She had been a close friend of both our families. She and her husband, David Tannenbaum, an attorney, picked us up, drove us to their home for lunch, then gave us a sight-seeing tour of Beverly Hills. It was a warm and clear-skied day — all blue, white, and green. Our first view of the suburb of Westwood remains a clear 3-D color picture. There was a cluster of buildings, each one white-stuccoed and roofed with red tiles. The master plan of the developers of Westwood was to create a model suburb with the center of the town designed to house shops, filling stations, food markets in the same-styled buildings. For years they succeeded, but the pressure of the booming population surge buried the plan. Today, most of Westwood is schlock with only remnants of the original dream town visible in the mass of chrome and glass emporiums housing ice cream, hamburgers, gas, radios, and so on. It is the UCLA college town, jammed with students, faculty, visitors, and merchants. Motorcycles, bicycles, and autos duplicate the traffic snarls of any modern city.

It is now fashionable to scoff at memories as being illusions of beauty and peace and security. But the fact is that cities have changed. We were fresh from a grimy, grim, cold eastern city environment where lines of hungry and desperate people waited for handouts from soup kitchens; apple sellers were on the street corners hawking for nickels; the big hit song was "Brother, Can You Spare a Dime," and it was for real. In Hollywood and its environs, there were no such signs of the depression. The Roosevelt boom had already begun solely on campaign promises. There were few empty storefronts. A building economy was burgeoning and a surefooted air came with it. Property was low-priced and buyers were picking it up in bundles. It was Disneyland blanketed by sunlight.

That night, the Tannenbaums took us for dining and dancing at the Miramar Hotel in Santa Monica. The Miramar was an early-day Ciro's, Trocadero, and Chasen's rolled into one.

We were joined by one of David's clients, Carl Laemmle, Jr., a fresh-faced young man, known to me by reputation as the heir apparent to the Universal Pictures empire. Hardly had we recovered from this first flush of hobnobbing with celebrity when our first look at a sex symbol of the industry was presented to us by Junior — Jean Harlow. She was smaller than I thought she would be and not nearly as coarse looking but rather frail looking, beautiful, and gracious.

Meeting her was a sudden blow to Miriam. She was again conscious of her facial paralysis and for the first time since our departure from New York I noticed she was sitting back in her chair, her head lowered, her manner quiet — sure signs that she was unhappy. However, she fought her way out of it and before the evening was over, food, champagne, and excitement had driven Harlow out of her thoughts. I assured Miriam that she had a better figure than Harlow — and she did.

Monday morning we four visitors from the faraway planet checked into Columbia Pictures. A studio policeman took the case of Scotch off my hands and conscience and we lingered for our meeting with Mr. Harry Cohn. After a long wait, we were escorted into an inner courtyard surrounded by four walls of offices. We were assigned first-floor cubicles that had decorative iron bars on the windows — sort of a classy San Quentin.

Some time later, young men appeared with pads, pencils, pens and ink, typewriters, information sheets, and the like. Next door to my cell was a chubby, moon-faced man who waddled into my room and introduced himself as Bill Kay, "a wanderer in the lotus land of Cohn, Briskin, and Jaffe. Relax, dear boy, trusties such as ourselves are allowed to return to our homes each night." For the time he remained at Columbia, Bill Kay was given no assignment and spent most of his stay composing marvelous memos and letters to cheer me on with predictions of my success.

By late afternoon that first day, the four of us had broken security and gathered in Larry's office to decide whether we should leave for our lodgings or wait out the night. Gilbert was outraged at the "typical rudeness" of Hollywood executives. Levenson, slumped in a chair, was working on a chess problem. Larry, bright-eyed, argued that we were getting a hundred a week and had no reason to be arrogant or prideful. I really didn't give a damn. My normal curiosity had kept my interest at a high key. Having studied personnel sheets, I had learned that other writers employed currently with us included Norman Krasna, James Cain, Joel Sayre, Jo Swerling, Sidney Kingsley, Robert Riskin, and James McGuinness. I concluded that if this was good enough for them, it was good enough for us.

At five o'clock, we received our summons to the throne room. We left the courtyard and walked up a flight of steps into Mr. Cohn's reception room, where a perfectly stunning secretary was waiting to lead us into the sanctum sanctorum. Gilbert, one hand in his jacket pocket, preceded us, followed by Levenson, Pohle, and me.

Inside the office were Mr. Cohn, Walter Wanger, Frank Capra, Sam Briskin (who had signed our original contracts), and Robert Riskin, who, teamed with Capra, had earned a great reputation as a dedicated and highly talented screenwriter. Cohn introduced us with nods. Waves of hands were exchanged. Handshakes between us would have developed into a comedy scene. Larry had sat down into a large soft couch, Levenson plopped next to him, and Gilbert took a position of nonchalance near the piano, his hand still in his jacket pocket. I chose to sit on the arm of the sofa nearest the door. Wanger thanked me for bringing the Scotch. I saluted, and while I was tempted to suggest he pay me for the extra tips the damn box of booze had cost me, I kept my mouth shut.

Cohn lit a cigar, then turned to Pohle and asked, "What kind of writing you do? Whaddaya want to write?"

I winced as Larry, losing his poise, burbled, "I'd like to do a story about a gangster's moll. I believe these women have been terribly neglected in crime movies." He went on for a few more minutes. Being on an advantageous perch, I could read the quick, negative attitude of our audience. Levenson was next. Not having spotted any of the reaction to Larry's gaffe, he essayed that he would like to write a tough, honest, true, real, hard-boiled newspaper story. Since *Front Page* had already furrowed that territory, it seemed doubtful to the jury that Levenson could outdo Hecht and MacArthur. So it was two down and two to go. Gilbert was next at bat and he boldly declared, "I write like Noel Coward." That was three down and Cohn called on me.

I said that all day I had felt like a milk bottle waiting to be delivered and I would write what I was asked to write and do my best to make it good.

Cohn chuckled and said to the others, "I told you, Walter, he was no dame."

He got up, which was an obvious suggestion that we go. We said good night and this time I was first out. As Larry closed the door behind him, we heard the murmur of voices and some laughter. Gilbert, furious, said good night to us and rushed away. Levenson decided to hang back and talk to the lovely secretary, who was one of three. Larry and I walked out together and he shook his head and said, "You're the only one who didn't act like a horse's ass."

I answered that being last had given me an edge. I probably would not have done well had I been first.

My good humor lasted until I reached the apartment, then the held-in uneasiness, the strangeness, the strain of the trip and that first day brought on old symptoms familiar to those who know of William Ellery Leonard's *Locomotive God* — loneliness and apprehension, accompanied by a desire to hide and avoid the unknown danger.

I felt feverish and became savaged by nausea and diarrhea. Miriam reached the phone in the landlord's apartment and called Ruth Tannenbaum, who got in touch with a Dr. Immerman, who showed up rather quickly. He diagnosed my ailment as "gastric neurasthenia," gave me a shot of a sedative, prescribed medication, advised me to stay in bed for a day or two, and stated that the bill was fifteen dollars. After he left, I realized we had ten dollars and some change left for the rest of the week.

The sudden drainage of physical and financial resources sobered me up. I drew some deep breaths, fell asleep, and woke up the next day ready for battle.

That's the way it always works with me. First the jimjams, then a long night's sleep and I arise reoriented and prepared for new experiences, having shed my fears and alarms.

11

*F*or weeks, *I scribbled* original stories; one about FDR's plan for the CCC (Civilian Conservation Corps), one about baseball, another about automobiles. In the early era of talkies, there was a system of selling motion pictures called block-booking. A studio would list a series of titles for the following season's or year's program. The stories accompanying these titles were nonexistent except for a few "flagship" films. The salesman would pack his suitcase and go traveling the country to sell the entire ball of wax to the exhibitor. If the studio owned theaters it, of course, reserved its own pictures for first exhibition. (A foul was called on this system some years later.) New writers were given titles for which they were asked to dream up stories, or had to think up new stories for which titles might be found. My early screenplays were based on the following perishable titles: *Fury of the Jungle, Fog, Man of Steel.* I submitted a half dozen of my own titles and stories, among them *Strike One, Little Acorns, Big Trees,* and *The Iron Sleep.*

Someone must have read them, but I never heard a word from anyone. Edwin Gilbert, utterly disenchanted, left before his first option was due. He hated Columbia and hated screen writing. In a letter he sent on his return to New York, he offered some patronizing observations to Larry and me. He suggested that we were suited to Hollywood's low standards but that he was headed for the theater. He wished us luck. Larry and I returned the good wishes.

Larry embraced Hollywood with unfettered affection. He adored the climate, the oranges, the cleanliness, the opportunity, and the weekly check. Both he and I were notified that our first option had been exercised provided we agreed (because we still had no screen credits) to renounce our raise to one twenty-five a week and remain at one hundred dollars. Like Barkis, we were willing. Larry would have stayed for less.

I had already dug in for a stay; like a homing pigeon, I had discovered the Jewish Community Center in Boyle Heights and had begun to organize a theater group.

Lou Levenson's option had not been picked up, so it was Larry and me against the tide. California was expanding and the automobile was a necessity. Walter Hart, the director, who had been in California for a short time waiting for a chance to work, was fed up and decided to hie back to the Big Apple. He owned a Ford and offered it to me for two hundred fifty dollars, payment deferred. That was an offer I could not refuse, even though it raised my national debt.

FDR was sworn in and his memorable "We have nothing to fear but fear itself" quickened our resolve, but when the banks were shut to forestall a headlong slide to oblivion, the panic caused by the closing precipitated a countermove by the studios that taught us we did have something more to fear than fear itself: studio shenanigans.

At each studio enclave, employees were summoned to a mass meeting, told that the business was in jeopardy, theaters might close, studios might be shut down, and as a consequence, it was necessary for each of us to share the burden of those dangers by accepting a 50 percent cut in salary, if we were earning one hundred a week or more, for a period of eight weeks, at which time the crisis should be at an end.

We were sheep with no shepherd to guide us, so we submitted to the shearing. However, the fleecing led to the organization of guilds. In union, we decided, there *was* strength. So we began our call to arms. The leaders of the screenwriters included John Howard Lawson, Philip Dunne, Howard Estabrook, Ernest Pascal, Dudley Nichols, Wells Root, Oliver H. P. Garrett, Allen Rivkin, and other stalwarts. Actors and directors and craft unions also began their assemblies. The studios at the end of that year's first quarter showed greater profit than ever. It became so obvious that we had been euchred that some of the studios shortened the period of the cut, but that did not assuage our determination. The line had been drawn and it was us against them in a drawn-out battle that lasted for years.

Along with my option pickup and the 50 percent cut, I received my first assignment — *Fury of the Jungle*. My collaborator, paired with me because of her experience and talent, was Ethel Hill, an extremely dear and generous woman who resembled an early-day Lily Tomlin. We worked well together. She had an interest in horses and often wore jodhpurs and riding gear to the studio.

On March 10, 1933, Ethel and I were plotting our story in her upper-level office. I had a sudden sense of dizziness, heard dogs barking, and felt the room shudder. Ethel gave me a startled look and said, "Let's get the hell out of here. It's an earthquake." We got the hell out of there. Arriving at our apartment, I learned that Miriam had been bathing and had become aware of inexplicable waves in the bathtub. She was standing on the lawn far away from the front of the house, dressed in a terry robe, worried about me as I had been about her. Mr. Taylor told us to go in and stand near doorways or arches — the safest spot to be in when more expected tremors and shakes came along. The radio blared early details and, as always, the first dispatches exaggerated the death toll and damages, though the final results were deadly enough.

Moss, who was living in Beverly Hills in a home he had rented to accommodate his brother, Bernie, his mother and father, and himself, telephoned and asked us to drive over. He was in shock, lying on a couch with wet cloths on his brow. Each tremor brought an afterword from Moss, most of them funny. Moss's mother believed it was the end of the world. Bernie thought it was more fun than a roller coaster and Pa Hart couldn't have cared less. He went to sleep after he said in his cockney accent, "I *don't* want to die with me boots *on*."

The temblors and tremors rattled on through the night and part of the next day but finally heaved off like mighty hiccups. The walls of our apartment had hairline cracks in them and the little chandelier occasionally swayed from the earth's shaking. Then all was still and the stories of terror, heroism, and casualties began to be authenticated. It was an experience that you were pleased to have survived but had no desire to have repeated.

Ethel Hill and I resumed our labors on *Fury of the Jungle* learning, as we wrote, of the Amazon River, piranhas, jungle rot, snakes, and rain forests, which information we ramrodded into our script, now assigned to Victor Jory as our star. To my chagrin and a sharp reappraisal of my value to the enterprise, I discovered that a small monkey we had written into our script was getting more per day than I was per week. I had no intention of forwarding that information to my father.

Our Amazon location was Lake Malibu, some fifteen miles from Los Angeles, but I never would have known it wasn't the Amazon. The production was my first contact with studio magicians, the technical staff that built the homes, castles, streets of Rome, New York, Paris, London, and Shanghai on studio back lots; the men who create the special effects of hurricanes, earthquakes, fires; who destroy planes in the air, shoot arrows into the necks of cavalry men, and who bring the dreams of writers and directors into life on screens throughout the world.

While the theater is a collaboration of a few of the creative arts, it is possible and often rewarding to see and hear a play on a bare stage without the contributions of a host of talents except for actors and a director. The play *is* the thing.

But motion pictures demand a fuller and more complex relationship involving the writer, the director, actors, producer, cameraman, sound engineer, decorator, designer, editor, electricians, composer, and the practitioners of at least three dozen other crafts, all of whom aid in the creation of an image that ultimately is shown in a large dark room on a flat screen and makes you cry or laugh or scares hell out of you. I was told that Sam Goldwyn once said that the trouble with making a picture about Lincoln was that everybody would know the ending. But as with so many apparent truths, the specifics prove them false; we know that Custer and his men were massacred, that the *Titanic* was sinkable, that we recovered from Pearl Harbor, that Lou Gehrig died of amyotrophic lateral sclerosis, that the Union was saved — yet films based on those facts and others proved the obvious point that it is not only what you do but how you do it. Despite the current devotion to the auteur theory, the hard fact is that a film requires the talents of a flock of magicians, all of whom start on their adventure after a script is placed in their hands. The director directs the charge but he needs the troops to carry the day. Recently Richard Gilman, the distinguished critic, observed with his usual calm perception that many directors have lost a sense of modesty. However, the nature of the making of films has always featured the director, from the days of Rex Ingram, Cecil B. DeMille, and D. W. Griffith, to the present front-runners Francis Ford Coppola, Steven Spielberg, George Lucas, and Michael Cimino, who do much of the screenplay writing. The most modest and one of the best of the new breed is Alan Pakula.

Eventually, *Fury of the Jungle* was shot, cut, and distributed into the maw of the hungry exhibitors. Then came another less than triumphant entry from Ethel and me, *The Most Precious Thing in Life*. After that, *Fog*, which was a solo script, and finally, *Man of Steel*.

By that time, I had received another notice telling me my second option would be picked up if I stayed on at the same hundred per week. Since I had no place else to go, I stayed. Meanwhile, the guilds were forming and acquiring new recruits, though rifts were apparent. A left wing and a right wing hardened positions for the future; at the extreme left and extreme right there was gossip about communism at one end and fascism at the other.

In April, Don Hartman wrote me that he was heading west and

planned to enlist in the growing ranks of screenwriters. When he arrived with no place to sleep, we made a deal with the Taylors for a two-room atelier. Don, with his share of the rent, had the limited advantage of the living room, while Miriam and I now enjoyed the luxury of a bed we didn't have to move each night. Miriam had tried to cook, but after her disastrous attempt at potting a roast and baking potatoes, which exploded in the stove, we settled for meals at nearby restaurants. Don went to work on his first original story, *Romance in Manhattan*. It was during this period that Don and I became fast friends. He was wonderful company, his humor grew sharper, and his considerable talent as a writer of comedy came into focus.

By now, Mother had given up the operation at the Y. With the help of Sam, whose fortunes had improved, Lil, who was running a decorating business, and my measly ten dollars a week, Ma was able to stop working and was living in an apartment with her father, my beloved Zayde.

My debts had been decreasing. I had paid off what I owed Columbia for Miriam's ticket and had reduced other debts by three hundred. We saw every movie we could get to so that I could familiarize myself with the work of other writers and actors, directors, and producers. It was a lively and healthy time.

Frank Borzage was filming *A Man's Castle* at Columbia, starring Spencer Tracy and Loretta Young. I had become friendly with Jo Swerling, who had written the script, and he had asked Borzage for permission to get me on the set (like Capra, Borzage was very tough regarding intruders).

Parenthetically, one meeting with Capra, beyond our first sketchy introduction in Cohn's office, had taken place one hot afternoon in the executive dining room, where writers were permitted to lunch (at prevailing prices). In this special room Harry Cohn had installed a chair, for the unsuspecting visitor, with a buzzer and not too gentle electric-shock device that was activated when the victim's body was lowered onto the seat. Norman Krasna, a friendly soul, had early-warned me to look under every chair before sitting down, and consequently I had never been subjected to the annoyance and embarrassment that followed the sound of the buzzer and the jolt to your behind.

On this late afternoon, I was alone in the dining room when Capra came in looking exhausted. He said it was too damn hot, asked for a long cold drink, and plopped down in the chair nearest him. The buzzer sounded. Capra did not jump up. He sat there and quietly sounded off, "Oh, shit! That stupid son of a bitch Cohn and his goddamn chair."

Then he rose, picked up the chair, and smashed it to the floor, shattering it into an irreparable mess. The waiter brought him his drink. Capra sat down, took a long swig of iced tea, and said to me with his infectious smile, "How's it going?" I answered, "Fine." We exchanged some more small talk about the weather and Harry Cohn and that constituted the beginning of our casual but always friendly relationship.

Addendum: Cohn replaced the destroyed chair with a new one, buzzer and shocker, but abandoned it forever when Victor Schertzinger had a mild heart seizure when he sat on it.

When Swerling walked me onto the remarkable "Hooverville" set of *A Man's Castle* I saw Tracy talking to some of the crew. I was about thirty feet from him. Jo walked over to talk to Borzage, who was waiting for electricians to finish relighting an area. I sidled into Tracy's line of vision and caught his eye. He looked at me and said, "Hello, kid." I greeted him, "Hi, Mr. Tracy." He beckoned me over. "How you doing?" I told him I was employed at the studio as a writer and that I had fond memories of *The Last Mile* in which I had acted under the name of Dore Schary. He laughed and said, "I'm lousy at names."

When I left in a few minutes with a so-long, he said, "Good luck, Dore."

Don Hartman was soon finished with a draft of his story, *Romance in Manhattan*, which was submitted to RKO. Al Persoff, the story editor, loved it, and the studio bought it for ten thousand dollars, part of which Don used to rent a house, send for Chick, their two daughters, Mimi and Donna, buy a car — all that in a spate of hurried decisions and joyous phone calls. Don moved from a new arrival out of work with no prospects to a hot "property" in record time. Miriam and I lost a boarder but gained a successful colleague.

At Columbia, I had written an original comedy designed, in my own estimation, for James Cagney. Columbia didn't want it, and released it to me. Warner's didn't want it either; as my hopes for selling it at a big price diminished, it made the rounds, winding up at Monogram Pictures. Lou Ostrow, a husky man with a surprisingly gentle manner, sent for me, and offered me one thousand dollars for the story provided I tossed in the screenplay. I weighed the matter carefully for a split second then asked, "When do I get the money?"

The answer was heartening: "Sign the contract." I did, got the check, went to the bank, cashed the check into one thousand one-dollar bills, took them to Miriam, tossed them into the air for a rainfall of dollars, and then gleefully stacked them up again. I returned to the bank, opened up my first checking account, wrote a hundred-dollar check for Mother, and reduced my outstanding debts by another two hundred. I was rich as Rockefeller.

Work disciplines came in handy as I spent the next two weeks writing the screenplay of *Born Tough*, which was immediately retitled by Monogram to *He Couldn't Take It*. The film was shot in seven days, Monday to Sunday inclusive (no overtime — no eight-hour days).

In a few weeks, the picture opened to excellent notices. On the same day I received word from Columbia that they were picking up my third option but only if I stayed at one hundred dollars per. Encouraged by the notices, I decided to ask for my overdue raise.

In answer to my request to see Mr. Sam Briskin, I was told to enter his office. Not being invited to sit down I launched into reasons why I thought Columbia was not being fair. (Tough executives never ask employees to sit. An employee standing and asking for anything becomes a panhandler with hat in hand and holes in his shoes.) My point was that I was worth more than one hundred each week. Briskin asked me what I thought I was worth. I suggested what the original contract stated, two hundred. Briskin smiled as his eyes narrowed into a hard glint. "You're fired at the end of this term. When you come crawling back looking for work, you'll be glad to get a hundred." He looked down at some papers on his desk and I shuffled off and out.

David Tannenbaum suggested an agent I might visit to line up a job before zero hour on September 30 when Columbia would close the gate. My appointment was with Arthur Landau, a small, successful, aggressive man who with some exasperation pointed out that no self-respecting agent would take on a client whose 10 percent fee would be a paltry ten dollars a week or even twenty. He suggested I go home — "by home I mean New York."

The possibility of returning to Newark defeated after a short skirmish of only nine months acted as a censor to bar me from considering that ignominious future; instead, I determined to face the challenge without the faintest idea of how to face it.

In three weeks, I would be unemployed. It was unlikely that my screen credits would break down any walls.

Someone had to open a door. Someone did.

M *iriam and I went to dinner* at Ada and Al Persoff's home. They and their friends were game-lovers as were we. Among their guests that night were Mr. and Mrs. Herman Mankiewicz. His national reputation as a newspaperman, wit, and scenarist was enormous. It was he who, when Harry Cohn ventured that there was no need to go see a preview of a picture in a theater since all he had to do was watch it in his projection room and if he became restless in his upholstered chair he would know the picture would not appeal to any audience, had said, "Harry, what gives you the notion that you own the monitor ass for millions of Americans?"

Also, it was Herman Mankiewicz whose wasplike retorts and funny improvisations appeared in Hollywood and New York columns and earned him awe mixed with enmity. In addition, he was a prodigious imbiber, also a reckless, notoriously bad gambler. This assorted bag of personality assets and liabilities had in no way lowered his perch as one of the most respected screenwriters at MGM. There was so much written and said of him that years later when his younger brother, Joe, came to Hollywood and earned his own distinguished reputation, he constantly had to contend with his older brother's record to a point where Joe used to say wryly, "When I die, they'll mark my headstone, 'Here lies Herman — I mean, Joe — Mankiewicz.'"

Meeting Herman was something special, spurring me to show off during parlor games the memory tricks at which I was quite good. During time-out, Herman asked where I was working. When I told him I was losing my job at Columbia, he suggested I call him the next day at Metro. When he left the party an hour later the Persoffs congratulated us, assuring Miriam and me that if Mankiewicz asked me to call, I was in like Flynn.

Whatever doubts I had (and there were many) disappeared when I called Mankiewicz, went at his direction to the office of Samuel Marx, who was then in command of the regiment of writers at MGM, and within a few minutes was told I would begin at Metro October 1 at a salary of two hundred a week. After a hurried trip to thank Mankiewicz, I rushed back to Columbia to dabble in a script. As instructed, I kept my mouth shut about my new job.

MGM was, in 1933, the premier studio, headed by Louis B. Mayer and Irving Thalberg, who shared an uneasy stewardship. Each of them wanted what the other had: Mayer, Thalberg's creative style and mind; Thalberg, Mayer's money and lusty power. Before Thalberg died in 1936, he had had a taste of Mayer's authority and position, but had given it up because of its physical drain; Mayer mourned him with crocodile tears and a building that bore Thalberg's name. Neither achieved what he wanted — Thalberg died young; Mayer only got more power, never made a movie, and learned too late that power is a chimera and that, like money, you cannot take it to the grave.

Metro's list of writers was endless: William Faulkner, P. G. Wodehouse, Paul Green, Mankiewicz, Morrie Ryskind were just a few; in addition to perhaps seventy writers there was almost a horde of directors, producers, and actors. To young writers, MGM was a land of milk and honey where patronage was handed out on the scale of the Medicis, even though the writer's building was a wooden barracklike structure that we sensed was a firetrap. We knew it had survived the earthquake but we yearned to be assigned to some other less rickety and less confining building.

When I started at Metro on October 1, I made the rounds and met some other neophytes — George Seaton was one, Robert Pirosh another. We each had a tentative assignment but did not take them seriously because we learned that assignments kept changing in MGM's writer-roulette game.

When the MGM job started, the Persoffs advised Miriam and me to get a new address — somewhere closer to Beverly Hills. We moved into a hacienda; courtyard, tiled walls, swimming pool with cactus, and sage gardens with a scent of desert flowers. We missed our old landlords, the Taylors, but we were much more comfortable.

My first Metro assignment was to write an original story for Marie Dressler and Wallace Beery. My collaborator was Vance Randolph, an authority on the Ozark Mountains, the locale chosen to take Minnie and Bill out of their tugboat environment. Vance, a veteran of World

War I, was a man who never dreamed anyone would pay him five hundred a week to work in Hollywood or anywhere else. He had a Guggenheim Fellowship earned by recording the balladry, language, and mores of the Ozarks in a number of books, which he gave me to study. Vance was a matter-of-fact, straightforward man. He had a lean face, a scraggly mustache, and a drawl that crawled. At work, he wore an old army shirt (a souvenir of his World War I career), carpet slippers, and a worn green cardigan sweater. He chewed tobacco. By special dispensation, he had obtained the use of a spittoon, which was placed behind his desk. His aim was flawless. He disliked being in Hollywood, cooked his own meals in a small hotel suite, and never went anywhere except home to lunch and dinner.

The producer of our script was Harry Rapf, once a part owner of Metro, who had been squeezed out when Nicholas Schenck, Mayer, Robert Rubin, and Thalberg took over the Culver City lot from Sam Goldwyn some years before. Rapf had a fearsome reputation among writers as a tough and cruel master; he also had an extraordinary nose, thin and long. A writer had once suggested to Rapf that he would like to do a realistic version of the Pinocchio story. As he began to tell Rapf the tale of the puppet whose nose grew larger as it told each lie, he belatedly realized he was heading for a box canyon; there was no escape. He stopped as Rapf became livid and fired him that instant.

When Sam Marx had given us the assignment, he told us that when the treatment was finished, we were to deliver the script to Rapf and wait to hear from him.

Vance Randolph and I worked our way through and out of a number of ideas but after many weeks, we began to form something we liked about moonshiners, federal agents, and bootleggers from Chicago.

After polishing and pruning, we brought the script to Mr. Rapf's office and waited for a sign. We heard nothing for two weeks, by which time Vance was edgy, chewing larger wads of tobacco. We played a lot of checkers until I grew weary of never winning. Then we played casino — I did better at that.

It was mid-December when we were called to Rapf's green and tan office that looked down on a long shot of the Metro studio. We entered his office to find him gazing out the picture window mounted behind his desk. We stood silently for a minute at least (a count of sixty is a long time in which to do nothing). Finally, Rapf turned to us. There was no hello, no invitation to sit down, merely one declarative sentence: "I read the story and it stinks." Since Vance ventured no answer, I asked,

"What do you think is wrong with it?" Rapf replied that it wasn't authentic. Vance, bestirring himself, delivered the following valedictory: "Mr. Rapf. I don't know if the story is good or not, but I am, sir, the country's authority on what is and what is not true about the Ozarks so you can't tell me that the story we wrote isn't authentic — so I tell you, you take that script and stick it in a hole the Good Lord provided for you." As I was beginning to recover from the first shock wave, Vance horrified me by unloading a stream of spittle onto Mr. Rapf's green rug. I watched in stunned wonder as the spot burbled, bubbled, and grew, hardly aware that Vance had left the office. I looked over at Mr. Rapf, who, pointing a long, bony finger at me, shouted, "You're fired." I believed him.

By the time I got to Vance's office, he had tied up his high-laced shoes, packed his belongings, and was on his way to check out of his hotel. I walked with him. He wasn't angry. Rather, he was relieved. He was sorry for me, wished me luck, said he was getting out of town by bus that night. We exchanged good-byes. I returned to the studio to call on Sam Marx, who verified that I was out.

For Christmas the following week, I got my closing-out check.

Vance Randolph and I stayed in touch for quite a while, then our correspondence faded. But recently I called Vance when I heard he was hospitalized, and we talked of those few weeks at Metro, and he asked, "Did you put in your book what I told Rapf?" I assured him I did. He said, "I'm glad you remembered."

13

M ankiewicz couldn't rearrange my dismissal from Metro, but he did lead me to an agent, young in years and in the business only a short time. His name was Nat Goldstone. He was a good-natured man who was positive he could help me. He was well-groomed, persistent, and sincere. He did have a habit of changing the subject of his conversation rapidly, giving one the sensation of chasing after a bus that would speed up just as one was about to catch hold; for instance, "I spoke to Universal today, Maury Pivar is a friend of my father-in-law Harry Curland and he and I owned some property, real estate — anyway — Benny Zeidman is a brother-in-law of — did you know that RKO is in trouble? You play tennis?"

To me, Nat was the only game in town. Luckily, he knew what he was doing, though often many of us wondered if he did.

Nat first mated me with Universal to work with Benny Zeidman to script a Chester Morris film, *Let's Talk It Over*. More important than the script was the beginning of my friendship with Leonard Spigelgass, the story editor.

Leonard had come to California a few years before, had worked for Sidney Kent at Fox studios, had shifted to Universal as a scenarist, and having earned the confidence of the Laemmle family, was elevated to his present job when he was twenty-four. Leonard when first we met was talkative, funny, knowledgeable, a marvelous teller of anecdotes, and a joyous gossip — he hasn't changed a bit beyond having been cut up by surgeons for a variety of ailments. While his life-style in some ways is very unlike mine, we shared devotion to rich desserts, preferably chocolate ones, all kinds of bread and rolls, pot roasts, fried onions with eggs, sour cream, and vegetables. Minus a good part of his stomach, Leonard is no longer able to drink or perform as a trencherman.

I believe we became fast friends because both of us are good listeners, but whatever the original reason, time and circumstance have kept our relationship close; we, with our oldest mutual friend, Allen Rivkin, have shared sorrows, awards, successes, failures, losses, enemies, meetings, conventions, and quarrels. In recent years Lenny has become a quick crier — I laugh at him, then he laughs at me, because I too cry quickly. Allen growls at most anything.

Let's Talk It Over, the first assignment Leonard picked for me, was a light-minded, low-budget picture, the first of a long string of quick assignments that took me to Paramount, Fox, Warners, back to Columbia, Monogram, Republic, and to independent producers. Almost every assignment brought a fifty- or twenty-five-dollar raise based on a not extraordinary skill that fortunately was an asset to producers — I was quick, facile, and could get the job done. Good or bad (there were some of each), the scripts had a beginning, middle, and end.

During the next few years, I dashed from one studio to another gathering credits on pictures few people saw, except my father, who went to all of them. He became a fan with my first screen credit. Not all the assignments were successful or pleasurable, but they were plentiful. During one hectic period, Don Hartman and I were hired to work on the Jimmy Durante radio show.

Nat Goldstone arranged this one. Don and I each got two hundred seventy-five per week — the money was good and we met Jimmy, a darling man, his father, a former barber who would cut your hair if you sat anywhere near him, but best of all we met Lou Clayton.

Lou, a famous dancer, was street smart and tough as steel. He had been Jimmy's partner along with Eddie Jackson, and the trio had gone from vaudeville to nightclubs to special appearances, but now Clayton was Jimmy's manager. Lou was an expert at card games, an unbeatable money player at golf, and a relentless and murderous street fighter — a proud and angry Jew who once flattened Frank Fay backstage at the Palace when he heard Fay say something insulting about the Jews. Fay, having lost five teeth during the punishment Lou gave him, was out of action for a couple of weeks.

The relationship between Jimmy and Lou was what is written about in stories you don't believe. When Lou died Jimmy took a pair of Lou's shoes, placed them on the bottom of the clothes rack in his room, and draped the rack with one of Lou's suits, a shirt and tie. When Jimmy used to say, "Good night, Mrs. Calabash, wherever you are," he was talking to Lou.

Lou was a sentimentalist who, if you got out of line, would knock your block off.

The moonlighting stint for Durante increased our income but diminished our energy. While Don and I were not responsible for Jimmy's departure from the air, we certainly did not help extend his radio career. The fact is, Jimmy had to be seen to be loved. That became clear when he moved to the screen. Lou didn't blame us for Jimmy's failure to score on radio — which was a lucky break for Don and me.

While I was on the script-writing carousel, I took a few nasty falls. One of the first followed my first picture at Universal. Goldstone peddled me to a new film company called Mascot, headed by an energetic man, Nat Levine, whose speech, full of "pernt" instead of "point" and "cherce" instead of "choice," bespoke his Brooklyn youth. The deal was for me to receive one thousand dollars for a four-week job, thereby establishing my salary as two hundred and fifty dollars a week. I checked into a dreary office on Santa Monica Boulevard. When I was given the contract to sign, I noticed that Levine had changed the total sum to seven hundred and fifty dollars. Unable to reach Nat Goldstone, I tore up the contract, left it on my desk, got into my Ford, and headed for a ride up the coast. The four-hour drive calmed the churning of my stomach. I returned home having scared hell out of Miriam and alarmed Goldstone, who had been trying to track me down to tell me that Levine was going to sue for breach of contract.

Miriam and I had moved from the hacienda apartments to a small cottage with a white picket fence, knotty pine panels, fireplace, green lawn — the works. Final touch — our first dog, Toughy, named for *Born Tough*, a wirehaired Scotch terrier. The rent was cheap, I had saved a few dollars and could sweat out Nat Levine's threat. He tried but lost.

Back I went to Universal for an epic called *Chinatown Squad*. (A few years ago, my son, Jeb, called me at one in the morning to ask, "Dad, did you *really* write a picture called *Chinatown Squad?*" When I confessed, he told me it was on the late, late show and he would never again acknowledge me as his father.)

The second Universal job was followed by a call from the same Nat Levine, who now was located at Monogram studios. He wanted me for a rewrite of a William Haines picture dubbed *Young and Beautiful*. I told Nat Goldstone I'd do it as a ten-day job — a hundred dollars per day payable in cash each day. Levine agreed. On the tenth day, Levine had his script and back I went to Universal for another job, *Storm over the Andes.* When I checked in, Maury Pivar, the producer, showed me a telegram from Levine warning Pivar not to hire me — that I had not finished Levine's script and I was not to be trusted. Pivar gave me the telegram and told me not to be bothered with it. I nodded, left his office, and sped to Levine's new offices only a short distance from Universal.

I rushed into Levine's outer office, frightening his secretary. She called out to Al Le Voy, who was Levine's aide-de-camp, as I burst into Levine's private office, which featured a stained-glass window. When I stormed in, Levine half rose and shouted, "I'm the president of this company." I didn't laugh. I called him a son of a bitch, threw the telegram at him, and told him if he didn't sit down, I'd throw him through his window. A number of hands reached me at this time. They belonged to Le Voy and two studio policemen. Levine screamed, "Throw him out. He's a troublemaker." They took me to the studio doors, by which time I had stopped struggling, and out I went, again wondering, "Why the hell did I do that?" But I knew. It was Pa's temper still thumping inside of me despite Ma's restraining hand.

Completing the Universal script, I resumed my appointed rounds, this time going to the "B" picture lot of Fox studio, which was located on Western Avenue, far removed from what would one day soon shine with pristine glory — Darryl Zanuck's Pico Boulevard Twentieth Century–Fox "A" picture bailiwick. Once again, Levine called. He had bought Monogram studios and wanted me to join him as studio story editor and executive producer. He offered to rename a studio street for me. I declined, staying on at Fox to do two jobs for Sol Wurtzel, a man with a perpetual grimace that might be either a smile or a threat — it was impossible to tell which. Wurtzel fired me when I had completed three assignments, after which I was hospitalized following an auto accident while I was working on my fourth Wurtzel film. I had lifted the front end of a car and torn some ligaments in my back. Wurtzel pragmatically reacted by telling Rivkin, who was producing, "I hired a writer, not Jean Valjean."

While all these events were going on in rapid-fire sequence (Charles Brackett and I once shared a dubious record — we each had eleven screen credits in one year), other things were happening.

One of those things was an invitation from Norman Krasna to have drinks at his home and join some of his friends in a poker game. Norman, who had moved over to MGM, thought it would be of benefit to me to meet some of the Metro brass.

While I had never played poker beyond a twenty-five-cent limit, I decided that a twenty- or thirty-dollar loss would be worth the opportunity to, as Norman said, "mingle. It's like socializing in the Borscht Belt — but the returns are better."

Norman's house was in exquisite taste, full of antiques and good paintings and prints. The food was first-rate. I wore my Bar Mitzvah apparel — blue suit, white shirt, and maroon tie. The other guests were less formal. I knew their names but never had met them — Eddie Buzzell, a director and Norman's closest friend; Hunt Stromberg and Larry Weingarten, first-flight producers at MGM; Sam Marx (I knew *him*), in charge of the writers at the same studio (he had hired and fired me the first time around at MGM); Joe Mankiewicz, who was comparatively new but on his way to his celebrated career; and Sam Katz, a major executive who had quit the exhibition business with Abe and Barney Balaban in Chicago to enlist at MGM.

I ate sparingly — drank water — smiled cheerfully, and contributed nothing to the conversation. Then we sat down to poker. Buzzell handed out the stacks of chips and I almost went into cardiac arrest when it was announced that each stack represented a thousand dollars. I was able to nod without fainting. Recovering quickly, I calculated that if I lost I would borrow the money from Krasna on the justifiable grounds that he had led me into bankruptcy.

The game began. I noticed a few things. Each man had an odd tic. Katz rattled his chips; Marx twitched his neck; Stromberg squinted his eyes and opened his mouth simultaneously; Weingarten opened his eyes as if he had just awakened and kept adjusting his eyeglasses; Krasna kept talking; Eddie Buzzell whistled or sang snatches of songs; and Joe kept fiddling with his pipe.

Absorbed and distracted from the game by the clicking, rattling, whistling, smoking, twitching, and talking, I soon was three hundred dollars in the hole. Then, facing disaster, I began to concentrate on the poker habits of the players. I also got lucky, and by the end of the night I went home with over six hundred dollars in cash. I was trembling and decided never to go back.

Norman was delighted on two counts — that I won and that I didn't come back.

During my tours of duty at the studios I was forming many new friendships, among them those with Julie Epstein, Norman Krasna, and George Seaton, lasting to this day. However, some were transient and were amortized very quickly.

The Screen Writers Guild was growing in strength but had neither recognition from nor negotiation with the producers.

While we were aware of Hitler and Nazism, it had not reached into our guts; even refugee veterans from the German movie colony were not alarmed, being certain that Hitler would fall under the "sturdy common sense of the German people." There was not much talk about work camps and no reports of death camps. That came later.

The Spanish civil war had not yet been joined and FDR had done some wondrous things.

So there was time for elaborate practical jokes and imitations of "der Fuehrer." We writers saved some money, got new convertibles, moccasins, scarves, sport shirts, and spent weekends at Tijuana or Palm Springs.

Most important, Miriam and I had decided we wanted a child. By October, 1935, Miriam was pregnant. My mother had come to live in California. She, Miriam, and I refused to get into a conventional trap. Mother wanted her own "workshop," so after a short spell of living with us, she moved to her own apartment and we rented a larger house to accommodate the baby when it arrived.

By 1936, most of my friends were alarmed and getting involved in taking rigid political positions. The right and the left were drawing up partisan and emotional barricades. The right wing viewed the growing tensions as an injunction to get rid of the Communist menace. The left wing and the liberals were more concerned about Hitler and fascism. The name-calling from both sides became shrill.

It was during this time that I became interested in the work of the Anti-Defamation League. As a member of B'nai B'rith, I knew something of their activities but was not aware of how much work was going on in chronicling, verifying, and exploring the shenanigans of overt anti-Semites who were growing bolder as Hitler grew stronger.

Recognizing that there would be greater demands on my free time, I felt it was imperative to be well organized. There were frequent meetings of the Writers Guild, which was now closing ranks to face up to the producers as a solid union phalanx; meetings of the ADL; political meetings to work for FDR's reelection — all this in addition to fun and games and work on screenplays and two stage plays. One of the latter, *Man of Ideas*, was produced in Hollywood by Lela Rogers with her niece, now Phyllis Cerf Wagner, as the ingenue; the other, *Violence*, based on the San Jose lynchings, kept being optioned by New York producers who first expressed enthusiasm, then mumbled lack of interest.

Miriam was in full bloom, adding weight by the day and growing more beautiful and radiant.

Leonard Spigelgass had been selected as a godfather for the unborn child and was apprehensive about it because he took it so damned seriously. He had moved out of his job as story editor and had joined the ranks of scenario scribes just in time to welcome a crisis.

Convinced we had to lay down a challenge, the writers voted not to sign any contract for employment that ran beyond June 30, 1938. The news hit the papers; the producers hit the ceiling. Headed by Irving Thalberg, the studio heads announced the formation of the Screen Playwrights, a rival union that was granted immediate recognition by the producers as the bargaining agent for all writers and immediate recognition by the Writers Guild as a company union.

The carnage began. Writers were called in and offered long-term contracts and raises to quit the Guild and join the Playwrights. At Warners, Jack Warner addressed an assembly of writers in a manner that was duly and fortunately recorded by a number of witnesses who knew shorthand: "We're not going to use coercion or threats but if any son of a bitch is a member of the Guild, by tomorrow he'll be out of work."

It was this same light-handed touch that, some years later after a few strikers were shot during a demonstration at Warner Brothers, inspired Julie Epstein to suggest changing Warners' slogan from "combining good picture making with good citizenship" to "combining good picture making with good marksmanship."

The pressure on writers to join the Screen Playwrights was insistent and many grabbed at the lure. Others simply dropped out of the Guild. Others soon found themselves out of work. The president of the Guild during those rugged days was Ernest Pascal, an intense man, short in size, tall in courage. Ernie would flush when angry and his slight lisp would become more pronounced. Our last official meeting, which adjourned *sine die*, represented only a handful of veterans who had kept their front-line positions.

But our casualties were heavy, the battle was lost, and Ernie advised us to take down the flag and fade out of sight until we could raise it once again in battle.

The Screen Playwrights represented the right-wing political view though there were men among them who were conservatives, rather than radicals, and who did not maintain a hysteria about American communism but did view the Guild as a nuisance.

However, others such as Morrie Ryskind, a "reformed" liberal, and James McGuinness became hard-nosed Red-baiters and reckless wielders of verbal shotgun attacks. This period of time formed the first part of the jigsaw puzzle of Hollywood political warfare that in later years became an ugly portrait of bitterness, deception, and cowardice costing the livelihood and reputation of many creative people.

By now, Miriam and I had a circle of fast friends with similar, but not identical, tastes. We were politically allied to the left and the middle ground, spent many evenings together talking and playing parlor games, went to clubs for dining, dancing, and entertainment, and traveled together for weekend holidays. Lenny Spigelgass, Don and Chick Hartman, David and Ruth Tannenbaum, Allen and Ruth Rivkin, and Ralph and Betty Rainger formed the center of our group. Ralph had preceded us to California after his success in New York as the composer of "Moanin' Low," which acted as a skyrocket both for Ralph and for Libby Holman, who sang it in *The Little Show*. I had known Ralph back in the days of Schary Manor in Newark. He had played piano in an orchestra while studying and heading for the law profession. Being five years older, he took my passionate interest in any form of theater with a cool but friendly attitude. Later on, his own interest heated up and he gave up the law and a few steps later found himself in Hollywood with a pretty wife and a booming career in films as a composer.

One night in our home, he doodled fragments of a new song he was writing, trying to find the "release," that part of a song that corresponds to a second-act curtain and leads you to the triumphant end. To his delight and ours, he found what he wanted, and there was "Thanks for the Memory." It came after "Love in Bloom," and Ralph's career zoomed. Ralph was a lean and gaunt man, with light brown curly hair, small features, a rather prim expression, marvelously expressive hands. His manner was precise and often clinical. However, he loved to play cards, backgammon, and paper games and could, after a few drinks, "rowdy" it up with the best of us. Betty was a dark, handsome woman given to unpredictable moods. She had an explosive temper, was an excellent dancer, but had a haughty manner, which dissolved one night at a party when she removed her girdle in front of all of us and joined us in a sexy fandango. From that moment on, she was a hell of a lot more fun.

In the early hours of May 30, 1936, as Decoration Day began, I called our friends and our families to tell them that Miriam had given birth to Jill. Mother had sat in the waiting room with me, knitting away on a tiny pink jacket, knowing for certain that the baby was going to be a girl.

When I called my father, I invited him to the Coast to get a look at his new granddaughter. He had been ill with a ruptured hernia, so delayed the journey for a couple of months.

Having just finished three scripts for Emmanuel Cohen, an independent producer for Paramount Pictures, I had to make a choice. Two recent films that I had scripted, one for Walter Wanger, who was now an independent producer, had received good reviews and a few assignments were offered me. I chose the one from Norman Krasna, the Columbia alumnus, who was producing at MGM. I liked the idea of going back on the Metro payroll, perhaps to see if the tobacco stain dropped on Harry Rapf's rug by Vance Randolph had disappeared. (I discovered that the mark, faded and almost as green as the rug, was still visible.)

Norman's picture, *Big City*, was for Spencer Tracy and Luise Rainer. Frank Butler, a collaborator with Don Hartman on the *Road* pictures for Bing Crosby and Bob Hope, had a son, Hugo, who was a new junior writer at Metro. Frank asked if I would lead Hugo into script writing by tying him into the *Big City* project. I was very fond of Frank and when I met Hugo and liked him, I spoke to Norman, who okayed the setup. Hugo and I went to work. For the first time since the short visit on the set of *A Man's Castle*, I met Tracy, and he remembered my name. Those of us working on the film had a marvelous time — a happy time — but while the trade reviews were good, the picture simply didn't work. Perhaps Sam Goldwyn in his infinite wisdom was right when he said, "A happy set means a lousy picture."

The Spanish revolution began in July. Rallies and fund raising accompanied the formation of the Lincoln Brigade. The conflict hardened opposing camps in Hollywood. Members of the right called for the United States to back Hitler and fight the Reds. Others wanted Russia to win. Most forgot that it was a Spanish revolution, which was serving as a training area for Soviet and Nazi armament.

Many liberals were quite aware that some of the support for the Loyalist cause in Spain was coming from members of the Communist party or their devoted friends. But we also knew that Red-baiting was a chief weapon of the radical right, used effectively to smear and in fact destroy those who walked the middle of the road, maintaining that neither communism nor fascism was the future. However, we were also aware that the Communist party line could shift rapidly and yesterday's "truth" could become tomorrow's "lie" without a blush or a tear.

During the time *Big City* was being written, Miriam and I determined to move from the cramped quarters of our home on Lake Hollywood Drive to North Las Palmas in Hollywood. This time we would buy our own furnishings; a good deal of them on time. I had been saving some money and making friends not only in the movie business but in law, medicine, education, and community affairs.

Pa showed up for his visit to meet Jill, who was, even at three months, a charmer — blond, happy, and playful.

Pa, who had not believed me when I had told him I had been hired to write for Columbia for one hundred dollars per week, had seen my name on a score of pictures and by now was convinced I was doing very well. After his first dinner with us he asked if I would tell him what I was now earning. I said, "Well, Pa, I'm now getting six hundred dollars per week." Pa eyed me steadily and said, "Don't lie to me, son. I know a man in your position must be earning at least fifteen hundred a week." When I showed him my week's salary check, he said, "You're underpaid." Pa would have been a hell of an agent.

There had been more inquiries about my play *Violence* but no firm commitment and I had resigned myself to its nonproductive state. One evening I received a call from someone who identified himself as Jed Harris. It was obvious this was a practical joke because (a) the play had not been sent to Harris, (b) I didn't know him, (c) he wasn't calling long distance, and (d) a group of us were continually playing phone jokes on one another. Therefore, when the joker said, "This is Jed Harris," I answered, "Well, how are you, Jed old boy?" He didn't tell me but went on, "I've read your play. I like it. I want to talk to you about it."

I suggested it wasn't his kind of play.

He answered he would be the judge of that.

I said, "Come off it. Who is this?"

He said, "Jed Harris, you stupid jerk."

I said, "Harris Schmarris — go fuck yourself."

He hung up, leaving me angry at whoever was playing the crummy gag.

The phone rang again. It was Eddie Chodorov.

I told Eddie he had pulled a rather unfunny practical joke. But seriously and truthfully, he told me that Jed *had* come to Hollywood, *had* read the play, *had* liked it, and *had* called to express interest in doing it.

Why hadn't Eddie first spoken to me?

Jed wanted to surprise me.

Now Jed didn't want to talk to me — or see me — and was convinced I was an eighteen-carat idiot. I asked Eddie to explain that I simply had been flabbergasted and could not believe I was being complimented by getting a call from Jed Harris, the great producer — I went on with other flattering excuses. Eddie spoke to Jed as I listened and I could hear Jed explode, "Tell him *he* can go fuck himself." Eddie was sorry. I was sorry. That was that. Of course, I blamed Eddie, forgetting that I *had* behaved like an eighteen-carat idiot.

A short time after we moved into our newly interior-decorated home, which sparkled, smelled, and looked like a department-store model home, I heard that Carly Wharton, a producer new to New York, wanted to present *Violence* on Broadway.

Carly came to California with a check and ideas for the production. She had spoken to Garson Kanin, recently arrived in Hollywood to aid Sam Goldwyn. Garson, an actor and assistant to George Abbott, had read the play and wanted to direct it. I liked Gar. We both wanted Chester Morris to play the leading role, that of a young man who is opposed to violence but who, victimized by the raw emotion of a mob, is responsible for killing a man accused of kidnapping and murder. Morris had picture assignments; in his place, we cast James Bell, who had played in *The Last Mile*. One of the first moves was to change the title from *Violence* to *Too Many Heroes*. The easiest contribution to picture or play making is to change titles.

We were to go into rehearsal in October and open cold in New York on November 15. It was spring, 1937; I was busy working on a *Broadway Melody of 1938* script that would occupy my time until we went to New York for casting late in the summer. Mother moved into the house with us, and would stay to protect the fortress while we were away. Aiding her would be Jill's nurse and a houseboy, Cirilo Mantilla, an ex-boxer with an incredibly sweet nature and an accent that made his English unintelligible until you penetrated his sentence structure and diction. Item: "Boss, Fleemout go study wha our?" Translation: "Boss, are you driving the Plymouth to the studio and at what time?"

In early August we landed in New York. Ralph and Betty Rainger had been there for a while to see if Ralph could cook up a musical show to fill in the time until musicals would make a comeback in Hollywood. They were both a comfort to us. Lil had set up quarters for us at an apartment hotel and I went to work with Gar and Carly, cutting the script, rewriting, and casting. Jo Mielziner was to design and light the play.

Mixed with the excitement of the work was the enjoyment that came with making new friends — like Jim Backus, who was signed for a small part in the play along with Jean Barrere. Shirley Booth and Elspeth Eric, who played the feminine leads, also became friends. Then there was Paul Stewart, who was developing celebrity with Orson Welles's Repertory Company. Also among the group who habituated the Tavern (a coffeehouse that warmly welcomed show people) were Sam Levene, starring in *Three Men on a Horse*, and Robert Ardrey, whose plays were receiving notices that drive young playwrights crazy ("While Mr. Ardrey is a writer who must be counted on in the future, this new play of his is simply . . ."). Bob, weary of being counted on for the future but counted out for the present, finally left, went to Hollywood, earned many credits, and then gave it all up to become a highly respected anthropologist. The two months before we went into rehearsal included some of the best times I have had working in the theater. It is the im-

[*91*]

mediacy of the theater that is so captivating. In front of you your play is being shaped, polished, and refined. The production is chancy — fraught with danger — your leading actor may get hurt, the scenery may fall, but the climax is heavy — the decision is quick — you go home a hero or a bum — there's not the long wait that goes with picture production.

The cadre of men with whom I was working, the new friends and old friends like Moss and Lester Sweyd (a loyal fan of Moss who believed in both Moss and me) and Frieda Fishbein, were providing me with an excitement that was stimulating and nourishing. Gar approached his first directorial job on Broadway with supreme élan and an authoritative manner that he has never lost. When I entered the backstage of the Hudson Theatre for the first day of rehearsal for *Too Many Heroes*, I was avid, tense, and virginal. This was my first experience with the toboggan ride that is mounting a play for Broadway. Once the date is set, the sled is on its way. There is no way to stop it. The effort and tension were too hectic for my colon, which rebelled, bringing on painful colitis that sent me to Doctors Hospital, scaring me and convincing me that I would not live to see the opening of the play.

But I made it.

The first act was a triumph. Moss, accompanied by George S. Kaufman, came backstage at intermission and predicted a Pulitzer Prize. We never should have brought up the curtain for the second act — the play sagged and ran out of steam as we discovered that most people in New York were against lynching and couldn't care less about the play.

Recently, I've looked at the critics' reviews written in 1937 and the strange and interesting fact is how much the theater has changed. The chief attacks on *Too Many Heroes* were aimed at the violence of the lynching and the "rough" language (the most explicit words were *damn, hell, bastard,* and *son of a bitch* used sparingly). It is odd that the point of the play, which Gar so brilliantly staged, was that violence *was* horrible, cruel, and debasing, and yet only one or two reviewers recognized what we had done. Kelcey Allen, writing for *Women's Wear*, was the only one who gave us a complete rave. Some of the other reviews were kind but extremely qualified. No customers came and after three weeks, the show closed. By that time, we were back in Hollywood, where most of my friends, having read only the local trade paper that had printed a glowing notice, assumed I was the author of a smash hit. So did the Metro executives. Norman Krasna advised me not to tell anyone the play had closed: "Keep quiet. A year from now they'll still think it's a hit. They don't read anything."

My new assignment at a salary of seven hundred and fifty dollars per week was to do a story for John Considine, a producer who had the idea that there was a good movie in the history of a little-known institution called Boys Town near Omaha, Nebraska, founded and governed by Father Edward Flanagan.

John Considine was a burly, handsome man with the stereotypic features of the Irishman — short nose, long upper lip, heavy jaw, broad shoulders, and wide chest. A creative producer, he had been disappointed in previous work that had been done on his idea. He informed me that Father Flanagan had rejected early story ideas. The film *Boys Town* was designed to star Spencer Tracy, Freddie Bartholomew, and Mickey Rooney.

After reading what had been written and studying the history of Father Flanagan's unique institution, I told Considine that the error holding up the project was casting Freddie Bartholomew in an atmosphere where he clearly did not belong. My suggestion was to do away with the character completely and concentrate on the relationship between Tracy as Father Flanagan and Rooney as the rough, unmanageable new recruit into Boys Town. Considine agreed and sent me to Omaha to meet Father Flanagan.

When I arrived, it was bitter cold. I found my way to Father Flanagan's home, but I was practically frozen — also deeply concerned about how to behave with a Catholic priest. Father Flanagan joined me in a moment or two and relieved my chill and my tensions by offering a long drink of straight Irish whiskey. After we each had two of these generous appetizers, I was warm and captivated by the tall, craggy priest, who spoke with a slight brogue but with no affectation. He didn't look a bit like Tracy but he had Tracy's charm, his smile and twinkle. He was going to be a cinch to catch on film.

He was very pleased with the outline I had already worked out without having seen Boys Town. He told me that the weather might be milder the next day but for that night we would just have dinner together and talk. Later at the hotel I spent two or three hours writing some of my impressions of this interesting and committed man. My stay in Boys Town was short but productive since the story elements flowed quickly and surely. When I returned to the studio, Considine was extremely pleased. In a few days, Jack Ruben was scheduled to direct and I began work on the screenplay. Within two weeks, accompanied by Jack Ruben, I was on my way back to Boys Town.

Both of us were so impressed by what we saw during these next few days of activity that we called the studio and asked for permission to buy the Boys Town basketball team new uniforms. This marvelous squad of kids, who had played some forty games without ever losing, wore uniforms that were ragged, torn, dirty, ill-matched, and ill-fitting. Eddie Mannix, the general manager of MGM, approved our idea. We sped to the nearest sports store where we ordered the suits and top-flight knee guards, basketball shoes, and so on.

When we arrived back at the studio, we learned that the team, all dressed up in their new uniforms, had lost their first game. I called Father Flanagan to extend my condolences, but he assured me that within a couple of games the uniforms would be dirty and torn once more and the boys would resume winning.

As the script of *Boys Town* neared completion, Jack Ruben, a young, healthy, athletic man, suddenly took ill with endocarditis, an inflammation of the lining of the heart, and suddenly, sadly, he was dead. Norman Taurog, a rosy-cheeked, roly-poly man who had earned fame as the director of *Skippy*, was assigned to take Jack's place. However, Tracy had some resistance to playing the part of Father Flanagan since he once before had played a priest in *San Francisco*. After some weeks of stalling, Tracy flatly turned down the assignment. During this period, Tracy had a drinking problem and the studio executives treated him gently rather than bring on a crisis.

So *Boys Town* was shelved and Tracy went on one of his Homeric binges. John Considine had no other assignment for me but other producers were interested in my services, particularly as a script doctor, so for the next few weeks I jumped from one assignment to another, patching, mending, contributing ideas, and rewriting. One day Eddie Mannix sent for me to look at an unfinished picture directed by George Fitzmaurice. During the conversation, Mannix, who was a good friend, asked, "How does it feel to be the fair-haired boy?" I said I had been in Hollywood long enough to know that one's hair turned a different color very quickly. Eddie slapped me on the shoulder and said, "You better believe it." The exchange stayed in my mind because a short while later a series of shocks hit hard.

Eddie Mannix's wife was killed in an auto crash, a brother of his died suddenly, and death came to his father and mother a week or two later. Eddie took a long leave of absence from the studio. Meanwhile, I was continuing my various tours of duty. One Friday, Harry Rapf asked me to read a script and report to him on Monday. I read the script, disliked it violently, and reported this to Mr. Rapf on Monday morning.

Mr. Rapf was furious when I concluded my remarks by suggesting that he not attempt to make a picture out of the script. Rapf explosively said it was none of my business which picture he did or did not do, that I had wasted a weekend of MGM salary, that I was a writer and not a producer. He ended the tirade with the news that as of that moment, I was fired.

I reported to Edwin Knopf, now in charge of writers, who told me he regretted Rapf's decision but that there was nothing he could do about it since Eddie Mannix was not available to counter Rapf's temper seizure. It was at this point that I remembered my remark about hair changing color. My hair was back to its normal shade. I had been fired twice at MGM — both times by Rapf.

I was out of a job, Miriam was pregnant again, but the future did not seem bleak. My optimism constantly jumps up and kicks me in the rear.

N *at Goldstone's efforts* to obtain assignments for me hit a snag. The problem was that my current salary of seven hundred and fifty per week was rather high for B-picture scripts. My only A-picture credit was *Big City*, which had failed, thus precluding other jobs on larger-budget movies. Nat argued that if we became panicky and began to lower the salary, the sharks would begin chomping me down. Panic was averted when Leo McCarey signed me to work with him on an original story he had titled *Love Affair*. We worked for a week at Leo's chalet at Lake Arrowhead.

The first two days were spent searching for character relationship. Leo's male character was to be a diplomat whose career would cause a separation from the woman. But as yet, we hadn't characterized her. During the third evening, the notion occurred to me of having the heroine badly hurt and permanently crippled, thus preventing her from pursuing her beloved and him from finding her. This satisfied Leo and after much additional plotting we went back to Hollywood. The following Monday, Leo told me he was going to hire Donald Ogden Stewart to do the screenplay. Leo and I were to share credit on the original story. But production was some time away, "So good luck, Dore, and thanks for the ideas."

Back to the doldrums of waiting for Nat to call. He did, but there were no jobs. That was nice of Nat. He would call to keep your spirits up. I had many appointments but no assignment.

Rather than bite my nails, I wrote some original story ideas but none of those caught fire. Meanwhile, our expenses cut sharply into our reserves. The furniture payments were large, the two cars had been bought on bank loans and those payments dug deep. I sold one of the cars and advised my secretary, Babette, to start looking for another job. I began to face the possibility that the wisest course might be to settle for whatever equity we had in our possessions, rid ourselves of debt, and drive back to New York to make a fresh start. During the fallow months of spring and early summer I had been aware that Spencer Tracy had been found sleeping in the stable with his polo ponies. Dried out after a short spell in the hospital, he had asked to go to work. There was only one script ready for production — *Boys Town*. Tracy said yes, and by now the picture had been shot and was in its editing stage. However, I had not heard from Considine, nor did I know if Mannix had returned to the studio.

Miriam was in her last month of pregnancy but she faced the probable move back to New York with courage and poise. I had spoken to Lil, who was scouting for an apartment for us. My thirty-third birthday was rolling toward me, an anniversary that was making me feel like fifty-three.

A few days before August 31, John Considine called. There was to be a preview of *Boys Town*, which he wanted me to see. For the first time I learned that I shared credit for the original story with Eleanor Rankin and screenplay credit with John Meehan. That news revved me up, and so Miriam and I went to the preview in Inglewood, a few miles from Culver City.

Nunnally Johnson, once pressed for a definition of a preview, said, "Well, after a year's work on a picture that costs a million dollars, a squad of high-priced professionals pile into a convoy of black limousines and travel to a small town to exhibit their product to an audience they assume know more than they do, who will at the conclusion of the picture go into the lobby and scrawl on preview cards the verdict, 'It stinks.'" However, previews have to be endured. They do provide the only measure the creators have for knowing if they have done what they intended to do; if they, representing many crafts, have arrived at a monitor image that says to the writer, producer, director, scene designer, cutter, cameraman, actor — "Yes, that's what we had in mind."

As *Boys Town* unreeled at Inglewood, the audience responded with laughs, applause, and tears; at the end, they cheered. As we filed out of the theater, Considine gave me a bear hug, pounded me on the back, and pushed me toward Eddie Mannix, who was standing in the theater lobby with a few other executives.

Mannix was euphoric and wanted to know what script I was working on. My answer was stifled by the host of people; Norman Taurog, the director, Considine, the producer, and others tied in with the picture were being congratulated, assured they had the picture of the year. Someone suggested that a prizefight scene be eliminated. Considine frowned at that and told me to be in his office the next morning. I was trying to prevent Miriam from being pushed by the happy throng while I simply kept beaming. This, I knew, was my first real success — after a swarm of small films, most of which had been received with no great degree of appreciation — this one was to be the film that moved me up. Before we left the theater lobby Mannix told me to come to his office the next day.

Miriam and I barreled home and laughed and cried. Joined by Mother, Cirilo, and Babette, who had seen the preview, we opened a bottle and drank a toast of thanks. Jill, at the age of two, wasn't quite sure what was going on but having been wakened, she enjoyed the fun. She's enjoyed going to a party ever since.

The next day, Considine, Taurog, and I fought off the changes that some of the company wanted to make, which would have damaged some of the quality of the picture. Later that day, I met with Mannix. He had heard the story of how Rapf had dismissed me. He raised my salary to one thousand a week and called Knopf to put me on the payroll as of that day.

Two weeks after my happy birthday celebration, Miriam went into labor. Once again, Mother sat out the event with me. When we took our first look at the new baby girl, a merry and happy child from the moment of her arrival, we knew she had to be named Joy — Joy for everything that had happened to us in the sudden turn from despair to renewed hope.

Shadows from the Munich accord dampened our spirits and raised fears even as we attended dinners and rallies on behalf of the Anti-Nazi League.

One such dinner stays in my memory. It was to honor Thomas Mann. We did not have heavy resources but prevailed on a rich patron to pay for the cost of the meal. The *quid pro quo* was that the patron would be given the privilege of introducing the famed writer and refugee from Germany.

We sold out the tickets, and because of my diverse activities I was selected to act as MC, a chore that required me to call on others who introduced the speakers. The compensation for my job was a bonanza — I was seated next to Thomas Mann.

After dinner I kept getting up and sitting down, introducing the introducers, and finally it came time for us to listen to our patron, who had bargained for the right to present Mann to the assemblage. He rose and spoke slowly and shyly, saying that he had no idea why he should have been selected to introduce this great man, Thomas Mann. "After all," he said, "I've done nothing to deserve this honor. I am a pygmy chosen to introduce a giant." This self-estimate went on for a few minutes, during which time Mann leaned toward me and whispered, "Mr. Schary, what has the gentleman accomplished that he can be so humble?"

I don't know if Mann had ever used the line before but I've used it since — and whenever anyone is described as humble I wonder if he truly rates the designation. My preference is for a man such as L. B. Mayer, who at an Academy Award dinner presented his son-in-law, William Goetz, with the Irving Thalberg Award and said, "I'm proud of you, Bill, and someday if you keep it up you'll be as great a man as I am." At least he was honest about his self-opinion.

While we were depressed by the prospect of a war that seemed inevitable, we did feel secure in the faith that England, France, and Russia allied with the United States shared so much power that Germany could not win such a war. There were not as many jokes about Hitler, but Mussolini had taken his place as a favorite target for the mimics.

The Writers Guild was still a pariah. Even though the Screen Playwrights were fading fast because of flaccid organization, the Guild was inoperative and certainly nonexistent so far as the producers were concerned.

Boys Town developed into the hit the studio had reckoned it would be, which enabled John Considine to get approval for a project he had harbored for a long time, two pictures based on the life of Thomas Edison: the first, dealing with his youth, *Young Tom Edison*, starring Mickey Rooney; the second, a chronicle of Edison's adulthood, *Edison the Man*, starring Spencer Tracy. John assigned me to research and write the scripts and I recruited Hugo Butler to work with me.

But Considine had prior projects to attend to; Hugo was finishing up another script; and I was called in to tie up some loose ends in the script that later became *Broadway Melody of 1940*, distinguished because of the extraordinary dancing of Fred Astaire and Eleanor Powell. I have not the faintest memory of any part of the story, which is a blessing.

However, my work on *Melody* brought me to the attention of Sam Katz, the once powerful Katz of the Balaban and Katz theater circuit. Katz was a polished, well-groomed man with a mellifluous voice and an engaging smile who asked me to write a musical about Irish-Americans. He had in mind a cast of George Murphy, Eleanor Powell, Mickey Rooney, et cetera, et cetera. After burrowing in my den for two or three weeks, I came up with a story of Irish immigrants who arrive in New York in the early 1900s and, using their considerable talents, make a mark in show business. Mr. Katz was pleased I had something to report and asked me to tell him the yarn.

This practice of storytelling to executives was inaugurated by Mayer, who seldom if ever read anything. Since Thalberg's death in 1936, Mayer had devised a unit system with executives in command of a group of producers. Mayer was commander in chief. The executives — Bernard Hyman, Sam Katz, Al Lichtman, Larry Weingarten, James Mc-Guinness — were field generals. Producers and directors were colonels, majors, and captains, depending on their credits. Writers were privates. The unit idea was designed to prevent any one executive from developing the threat Thalberg had been to Mayer's seat of power.

Each week the staff officers would meet and listen to stories that might be potential films. These tales would be related by talented Scheherazades who were excused at the conclusion of their performances to permit the staff, which included the head of the story department, to decide yea or nay. In some circles, this decisive screening group was known as the College of Cardinals, with Mayer designated as Pope.

Therefore, when I went to see Katz to outline my Irish saga, I had prepared it to be heard, not read. As I left the starting block, Katz greeted the first sequence with a smile and a nod of his head. The smile grew wider and the nodding continued as I went through the twenty minutes it took to complete the job. At the triumphant finish, Katz looked at me with a broad grin. He spoke: "I don't like it." Still with a half smile he went into detail. He disliked the characters, the story, the period (he wanted it modern), and I sensed he didn't like me. I did manage to say, "You had me fooled. I guess it was the smile." He nodded as he smiled; "I'm always polite."

After that fiasco, David Hertz and I were assigned to put together some sort of tropical romance for Joe Mankiewicz, who was then a producer. The intended cast was Hedy Lamarr paired with either Gable or Bob Taylor. We tried and failed but we did become fast friends because we laughed a lot at our attempts to write a serious story about the tropics, where we had never been, and about characters in whom we had no interest. We told Joe we were miscast. He removed us from the assignment with no hard feelings.

During these early days of 1939, the Spanish revolution was collapsing, Hitler was obviously becoming stronger and more aggressive, and there was a growing conviction that, because of the disastrous 1938 off-year elections, FDR would run for an unprecedented third term to protect the New Deal against dismemberment. The "arsenal of democracy" speech Roosevelt had made was the tip-off. The America First-ers were furious. We talked about all these matters in living rooms and offices and remained as active as possible. I was writing material for the ADL and in speeches was lambasting Father Coughlin and Congressmen Bilbo and Rankin, along with the German-American Bunds.

Then personal tidings came. The Academy nominations were announced and I was named for both the story and the screenplay of *Boys Town*.

By then, I was working with Irving Brecher on a Marx Brothers story — *A Day at the Races*. I had little interest in the story and since the talented Brecher was much better than I at inventing material for the Marx Brothers, I copped out.

At home, Miriam, an accomplished pianist though shy about playing for an audience, had resumed her work as a painter, a career she had prepared for at the Art Students League years ago. While she had worked with charcoal, pen and ink, and pastels, she had worked only sporadically with oil, and now concentrated on that medium. We had plenty of room in the house and Miriam was turning out pictures by the dozen, tossing most of them away as inferior; but despite her frequent dismay, her work was developing an original imprint. She had made a commitment, which she kept until recent years when rheumatoid arthritis crippled her hands.

Our two daughters, Jill and Joy, were a constant source of fun, and Mother was happier and more comfortable than she had been in her life. Lil had come in for a visit to meet our new daughter and spend time with Ma. Lil's marriage was getting rockier by the week and would last only a few months more.

The night of the Academy Awards, since I was a nominee, Miriam and I had been invited by MGM to attend. I didn't know that, a few hours before the presentations, the press were given the results before anyone in the ballroom knew who had won. In those days, the Academy Awards were held in the Biltmore Hotel Ballroom, a tiered hall that was designed for good seating and viewing. The awards were handled more informally, nominees were not limited to a few hurried seconds of thanks, and the atmosphere was more congenial and less structured than the television spectaculars have become. You didn't have stars introduced who would then introduce other stars who would read the names of nominees, announce the winner, and disappear for the evening.

At six o'clock I received a call from Howard Strickling, chief of publicity at the studio, who whispered I had won the Oscar. We all whooped and I told Ma and Lil to get dressed up and come along for the occasion. Strickling said he'd arrange to seat them.

Miriam and I were seated at a table with the other writing nominees. I had been warned not to tell anyone I had grabbed the brass ring, and consequently the hours while dinner was being served were damned uncomfortable. We were wishing the others luck with false smiles and genuine hypocrisy. I regretted I had been told — but when the moment came, regret fled. I strode up, took the statuette, and told everyone that for me the Oscar was Father Flanagan. The rest of the night was a blur. A happy blur.

A bonus was in store. Spencer Tracy won the award for his performance as Father Flanagan. Later, I went to greet him with congratulations. He said, "You know I didn't want to do this one — but sure as shit I'm glad I did." Then he gave me a slap on the back and thanked me.

A few days later, Leo McCarey called to tell me that he was taking my name off the credits of *Love Affair*. He said, "You won your Oscar — now I want mine." His directness stymied me and I mumbled something, like, "Well, good luck." Leo asked if I was putting the "witch's curse" on him. I didn't answer. I hung up.

There was nothing I could do about the situation. Indeed, nothing I chose to do. Producers or executives made the decisions on original story credits. The Screen Playwrights were fading; the Writers Guild was still realigning its strategy for recognition and still being rejected by the producers.

It was at this time that John Considine called to tell me that he was free to begin work on the Edison pictures. Hugo was free of his chores, and he and I began our research.

First we dug for gold in the biographies of Thomas Alva Edison; while we found some flashy ore, we wound up mostly with slag. Edison, a genuine hero of American invention and enterprise, had been mummified and placed in a sarcophagus tightly latched by legend, respect, and awe, making it difficult to know the boy and the man as he really was — unless, of course, the real man was not as complex, humorous, or fascinating as we wished him to be. Clearly, it was necessary to talk to a few people who knew Edison.

Considine decided that he, Hugo, and I should go east to do some mining. We traveled to Menlo Park, abutting the Oranges in New Jersey, where we lunched with Charles Edison, the inventor's son, who later became governor, and Ed Walsh, a former aide of Edison's who was still functioning as a caretaker of the Edison interests. Walsh was a fresh and amusing man with an absurd but rather fascinating gift for clasping his palms together and massaging them in a manner that produced music. We spent time in the Edison library and workshop, Walsh pointing out the large clock that is supposed to have stopped at the exact time Edison breathed his last. Charles Edison was a quiet and courtly man, quite reticent about his father. We gathered that the Edison family was a reclusive clan. Later, Considine, Hugo, and I agreed that we would have to dig a lot deeper for the mother lode.

We began to mold *Young Tom Edison.*

16

*A*s I recall the flow of the years 1939, 1940, and 1941, I realize they
set me on a road I had not contemplated walking. To piece this
together is much like tatting lace; while weaving a design with the thread
of events, it is unnecessary to fill all the interstices.

After Hugo and I finished the script of *Young Tom Edison*, I moved
on to *Edison the Man*. Hugo and I had quarreled. Hugo had drifted to
the far left — was now in agreement with a party line that accused liberals of being premature anti-Nazis. Our friendship ended with a bitter
scene during which Hugo said that Nazi anti-Semitism was largely a fig-
ment of Jewish imagination.

John Considine sent me to Detroit to meet with Edsel Ford, who
was running the Ford empire. Mr. Ford was a finely featured gentleman
with a charming gift of wry humor and an interest in the theater. Obviously, he was badly cast as a tycoon. He seemed better suited to be head
of a university.

The Ford family, inspired by Henry Ford's friendship with and admiration of Edison, had re-created the Edison workshop in an incredible
duplication of Menlo Park. It was to obtain their cooperation that I had
been sent to Detroit.

Edsel Ford spread a gourmet lunch in the executive dining room
and then escorted me on a tour of the River Rouge assembly plant with
its smelting vats and foundries. The shocking impact of the roaring
clangor, the smashing, riveting, and crashing, hammered at my senses.
Choosing an opportune moment, I asked for the key to a men's room,
dashed into it, and threw up the elegant lunch. Fortunately, Mr. Ford
then took me for an open-air walk that aided my recovery. I told him of
my amazement at the massive dimensions of the Ford industry. When I
asked how such a vast enterprise was run, Mr. Ford said, "It has to be

run efficiently — the more efficiently, the bigger it gets; the bigger it gets, the more efficient it needs to be, then it gets bigger . . ." He smiled and added, "I often wonder how long I can do it."

I met Mr. Ford on other occasions. He was a sensitive man whose will and interest were totally destroyed by Harry Bennett and his goons, who had usurped Ford's power and taken control of the Ford operation. Ultimately, the hooligans were literally bounced out by Edsel's son, Henry, who had the gristle and muscle to take back his family's control. I have always thought that the irony of the ugly seriocomic failure of the Edsel automobile was that it bore the name of a tasteful and dignified man.

Angry political currents had been stirred up by the announcement that Stalin and Hitler had signed a nonaggression pact. While many of us did believe that this alliance was designed merely to give both Russia and Germany time to prepare for an all-out war against each other, what irritated us was that so many of our associates touched their fingers together and spoke piously of peace. The local Communist party liners accepted or at least broadcast the myth that England, France, and the United States were planning an alliance with Germany that would turn on Russia and destroy it. Concurrent with that conspiracy theory, we were told that the Anti-Nazi League was no longer relevant. Czechoslovakia ceased to exist; Russia was "defending" itself against Finland by a massive attack, which was being nobly resisted by the Finns; but all the startling danger signs were eloquently dismissed by the party boys.

These political crises ruptured many friendships. The meetings of the board of the Screen Writers Guild became strident and harsh as we also were strained by the evidence that the producers were avoiding granting us recognition on the pretext that we were governed by Communists. While we were well aware that a number of our members had hewed to the party line, we felt that Red-baiting would be counterproductive by probably breaking us into two guilds, rendering each one ineffective in the struggle for identity and recognition. So we quarreled and argued but agreed that our objective was to avoid an amoebalike separation.

By now, I had handed the *Edison the Man* script to Considine, who assigned John Meehan to work with Clarence Brown, the director, on a rewrite. Considine then shipped me off to Syracuse, New York, to see the family of Warden Lawes of Sing Sing to persuade them to permit MGM to film an account of the warden's courageous and certainly controversial life. They agreed, provided we used a name other than Lawes.

We selected Osborne, received a quitclaim from the family, and I started scribbling in early January, 1940.

Miriam and I knew that she was pregnant again, and due to have the baby in September. The two girls, Jill and Joy, were adorable but I was hoping that the next child would be a boy. In Jewish families it is a matter of conceit to have a son to carry on the "family" name, but it is also important (another conceit) to replace yourself with another male Jew to provide a *Kaddish zugger* to say the prayer of faith as a memorial to you when you die.

While working on *Osborne of Sing Sing* I accepted the chairmanship of a committee, Hollywood for Roosevelt, to work for FDR's reelection for a third term. Since Roosevelt was being dubbed a "warmonger" by the left as well as the right, our committee worked harmoniously and energetically without having to contend with the endless forensic tactics of the left wing.

I met Mrs. Roosevelt for the first time when she visited Los Angeles and, of course, fell in love with her. Having been selected to introduce her to a large gathering, I had the opportunity to say much of what I felt about her and FDR. The occasion also was my first tentative contact with national political figures.

Being inquisitive and curious, I have always responded to new challenges and experiences; therefore it was inevitable I would say yes when the League of American Writers invited me to give a course in screen writing. During that stint, I came to know Carl Foreman, whose talents were bright and abundant, a prize student who developed into a major creator in the motion-picture industry. Another student with rich ability was Paul Jarrico, who never reached his full stature once the blacklisting began. I enjoyed the night sessions at the school, working with the students without involving them, or myself, in partisan politics. But in the late spring of 1940, John Howard Lawson submitted a petition attacking FDR's South American "Big Brother" policy that each teacher was asked to sign. I told John that I would sign no such petition. Later that evening, Donald Ogden Stewart, also teaching at the school, tried to persuade me to go along with the rest of the staff. He told me that the faculty members would have to sign or resign from the staff. That made it easy. I quit.

This experience with the League persuaded me that a council of guilds might be a worthwhile device to develop a middle-of-the-road policy designed to keep both the right and left wings of Hollywood from dominating any guild.

The Guild Council represented creative and labor unions, and during our first meeting someone suggested that the first order of business be a statement condemning Roosevelt's "Big Brother" policy as a capitalist ruse. Echoes of the League of American Writers were loud and clear. There was some support for this troublesome, divisive suggestion. I countered by threatening to break up the council just as quickly as I had helped organize it, pointing out that the proposed resolution exactly demonstrated what we had organized to prevent — a political rather than a labor-oriented council. The proposed statement was defeated.

A few days later, Miriam stopped knitting and told me to take her to the hospital. Some hours later, our son, Jeb, was born. We named him so not to honor Jeb Stuart but to remember the hero of my play *Too Many Heroes,* whose name was Jeb Williams. I hoped that Jeb would have the virtues of the stage character — courage, integrity, and honor.

When we brought Jeb home from the hospital, Mother decided that our place was getting a bit crowded. She believed she should have her own apartment. When Mother found one she liked, Miriam helped her set up her own *wirtschaft,* workshop.

The Writers Guild bargaining committee had been rejected for the fourth or fifth time, and at a meeting of the board, at which I was not present, it was suggested that those members of the committee who had any taint of the "Communist" label bow out of the committee, removing one of the excuses the producers were making for not negotiating. Those members did so quite freely. I was asked to serve on the committee in place of John Howard Lawson. The other members were Charles Brackett, Sheridan Gibney, Dudley Nichols, and our attorney, Robert Tenney.

At the same time, I was assigned to write a script, *Married Bachelor,* to star Robert Young. My collaborator was Lionel Houser, who, plagued with phlebitis, was confined to a wheelchair. Lionel was a breezy, cheerful man who during his long illness had become a whiz at pitching cards into a hat. Writing a scenario leaves many free hours during the day and those idle spells were used to teach me the art of tossing cards — eventually with my eyes closed — into a hat or a wastebasket. My skill at this parlor trick has won a few bucks in a couple of hustles and later on in *Lonelyhearts* my hands stood in for those of Monty Clift, who had to toss cards when we made that film.

Lionel and I had fun working on *Married Bachelor.* As a result, the script came to life in very short order. Eddie Buzzell was drafted to direct the picture and Lionel and I finished this one up by ourselves without other writers being called in to polish or rewrite our work.

Writers at Metro and most every other studio were constantly in a rage because of the arbitrary use of their talents, which resulted in the multiple credits that appeared on the screen, such as: Original Story by Joe McGiffen, Based on an Idea by Joe Blow, Screenplay by Joe Smith and Joe Doe and Janet Blue, Continuity by Joe Kelly, Additional Dialogue by Joe Moe. The lineups were humiliating, often giving credit to writers who didn't deserve any and depriving others who had made major contributions.

During the time Lionel and I were working, the producers agreed to meet with the Writers Guild's new bargaining committee. The neutral ground chosen was a new private dining room at the Vine Street Brown Derby.

Among the producers in attendance were Eddie Mannix (Metro), Harry Warner (Warner Brothers), Y. Frank Freeman (Paramount, and the president of the Motion Picture Producers Association in Hollywood), Ben Kahane (Columbia), Cliff Work (Universal), Charles Nolan (RKO), Lew Schreiber (Twentieth-Fox). They were accompanied by a battery of tough-minded and skilled lawyers headed by Mendel Silberberg, a legendary bargainer, negotiator, and, as attorney for the Motion Picture Producers Association, the protector of the iron gates to the the studios. It was a formidable group that not only outnumbered us but outgunned us with experience and power.

We were a small group: Brackett, Gibney (the Guild president), Nichols, Tenney, and me. First we ate and exchanged pleasantries designed by them to soften us up and by us to show them we were sober, respectable gentlemen and scholars.

After dinner, we sat down with smokes and some liquor and got down to cases; Mendel Silberberg pulled the first cork out of the bottle. He assured us the producers were willing, at some time, to reach an agreement — "See how many of us are here?" — *but* — the *but* alerted our tiny but valiant group — *but* as we surely knew, FDR's plan to gear up for possible trouble (the "phony" war was on) was likely to cause hardship for the industry. Lumber, nails, all sorts of products needed for making films might not be available to the studios. Therefore, it was possible the picture business might have to shut down. This was no time to negotiate. Our country had to be served come what may.

Those of us who were veterans of the 50 percent wage cut had heard that sad song once before. As Mr. Silberberg quietly and almost persuasively continued, my mind wandered and I got an idea. I whispered to Bob Tenney to ask for a recess so that we could meet for a short time to react to what had been said. Bob nodded and suggested to Gibney that we take a break.

We retired to a small anteroom, where I broached my notion. I proposed that we agree that the times were fraught with danger and that we did not wish to add any financial burdens or risks to the studios, *but* — now we had our *but*, and better than theirs — *but* that there was no reason why they could *not* recognize us as the sole bargaining agent for all writers; why they could *not* give us the right to determine final writer's credits; why they could *not* permit us a 70 percent (not 100 percent) guild shop; why they could *not* agree to discuss a minimum-wage clause in the future; and why they could *not* accept these basic terms, since none of those items cost a dime and would once and for all determine our right to exist as the accredited bargaining unit for writers.

The committee agreed it was an interesting ploy. Bob Tenney was absolutely certain that we had them over the well-worn barrel. The others were not quite as sure but were willing to gamble. As we began to move toward the door Dudley Nichols help up a hand, smiled, and said, "Brothers, let us pray." We laughed and returned to the bargaining room.

Sheridan Gibney quietly (he is a calm, reasonable man at all times) told the producers what we thought and summed up by asking for this minimal contract. There was a hush. For the first time we sensed tension. Harry Warner got up, crossed to Sheridan, and asked, "Is that all you want?" For a moment, I thought we'd sold too cheap. But when Sheridan answered Warner, "Yes — we think that's fair," Warner exploded. He turned to his colleagues. "That's all they want! They want blood!" Now he turned to us: "That's all you want, you goddamned Communist bastards! You dirty sons of bitches. All you'll get from me is shit!" He continued his tirade with a series of other curses and repetitive screams, his face growing livid as the color fled from his cheeks. All of us were stunned, producers as well as writers. Mannix and Freeman rose and took Warner by his arms and tried to quiet him as they escorted him out to the parking lot. There was an embarrassed silence. No one knew what to say. The producers edged over to one side of the room, we to the other. After a while, Freeman and Mannix returned sans Warner.

Freeman told us that Warner had left for the evening and asked us to retire to our room away from room. We did.

When we were alone, Sheridan, still white-faced, merely said, "That man Warner is stark raving mad."

Bob Tenney said, "The question is — what about the others?"

In a matter of minutes, we were asked to return. Silberberg spoke for the producers: "We regret what happened. However, we agree your request is reasonable. Based on Mr. Gibney's points, we are pleased to advise you that you have your contract."

There were handshakes, a couple of more drinks, then we got away by ourselves to drink the wine we'd been thinking of since 1933. Then we each hit the road for home, and telephones rang in many writers' homes for hours. The battle was won. We had our first deal — scrawny and weak, but our first.

Footnote: As of 1978, the Writers Guild had received and processed more than 110 million dollars in television residuals and motion picture benefits for its members.

A group of screenwriters who fought hard for the Guild now abide in Writer's Heaven, where all plays, novels, and scenarios are reviewed ecstatically. Having known them, I can see and hear them — John Howard Lawson, Charlie Brackett, Dudley Nichols, Dalton Trumbo, Ernest Pascal, Oliver H. P. Garrett, Ralph Bloch, Edward Paramore, Doris Malloy, among many others.

They are very happy.

17

*J*ohn Considine's next idea for a film was to do the story of Simón
Bolívar. When he assigned me to it I knew little or nothing of the
life of the South American liberator. For the next few months my reading of his life in libraries in California and at the Pan American Union
in Washington, where I began a warm and cherished friendship with
Father Sheehy, an authority on Bolívar, gave me a solid education of the
times, manners, triumphs, eccentricities (mental and physical), failures,
and sad death of this baffling and brilliant man.

The lengthy treatment of his life that I wrote is, I believe, a first-rate
motion picture outline. But the film was never made. In Washington I visited a number of South American embassies, all of which had objections.

The Colombian ambassador was dismayed that I had dealt with the
attempted assassination of Bolívar by Francisco Santander, who in later
years had become the first president of Colombia, and so, of course, the
dramatization of the incident would not be well received.

The Argentine embassy reviewed my script, particularly that section dealing with General José de San Martín, the liberator of Argentina,
who shared an ambition with Bolívar — to free Peru from Spanish rule.
With their armies both liberators arrived for the deliverance of Peru at
the same time and place. A meeting between the two leaders was arranged
at Guayaquil. No other person was present in the room where the two
met. At the close of the conference, San Martín and Bolívar exchanged
gifts, San Martín went back to Argentina, Bolívar liberated the area, part
of which now bears his name, and a short while later San Martín returned
his medals and awards and left the Argentine forever. No one has ever
come up with a valid or confirmed explanation of what took place in that
room at Guayaquil.

The Chilean government reminded me that their homeland was liberated by Bernardo O'Higgins. They did not view Bolívar with affection.

Because of the questions raised by the South American governments, the studio decided to shelve the production.

The two films I've most wanted to produce were both stymied by political protests: *Forty Days of Musa Dagh* by Turkish interference and threats; *Bolívar* by the objections from Chile, Colombia, and Argentina.

During my work in Washington on the Bolívar project, before my tour of the embassies, I met with Sumner Welles, almost a doppelgänger for Lou Calhern, a tall, glacial, lean slash of a man, who was the first to caution me that it was unlikely we would ever make the film.

In the case of *Musa Dagh*, some years later, when I made an attempt to move the property into production, Turkey, Great Britain, and the United States joined in frowning on the proposal with the warning that if it was produced, all MGM films might be boycotted in "certain areas." The only area I could think of where such a boycott might have been launched was Turkey. I did not believe that Metro, or indeed any other movie company, would be placed in financial jeopardy by being banned in Turkey, but the New York office said "nyet."

However, in regard to *Bolívar*, as a writer, I could only file my protest to Considine, who fumed and fussed; but his efforts were as futile as mine.

There was nothing to do but heave a sigh and look for something else to do. We tried to revive our lagging interest in *Osborne of Sing Sing* but realized that both of us had lost faith in the script, and with good reason. While Considine and I were marking time it gave me the opportunity to move the family to a new and better home.

Shortly after Jeb's birth, we had begun to look for a home that would provide the family with cleaner air, more greenery, and greater security. After some months, we found precisely what we needed in Brentwood. Situated on a plot of about half an acre, our new place, much like an English farmhouse, had a tennis court, beautiful trees and flowers, and was surrounded by high, thick hedges. The acreage was elevated above the street level, giving us a barrier against noise, low fog, and casual intruders.

There was an additional endowment: a small but serviceable studio for Miriam, whose work was beginning to develop an original representational color and line.

All this for a rental of two hundred fifty dollars per month. We discarded all of our Chinese Chippendale modern junk and went in for English and early American decor.

Brentwood in 1940 seemed far removed from Hollywood and Beverly Hills. We moved from our house by traveling due west over Sunset Boulevard, past the still rather quiet Sunset Boulevard area with the oasis of the original Schwab's drugstore, past the nightclubs and the Colony gambling parlor, past the beautifully gardened Beverly Hills homes and the Beverly Hills Hotel, past the rich Holmby Hills area, where the very rich and swank elite parked — Beverly Hills was Cadillac and Lincoln territory, Holmby Hills was Rolls-Royce and Bentley.

Then we moved into open country with vast fields of poinsettias aflame before the Christmas season. Finally, Brentwood Circle bisecting Sunset and one block south was home, where we would spend the next eighteen years.

Many of our friends felt we were moving out of their lives. However, once they saw the tennis court, business improved as did my game, which on a scale of one to ten never got above three . . . on exceptionally good days.

We moved in late November. The night we checked in our phones were still not connected, which forced Lenny Spigelgass and Allen Rivkin to come to our home at one in the morning to rouse us with the scary news that Mother had had a severe heart attack. Grabbing a pair of pants and a sweater, I dashed out, telling Miriam to follow in Lenny's car, and raced to Mother's apartment. Dr. Moe Nathanson had already gambled by injecting a huge dose of adrenalin directly into Mother's heart muscle, reviving her and improving her chances for recovery.

Weeks later when she was able to sit up, Mother said she'd like to go back east to spend time with Lil. We dismantled her apartment and sent her to New York accompanied by a nurse. She was to stay east for two or three months and then return to California.

I kept reading synopses from the studio file, novels, biographies, and magazines in a search for a story that would excite me. The yarn I found was one by Paul Gallico titled *Joe Smith, American*. It had a good tense plot, a patriotic theme that fitted into FDR's preparedness program, and a cinch role for a star. Before telling Considine about it, I worked out a complete continuity, thought up a finish that was lacking in the original, and came to the conclusion that I would like to write and direct the film. I rehearsed the story for Miriam and Ralph and Betty Rainger, who loved it. What else could they say? It was clear to them that I would not have listened to any negative vote.

Then on to Considine, an emotional man who was in tears as the end of the story was reached. He ordered Kenneth MacKenna, now in charge of the story department and writers' brigade, to buy the short story, but told me that he, Considine, could not approve me as director. Only Mayer could make such a decision. He called Mayer's office, told him it was urgent, and before I could develop doubts or insecurities, we were in the Vatican in the Pope's office.

I had never met Mr. Mayer. His office was huge and white. A large semicircle of desk surrounded him. It was loaded with intercom devices on one side, a couple of telephones on the other. Mr. Mayer was chunky, immaculately dressed, white-haired with deep brown eyes that were slightly magnified by his glasses. There were a few papers neatly stacked on his desk. Pictures of his favorite friends were placed on a credenza in back of him, the ones of Herbert Hoover, Cardinal Spellman, and J. Edgar Hoover most prominently displayed. Mayer radiated power — physical and psychological. He held out a hand, short fingered and well manicured, then settled into his chair sideways in what I came to know as a typical position and indicated that Considine should explain the urgency. After that was done, Mayer asked me to tell him the story. This was the third performance and I played it like opening night.

Mr. Mayer said, of course, buy it — but (always, ever, there's a but) he wasn't sure that he would let me direct it. To begin with, why did I want to direct rather than produce? Mayer preferred producers — to him they were the captains of the armada, and the writers, actors, directors merely members of the crew. His attitude undoubtedly stemmed from the early days when directors might simply disappear with cast and crew and do what they wished with no interference from the producer or executive. Writers? MGM had a hundred under contract.

My reasons for wanting to write and direct, I said, were based on my feelings as a writer, which had led me to the conclusion that I would enjoy putting my scenario on the screen in the way I had written it. Purely personal — purely possessive. Finally, to cushion possible loss, I pointed out that this would be a low-cost film.

Mayer's next question was, "Why a B picture rather than a big one?"

I answered that a B picture didn't have to be a bad picture, a conclusion most people reached simply because it was dubbed "B."

That stirred Mayer to ask if I believed MGM's B's were bad. My answer was that I thought they lacked punch and point. "I believe," I said, "that low-cost pictures should dare — should challenge — that they also should be used as a testing ground for new talent — directors, writers, actors, producers."

Since the B pictures made for $250,000 always returned their cost, which included overhead, they satisfied everybody — but I believed that they had a greater potential, and told Mayer so.

He ended up being noncommittal and said he'd be in touch the next day and give us an answer.

When we left the office, Considine shook his head. "You blew it. You talked too much. Why can't you keep your goddamn mouth shut?"

"He asked me, I had to answer."

"You could have said something nice about the Andy Hardy pictures."

"I didn't think of them. I should have."

"You blew it, believe me, you blew it," Considine repeated as we parted.

He convinced me I had. I told Miriam the unhappy saga of the interview. Her only response was that she didn't like Andy Hardy pictures.

The next morning I heard from Mayer's office. I was to meet him in front of the Thalberg Building at two o'clock sharp. An image came into view: a lineup of writers standing at attention, a muffled drum serving as background scoring; I am forced to hand over my pencils and am booed as Generalissimo Mayer orders me to leave the Metro fortress.

However, undaunted, I was on time for my rendezvous. So was Mayer. His car was waiting. He beckoned me in and told me we were going to the Hollywood racetrack to see one of his horses run. On the way he talked of horses, his early life in Canada, his mother — but not a single word about *Joe Smith, American* or my request to direct it.

While I nodded in the manner of a Christmas tiger, little of what he said stuck in my memory. I kept waiting for a segue into what interested me. Quite clearly, I wasn't going to be fired, but I sensed he was going to try and talk me out of directing. Then I wondered why he had not simply told Considine to forget it — why was I being escorted to the races, a sport in which I had no interest?

We arrived at the track, saw one race, in which Mayer's horse ran far behind, then back we motored to the studio. During the journey I was told something more about horses, stables, and how you win some races and lose some.

I had noticed that Mayer moved rapidly in short, choppy strides approaching the car, popping out of it, getting into the grandstand and leaving it. When we moved into the studio he went at the same pace, talking as rapidly as he walked. Once we got into his office, he sat down, shifted his weight to his left hip, placed his right hand in his frontier style pants' pocket, and broached the subject so quickly I was flabber-gasted, which I would have been even with some conversational overture.

"Did you really mean what you said yesterday," he asked, "I mean about our B pictures?"

"Yes, I did," had to be my answer.

"All right." He held me with an intense look, then half smiled. "All right, you're in charge of all the B pictures."

I was unable to answer. Mayer continued.

"You'll pick your own stories, casts, directors, we won't get in your way. Sink or swim."

I mustered enough voice to question if I had the ability to do that. He assured me I did. I had heard that Mayer applied animal features to people — stars were like thoroughbred horses, people who were too am-bitious were wolves, cheap women were alley cats — and now he said I was like an elephant (a disappointment — I'd have preferred being called a horse), strong, big, surefooted, firm. He threw a slider at me: "I'll put Harry Rapf with you to bother about budgets — he'll have nothing to do with the pictures. He's doing nothing — he'll be grateful."

By now I was bold enough to ask a few questions. Would I really be in charge? Yes, provided that I stayed within a prescribed maximum budget of $300,000 for any one picture, but the films should be geared for $250,000 or less. Any budget above the maximum would have to be approved by Mayer.

There was only one thing for me to say: "I'll have to think about it."

Mayer answered, "You either believe what you said or you don't. Here's your chance to prove yourself."

I ducked. "I'll have to talk it over with my wife." He liked that and concluded by telling me to let him know the next day. We shook hands, I thanked him for an interesting day, drove home, and burbled the in-credible news to Miriam.

To accept the responsibility would mean a change in some areas of our family life. Accustomed to working at home, I'd be chained to the office. Instead of having a nightlife that kept me reading or working until two or three in the morning and permitted me to sleep until ten, I'd have to be up by seven-thirty or eight. But I would not give up being home for dinner and eating with the family.

Miriam suggested a conference of friends. That evening Ralph, Allen, Leonard, and Don trooped over to answer what they had been told was an urgent request for help.

As I told the story of the day's events I could read their answer.

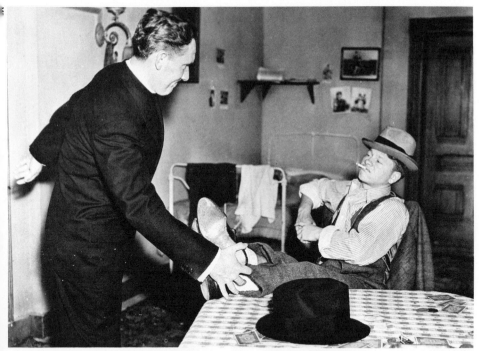

Spencer Tracy is about to slap some good manners into the insouciant Mickey Rooney in Boys Town

The original Lassie in 1943 with her director Fred Wilcox and trainer Mr. Weatherwax on Lassie's right front paw

The extraordinary Margaret O'Brien in her introduction to films as the orphan in Journey for Margaret. *Robert Young, eons before Dr. Welby, comforts Margaret.*

The only picture extant of L.B. and me in serious discussion

Sinclair Lewis is acting up a storm pretending he is reading our script Storm in the West

They were all smiles. Lenny made the first observation: "Let's get one thing out of the way quickly. You intend, of course, to hire all of us." With that joke over the talk became serious, candid, and sincere. Ralph was certain I would be a good executive and would more than likely become head of a studio. Don had reservations about whether or not I'd like having to fire anyone. Allen said, "You're the best damn script editor in town." Lenny thought it was a marvelous opportunity to prove a number of things.

Miriam had reached her decision: "You've talked for years about how things ought to run — well, now you can run them." That appeared to sum up my own feelings. I had waited for hours in producers' offices and then been told to come back the next day. I had been bilked out of credits — been fired for expressing differing opinions. Every writer I knew had gone through similar exasperating experiences. Perhaps I could change things.

The next morning I called Mayer's office and asked if I could see him before noon. I was told he'd see me at eleven.

When Mayer greeted me, I saw he was studying me to detect my decision. The fact was that while I wanted to accept the offer, I was prepared to reject it if I could not have the job on the terms he had implied.

In answer to his question, I said that I was ready to say yes but I wanted to review the ground rules. Was I in charge despite Rapf's position as guardian of the budgets? Reply — yes, and if there was a difference of opinion, Mayer would act as final arbiter. Could I truly choose the stories, writers, directors, and actors with no interference? Reply — yes, if the contract players were available, and yes, if outside talent did not break the budget barrier, and no, if the top stars flatly refused to play any of our scripts. Would I have the last word on scripts and final editing of the film? Reply — yes.

Last question: Had Mr. Rapf been told and had he agreed if I did take the position?

"Of course," said Mayer. "What else would he say? You want me to call him up here?"

I thought it would be better if I went to Rapf's office.

Mayer stood up, extended his hand, and we shook on our bargain. He told me that my agent, Nat Goldstone, should talk to Eddie Mannix regarding a long-term contract. While the security such a contract offered was attractive and a week-to-week job was a risk, I was also aware that a contract could be abrogated or made so untenable that, in Goldwyn's immortal observation, "an oral contract isn't worth the paper it's written on" — and neither of course are most that are written.

I decided to gamble by telling Mayer that if I flunked out my dismissal would be less bloody without a contract — if I did well, I could bargain for a contract with better terms than would be offered at this time. Mayer said that made sense and sent for Eddie Mannix, who was pleased and congratulated me with obvious warmth.

Mannix wanted me to go to his lair so that he could send for decorators; the building superintendent; Howard Strickling, the head of public relations and publicity; and others, all of whom would take over my conversion from writer to executive.

First I went to see Harry Rapf.

He was sitting at his desk in his new offices in the Thalberg Building and as I entered he got up and said, "L.B. just told me." Then he started to cry, the tears tumbling out of his pale blue eyes. He told me how grateful he was to me for accepting this new arrangement, and as he went on my embarrassment permitted only short responses — "It's okay," "Don't worry," "It's going to be all right," "Let's have no tears."

By now Rapf was wiping his eyes, blowing his nose, and had begun to smile. Explaining that I had to go to Mannix's office and that I would see him the next day, I left Mr. Rapf.

On the way to Mannix, I felt sorry for Rapf. I thought, this is my first experience with power. Here's a guy who bounced me out of the studio twice and now he's willing to kiss my ass. Upstairs, a group of men wait to flatter me, brush my coat, obey my wishes. Now I'm in a spot that has some real clout.

I knew my pulse was fast. I felt good — but at the same time I was fighting back panic.

I knew that power is gained in one of three ways or in a combination of two or all three of these ways: by aggression, by persuasion, or simply by the gift of authority . . . elective or appointive.

The power settled upon me came through the certification of L. B. Mayer. I knew that if you accept a position of authority you must use it; if your decisions are right, fortune smiles — wrong, Bye-Bye Blackbird.

Therefore, when the decorators, electricians, painters, and staff paraded into the capacious executive suite assigned to me on the second floor, I chose the decor, style of desk, chairs and sofa, thereby making it clear I was in charge. While Harry Rapf and I were supposed to be a team, the arrangement that I was in charge had been outlined to Rapf. His job was to keep an eye on budgets and sound alarms if we were exceeding our allotments.

When the gate sprang open, the first picture to break free was *Joe*

Smith, American. I assigned Allen Rivkin to do the script from the out-line I had already prepared. Jack Chertok, with an enviable record as executive of short subjects, was the first producer in our unit. We wound up with six others: Samuel Marx, former chaplain of writers, who wanted to be a producer; Benny Zeidman, a producer for whom I had worked at Universal; Bernie Fineman, a rather elegant man, snobbish but with taste, who at one time had made films at RKO; Irving Starr, a warm, chubby man with a sense of humor and a devotion to horse betting and gin rummy; Richard Goldstone, also drafted from the shorts department, who had lively ambition and a good sense of how to develop a screen-play. Completing our roster was William Wright, a Hoosier with dry wit, talent, many enthusiasms, and a flair for offbeat tales.

These seven soon became an active unit of workers. The writer's table, where I ate, dubbed them the Seven Dwarfs, giving each one of the men a special designation from Disney's flock. I've long forgotten how the producers were matched with the dwarfs.

Rapidly, our program fell into shape. We hit a few jackpots on the first pulls of the lever. *Joe Smith, American*, starring Robert Young, directed by Richard Thorpe, picked up wonderful reviews, big business, and a stack of awards. It was at the preview of *Joe Smith* that Harry Rapf grabbed my shoulder and whispered in triumph, "Believe me, this is going to be a feather in our eye."

Sam Marx, a husky fellow with a shaggy head of hair and a slight tic that caused a shrug of his shoulders and a flick of his head, lumbered in one day with an idea he and Hugo Butler had to film Eric Knight's *Lassie Come Home*. We got permission to raise our budget to $400,000 and came in with a $4-million grosser directed by another new director, Fred Wilcox. I never dreamed Lassie and her descendants would achieve Hollywood immortality, along with a young girl, beautiful and dear Elizabeth Taylor.

Our apparent success brought in high-salaried writers who volun-teered to write scripts in tune with our budgets since they knew I had established a policy of choosing screenwriters who were capable of do-ing a script from start to finish and guaranteeing them that their work would not be watered down by a squadron of rewrite men.

David Hertz, the brilliant and charming man who had shared the few weeks with me on the Hedy Lamarr story we had abandoned, came in with *Journey for Margaret*, which he had read and offered to script in two weeks. Willard "Woody" Van Dyke, a mercurial yet gifted director, took on the direction. Herb Kline, once slated to direct, searched for weeks for the right little girl until Margaret O'Brien, escorted by her mother, showed up and proved she could cry as readily as a modern Tiny Tears Doll. This odd talent plus her adorable looks and appeal made her an MGM star. The film was an enormous success.

We followed up with *Pilot No. 5*, this time an original by David Hertz that dealt with a Huey Long counterpart. I believe it was the first film to deal with the specter of American fascism. The cast included Gene Kelly, Van Johnson (a new recruit whom I had seen on Broadway and signed for the studio after he spent six empty months at Warner Brothers), Franchot Tone, and Peter Lawford. Again, we gathered excellent reviews. This one was director George Sidney's first film. By now our B pictures were at times outgrossing some of the Metro A pictures.

With our good fortune rising like a good soufflé, Rapf began to feel secure, a feeling that suddenly activated his harshness, which had not disappeared but had been hibernating.

He, of course, had been welcome each day when we viewed the daily rushes of films we were making. Present at these screenings during the lunch hour were the directors, producers, writers, and film editors of the pictures in work.

When the screening was over, I'd make comments to those involved, reserving for later conferences any disagreeable criticisms since there is nothing quite as fragile as a creator's pride when he is attacked in public.

This one Friday we were running film on pictures being directed by two new directors, Jules Dassin and Fred Zinneman, both of them moved up from the shorts department, where I had spotted their work.

Dassin's film was *Nazi Agent* starring Conrad Veidt, and Zinneman's was *Kid Glove Killer*. (A parenthetical note. The original title of Fred's picture was *Along Came Murder*. Howard Dietz, head of MGM's publicity and advertising, jettisoned the title, explaining that the word "murder" kept people out of theaters. Later he slipped us the final title, *Kid Glove Killer*. I called Dietz to ask him where in the Talmud it was written that "murder" kept audiences out and "killer" brought them in. Dietz was not amused. He simply suggested I make the pictures and he'd pick the titles.)

In the projection room as the Dassin and Zinneman dailies unrolled, I suddenly was aware that Rapf was reaching over to buzz the projectionist to stop the film. The lights went on, the pictures came to a blurred halt, and Rapf announced, "These rushes are lousy. I wouldn't let these two guys direct traffic."

The only thing that made sense was to tell everyone except Rapf to leave the room. Then I turned to their critic and asked what the hell and why the hell. He was brusque and said it was about time he spoke up. He wasn't an office boy — "I used to own part of this studio." That was true.

I reminded him of the arrangement for our unit worked out by Mr. Mayer, said that I had no intention of changing it, and if he was planning to ad-lib any other comments during the running of the rushes, he was no longer welcome. When Rapf grew angry, his nose got red and his cheeks pale, which was happening as he got to his feet and said, "We'll see about that," and stalked out.

A minute or two later, I left and found the assembled staff members waiting for me. I told them I disagreed with Rapf and for them to go back to work. That all would be well.

My confidant at the studio was Eddie Mannix, and after lunch I went to see him and told him we might be heading for trouble. He said that Rapf would cool down and for me to forget the entire *shmeer*.

Before returning to my office, I checked to see if Rapf was in. Perhaps a less hectic meeting could quiet the sonic booms of temper. His secretary advised me he had left word that he was going away with L. B. Mayer for the weekend. I assumed that Rapf was going to throw the first punch.

Well, the weekend was open for tennis. Perhaps I could improve my backhand. The kids would want to go to the merry-go-round, we would see some films, the Raingers were having a dinner party on Saturday, the time would go quickly.

Monday morning when L.B. arrived at his office, he sent for me. He greeted me with a big smile, asked how I was feeling, how were the children, Miriam. I could see no storm clouds.

Then he said, "Eddie told me you had some trouble with Harry."

I said I had thought Harry would have told him about that over the weekend.

"No," Mayer said. "Not a word."

"He'll get over it, I'm sure," I said.

"*He'll* get over it?"

Mayer pressed a lever on his intercom. Rapf's voice responded, "Yes, Louie?"

"Get up here right away, now!" Mayer's voice was a threat, an order, a clap of thunder.

Not wishing to witness Mayer's temper, of which I had heard a great deal, I said there was no reason for a quarrel.

Mayer then started a short lecture about old dogs never changing bad habits — that it was necessary sometimes to punish them. Before he was thoroughly warmed up, Harry Rapf entered and the roof caved in on him.

Mayer opened with a barrage of abuse. "Goddammit, Harry, you spent a weekend with me and never breathed a word. Mannix told me all about it. You stupid kike bastard — you ought to kiss this man's [pointing to me] shoes — get on your knees."

I got up as I started to tell Mayer there really wasn't any need to . . .

But Mayer waved me down into the chair.

Through the years I had heard many of the top-drawer Jewish studio executives lose their tempers at meetings or in card games and I was always dismayed when one of the first pejorative terms they used was "kike" — usually "dirty kike." It must have been an attempt to assert their superiority in the same way that blacks will call one of their own race "nigger" or Italians will whip out the name "wop." As a boy, I endured some lumps as I was called "kike" or "sheeny," and consequently either of these monikers still raises my hackles.

Rapf's jaw had slackened as Mayer continued to bombard him. He didn't utter a word. I felt myself getting ill as Mayer kept pummeling Rapf with curses and then suddenly L.B. pointed a finger at Rapf and declared, "Get out of here, you're fired, get out of your office. You had your last chance, you son of a bitch."

Rapf turned and hurried out.

I told Mayer I had to leave; that there was no need for him to have fired Rapf. Mayer answered by telling me I had to learn to be tough. "If you have to cut, cut fast, finish it quick."

When I got out of Mayer's office, I dashed to the men's toilet and threw up my breakfast.

After that I went home.

Obviously, I had committed a blunder by telling Mannix about my scene with Harry. I was sick with remorse and still shaking with having seen Rapf cut up.

An hour or two later I called Mayer and told him I could not accept his firing Rapf. If he did not reinstate Rapf, I would not go on with my job. Mayer now told me not to be stupid, but I insisted that Mayer's punishment had not fitted Harry's crime. He told me to sleep on it.

I didn't. I couldn't.

I kept seeing the scene run and rerun like rushes in a projection room.

The next morning my first resolve had hardened and when I met with Mayer, I repeated my determination that Rapf stay on. Perhaps because Rapf had not really quarreled with him, L.B. decided to be generous. He said he'd talk to Rapf. In two days Rapf, chastened, returned to his office. The trade-paper stories about the ruckus were soon forgotten and Harry apologized to me and swore he would never again behave as he had that Friday.

My private vow was that if Rapf ever again popped off the reservation, I would not tell a soul.

The unit resumed work on a schedule of eighteen pictures a year.

The Japanese attack on Pearl Harbor put an end to internal problems, though Mr. Mayer's understanding of it seemed a bit askew, as witness his toast on the occasion of the yearly pre-Christmas luncheon for producers, directors, writers, stars, and executives.

Before we were served food, he asked us to rise and lift our wineglasses. He gave a short speech; it went something like this: "This is a sad time. Many of our young men will be going to war and some will die. But we who stay at home must help all we can. Please join now in a toast," we raised our glasses as Mayer wound up, "to our president . . . Nicholas Schenck."

Perhaps it was natural that L.B., as former Republican chairman of California, had, since Herbert Hoover left office, only one president to whom he could relate — the president of Loew's, Inc.

The tension created by Rapf's interference and my blunder eased off as work resumed. Our program of pictures rumbled out as new directors — David Miller, Joe Newman, Bob Aldrich — joined the ranks. Barry Nelson, Dane Clark, Marsha Hunt, Steve Forrest, Bob Walker, our new players were soon flanked by MGM stars Robert Taylor, Robert Young, Fay Bainter, Frank Morgan, Laraine Day, George Murphy, Van Heflin, and Lew Ayres, for whom we were supplying good roles in successful films.

Bob Walker had come to us via a test made in New York. Tay Garnett had signed in to direct *Bataan,* a remake of John Ford's film *The Last Patrol.* Robert Andrews had brought us the idea of changing the English soldiers to Americans and the Arabs to Japanese. For one role we were looking for someone young, vulnerable, naive. We brought Bob out, Tay tested him for the role, and Bob's career got off like a jet fighter plane.

Wanting to break the color barrier in American war films, I cast one of the soldiers as a black. Andrews was never told which character it was to be — I didn't want any speeches about the white man's burden or other items dealing with race.

The picture was a hit. Though I was criticized by some of the executive staff inside the studio for using a black actor, we did get awards for having made the film.

As the list of our successes grew, one could observe the warning signs of the chronic Rapf infection. He began to call in producers for story conferences, send acerbic messages to directors, and again muscled his opinions into the projection room sessions.

During this time my friend Ralph Rainger, distinguished for his songs "Thanks for the Memory," "Love in Bloom," "June in January," "I Wished on a Star," and a host of others, took off for a trip to New York and was killed in an airplane accident occasioned by a stupid rendezvous arranged by the pilot of an army plane and the pilot of a passenger aircraft. Everyone in the commercial plane was killed. Ralph's death was a deep loss and left a permanent scar.

By the time Rapf's second spasm of erratic behavior activated a crisis, the B unit had turned out twenty-four high-quality films in eighteen months. However, seeds of disarray had begun to sprout. Some of the directors were being drafted from the unit and writers were also being tapped for membership in the A units to help aid the cause.

There were other problems, including inside and outside politics. Since I was head of the unit, our success focused to a great degree on me, stirring up jealousies. Gossip swirled around but I took the position, which I've kept to this day, that if I am told that someone has spoken ill of me, I want to know if the talebearer is willing for me to use his or her name in any subsequent confrontation. Since most refused, I paid little or no heed to the buzz-buzz.

But one day Sam Marx told me that at lunch James McGuinness had referred to the writers of our unit as "the Yeshiva." The implication was clear. Sam told me I could quote him.

I called on McGuinness, who was an editor for one of the A units, and related what Sam had told me. He admitted he had used the term because all the writers working for me were Jews. I challenged him to produce his list of writers and compare it with mine. When he did, we both saw that he had as many Jews working for him as I had. I also, for the record, indicated I had as many Irishmen as he. He expressed surprise at the facts but did not apologize. From that point on, McGuinness and I would exchange hi's but I knew he loathed me. I, in turn, had contempt for him. That fruitless relationship led to trouble later on.

Not wishing to repeat the embarrassing sequence of events with Mayer and Rapf, I played Goody Two Shoes. When Rapf's didoes became unbearable to me, I went to Mayer and registered my desire to move on and make some A pictures. I said the point had been made about B pictures, now I wanted to play with the big boys. Mayer agreed it was time for me to move on. He insisted I sign a contract, asked if Rapf could handle the unit ("Of course," I said), and called Howard Strickling to herald the news in the trade papers.

Mannix, who got the less than earthshaking item from Mayer, looked at me suspiciously and asked me about Rapf. I told him all was copacetic, knowing damn well that if I revealed what Rapf was doing the information would be telegraphed to Mayer and we would go back to the two slices.

When I met with my producers to wish them farewell, I learned a primary lesson regarding power. The boys said they were sorry to see me go, but were eager to shake hands with Harry Rapf and assure him they would continue the same run of success. The phone calls abated, the invitations dropped off, the fun memos disappeared, and my former cadre seldom dropped in to pass the time of day. For a while this sudden breaking of contact bothered me until I realized that they had their problems and that I too was guilty of contributing to the process of separation. Moreover, in quick order, the unit dissolved, Rapf retreated to his quiet empty office, and most of the Seven Dwarfs dropped out of action.

In the new job as producer the first subject I took on was a movie about movies — a fiction story backed by history. It never had a chance. It failed to take root and I dropped it. One night I had an idea to do a picture — it was 1943 and while there were many war pictures being made, my notion was, I believed, a unique one. I was going to tell the story of Hitler, Churchill, Mussolini, and the United States as an American Western epic.

The locale was to be a large Western territory; the shape of the area looked a bit like Europe. The time was a few years after the Civil War.

Hitler, Goebbels, and Goering were to be three escaped convicts. From that point on, I was going to tell the story of what had happened, was happening, and what would happen.

I wanted someone to work with me. Sinclair Lewis's name came to mind. I called him (he was in New York), told him the notion, and asked him to come out for a week to listen, think, and then decide yea or nay. He agreed.

When I told Mayer about the story and who would, I hoped, work with we, he was excited and delighted.

Lewis arrived in a few days. He was on the wagon. His only liquid refreshment during the hot summer days we were suffering and working through was iced coffee — heavily sugared and whitened with cream. He drank pitchers of the stuff, which propelled him to the toilet, from where he would return most often with a remark such as, "While standing at the bowl relieving myself, I had the following thought . . ."

Before the first week was over, Lewis agreed to do the screenplay with me.

His first job, he said, was to get the names of the characters in his head. For days we labored over names. He would take his urinal breaks by saying, "As I piss, I shall ponder."

The work, the pissing, and the pondering took about two weeks — "Red" Lewis was persistent and patient regarding the chore — and we came up with the following cast of characters:

> Hygatt — Hitler
> Gerrett — Goering
> Gribbles — Goebbels
> Mollison — Mussolini
> Chancel — Churchill
> Chambers — Chamberlin
> Ulysses Sanders — United States
> "Chuck" Sloane — Czechoslovakia
> Slavin — Stalin

The story was titled *Storm in the West*.

The story line we knew. Red had a great ear for Western idiom, I knew how to put a screenplay together, so between us we worked quickly and happily. Our ending, written in 1943, had two curious prophesies. One: in the final battle between the ranchers and the villains, Mollison is shot while trying to escape and as his horse gallops away, Mollison's boot is caught in the stirrup and his dead body hangs head down as he is dragged in the dust. Two: Hygatt is shot and falls into a flaming building and dies.

Red left California when we finished the job and I sent the script to all concerned. McGuinness reported to Mayer that the script was full of Communist propaganda. Witness: when Slavin (Stalin) first appears, his work wagon carries a hammer and a sickle.

Mayer decided that a war story was not important — after all, we were fighting a war. There were too many other war movies.

Some liked it, other disliked it. Mayer was going to send Lillie Messinger to New York and she would discuss the project with Schenck. She would report the decision to me.

The entire sequence of events that followed is most economically told in the following telegrams and letter.

I wired Lillie Messinger on October 20, 1943, a few days after she had gone to New York:

PLEASE ADVISE ME IF YOU HAVE RECEIVED SCRIPTS AND WHEN YOU ARE TO TALK TO MR DIETZ AND MR SCHENCK VERY ANXIOUS TO HEAR BEST REGARDS.

On October 22 this question was sent:

WELL?

On October 27, this one:

BOY, GIRL, TWINS, OR TUMOR?

The same day came the answer:

ASSUMED MR MAYER HAD TOLD YOU HIS TELEPHONE CONVERSATION
WITH NICHOLAS SCHENCK LONG DISCUSSION DIETZ AND SCHENCK FINALLY
LED TO DECISION AGAINST DOING PICTURE FEEL BADLY ABOUT YOUR DIS-
APPOINTMENT REGARDS

LILLIE

There it was. No periods — all capital letters — no commas.

When I met with Mayer to tell him I wanted a release from my contract, he asked if I wanted more money. Did I have another job? Both
answers were no.

I wanted to leave because I wasn't happy. Mayer said he'd think about
it.

I wrote Sinclair on November 4:

Dear Red:

This is what has been happening: The studio has decided not to make
the film. I have decided to leave the studio. I am waiting for an official
release from the studio.

There was no sense of writing you all during this period because too
much was going on, and a thousand and one delays that a producer's
flesh is heir to would only have confused you. Further, I was in no mood
to write anybody.

Once I get clear of here and I have some time I will sit down and write
you the whole story — to conclude with an understatement — I'm mad.

Every good wish.

A week later, Mayer told Mannix to give me my release.

My agent, Nat Goldstone, said he doubted that he could get me a
job. I did not have my name on any of the B-unit pictures, both my
A projects were on a shelf collecting dust, and my fifteen-hundred-dollar-
a-week salary was a liability.

The message was clear. Nat had many clients at Metro. The word had gotten to him — forget Schary.

Through Horace McCoy, who wrote *They Shoot Horses, Don't They?*, I had met Lew Wasserman when he and his wife, Edie, had first come to Hollywood. Lew had prospered as the head of the MCA agency.

Out of work, abandoned by Goldstone, and scared that his summary of my *extremis* condition was correct, I decided to call Lew and ask if he'd take me on.

When Lew came to our home, he listened to the saga of my MGM tenure. He has always been a good listener, eyeing you intently, making sure that you are telling him the truth. Sometimes he has the disconcerting habit of watching your lips as you talk. Always, he had and has (though I have not seen him often in recent years) an air of complete confidence with a penumbra of wisdom and assurance that impels you to place your career in his hands. Once, years later, Nicholas Schenck, president of Loew's, told me that Lew was the smartest man he'd ever met and added, "I never see him after twelve noon, I'm too slow to take him on after that."

When I finished sketching out what I believed was going to be a hairy time for me, Lew asked if I was in need of money. I said there was no worry on that score. I didn't tell him that actually I was secure for only about ten weeks, but I believe he sensed I was boasting. He told me to relax, that he'd look around, ask some questions, and be in touch. Before he left, he asked me to name a list of the pictures the B unit had produced. He nodded, made no notes, and said good-bye.

While I do have confidence in myself, I often gather that others believe I am too easygoing, too amiable; not steely enough. Therefore, when Lew rode off, I suddenly felt that he had been kind, generous, patient, but that I wouldn't hear from him except to be told he'd struck out.

A few days later Lew rang to ask if I could make myself free for the entire following day. Of course he knew I could but he gave me the courtesy of protecting the shredded dignity most of us have when we're out of work.

He was to pick me up. We had three dates: Charles Koerner, head of RKO, was at 10:30 in the morning; David Selznick, 12:30; finally, Henry Ginsberg at Paramount at 2:30 P.M.

The meeting with Koerner, a handsome gray-haired man with tanned skin and the bulky look of a capable boxer, went well. Koerner was frank in saying he'd like me to make some films at RKO and was willing to pay the going rate. There were a few manly jokes, hard handshakes, and we left. Lew's comment was, "Could be. But I'm not sure that's for you."

The next stop introduced me to David O. Selznick, a legendary figure for whom I had enormous respect and admiration. I had been present at the opening night of *Gone with the Wind* at the once handsome Cathay Circle Theatre in Hollywood. At intermission, I had heard the sour jokes and the drear estimates — "This should be called *Gone with Selznick*"; "David's a dead duck"; "This one is four hours too long"; et cetera, et cetera. I had loved the film and knew his other work, *Dinner at Eight, David Copperfield, Viva Villa.* When *Gone with the Wind* swamped the competition at Academy Award time I was, as a fan, happy and amused to recognize some of the opening knockers applauding their hands raw.

Selznick and I had met briefly just once at the Academy Awards in 1939 when he came by and congratulated me for *Boys Town.*

Now here he was. A big, toothy grin was accompanied by an involuntary nod of his leonine head. His eyeglasses made his eyes look larger than they were. His offices were tasteful and comfortable, rather uncluttered with memorabilia. I liked Selznick instantly and hoped I could work for him, but wondered whether his father-in-law, L. B. Mayer, had laid an ax to my head. With Selznick was his executive vice-president, Daniel T. O'Shea, a feisty, humorous man with a lopsided grin, premature gray hair, and a no-nonsense manner. I didn't have to wonder too long about what Mayer had said. "L.B. told me you're a maverick," Selznick said. "Don't like to take orders. Tough to deal with." He smiled. "I told him you sounded like me."

Selznick said that he knew of the films I had supervised and that he wanted to have someone make low-budget films for a new company he had formed called Vanguard Films. He, Selznick, would continue his Selznick International schedule and the new boy in town would be boss of Vanguard to make six or seven pictures a year on budgets ranging from five to seven hundred thousand each. "I would approve of the basic idea, then I don't want to have anything to do with any of the pictures till you show them to me in rough cut."

I was happily aware that he had slipped into referring to me as the potential head of his new company. "Wonderful," was my searching and compelling observation.

We exchanged grins. "You can be charming, can't you?" he said. "Well, you're not so bad at it yourself," I answered.

David then asked Lew to talk to Dan O'Shea and see if something could be worked out.

Lew and I moved into O'Shea's office and Dan, with his special style, pixieish and Irish, launched into his need to have a hard-nosed picture maker in the lineup who could help bring in money to finance David's multimillion-dollar adventures.

After a while, Lew looked at his watch and explained we had a date at Paramount. O'Shea said to me, "We'll be in touch. You'll have it good here if we can work things out."

I told Lew as we drove to Paramount that I wanted the Selznick job. Lew answered, "First, we'll see Ginsberg." We went to that gentleman's office. He came directly to the point. "You're welcome to come here — if Lew doesn't make the deal too rich." Lew got up, asked Ginsberg to please tell anyone if they called that he and I were having lunch nearby at Lucey's; "Thanks, Henry." Then we went to Lucey's, where we talked and ate.

A half hour after we arrived, there was a call for Lew and they jacked a phone into our booth. Lew answered, covered the phone, and whispered, "It's O'Shea."

The conversation went like this: "Hello, Danny. . . . Dore likes the idea too. . . . No, Danny, it's not complicated . . . fifteen hundred a week . . . he needs a staff . . . an assistant, reader, two secretaries and one of the bungalows . . . a five-year contract — we can talk about yearly raises . . . and that's about it . . . except for fifteen percent of the profit on each picture he makes. . . . Danny — he wants to get going . . . Ginsberg and Koerner have both offered setups. . . . I'll hang on . . ."

Again, Lew covered the phone. "He's checking with Selznick." I pleated my fingers as Lew got back to O'Shea. "Yes . . . yes . . . right . . . okay, Dan — tell Dore." I took the phone and said, "Hello, Dan." Dan's voice was dry. "You got a hell of a good deal — but we're pleased. When can you start?"

"Say when."

"Tomorrow."

"Good. Thanks."

After I hung up, I looked at Lew, who was giving me one of those half grins I came to know so well.

I said, "Thanks, Lew."

"Let me ask you a question," he said. "Tell me, do you really know how to make a picture?"

19

*E*ven *if I had known* everything about how to make a picture, I would have had my education widened by working with Selznick.

He had asked me to work on a group of films designed for lower budgets than his Selznick International efforts. I was to work rapidly — get some pictures on the stages — complete them, and the Selznick releasing company would place them into distribution as soon as possible, bringing in money to help eat up the heavy overhead carried by Selznick's major films. That was the plan . . . simple and neat as "There's no place like home."

One of my failings is that I am an eternal optimist who believes almost everything anybody tells me — however, I don't believe them the second time if they change the game. Once hustled, I hand over the dice and walk out.

So I followed the plan Selznick laid out. Within a week, I had read scores of stories or listened to radio sketches or talked to writers who had ideas for movies. In the second week, I listened to a radio sketch called "Double Furlough," a story of a veteran who was undergoing treatment for what in 1943 was called "psychoneurosis" (instead of the World War I "shell shock" and the later more opprobrious identification "Section Eight"). The soldier, on leave from an army hospital, meets and falls in love with a young woman who is on furlough from a stay in prison. These two fall in love.

After sketching out to Selznick how I wanted to do the story line as a film, I bought the sketch, assigned Marion Parsonnet to write it, told the story to Joe Cotten, who was under contract to Selznick, and went to work.

Four weeks later I gave Selznick a complete screenplay on which

Marion and I had worked day and night. I believed it would make a good picture. The following day I received my first memo from D.O.S. It was long — it was murderous. He castigated the script — said he would not allow me to make it . . . that it was sloppy, hurried, and immature . . . for me to forget the project and look for something else. And forget Joe Cotten — and in any event, no star would ever play in the film because the film would never be made. In short — no compromise — junk it.

I spent that night at home rereading the script and rereading the memo. Then after digesting both, I wrote Selznick a lengthy memo — but not as long as his to me. In it I challenged him to play the game we had agreed upon or let me go.

I reminded him I was to pick the stories and produce the pictures in order to free him to work on his large-budget projects — that he had agreed to gamble on my judgment until I had proved he had made a wise choice or a bad one. I wrote that I wanted to be as good as David Selznick but not like him — that I wished to be my own man. I offered to buy the script from him for whatever he had invested. I sent him the memo by hand.

The next morning Selznick called me at my home and asked me to come to his office. It was raining heavily and I felt particularly forlorn and begged off rather sulkily by telling him I did not wish to be excoriated in person. He said he'd come by to see me in the late afternoon.

He arrived during a teeming storm and asked for a long drink of Scotch. His manner was affable; after a swallow or two, he reported that his wife, Irene (née Mayer), had read my memo and had said, "Whether you like the script or not, Schary is right. You made a bargain — you ought to keep it."

Moreover, she had read the script, liked it, and thought it would be an effective movie. David told me that I could make the movie but not spend more than $750,000. I could not use Joe Cotten — or any Selznick player — only outside talent.

He smiled and concluded, "I bet you'll never get a star to play either part." I disagreed. We bet one hundred dollars. I thanked him for his decision and his courtesy and vowed I'd work like hell not to let him down.

He laughed and said, "You'll have to."

Then he was gone.

Dan O'Shea, aware of the exchange of memos, had read the script, and he urged me to get a solid and experienced director. The man I picked was William Dieterle, Germanic, heavily built, addicted to fawn-colored gloves and (unknown to me) a devout believer in the stars. David approved him, though the price was greater than the sum that had been budgeted.

Next I sent the script to Ginger Rogers. She adored it. Her price rocketed the budget to over a million. Selznick okayed that and paid off his hundred-dollar bet — then predicted that with Ginger in the setup, no male star would play it. Another hundred was the ante.

When Alan Ladd agreed to do it, Selznick argued that it would be absurd to pay Ladd his going figure when Joe Cotten was available for the film at half the cost of Ladd. Willingly, David paid off the other hundred. The picture finally was budgeted at $1,300,000 when David added Shirley Temple to the roster in a minor part.

David thought "Double Furlough" was a dull title. He liked my idea of using Noel Coward's song "I'll See You Again." That was not avail-' able but Sammy Fain's tune "I'll Be Seeing You" was, and we went with that one.

Then, David began to send memos — long ones — exceedingly long ones — with suggestions, criticisms, and general observations about films, life, and art. He had a habit of asking you to respond — "Let me hear what you think" or "Do you agree?" or "Let me know your decision."

It was Dan O'Shea who advised me how to handle the stream of memos that flowed from David's office: "Answer them — meticulously — then instead of questions make statements — 'If that's all right with you, I'll go ahead' . . . 'If I don't hear from you, I'll assume you agree.'" I followed Dan's suggestions. Since David preferred to write rather than read memos, confrontations were avoided.

However, there was much Selznick did contribute. David was the most compleat producer in Hollywood — the smartest and most gifted of them all. He knew scripts, direction; was a master of film editing; had exquisite taste, energy to spare, a glowing gift for publicity and advertising, and a willingness to dare. His films *Viva Villa, David Copperfield, A Star Is Born* (the original), *Tale of Two Cities, Dinner at Eight, Rebecca,* and the lodestar of filmmaking, *Gone with the Wind,* are a permanent testimony to his talent.

As we exchanged memos, I kept learning. My problem during the actual shooting of the picture came not from Selznick (that was mainly fun and education) but from Herr Dieterle. It began with our first day of shooting. At nine o'clock the crew was ready, the cameraman had lined up the first shot, the actors were in place, and I was wondering why the devil Dieterle wasn't calling "Action." His assistant, Victor

Stoloff, tipped me off. The stars in heaven indicated Dieterle was to call for the first rolling of the cameras at 10:05 — exactly. From that day on, Victor told me, we'd start at 9:00 A.M. as scheduled. I took a deep breath and waited. At 10:05 exactly we made the first shot.

The early days went well; the daily rushes were good — hard and realistic — and the changes I had to make on the set seemed to work. Then one afternoon, I noticed a long debate going on between the cameraman and Dieterle. I also became aware of three Chinese dressed in Japanese soldier uniforms. There were no war scenes in the script and since I knew we had begun to move the Japanese army back in the Pacific, it was clear we were not being invaded.

When I asked for an explanation Dieterle, speaking to me in the manner of a professor talking to a cretin, described his decision to photograph the faces of Japanese soldiers, which would appear on the dinner plate of our poor hero while he was having dinner at the heroine's home; these faces would be a demonstration of the soldier's neurosis. Well, I didn't like that. When Dieterle went on describing some of the other "nightmares," my dislike turned to hate. But I agreed to look at the dailies the next morning . . . after which I hurried to the set to see Dieterle.

It was 11:15 A.M. when I approached Der Fuehrer, who was waiting for the crew to light the next scene. When I said I wanted to talk to him he yelled, "Lunch," and started to walk off the set. I faced him and said, "If you leave the set now — don't come back." He left and I told the crew to get on with their work. Victor Stoloff briefed me on the scene we were preparing and I began plotting it out with Cotten and Rogers.

Some minutes later I was called to the phone. David Selznick was waiting to see me in his office.

Not only David was waiting but also Dieterle. David asked me to tell my side of the farrago — Bill Dieterle had already told his.

Our stories agreed with one exception — Dieterle had referred to it as his picture.

David quietly announced his decision and I was devoted to him from that moment on. In substance he said, "Bill, I don't like this picture — I personally would not make it. But I agreed that Dore could. It is *his* picture — his neck is out to here." (An appropriate gesture showed how far out.) "It has to be done *his* way. So Bill — it's up to you. Go back and do it as he wants it done — or quit."

Bill went back.

The picture turned out very well. David was so pleased he decided to call it a Selznick International film. It received beautiful notices and had a gross of almost $7 million, the equivalent of a $35 million gross in 1979.

One of the weekly magazines in praising the picture referred to it as another Selznick triumph. In a way, it was, since he had allowed me to do it.

My term with Selznick lasted three years, during which he pampered me with extravagant publicity, lavish compliments, and a warm personal relationship. He had a sharp sense of humor and a gambler's temperament, which at one point almost reduced him to penury.

Politically, he was a liberal Republican who inveighed against FDR and Truman. His toothy grin and shock of grizzled hair, which he rumpled as he talked, were often disarming as he voiced outrageous opinions. Yet when the far right wing had become active prior to World War II, he had belted them with the same lusty sarcasm he leveled at the far left. He was taken in by Madame Chiang Kai-shek but turned against her when he heard of her queenly and demanding behavior.

During my three years with him — November, 1943, to December, 1946 — the living was easy, like summertime.

The success of *I'll Be Seeing You* was followed by *The Spiral Staircase*, which had been designed for Ingrid Bergman, who rejected it. Dorothy Maguire jumped at the script and the cast included Ethel Barrymore, George Brent, and Kent Smith. The script was based on the book *Some Must Watch*, a good thriller. However, the heroine was not a girl muted by shock.

Her disability came about during a story conference with Mel Dinelli, the screenplay writer, Paul Stewart, then employed as an assistant, and Laura Kerr, who was my story editor.

We had reached a cul-de-sac. The girl was trapped in a series of logical moves, but now the question I asked — "Why the hell doesn't she yell for help?" — had no appropriate answer. Finally, Paul, as we reached the dead end, laughed and said, "She don't yell because she's a dope — a dumb dame." Then came the pause that usually follows a forced joke and my eyes must have lit up like a pinball machine — "That's it — she can't talk."

Everything slipped into place. We had a better motive for the crimes — more suspense and terror and an emotional ending. Dinelli's script was a lesson in screen writing. It projected suspense and tension. The script itself reads like a good mystery novel. Our cameraman was Nick Musaraca, a brilliant cinematographer who gave us sharp black and white contrasts, and director Robert Siodmak caught the mood and style of the script accurately.

There was disagreement on the title. David thought the title was cheap and that it would hurt the film. I disagreed. We kept the title, and the picture was a success, critically and commercially.

However, another film was originally called *Suddenly It's Spring*, which I didn't like, but I despised David's title, *The Bachelor and the Bobby-Soxer*. We had arguments about it. I thought the title obvious and ordinary. David was positive it was attractive. I argued that with Cary Grant and Myrna Loy and Shirley Temple we had enough attraction — that we could call the film *Borscht* and do well. But I lost that set-to and we went into production.

Irving Reis, the director, was a mercurial young man who did not respond too well under pressure, and one day he blew up and left the stage. I took over for him and directed some scenes with Cary and Myrna. After a few days Irving returned, permitting us to establish a modus vivendi in which I could work closely with the actors while he worked on camera setups and movement. This arrangement satisfied Cary, who had found Irving too complicated a director. Cary was a brilliant romantic comedy actor who was aware of what he could do best, how best to do it, and who could help him achieve the best.

Cary is a fad man — when he gave up cigarettes he played with LSD, then quickly abandoned it. He was the first man I knew to suggest shoulder bags for men, Nehru jackets, various health diets, Chinese wardrobes (which give you room to breathe). He remains in superb condition and if anyone I know lives to be one hundred, it will be Cary.

He loves to watch travelogues, eats sparingly, avoids "the social ramble" as suggested by Satchel Paige, and is a fountain of esoteric and amusing information. Finally, he's easy to work with — demanding — but easy and malleable. Among his charming and individual tricks are those almost subliminal sounds he incorporates into his scenes of surprise or frustration — *um*s, *hum*s, *aaah*s.

Working on films with actors of talent, humor, and good disposition is a joy — certainly Myrna Loy, whom I adore, Cary Grant, Richard Widmark, Spencer Tracy, the late Robert Ryan, Mel Douglas, Dorothy Maguire, and Loretta Young fit that description.

The Farmer's Daughter preceded *The Bachelor and the Bobby-Soxer*. It was based on a Finnish play and Selznick had read a synopsis and passed it on to me. I liked the idea and believed it would make a good comedy with a strong point of view.

Even studio executives got the glamour treatment in the 1940s

Peter Rathvon ran a tented soiree for my arrival as production VP at RKO. He's at the left. My dear and admired friend David Selznick is in the center holding my back in a comforting embrace.

Location at Petaluma, north of San Francisco, was cloudy and rainy for days. We sat, ate, bemoaned our fate, but Loretta remained the beloved "Farmer's Daughter."

Taken on location for The Bachelor and the Bobby-Soxer. *I played a vignette and Cary gave me this copy of a picture I gave him.*

Bob Ryan, a former intercollegiate boxing champ, shows his skill in The Set-Up

Since it would deal with politics in the state of Minnesota and since Allen Rivkin was formerly a newsman in Minnesota and had been involved in politics all his life, I assigned him to do the adaptation and screenplay with his wife, Laura Kerr. They were a good choice. Allen had the hard-nosed, thick-skinned approach of a tough political boss and Laura the soft, sophisticated touch of a sharp steel razor that could cut you before you knew it had snapped open.

Allen, who resembles Doc in "Gunsmoke" or the wagon master in "Wagon Train," is a very special man. His opinions are educated; his ailments are endured with little or no complaint; he is orderly, neat, and talks like a city-desk editor. His loyalties are sturdy. He does not abide fools and he loathes poseurs.

Laura and he are a devoted couple with interests that mesh, humor, and a kind of courtliness in their home that is refreshing though Laura seems to bridle if a chair is moved too far from its original position.

Between them they wrote an excellent script with a juicy set of characters that the actors were delighted to play.

The entire company of *The Farmer's Daughter* was special; Ethel Barrymore, Joseph Cotten, Charles Bickford, Rhys Williams along with Loretta Young performed as an experienced unit under the direction of Henry (Hank) Porter. Miss Barrymore really *was* a baseball fan and a fascinatingly intelligent woman; Cotten has a flair for sardonic humor and reckless behavior (he once kicked Hedda Hooper in the behind to even the score for some things she'd written about him) combined with discipline and a wide-ranging talent.

Ingrid Bergman had been slated to do *Katie for Congress*, the original title for *The Farmer's Daughter*, but when I went to Paramount to talk to her about it, she brushed me off along with the script.

While I loved Dorothy Maguire, whom David suggested as a substitute for Ingrid, I pointed out that she had done two films for us, *The Spiral Staircase* and *Till the End of Time*, a film about the postwar problems of three veterans — Robert Mitchum, Bill Williams, and Guy Madison.

I suggested Loretta Young.

David wanted Sonja Henie.

In a memo dictated to Selznick on March 19, 1946, from Arizona, where I was taking a short holiday, I concluded:

> I honestly feel with deep conviction that Loretta Young could approximate much more of what we want, and in the company of the rest of our cast she would make a far, far better picture.

Please, fellas, don't brush this aside as a producer's frantic fear. I am sure that if this picture was going to be a Selznick International Picture we would never take Sonja Henie. Don't sell me Henie and bet on the Yankees. Sitting down here on my heinie — I am convinced that Henie won't do.

With all good wishes, I remain

Sincerely, your obedient servant
Dore Schary

Selznick wired back.

OKAY FORGET HENIE BUT DON'T COME AROUND TO ME WHEN YOU WANT SOME SKATING LESSONS

DAVID

Now all I had to do was get Loretta.

When I made contact with her she expressed serious reservations about her ability to fashion the Swedish accent. She loved the script, loved the part. We had our meeting at Lucey's, the restaurant near Paramount, and as we talked Loretta ate. She astounded me. There were two tall glasses of milk, a bowl of soup, lamb chops, baked potatoes, green peas, stewed tomatoes, rolls and butter, apple pie and ice cream. Loretta's metabolism must be perfect — she eats that way all the time.

As we talked, it became clear to me that her beauty, her directness, and her willingness to dare would be ideal for Katie. Pressing my argument, I told her that it was a gamble for her but if she played the part she would win an Academy Award. It was not a ploy — I believed that if she did bring it off with simple clothes, little makeup, and her invulnerable honesty, the uniqueness of Loretta risking such a role could win her an Oscar.

She plunged into the role — took lessons in Swedish accents, wore clothes from the wardrobe rack (except for the last suit she wore in Washington), stood up to the tough competition of Joe Cotten, Ethel Barrymore, and Charles Bickford, and when Oscar night arrived, she won the award. As Loretta accepted the statuette, I thought back to the argument over the title I had selected — *The Farmer's Daughter*. David finally permitted me to use the term, which he thought was vulgar, redolent of cheap traveling-salesman stories. The next day David still guyed me about the title — I guyed back by reminding him he hadn't thought Loretta Young could bring it off.

No matter — we both did well — the notices were good and a new boy, James Arness, made his debut and turned out years later to be Matt Dillon of "Gunsmoke."

It was during the making of *The Farmer's Daughter* that my father, troubled by three previous heart attacks, had a massive coronary seizure, and I left for Paterson, New Jersey, where he had been living since his second marriage in 1936. When I arrived he was in a disoriented state and did not know who I was. I talked to him for a while hoping to reach his consciousness. I was told that was no longer possible.

Sitting on a chair near him I studied his face, now heavily creased. His eyes, whenever he opened them, stared aimlessly, his white shock of hair was rumpled, and his color was waxen. I sat for a while thinking of the past, of his vigor, his ambitions, and the proud figure of the man he was so long ago.

Then I left. He did not know I'd been there — he did not know I had left.

That afternoon I started back to California by train. When we stopped at Harmon, New York, for an engine change I was notified that Pa was dead. I returned to New York. Pa was buried the next day in Newark, New Jersey, in a plot next to Frances.

Mother was not told of Pa's death until I returned home. I read her the eulogy I had written for him. She said, "It's very right. He was quite a man." Then she paused for a breath. "It's very strange. I seemed to know just when he died. I guess after you've been married to someone for thirty-nine years you know when he has died."

When I dream of my father I always see him in his best clothes, smoking a cigar stuck into his amber holder, and he is in one of his expansive moods, smiling and in charge of the "cermonies" — Pa never learned to say "ceremonies."

By the time my films were into production Selznick was immersed with his own *Since You Went Away* and his plans for *Duel in the Sun*. One night when he was bedded with flu, he asked me to come to his home and help map out a scene for *Since You Went Away*, which was in production. He was sitting in his king-sized bed, an ocean of script pages spread about him. An ashtray loaded with half-consumed cigarettes was perched near him and his pajamas were flecked with ashes. He looked feverish and kept running his hands through his hair.

After three hours of work, we agreed on a scene structure and I told him I'd go home to write it. He wouldn't think of that — we'd do it together. I mentioned that he looked tired and acted exhausted. "I feel great. Working makes me feel good," was his answer. Just then he picked up the phone and said, "Hello — hello! Hello — for Christ's sake —" Then he slammed the phone down. "Why the hell do people ring a phone and not answer?"

I asked, "Did you hear the phone ring?"

"Of course," he said. "Didn't you? Are you deaf?"

"No — I'm not deaf — and I'm not sick — but David, if you heard the phone ring, you're worse off than I thought. I'm going home."

David murmured, "Oh, shit," or some such thoughtful remark, and fell back on the pillows. "I feel lousy. Go on the set tomorrow and give John Cromwell the scene." By the time I had gathered up the pages and started out, Selznick's eyes were closed.

David called after he returned to the studio and asked that I read an article published in *Reader's Digest* that sketched out the story of the famous Indian athlete Jim Thorpe, a national hero who was unjustly deprived of gold medals he had won in the Olympic games because of one baseball game he had played for which he had received a small fee — which in the eyes of the officials made him a professional. The article dealt with Thorpe's bouts with bigotry directed at him, his fading career after the Olympic games, the fight and the failure to regain his medals, and his present skimpy occupation as a movie extra.

I liked the potential for making a picture that would take a roundhouse swing at prejudice but believed that the picture would slide downhill as we portrayed Thorpe sinking lower and lower. I told Selznick that it could make a good movie if we could end on a note of triumph and redemption at the end. I suggested that Selznick use some of his clout to start a public fuss to get the Olympic authorities to return the medals to Thorpe.

Selznick dismissed that notion as harebrained and asked me to see Thorpe and talk to him in the hope I could find a handle for the end of the picture — if we made it. We located Jim Thorpe and he showed up for our appointment only ten minutes late.

My first look at one of my boyhood's Supermen was a letdown. The years had not been kind to him. Thorpe was shorter than I had imagined, he was puffy, and his stomach sagged over his trousers belt. There was no spring in his movements — disappointment, age, and booze had battered him down. It was like seeing a reflection of his young self in a trick mirror in an amusement park.

We talked and he seemed interested but wanted to know what part of his life we'd concentrate on. As I gave him some idea of our desire to deal with his years at Carlisle College, the bigotry and prejudice leveled at him, his exploits and triumphs and what he believed to be the injustice of the Olympic game rulings, he kept nodding his head and told us of what he had gone through simply because he was an Indian — how people had shut him out, abused and deprived him. He was all for punching out at bigotry. Then he asked who we had in mind to play him.

At this point we had no one in mind. He thought Spencer Tracy would be ideal. I explained that Tracy could not possibly play a track star in his teens or twenties. "Well, then, what about Gregory Peck?" I liked Gregory Peck but I didn't believe he had the body of an athlete. Having collected pictures of Thorpe in his prime I didn't think Peck had the musculature the role would need.

He thought the actor should be a star.

I said that I didn't think that was important. The necessities were that the man be young, look like an Indian, be strong, and have the look of an athlete, who could run, jump, and move with grace. When he asked for an example, I thought of Anthony Quinn, whom I had gotten to know while at RKO, where I had shot three of the films for Selznick. Quinn at the time was being hemmed in, playing cowboys, mostly bad guys, Indian warriors, or Mexican bandits. It occurred to me he'd be ideal so I answered Thorpe's "For instance?" by saying "Anthony Quinn."

Thorpe grimaced and spit out, "Tony Quinn, a lousy Mexican? You might as well get a nigger."

That concluded any form of communication except for me to explain I had another appointment and "We'll be in touch."

When Thorpe exited I called Selznick, reported the meeting, and handed over the assignment to him. "David, it needs your kind of talent."

David laughed. "I think the subject is too big for both of us. Forget it."

Years later Burt Lancaster did play Thorpe — he was excellent as the young Thorpe and the picture was effective during the early reels but faded away. It was a failure. I've always had the feeling that if Thorpe had liked the idea of Tony Quinn I would have made the film and I think Quinn would have brought an inner quality that along with his natural looks would have given the story a better shot at success. But then, I thought the idea of doing *Snow White and the Seven Dwarfs* as a cartoon feature motion picture would lead to disaster.

20

*W*e are all *potential victims* of our virtues. If we are stubborn, we may become obstinate. If we are generous, we may also be profligate; disciplined — unyielding; critical — unforgiving. David became such a victim. He was a careless card and roulette player. Once I sat in a poker game with him and learned that he operated on the principle that if he had two pair — twos and eights plus a stack of chips in front of him — he could bluff you out of four aces. It was a ruinous course of conduct that cost him millions and helped turn Danny O'Shea's hair prematurely gray.

During the period of David's profligacy, he began work on *Duel in the Sun*, starring Jennifer Jones, Gregory Peck, Lionel Barrymore, Joseph Cotten, and a host of others. He shuffled directors on and off the set, finally settling on the redoubtable King Vidor.

When O'Shea assumed the picture was completed, David came to the decision that it was not. He asked Dan and me to attend a lonely screening in his projection room, screening time 9:00 P.M.

We saw a rattling good Western and then adjourned to David's office, where David kicked off his shoes, shed his jacket, and padded about the room asking us questions. "How did you like it?" "Was it too long?" "Were the characters real?" "Did you believe it?" "What was wrong with it?"

O'Shea and I were in agreement and our answers to David were (1) we liked the picture; (2) we thought it was a bit too long; (3) we thought the characters were real; (4) yes, we believed the story; and (5) we did not believe there was anything truly wrong with the film. We thought it needed trimming — obviously a good musical score would be an asset — and we both believed it would be a smashing success.

Danny wanted to know why there *should* be something wrong with it. David accused us both of being kind and not helpful. "It needs a hell of a lot of work," he said. "I want to do a new opening — giving the audience Jennifer's early story — her relationship with her father — it needs big scenes — a train wreck — confrontations — action —"

We argued there was plenty of action in the picture. I said that if he added too much, he could hurt the film.

That led to David's theory about picture making: make them big — surprise the audience — tell them all they wanted to know — and more.

O'Shea, sensing more millions were going to have to be raised, disagreed. I disagreed because I've shied from the belief that bigger is always better.

We went on and on with parables and illustrations illuminating our points; we testified quietly, then testily, then pleadingly. Finally after hours of the argy-bargy, David plopped down on the couch like a deflated life raft. "I know my trouble," he confessed. "I know that when I die, the obituaries will begin, 'David O. Selznick, producer of *Gone with the Wind*, died today,' and I'm trying like hell to rewrite them." He looked at his watch. "Christ, it's three-thirty. Let's go home."

As Dan and I staggered to our cars, Danny ventured, "He's right about that obit — and it's going to cost him."

However, Selznick persisted, and added many sequences to *Duel in the Sun* — reshooting some of them many times over. The exploitation on the film was staggering. Paul McNamara, the press man, had a field day.

Finally, the picture was finished and while David had not made another *GWTW*, he had made a highly successful *Duel in the Sun*. The reviews were mixed — some of them hostile — but it made millions, which David decided to siphon off to various games of gin rummy and roulette, an aberration that culminated in a divorce from Irene and marriage with Jennifer Jones.

During the three years I worked with Selznick, he indulged me with enthusiasm for my work, which was bringing in large sums of money to David. He had made a deal with RKO films, which financed the pictures I made plus Alfred Hitchcock's *Notorious* with Cary Grant and Ingrid Bergman. For Hitchcock's services and mine, David got 50 percent of the profit — I got 7½ percent of David's take. I don't know what Hitch's share was, but it has to have been more than mine.

About this time, Charles Koerner, in charge of production at RKO, took ill suddenly and died of acute leukemia. One day Peter Rathvon, the president of RKO and the only head of a film company stationed in California, asked me to lunch. Peter was a cultivated man with style and taste — totally outside the mold of the then studio heads. After we ordered our food, he hit me with the bulletin that he and Floyd Odlum, the chairman of the board, had voted to offer me the vice-presidency of RKO as head of production. I stopped eating.

I told Rathvon I had no such ambition . . . that I was under contract to Selznick, enjoyed what I was doing, and would have to tell David immediately that I had not asked for the job and did not want it. I thanked Rathvon for the offer. After lunch, I drove to David's quarters to tell him the news.

He said he suspected that RKO would make the offer. "Why not?" he added. "You've been doing a good job. You should take it. If you don't, you'll always regret you didn't."

When I said I felt obligated to him for two more years, he smiled. "Don't worry about me. They'll pay a good price for you — I'll make my deal with them." He gave me a heavy slap on the back. "You'll do a hell of a job."

Dan O'Shea didn't want me to go but had to accept David's feelings in the matter. When I told Miriam, we called a meeting of my close friends — Don, Lenny, and Allen — to ask for a reading of their opinions. That was a waste of time — they all said go.

I called my mother and told her the news — she was delighted.

Later, alone in my room, I thought of Ralph Rainger and his strong conviction that one day I'd run a studio.

I was to begin doing that January 1, 1947. Another door was about to open.

21

*B*y *then I knew* a good deal about studio heads. Having met the Carl Laemmles senior and junior, Harry Cohn, Darryl Zanuck, Jack and Harry Warner, and Y. Frank Freeman at various charitable functions, Guild negotiations, and Academy Award ceremonies, I had some idea of their party manners. Having worked for Cohn, L. B. Mayer, Junior Laemmle, and assorted independents and executives including Walter Wanger, Manny Cohen, Nat Levine, and Sol Wurtzel, I was provided with a firsthand knowledge of their office behavior, quite different in mode and substance.

The men who had fashioned the studios — Mayer, the Warners, Cohn, Laemmle, Zanuck — were *padrones* who viewed their *ranchos* with passionate pride of possession. Each stage, light bulb, chair, prop was theirs to own and cherish. Contract players, writers, directors, producers were members of the household staff to be pampered when the service was superb, tolerated if it was fair, and penalized or discharged if found incompetent, rebellious, or insubordinate.

They were men who enjoyed the success that had brought them palatial homes, fleets of cars, tailor-made suits, shirts, underwear, ties, coats, and shoes, and available attractive women for empty hours.

They reveled in the power that was actually circumscribed to their domains but exaggerated by them since Hollywood was a glamorous area and the chieftain of a studio could demand the front table in the best restaurants, the fourth row center in the theater, an entire Pullman car if he traveled by train, or a chartered plane if he so desired. A limousine was available day or night in California or New York or London, Paris or Rome.

These men had scrabbled up the mountain by courage, ingenuity, and vision, and often by cold strokes of cruelty to weaker men. They came on the scene when movies were new and primitive. Show business had always been viewed as attractive albeit slightly degenerate, but audiences had almost contempt for the "flicks." Movies were an illegitimate child whose parents had questionable certificates. Since others lacked imagination, the Zukors, Mayers, Schencks, Goldwyns, Laemmles, Warners, Cohns, Laskys rushed in to stake out claims. What they brought with them was a thirst for power and position to keep them out of the earthy professions in which they had labored as junkmen, streetcar conductors, butchers, glove salesmen, or band musicians.

The dreams came true for many; other dropped out — died — were destroyed; but because of those hardy men who survived, the big studios came into being — Metro-Goldwyn-Mayer, Warner Brothers, Paramount, RKO, Columbia, Fox, later Twentieth Century–Fox, Republic — and with them the greatest era of patronage since the Renaissance was born. Universal became Universal International, then back to the Universal of today.

Pathé, Lewis Selznick, Tiffany, Eagle-Lion, Hal Roach Films, Monogram, Republic lie a-moldering in their graves.

United Artists had no studio structure but only a group of offices in New York run efficiently by Arthur Krim and Robert Benjamin — until they regretted selling their stock to Transamerica and losing a degree of their autonomy. They then formed an independent unit, Orion, a new financing and packaging motion-picture-production organization tied to the Warner Brothers distribution company.

Directors were the first to be cosseted but dropped back as pressure grew to feed the demand for product, bringing the producer up into the front rank. In recent years, the director has muscled back in as the number of pictures has diminished and directors have had to be coddled. To paraphrase Jack Kennedy, "Success has many fathers, failure is an orphan." Partly true, except in films. Success today is always credited to the director, glorified as the "auteur" unless the producer has an influential, active, inventive press agent. However, failure always has a father — the writer. To the dictum "When the going gets tough, the tough get going" should be added "and the tough always go for the writer" — the *schlimazel* of motion pictures. He is the first to be sprayed with the odor of failure.

Despite the continued lack of identification of most writers for films, a few hardy souls, beginning in the early forties, recognized that the way to get identification was to perform in a dual capacity as writer-director or writer-producer, and these stalwarts led the parade that in time included Joe Mankiewicz, George Seaton, Norman Krasna, Billy Wilder, Charlie Brackett, Lamar Trotti, Richard Brooks, Nunnally Johnson, Delmer Daves, Ernest Lehman, and, of course, the more recent figures such as Spielberg, Coppola, Lucas, Stanley Kubrick, and William Friedkin. But in the thirties it was difficult for writers to move out of their prescribed circle of endeavor.

One of the most prolific and talented writers of the past was Grover Jones, who spent years at Paramount turning out innumerable scripts. Grover was an engaging man with rich humor, barrels of energy, and a growing and consuming ambition to write and produce a film that would be his and his alone.

This was a period of time when Paramount changed studio heads as often as Zsa Zsa changes husbands and as each new sachem arrived in the head man's office Grover would arrange an appointment to discuss his plan for the future. But Grover was so skilled and so quick with his pen that time after time his request was put off as he would be called upon to rush in and do a script for Jack Haley or Alan Ladd, Bing Crosby, Bob Hope, or Brian Donlevy. After completing each one of those emergency assignments, Grover would ask, "Now?" and always the answer was, "Grover, right after you finish this one."

Finally, Grover Jones's patience was worn to the last thread and when he was told that if he accepted another rush job he would be given an opportunity to do his own production, he warily insisted on meeting with the studio executives so that they could hear his story and his plans for his original production. He said that he would satisfy their panting request for him to do another comedy provided they would approve what he wanted to do for himself. The top brass agreed, set up a meeting, and Grover went into the conference room and faced the convocation of executives who were to listen to his tale.

"I want to do a simple morality tale — pure Americana," Grover said to the assembly with proper gestures and emotion. "We open on a small farm — a white picket fence, beautiful trees, a lovely clapboard house, a small silo. It is a lovely mild summer day — it is the haying season. The hero is the classic all-American man — tall, handsome, strong. His young wife is apple cider and roses. His mother, who lives with them, is a model for Whistler, and the little child just two years old is the kind of child poets sing about. But now, now the villain appears and he is mustachioed, riding breeches, boots — the personification of greed and evil. . . . He demands payment on the mortgage — the hero explains that he needs some weeks before he can make the payment. The villain declares that he will take over the farm and that this wonderful family must leave, he doesn't care where to. When the hero protests and says he will fight to stay, the villain takes out a derringer and shoots and kills the hero. When the wife screams and runs toward the villain he knifes her in the heart and she falls near her husband, reunited with him in death. . . . As the baby starts to cry the villain reaches down and breaks the child's neck. Now the hero's mother rushes at him with her cane, prepared to struggle, and the villain takes up a pitchfork and kills her."

Grover took a long pause, gazed directly into the eyes of the rather confused executives, and finished up, "Then the villain turns toward the camera and says to the audience in a big close-up — 'And fuck you too!' "

With that Grover turned away, walked out of the conference room, out of the studio, and retired to his lovely estate in Pacific Palisades, where he spent the rest of his productive and happy life. During the years, I have known many writers who would have liked to say the same thing to a group of their tormentors. But usually the tormentors get in a blow before the writer gets up enough steam.

In many cases the director and the producer also had to worry about their security because the big daddy of the past, the commanding general, the dictator, was the studio head. Not just a production chief but head of the entire studio operation.

At present the only one extant is the man who dreamed up the present Universal spread — Lew Wasserman. He's feared and respected. He's loved and loathed. He has his favorites and his blacklist. He travels to New York or London with only a briefcase — his apartments in different cities have duplicate wardrobes.

He is the last of the truly big wheels. Cool, calm, tough — unlike the former screamers, he speaks softly but can shed ice cubes if he chooses.

The others just have jobs. They are part of the corporate musical-chairs routine. Tenure is not guaranteed. One losing season and a head rolls.

Lew is the only one who could have boxed in the ring with any of the former champs — the others would never have gone the distance.

Because of my experiences as a screenwriter, an executive of B films at Metro, and my three years with Selznick, I was prepared to take on the responsibilities of running studio production. Having produced four of the films I made for Selznick on the RKO lot, I was familiar with the crews and the creative staff. I was also aware of a bevy of five young ladies who, although under contract as "starlets," had not appeared in a single film but had made personal appearances in various bedrooms for visiting board members and dignitaries who began to itch as soon as they arrived in Hollywood. Sex is a glorious experience but since I view it as a private enterprise rather than a public utility, it seemed consistent to me that the five starlets be freed to pursue their careers elsewhere. None of the board members complained directly to me, probably because they did not choose to reveal prior adventures. I didn't give a damn what they said to others.

Young directors who had not had a chance at bat were lined up for assignments, among them Nicholas Ray, Joe Losey, Norman Panama, Melvin Frank, Ted Tetzlaff, Mark Robson.

Edward Dymytryk had proven himself with a few films and he and Adrian Scott, who was a producer, approached me with a script by John Paxton that had been rejected by the late Charles Koerner, Peter Rathvon, and the head of sales, Ned Depinet. It was called *Crossfire*, an adaptation of Richard Brooks's novel *The Brick Foxhole*. Paxton, Scott, and Dymytryk had kept the basic theme of violence directed against the outsider but had altered the victim's identity from that of a homosexual to that of a Jew.

During the war, I had gone into army camps and lectured on the causes of anti-Semitism and had seen and heard of virulent bigotry in army ranks. Following those assignments, I had been asked by the chaplain corps to give seminars to young Catholic and Protestant members of the corps who were entering the army. Most of these priests and ministers had only recently been ordained. Not just anti-Semitism was discussed. It developed that the young Catholic priests bore open hostility to the Protestant ministers, who in turn displayed their annoyance with Catholic rigidity. At one of the seminars, the loud voice of a colonel prevented a full-scale Battle of the Boyne.

For years I had worked in the fetid field of combating anti-Semitism and I knew something about the steamy current of hatred.

Therefore, I liked *Crossfire*, and told Peter Rathvon I was going to put that into production as soon as possible. At the same time, Dudley Nichols was already involved in his personal production of the Sister Kenny story starring Rosalind Russell. Ned Depinet, determined to convince me not to make *Crossfire*, had an audience research company compare what was dubbed the "Want to see" quotient of both *Kenny* and *Crossfire*. Results: 70 percent wanted *Kenny*; 8 percent, *Crossfire*.

This depressing result did nothing to deter me from making the picture. When it was announced for production, Depinet advised that the Warner *frères* had called to issue the proclamation that *Crossfire* would not play in any of their theaters.

Dymytryk had agreed to a twenty-day shooting schedule and our budget was under $500,000. There was work to be done on the script, and we spent time pruning and refining it until it was strong and shiny as steel.

The cast starred three Roberts — Young, Ryan, Mitchum — and others in the company were Paul Kelly, Sam Levene, and Gloria Graham.

Meanwhile, Darryl Zanuck had bought *Gentlemen's Agreement* and expressed his annoyance at my having put *Crossfire* into work before his film. We exchanged a few notes — then a phone call during which I was compelled to tell him he had not discovered anti-Semitism and that it would take far more than two pictures to eradicate it. The conversation ended with both of us not having budged one inch. During the talk, he called me Door or Schar. I didn't correct him.

Crossfire was a big hit — even the Warner Brothers circuit played it. *Gentlemen's Agreement* was a bigger hit.

Footnote: *Sister Kenny*, a good film, failed. What audience research had not reckoned with was an outbreak of polio. Obviously, the picture did not attract an eager audience.

RKO resources had not been flourishing, and therefore it seemed sensible to make lower-budget films, using some of our rising stars to help attract customers, adding punch and content to the olio. Since *Crossfire* had proven itself, we placed *The Set-Up* into work starring Robert Ryan and Audrey Totter. It has become a classic film. Small, but classic. *The Window* followed and after that *They Live by Night*, starring Farley Granger and Cathy Downs, and *Blood on the Moon* with Bob Mitchum. We stepped up our pace and stretched out our reach with *Mr. Blandings Builds His Dream House* and followed that with *Berlin Express* and *I Remember Mama*. By then I had also traded Theodore Dreiser's melancholy *Sister Carrie* to William Wyler and Paramount for their priority rights to *Ivanhoe*. (There once was an agreement among studios to respect one another's intentions to produce properties in the public domain. I don't know if such an unwritten practice still exists. Considering the brouhaha over the remake of *King Kong*, I doubt that it does.)

Once we had *Ivanhoe* we began to draw an agreement for a joint venture with the Arthur Rank Organisation to produce the film in England.

While all this activity was burbling along, the first intimations of trouble became evident. I was visited by two investigators of the House Un-American Activities Committee. Both were rather gray-looking gentlemen, one of whom had the unprepossessing name of Leckie; the other one's name has faded from memory.

They had come to ask me about pending committee hearings and were interested in information I might have about some RKO employees. Bob Ryan? A former marine. Dymytryk? An excellent director. Adrian Scott? An excellent producer. Paul Jarrico? A very good writer. They said they detected that I was not responsive. I agreed, adding that since the days of Dies and Rankin I had had no respect for the committee and that the present group headed by Parnell Thomas had not abated my suspicion concerning them.

There had been groups of Yahoos baying about Communists in Hollywood but those of us who were aware of bearers of the left banner did not take them to be serious contenders for the acquisition of the motion-picture business, no less America. We had debated them during the days of the Russian-German pact, had defeated them when they tried to take over the Hollywood Independent Citizens Committee for Arts, Services and Professions (Hiccasp). Later, after the war, when the left wing refused to compromise, many of us departed, taking with us most of the financial support and many of the "important" star names. This withdrawal had finished off the basic purpose of Hiccasp, which had originally come into being as a Hollywood for Roosevelt group in 1936. We had not been bothered by the left wing until Russia was invaded in June, 1941, at which time the "phony" war had become the "People's War."

Not one of the men or women I knew who had almost unswervingly followed the party line had ever said to me, "I am a Communist," but even if they had I would not have avoided them or thought of denying them employment. I knew of anti-Semites, of hard-nosed right-wingers who would have gladly abrogated the Bill of Rights, of racial bigots who spoke of blacks in disgusting terms — yet those who were people of talent deserved to be working. The fact is that talent has no relationship to character, politics, or morality. There are gifted people who are monsters, charmers whose talents are excessively limited, but fortunately there are more than enough who combine the affirmative values of character and talent, thereby making life in the arts a joy.

It was also true that in the years immediately after the war, the violently anti-FDR forces released from the Roosevelt spell were attacking Truman and the Democratic party along with anyone who earned the title "liberal." "Liberal" was a synonym for "fellow traveler" or "pinko" or "bleeding heart." So began the era of lists — *Red Channels*,

Red Star over Hollywood, and the capricious intrusion of the American Legion into the minds of people in the arts. The digging for information went back to the days of the WPA and it was reminiscent of the Hoover regime when World War I veterans in Hooverville were all branded as Communists and burned out by troops led by Patton and MacArthur.

To us liberals then, planned investigations into the lives of our colleagues, even those we did not consider close friends, was alarming and required our opposition.

Ultimately, subpoenas were issued by the House Un-American Activities Committee, and among the "unfriendly witnesses" to be later identified as Communists were Scott and Dymytryk. What surprised me was that neither of them had been active in any of the groups I had been involved in and as far as I knew had not been part of any activity in left-wing action. Certainly, their work had been free of "radical" propaganda. When I received my summons to appear as a "friendly" witness, I met with Scott and Dymytryk. We joked about the summonses and they assured me that they had never been members of the Communist party. In return I assured that I wasn't a member of the Nazi party.

However, the joking stopped some days later when they asked me to meet for lunch with their attorney, Charles Katz, a short, sharp, smart man who some of us believed was an active supporter of the Communist party. Katz wanted to know what kind of statement I intended to make before my examination by the committee.

I intended to defend Scott and Dymytryk, criticize the committee, and prove there had been no Communist propaganda in films.

Katz said it was likely that the committee would produce cards indicating that both Scott and Dymytryk had been or were members of the party. I said that seemed odd, since they had vowed to me they were not. Charlie then said that it was almost a certainty they would also produce a card showing that I was a member. I answered I didn't believe they would — and if they did, then the jig was up for everyone in America; that if a congressional committee would deliberately make up false membership cards in any party, we were doomed. As Charlie persisted, I resisted and began to draw away from him, and when he asked if I would show him a copy of my statement before I went to Washington, I told him I would not — I sensed he was attempting to use me and I began to doubt Scott and Dymytryk's personal testimony to me.

During the time the investigative process was heating up, Bill Fadiman, the story editor, and I were searching for a war story. The best of the ones dealing with American soldiers had been *Walk in the Sun, The*

Story of G.I. Joe, Bataan, Thirty Seconds over Tokyo, and *Pride of the Marines:* all had dealt with either the war in the Pacific or the Italian campaign.

As we talked about the battles after the landing in Normandy, it occurred to me that the defense of Bastogne and the ultimate defeat there of the elite corps of the German Wehrmacht might give us fresh insights into that remarkable resistance, best typified by General McAuliffe's response of "Nuts" to the surrender ultimatum offered by the Nazis.

We met with Robert Pirosh, a veteran of the Bastogne battle, and he almost yelled with delight at the opportunity to do a story about that engagement — he said he had been making notes for years. In an effort to steal a march on other studios, which often rush in to join the parade in a new cycle, I told Bob to keep his assignment a secret. The working title was as far removed from the subject as possible, "Prelude to Love." I told Fadiman, "Don't even try to think of a final title, we might tell it to someone."

Then I broached the subject to Rathvon, who thought it a good gamble, and to Ned Depinet, who believed that the public was fed up with war pictures. He suggested, "Let's do a 'Want to see' profile." I reminded him of what happened to the *Crossfire* poll and the contradictory result. I suggested that we write a personal letter of inquiry to the heads of all our distributing offices and ask them to get a reading.

Two weeks later the results were toted up and the clear majority was in favor of "a war film." However, there were reservations — "It depends what kind"; "Where's the locale?"; "What's it about?"; "Who's in it?" We never answered the questions in our "thank you for your response" letters.

As Pirosh kept working, the 1947 House Un-American Activities Committee scheduled their hearings. I went to Washington for a meeting the night before my appearance. Among those at that meeting were Mendel Silberberg, the chief attorney for the Producers Association, and Paul McNutt, the acting attorney, retained because of his political background as former governor of the Philippines. McNutt was a handsome silver-haired gentleman but did not radiate glowing intelligence. He seemed lost in the company of Eric Johnston, the lean, voluble president of the producers, who was given to quick, chopping chirps of laughter that seldom seemed genuine. The others present included batteries of grim lawyers representing studios, who in the past few days had been dismayed by clients such as Jack Warner, Mayer, Cohn, and a covey of actors who had stumbled over each other in the effort to assure the committee they were one-hundred-percent Americans. The most vehement of the group was Adolph Menjou, the dapper, double-breasted, vested defender of the faith, who sat sidesaddle in the witness chair and gave the committee a series of charges concerning communism in Hollywood, most of which were as reliable as the tales of Baron Münchausen.

In addition to the hysteria ladled out to the committee by the so-called friendly witnesses, many of them actors, Johnston had become overwrought by the behavior of the producers, who had previously agreed not to fire employees who were Communists. I had read and had seen newsreel footage of some of the action in the cockpit of the committee room and assured my questioners that I would be firm in my determination to grant employment to anyone of talent regardless of political coloration, and I asked why the executives had not concentrated on the primary nonsensical charge that Hollywood films had been riddled by Red propaganda. I reminded them of the Nye committee hearings in 1941 charging us as warmongers for making anti-Fascist pictures — an investigation that was exploded by the tough defense of Wendell Willkie, who had been retained as defense attorney. He had made Nye look foolish.

I was told that McNutt was to accompany me to the witness table as a support unit. Despite my objection to that Johnston prevailed upon me to accept McNutt as representative of the concerted strength of the producers. By now I was not convinced of McNutt's ability to overcome any serious problem, but since Johnston and others had accepted my compromise that McNutt would not under any circumstances speak for me, I agreed to let him walk me to the scaffold.

The next morning, with considerable consternation and confusion, I listened as John Howard Lawson, Dalton Trumbo, Lester Cole, and Herbert Biberman railed at committee chairman Thomas and the committee's attorney (prosecutor is a better word) Pitkin. Having seen Lawson, Cole, Trumbo, and Biberman in action in other arenas, during which times they had been tough, lucid, articulate spokesmen, I wondered why they seemingly had collapsed in rage and frenzy over ordinary and stupid questions. The net result was that Thomas and Pitkin also began shouting and what was designed to be a hearing turned into a verbal free-for-all in which all the contestants became losers.

During the lunch break, some of the soon-to-be "Hollywood Ten" met with members of the Committee to Defend the First Amendment, who had flown to Washington to lend moral support. Humphrey Bogart, Lauren Bacall, William Wyler, John Huston, and Myrna Loy, all good solid liberals, were part of the group. I met with Scott, Dymytryk, and Charles Katz to tell them my impressions. Katz explained that when I appeared in the afternoon, I would be baited into the same behavior. I disagreed and suggested they were heading downstream and were going to be flushed out to sea.

Scott asked, "What alternative do we have? We've already been branded."

I argued that most of the newspapers and important columnists had not gone along with the reckless charges of the committee and had been impressed by the support of those Hollywood personalities who had formed the committee to defend the Constitution. Silly charges, such as the one that had attacked the film *Tender Comrade* merely because of its title, or the one made by Ginger Rogers's mother, Lela Rogers, who argued that in a film Dalton Trumbo had written (in a scene where three girls had agreed to share an apartment) the line "We'll share alike — one for all and all for one" was clear-cut Communist propaganda, had been laughed at and disregarded by thoughtful observers.

I suggested to Scott, Dymytryk, and Katz that I believed that they could keep the majority of public opinion on their side by avoiding the histrionics of those members of the Ten who had preceded them to the stand. I told them that if I were a Communist or accused of being one and had decided to invoke the First Amendment, I would get on the stand, quietly say I would not answer any question concerning my political beliefs, and add that while I was aware my refusal might place me in jeopardy in the minds of the committee, I believed the First Amendment protected me. Then I would add that I was not afraid or ashamed of my political conviction and that when I left the stand I would, with the other so-called unfriendly witnesses, call a press conference, where we would tell the press exactly what our political affiliations were and that we had refused to give that information to the committee because we didn't believe they had the right to ask us.

I insisted that their position would be respected by the press and could not be attacked by the industry.

Katz said my program was ridiculous. "If once they admit publicly they were or are Communists, they'll be kicked out of the industry."

"If that's true, and I don't believe it is, it's a better risk than the show they're putting on, for which they may get the ax."

Katz insisted I was naive. Perhaps I was. However, even now I am convinced that if the ten men had taken the course I suggested, the disaster that followed the hearings would not have taken place, despite Hedda

Hopper, Westbrook Pegler, and the Motion Picture Alliance for the Preservation of American Ideals, which was the wordy title dreamed up by strong right-wing opposition in Hollywood. I remain convinced that if the Roman-circus atmosphere had not prevailed, the Ten would not have been cited or convicted of contempt of Congress and the support of the press would have remained firm rather than fade away as it did.

My feelings then and now are that HUAC acted with malice and with no evidence of the American values that they were supposed to protect; that the Hollywood Ten were badly advised and provided an impetus for what happened following their appearance; that the producers behaved cowardly and cruelly.

My appearance at the hearings took place in the afternoon. From the moment Parnell Thomas greeted me, he was brusque. The fact that I had been called as a friendly witness cut no ice with Thomas. He had probably heard from his two investigators that I was actually "unfriendly." He and the committee's examiner eyed me balefully. Robert E. Stripling was cast out of a bad gangster movie. He was thin, dark, had plastered-down hair, and reminded me of Ed Pauley, an actor who always played the "heavy" in crime melodramas.

Stripling wasted little time in "exposing" me. He asked if I would hire a Communist. I answered that until the American Communist party was proved to preach the overthrow of our country by force and violence I would hire a Communist. The question then was repeated a dozen times in different ways. I kept giving the same answer, adding that I would judge a writer's qualification for employment on the basis of his talent, not his political opinions. Stripling and Thomas were sarcastic and appeared to be determined to irritate me in the hope that I would wind up being in contempt. My answers were loaded with *yes sirs* and *no sirs*. Finally, Thomas gave me a short lecture, asking me if I had read *Rip Van Winkle*. When I left the stand I thought of the answer I should have made but had not possessed the wit to think of it when it would have mattered. It would have been rewarding to have capped the exchange by saying, "Yes, Mr. Chairman, I've read that story. I am quite familiar with the art of fiction and the many uses of it."

Emmett Lavery followed me to the stand. Emmett has Jesuitical training, and he handled Thomas and Stripling with firmness and a touch of Irish wit. Emmett is a handsome man with a shining look of utter honesty. Using his legal skill and Catholic logic Emmett was the star of the proceedings. Stripling tried hard, but every time he threw one at Emmett it went sailing out of the park.

Emmett and I were the only two "friendly" witnesses who had not joined in the fox hunt.

Once the hearings ended and the Hollywood Ten were cited for contempt by the House, the Committee to Defend the First Amendment fell apart and Eric Johnston called a meeting at the Waldorf in New York. The meeting, November 24, 1947, was attended by the presidents of companies, and a regiment of lawyers. McNutt had been demoted (perhaps because his "political clout" had not had much clout) and replaced as chief legal sachem by former Secretary of State James Byrnes. In addition to New York executive heads, independents such as Sam Goldwyn and Walter Wanger were invited. Along with Ned Depinet I represented RKO; Nicholas Schenck, Mayer, Spyros Skouras, Barney Balaban, Jack Cohn, B. B. Kahane, Y. Frank Freeman, and Jack Warner were the big guns present. Zanuck was not there. A congress of attorneys were also in attendance. Johnston chaired the meeting. A sea change had taken place. Johnston had abandoned his previous posture and, seemingly panicked by what he saw as a drastic change in public opinion, was for a tough policy on the part of the industry. He talked to the seventy to eighty people who were in the room as if we were members of an industry manufacturing secret deadly weapons by employing Communists.

Johnston's opening salvo was followed by patriotic statements from Messrs. Mayer, Freeman, Skouras, and a few others. Sam Goldwyn was bold enough to suggest that there was an air of panic in the room. Goldwyn, ramrod straight, bald headed, and with a slightly Oriental slant to his eyes, spoke sarcastically and irritated Johnston, who responded with an angry speech concluding with the cliché question asking us whether we were mice or men. He insisted that if the motion-picture business wanted to earn the respect of the American public, the ten men who had appeared plus any known, or believed to be, Communists had to be discharged.

That was my cue to speak up: the men involved at the hearing were not yet proven guilty of anything — there was no law in the country denying the right of any citizen to be a Communist; there was no proof any of these men had advocated the overthrow of the government by force or violence; we had insisted there had been no Communist propagandizing in films, hence, the men in question could not be guilty of that arcane crime; we would dishonor and not honor our industry by an action that would inevitably lead to a blacklist.

My remarks provoked another angry outburst from Johnston and one by Skouras.

However, Walter Wanger demanded the floor and he barged into

Johnston, supporting my list of reasons for not rushing into a maelstrom. Then Goldwyn chipped in again, this time with anger and a statement that he would not be allied to any such nonsense as that proposed by Johnston.

The biggest surprise comment came from Eddie Mannix, the general manager of MGM studios. Eddie was once a bouncer for the Schenck brothers' enterprise at Palisades Park. He was a tough man, physically and emotionally, had a rugged temper, iron fists, and an enormous appetite for liquor and women. (Years later, following a series of ten heart attacks, after which he still kept up his drinking, cigar smoking, and womanizing, he said to me, "When I go, I want to be in the saddle humping, with a glass of booze in one hand and a cigar in my mouth." It was a complicated image of indulgence that I have never quite assembled in my mind.)

Eddie was one of those who believed it would have been sensible for the Allies to turn on Russia after Hitler was wiped out and finish them off while they were in a position to be had. Therefore, none of us expected Eddie to say that he opposed firing the ten men. But Eddie argued that there was a state law in California that prohibited an employer from firing anyone because of his political ideas, and Eddie added that he would not break the law.

It was now time for Jimmy Byrnes to speak up. He doubted that any government official "would argue with the decision of the industry to get rid of 'Reds.'" Not only that — the men could be relieved of their jobs because of the contractual "morals" clause on the basis that their behavior had brought disrepute on the industry. (This morals clause existed in all talent contracts and was a device that came in with the advent of the Legion of Decency but has, in view of present-day standards, become extinct.)

That heated up the meeting, with Goldwyn, Wanger, and me providing some of the coal. Finally, Johnston, who had been slapping his hotel key on the table as he made his arguments, became furious and threw his key down as a gage of battle and threatened to quit unless the industry came to its senses.

No vote was ever taken. It was Johnston's threat plus Byrnes's argument that had won the decision to discharge those cited. I said I would not be a party to the action — so did Goldwyn and Wanger, but we won no support. A committee was appointed to draft a statement. Mendel Silberberg, who was chairman, asked that I, as a spokesman for the opposition, be a member. It was an assignment I did not want, but Goldwyn whispered, "Do it — maybe they won't go crazy."

The statement (which appears in full on pages 369 to 370), is inconsistent, probably because I helped make it so by protesting the first four paragraphs and aiding in writing the last four, in the hope that I could persuade the guilds to form a defense barrier to prevent wholesale firings and investigations. That foggy hope served to make me a target for the right and the left. I should never have listened to Goldwyn.

One newspaper, in Los Angeles, ran a banner headline printed in bright crimson that proclaimed: STUDIO HEAD SAYS HE WILL HIRE REDS.

Later, when I appeared at the Writers Guild and stated that I opposed the studio policy but supported the effort to form some sort of talent guild council to stave off reckless indictments, I was clobbered. The nicest name I was called was "thief." Those bold members who stood up to defend me were either booed or silently rejected.

Floyd Odlum, the chairman of RKO, called me and asked for an explanation of my stand. Having been given the background, including Johnston's previous position for the industry to stand firm, Odlum wanted to know why the industry was not defending me against the rocks hurled at me. I had no answer for that. He informed me that there was to be a meeting of the RKO board in the Town House in Los Angeles in a few days.

Before that meeting took place eight of the now-called Hollywood Ten had been fired by Metro, Warners, and Twentieth-Fox, or if not employed, had been told they were unemployable.

I had not taken action against Scott and Dymytryk.

Peter Rathvon as president of the company chaired the board meeting and the matter in question was why I had not yet fired the two of the Ten at RKO. After I explained my position, Odlum said that he respected my point of view but disagreed with me and that there would be a vote of the board: to discharge or not discharge the accused men. When a vote was taken, I asked that my nay be recorded in the minutes. That done I told the board I would not execute the order to fire Scott and Dymytryk. Odlum was patient. He told Rathvon to do the firing. When the meeting was broken up, Odlum told me that the motion-picture business was one he would never understand. Two days later, he issued a statement defending me and by implication attacking Johnston for not publicly coming to my defense.

The entire episode was my first serious encounter with the heavyweights in the motion-picture structure, teaching me that in a clutch, if you swam against the tide, it was, "So long, Charlie, you should have hung on to the raft." There were those who thought that as a matter of principle, I should resign. I mulled that over and came to the conclusion that it would be more helpful to remain in the business and fight against the blacklisting; also, since the waters had been muddied by HUAC, the Hollywood Ten, and the producers, my resignation would in no way clarify the issue.

There is some doubt that this account will straighten the record. Perhaps it is just as well. Those who attacked me — Hedda Hopper, Jack Tenney, Westbrook Pegler, George Sokolsky on one side and spokesmen for the far left on the other — demonstrated what the position of liberals in politics has always been and will likely forever remain: they will be rejected for not having accepted the extreme alternatives.

Then along came Howard Hughes.

22

Despite the time eaten up by the HUAC hearings and their after-math, the job of making films was going on. *Mr. Blandings Builds His Dream House* was shaping into a first-rate picture. George Stevens had finally finished *I Remember Mama* (Stevens in later years was prone to overshoot and take ages to cut and dub) and it was slated for the Music Hall in New York. There was a major scuffle over the length of the picture — those at the Hall wanted it cut to measure exactly two hours but Stevens, after trimming out ten minutes to mollify the doubters, re-fused to cut any more of the remaining two hours and twelve minutes.

While I had the authority to take over and do the scissoring job, I had too much respect for Stevens; further, I had little respect for tailor-ing a film to two hours in order to satisfy a daily program schedule at the theater. I suggested cutting ten minutes out of the live show. Eventually, the picture went into the Hall with no further cuts.

Stephen Ames, some months before, had come to me with the short story "The Boy with Green Hair." I liked it and scheduled Joe Losey to direct as his first picture. (It was Joe who recommended to me the Stephen Vincent Benét story "The Sobbin' Women" as the basis for a musical film. We tried to get it, but Josh Logan had it under option for a stage produc-tion. Years later at MGM, after occasional inquiries, we learned the story was available. We snapped it up and made the musical Joe had suggested, but with another title, *Seven Brides for Seven Brothers*.) *The Boy with Green Hair* was in production. Waiting at the barrier was *Battleground*, the new and now public title for Robert Pirosh's "Prelude to Love."

I had talked to William Wellman about *Battleground* and had ap-proached MGM for the loan of Ricardo Montalban and Van Johnson. Billy Grady, casting director of Metro, advised me that there was no chance to get any MGM stars — the studio didn't like the script. Billy added gratuitously, "Believe me, kid, stay away from this one — it's a stinker."

Like children, who often assume characteristics of their parents, employees are inclined to take on the attitudes of their companies — certainly it was so with movie companies. MGM, the biggest and most powerful, had for years dominated the field. Twentieth-Fox under the freewheeling and daring leadership of Zanuck was issuing a worthy challenge; Paramount had DeMille; Warners had Cagney, Flynn, Davis, and Bogart; but Metro had most of the blue chips. Even though they had fallen into a recession after the war years, MGM still had the most stars, writers, directors, and producers, and all they needed was a burst of energy. What they had retained, undiminished, was the arrogance of power, which resonated from the white, large office of L. B. Mayer.

Many employees, such as Billy Grady, were a reflection of that arrogance. Cedric Gibbons, the designer, Douglas Shearer, the sound magician (slightly deaf), Ralph Wheelwright, press, Frank Whitbeck, the voice of the trailers, and the contract personnel, all had a slight swagger. They worked at the richest, most prestigious, and certainly the most publicized studio in history. So, Billy could with no sense of decorum advise me over the telephone, "It's a stinker."

Suddenly, to everyone's surprise, trade papers rumored that RKO was to be bought by Howard Hughes. Odlum, plagued with arthritis, was on his date ranch in Indio, and I drove there to urge him not to sell. I felt that Hughes, a picture maker in his own right, would interfere, eventually take control, and turn the studio into an ineffective operation.

Since my contract permitted me to resign if there was a change in studio ownership, I advised Odlum that I would quit if he abandoned RKO, leaving it in the hands of the mercurial Mr. Hughes.

Odlum was an engineer and a financial giant and had no affection for films. RKO had been an investment designed to earn him a profit, and the sale to Hughes was one way for him to leave with a profit and rid himself of what he termed an "uneasy relationship" with top motion-picture executives whose erratic behavior confused him. He viewed Johnston's conduct during the hearings as craven and irresponsible and he wanted out.

When the Hughes purchase of RKO was announced, there was some speculation about my remaining at the studio and whether or not Hughes would want me to stay. My own hunch was that Hughes and I would not be compatible.

Rathvon, who was still acting as president of the company, arranged for Hughes and me to meet in Rathvon's garden one late afternoon. Hughes waved a greeting and opened the meeting by saying, "I hear you want to quit."

This was a straightforward gambit and caught me flat-footed.

I had been eyeing Hughes, and this tall, lean Texan reminded me of a capable, quick gunhand one saw in Westerns starring Gary Cooper. I took a beat before answering and then told him, "I know you've made films — and if I were rich and bought a studio, I'd want to run it. That's what I think you'll want to do and I don't blame you. But you won't need me at my price to simply deliver your orders."

Hughes had leaned forward to catch what I said, and he assured me he had no intention of taking over. He wanted me to stay and let everything go on as before. He spoke quietly and sincerely. I agreed to remain in the job.

Rathvon and I talked for a few minutes after Hughes left. He was convinced the man meant what he said. "If he doesn't," Rathvon said, "I'll be out of there before you grab your hat."

For a few weeks the studio program rolled along. *Mr. Blandings Builds His Dream House* was finished, previewed, and readied for release. *The Boy with Green Hair* was being dubbed and scored. (We had bought Eden Ahbez's "Nature Boy" for the theme song.) Bob Ryan and Barbara Bel Geddes were making tests for a new film and *Battleground* and *Malaya* were being budgeted.

Studio personnel told me that Hughes was coming to the studio late at night to see the daily rushes; scripts were being sent to him; he was examining payrolls. After all, he now owned the entire spread and wanted to know what was doing on the range. He *was* numero uno honcho.

Hughes's activity did unsettle some of the studio people who had been pleased at the improved state of affairs. They kept watching me for signs of trouble. But my concern was my mother's health. She had had a second heart attack months before and now her heart was failing. Nurses and help were in attendance at her apartment, but I was spending most of my nights sleeping on the couch in her living room.

One early evening, after a particularly severe attack of weakness, Mother suggested to me that she would be pleased to see my sister, Lillian, and my brother, Sam. She assured me she wasn't frightened but she just would enjoy talking with them. The next day they arrived and my mother did seem to brighten up. She was cheery and funny. The following evening we were all in Mother's room listening to a radio program. Mother thought it was a bit corny. Then she said she was sleepy. As we got up to leave she asked me to stay for a minute.

She took my hands and held them, said some warm and lovely things to me, thanked me for bringing Lil and Sam to see her — and then she kissed me and said she wanted to rest. I left her and the nurse went in to keep the vigil. Within a few minutes, the nurse called us, we hurried in as the nurse went to the phone to call our doctor. But it was over. Mother was dead. Without thinking why, I ran to her dresser, picked up a hand mirror, and held it over her lips. There was no moisture — no sign of breath. Then I remembered that perhaps a year before Mother had asked me to make sure if anything "happened" to put the mirror to her lips.

During the seven days of mourning I did not go to the studio. I observed the ritual of *shivah*, the Orthodox period of grief and prayer that requires the family mourners to sit on boxes, not look into mirrors, not shave, not do anything but talk of the departed one. The house was swamped with visitors, day and night. Then after *shivah* one is enjoined to choose life rather than grief and to go back to daily demands.

When I returned to the studio I heard that the Arthur Rank deal for *Ivanhoe* had blown up. The reason given was the unstable condition at RKO, but there were persistent rumors that the Rank Organisation was having internal problems.

Within a few days I was again on a normal schedule, though one evening as I got into my car to go home, I asked the chauffeur to drop me at Mother's apartment. It takes a long time to alter muscle memory.

One night I had finished running the day's filming and was making notes to a tired film editor who had been working with me from eight until past midnight, when the phone rang. It was Hughes. He said he wanted to see me. When? At three o'clock. That seemed reasonable — except he meant three in the morning, that morning. That was impossible. I had to get some rest. We set a time to meet at one o'clock the next afternoon at a home he had rented from Cary Grant, who was one of his closest and most trusted friends.

But he asked that before we met I fire Barbara Bel Geddes, whom he did not like, and replace her with someone he would select; also, I was to take *Battleground* off the production schedule; also . . . I didn't let him continue. I told him he was doing what I had feared he would do — that he wanted a messenger boy, not a studio head. I ended by telling him that he had my oral resignation and that by morning my written one would be in his hand.

Not fearing my grandiose ultimatum, he insisted that I follow his orders before we met the next day. I repeated that I would not. He agreed to wait until after our meeting.

At one o'clock the next day I walked into Cary's unused house that

Hughes was temporarily occupying. There wasn't a paper, a cigarette, a flower, a match, a picture, a magazine — there was nothing except two chairs and a sofa. It had the look of a place someone had moved out of or was moving into.

The only sign of life was Hughes, who appeared from a side room in which I caught a glimpse of a woman hooking up her bra before the door closed.

Hughes beckoned me to the couch and sat next to me, his head bent forward a bit, his eyes seemingly focused on my shoes.

He asked me if I was quitting because I didn't want a boss — didn't want to take orders. No, I said, that wasn't the reason. Reasonably and quietly, he pointed out that he had to have men to run his enterprise who would take his orders. I understood that — then realized that I was beginning to feel sorry for him because I was quitting. Recognizing that the feeling was ridiculous, I took hold of myself and answered that it would be better for both of us if he let me resign without a sticky public quarrel.

He didn't answer for a moment but kept staring down at my feet. Then he asked, "Where did you get those shoes?" I mumbled, "I think they're Johnston and Murphy." "How much were they?" I didn't remember — I guessed thirty or thirty-five dollars. He said they were good-looking shoes; "Comfortable?" I said they were.

There wasn't much more to add to that part of the conversation, but then he pressed me as to why I wasn't willing to accept him as a boss. My answer was that if I were working for him in the airplane industry, I would obey his instructions, convinced that he knew more about the state of the art than I; but since I felt I knew more about motion pictures than he, our relationship was doomed to be a stormy and feckless one.

He asked if I expected a settlement on my contract. All I wanted was his word that he would allow me to buy *Battleground*. He agreed. He asked me to stay on for a week or two until he appointed someone to take over and we wished each other good luck and the conference was at an end.

The news of my departure was a one-day trade-paper item. Hughes was quoted as saying, "I saved myself two weeks' salary."

A few days before my mother died, she told me she did not wish her body to be buried in a plot she had bought in Newark, New Jersey. She had said, "It's a long trip back and I won't be able to see anything — also it would be better for me to be in the Beth Olam cemetery" (which was next to the studio) "so I can drop in to see you whenever I want to."

As I left Hughes, I remembered her joke and I suddenly felt regret — I was leaving a studio I had helped put back on a stronger footing; but I thought, with a smile, Mother would find me no matter where I wound up.

I had offers. One was from Gradwell Sears, a successful film sales executive, who was interested in organizing a group to buy United Artists and putting me in charge. That didn't seem attractive to me. Nor did a return to Selznick seem appropriate. I began to think about taking a holiday, or perhaps I'd write a play.

In a few days, I received a call from Lillie Messinger, who gave me the surprising news that L. B. Mayer would like to meet me at his home, if that was convenient, the following morning.

I knew that MGM since the end of the war had fallen into disarray, so I assumed I was going to be offered a job as a producer or perhaps to act as one of Mayer's executives in charge of a unit. I was willing to listen to the latter proposal but was reluctant to function as a producer. A unit head could veto story buys, screenplays, and casts and could do final editing on a film, which seemed to promise more action and less red tape. If I was to go back to MGM, I did not wish to place myself in the meat grinder of decisions by committee.

During my previous stays at Metro, I had never been to Mr. Mayer's home. I found it to be very large but also rather bare and uninviting. It lacked the comfort of a home well lived in. One wall was decorated with a full-length portrait of Mayer — perhaps a bit larger than life-size.

The chief impression was of a lack of form or a point of view, as if no one had determined what this home should be like. It had a catch-as-catch-can appearance much like an exceedingly large hotel suite that was in desperate need of an experienced interior decorator. Then I knew what was lacking — exactly what was true of his office — warmth. It was like a large urn of cold coffee.

Mayer greeted me with amity, offered me coffee, buns, orange juice. I had to decline because I had breakfasted. Mayer congratulated me on the work I had done for Selznick and RKO, then with no preface offered me the job as vice-president in charge of production. While the offer was unexpected, it didn't surprise me as much as when Rathvon had dished out the RKO offer. After all, I had been head of a studio. But being in charge of production at MGM would be like changing from guiding a span of horses to the complicated driving of the eight Budweiser Clydesdales.

MGM was ridden with conflict, envy, and rivalry. It was peopled with employees who had been there for years — spoiled and wasteful, and yet many of them talented but hobbled by the old College of Cardinals system inaugurated by Mayer.

I wanted no part of that system and told that to L. B. We then talked candidly. He spoke of his desire to resign in a year or two, of his weariness, of his inability to work with Thalberg, who, "believe me, was a genius but he was money mad. That was his problem. Money — money — that ruined him." Aware that Mayer for years had earned more money than anyone in the United States, I didn't pursue his analysis of Thalberg's "problem."

When he finished outlining his future plans, I spoke of my feelings about taking the job. My duties would have to be set down specifically in any contract . . . those duties would include my freedom in choosing the stories, the stars, the writers, directors, and producers. I would retain the approval of the final-cut version of all films.

While I would work in close touch with Mayer and Mr. Nicholas Schenck, president of Loew's, no other executives would have any control over my decisions. I would consult, listen, be open-minded — but if I were to be in charge of production, I would insist on being in charge of all that title implied.

I had decided to be clear and firm, because I knew that any other formula would lead to failure. Mayer told me to stick to my guns — he would speak to "the General" (Mr. Schenck) and I should be prepared to meet with them and their lawyers later in the week. That information led me to the supposition that Schenck had suggested that Mayer contact me; later Schenck confirmed the thought.

Mayer said he was happy "to have you come back home to MGM where you belong." I had been ordered out twice and had left "home" once before, but I thought — maybe that's were I do belong.

Miriam was ecstatic when I told her the news — which had to be kept absolutely quiet. The next day there was an item in the ubiquitous trade press that Metro was feeling me out about taking over as head of production. So much for "absolute quiet." My attorney at the time was David Tannenbaum, who for a few years had quit practice to take over an executive job with Walter Wanger. After the failure of *Joan of Arc* with Ingrid Bergman, David had returned to the less perilous business of handling a wide clientele. I also called Lew Wasserman, who had by now propelled MCA into a leadership position among theatrical agencies challenged only by the William Morris Agency, headed by the redoubtable Abe Lastfogel. While Lew was no longer my agent, he was my friend. His advice was, "Get rid of the whole bunch of executives — if you don't, they'll kill you — insist on cleaning house or don't take the job. Good luck." Allen Rivkin had volunteered the same thought when I had gone to RKO. I had not agreed.

Having neither the inclination nor the stomach to follow Lew's dictum, I concentrated on obtaining the prerogatives I had outlined with Mayer, convinced that those authorities would protect me from the palace guard.

Mr. Schenck arrived incognito on a weekend (he was avoiding being served a summons pertaining to a lawsuit — I didn't know what kind) and I was called to a meeting at Mayer's home on a Sunday. Present at the gathering were Mayer, Schenck; Tannenbaum and Morgan Maree representing me; George Cohen, a lawyer representing MGM; and Eddie Mannix, general manager of Metro. It was a warm sunny day and we met outdoors near the pool.

There were no problems regarding money. Four thousand a week for seven years, an additional two thousand a week deferred payment for seven years (provided I did not resign). The debate centered on definitions of my job and the proviso that if either Mayer or Schenck left or died, no other executive could be appointed unless he carried the vacated title "head of studio" or "president of Loew's." Schenck argued that even Thalberg did not have those strictures in his contract. Tannenbaum tactfully suggested that that's what caused the quarrels between Mr. Mayer and Thalberg.

George Cohen was fussing about other details. He was in a tough bargaining position because two years before, when Tannenbaum had been with Wanger, I had chosen George to represent me in the dealings with RKO. When I pointed out to George that I was asking only for what he had once obtained for me, he countered by saying that MGM was not RKO. David had the chutzpah to say that that was why their inclusion in the MGM contract was more necessary.

The meeting broke up with those matters still to be resolved. We were to get together the next day. Schenck suggested that the lawyers battle out the details and get back to him and to me for the yeses or noes.

The following morning Mayer called to tell me not to give an inch. "Schenck will give in — he has to — he wants you — I want you." I relayed that privileged information to Tannenbaum, then thought it over and realized that Mayer's message was a ploy to keep me on his side and insulate me against Schenck. Before I had the job, I was being cast as a shuttlecock.

Late that afternoon, Tannenbaum called. The deal was set. Cohen and Schenck had agreed — Mayer was pleased and by morning the news was out.

When I arrived at the studio two days later, my parking space had been set aside — I was welcomed, patted, congratulated, flattered — and loved every moment of it.

This was June, 1948. In December, 1932, I had arrived in Hollywood as a junior writer. Now I was to be executive VP in charge of production at the biggest studio in the territory.

In 1941 when I was debating taking over the small-budget picture unit at Metro, Ralph Rainger had said, "Do it — one day you're going to run a studio — maybe MGM."

That had seemed a silly prophecy, but now Miriam reminded me, "It happens to you — if you had kept going to boys' camps in summer, you'd have been a head counselor — you join a club, you get to run it — you make pictures, they ask you to run a studio — you run one, you get the biggest."

I thought about that, kissed her, and said, "My luck, Hughes will buy Metro and I'll be out on my *tuchis*."

I had made my plans and followed them through with Mayer's enthusiastic blessings.

I wanted to go away for a month with a trunk full of scripts — those in work, those contemplated — recent story acquisitions, plus a list of story material that had been abandoned along with a short synopsis of the latter group and a total of how much money had been spent on them.

With that information, I would need a list of all contract obligations with executives, stars, writers, directors, producers, and the average cost of pictures produced in the last two years.

When I returned from my holiday, I expected to have a projected program of forty films to be produced in the first twelve months. I would also have made decisions as to which stories should be permanently written off and which revived for production.

The "perks" of office came my way, and I refused some, accepted others. Mannix and Ben Thau, the executive in charge of contract personnel, had their suites next to Mayer's and suspected I might ask them to move — I didn't. I picked a suite at the west end of the floor. It had a private office, conference room, bath, and small dining room. I selected some fabrics, asked the decorators to avoid white or "moderne" furniture, green or rust rugs, and told them I'd bring my own pictures (Miriam had painted scads of lovely ones) and photographs.

We were to be escorted to the train (this was before Miriam and I began to use planes) and were to be met by cars in Cheyenne and driven to our destination in the Rockies, a hideaway near Denver that Tannenbaum had recommended.

The place was a disaster. The only item of interest in the day we were there was our encounter with a studio head sans wife and his lady, whom we also knew, sans husband. Embarrassment dripped all over the four of us. This was 1948 when it was still not embarrassing to be embarrassed.

We left our crowded quarters in the rustic lodge run by Hy Raskin (later to be a factotum in the Democratic party) and aided by a friend, Saul Caston, the conductor of the Denver Symphony Orchestra at the Red Rock Amphitheatre, we were guided to a charming place where we dug in for the good food, air, and water. And work.

When the four weeks I had allotted were past, I had selected a program based on all the properties I had examined. Our average cost of $2,200,000 per film could, if we increased our product and were more careful of cost, be reduced considerably — certainly to $1,500,000 if not less. More desirably we might come up with a few more pictures of merit.

I reported over the phone to Mayer and Schenck. Both were pleased. Schenck asked me to come to New York. He felt the first announcement of my plans would receive better coverage at a news conference from his office. Mayer was asked to join but he said he was too occupied. Further, he said that Schenck liked the publicity.

In New York, the trade press reported the plans enthusiastically. Schenck took Miriam and me to dinner with his wife, Pansy, a dear and bright woman with taste and a commitment to charitable causes. Tickets to the theater and a car each evening plus a lavish suite at the Sherry-Netherland were the perks in New York.

During the few days in Manhattan, there was an opportunity to see the contrast between Mayer and Schenck in mode and manner.

Mayer, while always well-groomed, was surrounded by a faint glimmer of crudeness. His language would easily lapse into primitive speech. He had on many occasions used his fists when he lost his temper — I knew of two such occasions, one when he had hit Sam Goldwyn and the other when he had clobbered Walter Wanger. He had also tried to tangle with Harry Warner when that gentleman had, at a charity banquet, described Mayer's donation as niggardly.

Mayer was also a protean performer. He would cry at will — feign heart pain — act out sentimental scenes. His body language was vigorous and he prided himself on his strength. He spoke often of his friendship with Herbert Hoover, Cardinal Spellman, J. Edgar Hoover, and Randolph Hearst. He used his power, as I had seen in his treatment of Harry Rapf, like a hammer.

Schenck was dapper, a small man, with heavy-lensed glasses. His skin was florid, had a sheen of moisture — Mayer's was pale and dry. Schenck moved with short steps, his body slightly bent forward. Mayer strode — ready for battle.

Schenck was not an actor. He did have a facility for appearing reasonable, yielding, quiet, and he was aware that he was very charming. But he turned his back on overt battle. He had other techniques. Schenck's language was mild. He had a slight Russian accent, as did his brother Joe. Schenck's manners in the office or at a restaurant were impeccable. He greeted you by standing up. Mayer seldom did. Schenck chain-smoked Parliament cigarettes. His style was quiet, reserved, gentlemanly. Those closest to him addressed him as "Nick." Everyone else called him "General." Those close to Mayer called him "L.B.," others, "Chief."

Both men were respected and feared by their staffs. However, it was clear from the history of these two men that if seriously challenged, L.B. would maul you to death — Nick would do you in with a cyanide cocktail.

Nick Schenck was pleasant to be with, warm and responsive. With Mayer, one always sensed a challenge — a peculiar insecurity, as if a word or an action might send him into orbit.

When I returned to Culver City and checked in with Mayer, I sensed that something was amiss.

The only one of the top executives with whom I felt easy was Eddie Mannix, and I selected him as my confidant. Ben Thau was and is smooth and cool, and in a short time I asked myself, "When will Benny thaw?" He never did. Louis Sidney, an aide to Mannix, was a big man with a heavy thatch of hair, hypertension, and extra weight. He was pleasant and funny (his brother was George Sidney, a well-known vaudevillian), but I knew he was subject to moods that would drift from euphoria to depression.

The hardest-working executive was Joe Cohn, built like a boxer. He was bald on top, prematurely gray, had a firm jaw, and was totally free of guile and concerned only with his work as executive in charge of all physical production. He played good bridge, aggressive gin rummy, and was like an automaton on the tennis court — he got everything and would lob his opponents to an early grave. Joe was representative of all the best that is implied by the description "a company man."

Marvin Schenck, a nephew of Nick, was sweet but used as a backup executive. I knew he functioned as an ear and eye for Nick — who I didn't believe would use Marvin except as an early-warning system.

Kenneth MacKenna became closest to me. He was in charge of writers and the purchase of stories. I had known him from my early days at Metro in the B unit. He was intelligent and well educated — had good humor — and was incorruptible. He had served in World War I and had gone back into action in World War II. We liked and trusted each other in fast friendship.

Billy Grady, the casting director, who had spent most of his lifetime at MGM, was aware of all the weekend or longer alliances between the sexes and would volunteer information at the drop of a pair of pants.

In baseball talk, that was the lineup when I reported in as field manager. Mayer was the business manager and Schenck the owner.

When after a few days, during which I saw Mayer each morning, I felt an arctic breeze, I asked Mannix, "Is there something I should know?" There was. Mayer was annoyed that Schenck had called the production meeting in New York and resented the publicity that had featured the story of my program for moving Metro out of its becalmed state.

It would have been foolish to let that irritation fester, so when I saw Mayer the next day I brought up the subject, pointing out that the announcement had carried both our names.

Mayer launched into the story of Thalberg and himself. He branded Thalberg as money mad and power hungry. He told me he knew Thalberg would die young — "that's why I wouldn't let him marry Edie" (his younger daughter).

He told of his scenes with Thalberg — of their fight for studio control — and of how, after Mayer had bowed to his demand, Thalberg had come to Mayer "and on his knees — begged me to take back the studio." From there L.B. spoke in a complimentary way of Thalberg's modesty — "he never wanted any publicity — neither did I — I won't talk to any reporters — you don't need any publicity — Nick likes it — and don't trust him. He'll bring you caviar when you leave New York and flowers in your room when you get back there — but he's only smiles and caviar and roses — and the rest of him is all shit."

I got the picture.

Then I went back to work and stayed out of Mayer's office for two or three days. I had a premonition I would hear the story of Thalberg and Mayer many times. I did.

Among the projects I had decided to buy was *Battleground*. Not wanting to spring a surprise on Mayer, I told him that I had called Hughes and he had agreed to keep his promise. Mayer was opposed to the purchase but knew I had left RKO because of Hughes's decision to junk the script, so after warning me that I was making a mistake — "Billy Grady read it and says it will be a disaster" — L.B. wished me luck. I had the feeling I'd need it.

But what I needed more than luck was to acquaint myself on this new level, as head of production, with the staff of producers, directors, and actors. I knew the writers on a level that needed no adjustment — having shared experiences with them, I knew their gripes and frustrations, and I knew how to eliminate them.

I started with some of the actors, the first of whom was Spencer Tracy. When he arrived for his afternoon two o'clock date he knocked on the door of my office and slowly pushed it open. Playing Uriah Heep he approached my desk rubbing his hands in a dry wash and said, "I don't know if you remember me. My name is Tracy." I love improvisations — I answered, "Of course, Samuel Tracy."

"No, no," Tracy said, "Spencer."

"Yes, of course, how stupid of me to forget."

"Well, sir," Tracy added, "you may remember that I was in a play with you called *The Last Mile*."

I nodded.

"Well, believe me, Mr. Schary, you can ask anyone in that play — I told all of them — just you keep your eye on that young fella who plays the reporter — one day he's going to be head of MGM." Then dropping Uriah like a dirty rag he said, "And so you are — you son of a bitch."

He had no complaints — no gripes. He had been on the wagon, felt good, and concluded, "Just send the stuff you want me to do. If I like it, I'll do it. If not, I'll tell you to get another player."

That was a good beginning.

I had a talk with Gable, whom I had never before met. There was a masculinity about him in the set of his body, the way his shoulders moved — he probably invented body language. He was not the chatty kind. He was a pleasant man but I heard little or no humor during our first meeting or all the others we had during the years. But he was an extraordinary personality.

Robert Taylor and Robert Young were old friends from the days when I had been making low-budget films, and we talked about the past rather than the future.

Gene Kelly and Van Johnson were veterans of *Pilot No. 5* and we had kept our friendships constant, which was also true of Keenan Wynn, Myrna Loy, and Judy Garland.

It was not possible to see each actor personally but I did introduce the practice of sending each star a flower arrangement, or a bottle of wine, or a box of candy along with a personal note wishing them good hunting each time a film went into production.

The musical producers represented the best array of talent ever assembled for the production of musical entertainment. There were three of them: Arthur Freed, Jack Cummings, and Joe Pasternak. Freed had the best taste and the surest touch. He was a lyricist and by reviving his songs in many of his films he kept a good ASCAP rating. However, his songs remain standards: "Singin' in the Rain," "You Are My Lucky Star," "Broadway Melody," "Pagan Love Song," "You Were Meant for Me" are a few of the tunes Freed wrote with Nacio Herb Brown.

Freed had been a protégé of Mayer's, and was responsible for a long list of hit films including *Singin' in the Rain, Gigi, An American in Paris, The Barkleys of Broadway, Easter Parade,* and *The Band Wagon.*

He had flair and a gift for choosing talented associates, all of whom made ample contributions. The supporting cast of creators who wrote, danced, and sang their way through the best years of Metro's musicals represent an honor roll of entertainment: Roger Edens, John Green, Conrad Salinger, Alan Jay Lerner and Frederick Loewe, Irving Berlin, Johnny Mercer, Harold Arlen, Cole Porter, George and Ira Gershwin, Betty Comden and Adolph Green, Stanley Donen, Gene Kelly, Debbie Reynolds, Cyd Charisse, Frank Sinatra — it is an endless list. Freed rates the post position. He was not a lovable man but was a hell of a producer.

Joe Pasternak is lovable but not as gifted as Freed. Joe, a sentimentalist and a romantic, lives in a highly original world that we used to identify even to him as the Land of Pasternaky. In this Land of Pasternaky all hotel suites were huge and lavish and shamed the best in the real world. His films were gentle, cute, and warm. He gravitated to Jane Powell, Red Skelton, Mario Lanza, Esther Williams, Ricardo Montalban, Kathryn Grayson, and captured artists such as S. Z. Sakall, José Iturbi, Lauritz Melchior. Joe's career took a big bounce with *The Great Caruso,* and with *Love Me or Leave Me* Joe entered the real world. I don't believe he ever recovered from the shock.

Jack Cummings, the last of this triumvirate, had talents that fell somewhere between Joe's and Arthur's. Jack had taken on the burden of proving he was more than L. B. Mayer's nephew. The burden ofttimes made him sensitive and quick to resort to truculence. He was the realist.

His last big success at MGM was *Seven Brides for Seven Brothers*. Jack had a good comedic sense and of the three was the best in the field of nonmusical films. *The Stratton Story* was his.

Freed was a sensual man, rather stout, flabby, and sybaritic.

Joe in his day was cute, fussy, ebullient, enthusiastic. He had a ready grin and was always certain of success. He never knew failure because he never recognized it.

Jack was lean, a good golfer, a tough and demanding man who dressed the best, always looked trim and showered.

No Three Musketeers they. I'm almost positive they endured each other with no affection and with no admiration.

But they, in the years from 1945 to 1958, built up a library of songs, stories, and dances that no other studio has ever touched in quality or quantity.

During the first months I managed to get to know almost everyone — actors, directors, producers. I already knew the writers. (Bennett Cerf once criticized me to someone for "hiring his friends as writers." The fact is that most of the writers were my friends. I could hardly avoid hiring them.) I also made friends with editors, policemen, stage managers, grips, electricians, but I never covered the entire staff of workers — there were thousands of them.

The priority of course was to get the studio back into productive action.

23

Another priority was my family.

I had received a small degree of celebrity during the days I ran the B-picture unit at Metro. Then my three years with Selznick and his generous handling of the five films I made for him, with extravagant advertising and publicity, had zoomed me up to the RKO job, which in turn had produced a continued flow of good pictures along with favorable press. The added excitement of House Un-American Activities Committee hearings and their aftermath plus the entrance of Howard Hughes into the scene had not made my name a household word, but certainly words of varying appraisals were attached to my name in Hollywood and New York and in the columns of those writers in other cities who followed show-business items. When the MGM announcement came, the news stories were longer but the household where it counted most was my own home.

At that point our three children actually viewed me as important. Jill, then twelve, wanted to meet the famous actors, see the costume department, and go to the picture premieres. Joy, ten, had the same desires with one addition: did the studio have a hospital for people who "get sick"? When I told her it did, she wanted to see it. Jeb, eight, wanted me to let him see how the movies were made — "How do they shoot the bad guys?" "How do the horses fall and then get up?" "When we see Gable in the plane, is he really driving it?"

To their friends the children went up a couple of rungs but our kids fought that off. Jeb was the most obstinate. He resented being driven to school. Jill was the least resistant — she liked the chauffeured escort, but could hardly wait to own her own roadster. Joy couldn't have cared less as long as she got to school on time.

The fact is that they were not spoiled despite the easy comfort of our home, which at its zenith supported a staff of a cook, a nurse, a kitchen maid, an upstairs maid, a butler, a chauffeur, and a gardener. Miriam and I tried to teach our kids not to take their luxuries for granted, because both of us had for a time been raised in surroundings where we had been able to call on servants to help us and then had seen luxuries evaporate. In Miriam's case, her family had gone broke during the depression, victims of bad advice and worse investments. I had been part of the work force that was wrapped around me. When my father went broke that fragile world of prosperity disappeared, but bad times did not destroy my mother and as a result did not destroy me.

Miriam and I prayed that any change for the worse would not damage our kids and often in our family exchanges we reminded our children never to take anything for granted.

We watched as they grew.

They had childhood illnesses but nothing severe. Jill and Jeb both had nasty allergies leading to asthma. Jill has retained hers — Jeb seems to have either lost his or controlled it. Joy was never plagued by allergy problems beyond eczema on her arms.

The three of them were exceptionally well behaved. They never made embarrassing scenes in front of company, and while they shared conspiracies that shifted from Jill and Joy allied against Jeb, to Jeb and Joy against Jill, to Jeb and Jill against Joy, none of these plots exploding into battles resulted in major injuries. However, the house rang with arguments and slammed doors.

The family played word games — spelling, definitions, charades, and public speaking. As a consequence, all three of our children are extremely vocal and articulate. Jeb has the toughest, most acerbic, and blackest humor; Jill the wittiest, most perceptive and searching style. Joy has the most florid speech (she speaks like a psychologist — nothing odd about that, she is one) and she always needed and asked less from us. She also has the freest and gayest laugh.

The children used to stage original plays and sketches for show nights. Joy in the early years was socially the most aggressive and would allot roles to Jeb, Jill, and their friends who sometimes joined in the performances. I remember an evening at Lake Arrowhead, where we were vacationing, when a turning point was reached that ended Joy's reign as production chief, writer, director, and star.

A pirate sketch was outlined with Joy as the beautiful Spanish princess, Jill as a freebooter captain who was her captor, and Jeb as a villainous pirate. Joy was to be captured and held hostage for thousands

Miriam and I celebrated our fifth wedding anniversary — March, 1937. The dress belongs to her — my outfit came from Western costume.

This was Miriam's first night out after Jill's birth. I think I've whispered something sexy to her.

Jill, age three, in a characteristic writing pose, in a photo taken by Val Burton in 1939. Jill was a lefty from the time she reached for her very first swig of milk.

Miriam is finishing a picture called Easter Bonnet. Jill had put the hat together and sauntered into Miriam's studio. Miriam dropped everything and went to work.

Mother at her seventieth birthday party. The date: July 4, 1945.

*It's possible Jeb's blast in L.B.'s ear ruined my relation-
ship with the alarmed titan*

The father of the bride escorting daughter Joy on the path to the altar

At Joy's wedding, I responded to music that heralded a Kazotsky

of gold doubloons. However, she was to be rescued by a daring young sailor, played by one of the visiting friends. (All the dialogue was ad-lib.) The show broke into shreds when, as the hero stormed in, Jeb blurted out to his pirate companions, "Cheese it, the cops."

Jill immediately resigned from the company.

Joy, however, was not dismayed. Another sketch followed starring Joy as an Irish gentleman smoking a clay pipe. Jeb, appearing as a hiker, asked a simple question: "Would you tell me how to get to Killarney?"

Joy took over, after asking the hiker to sit down, and for the next ten minutes, which seemed like a weekend, Joy answered the hiker with a monologue that included the sad details of a potato famine, a cholera epidemic, and a war.

That soliloquy brought about Jeb's resignation.

We were then left with weekly vaudeville shows. We were all enlisted into the program, including guest stars such as Walter Huston, Cary Grant, John Green, Norman Panama and Mel Frank, and Don Hartman and others less well known who visited us on weekends.

We did not produce a professional performer among the three kids, but the three of them learned poise, the art of conversation, and a straightforward manner of making friends.

Some of what we perceived when they were young has blossomed into their respective careers.

Jill was a flirt when she was five years old, she adored dressing up, loved posing (she was Miriam's favorite and best model), doted on visiting, enjoyed creating adventures for herself, was an expert fibber, wrote funny and beautiful letters, and noticed everything that others did not see — a missing button on a maid's jacket sleeve, a broken nail on a lady's hand, or the first wilting leaf in a bouquet of flowers. She was a hero-worshiper with eclectic choices — Clark Gable, Adlai Stevenson, Gore Vidal, and Cary Grant.

In the sixties Jill ran into trouble. An unhappy marriage led to her fall into the drug scene, alcohol, and psychiatric problems that terrified Miriam and me. A second marriage did further damage but ultimately led her to climb out of the abyss.

She has written of those years in her startling and beautiful book *Bed/Time/Story*, which required courage and stamina to write. She emerged as a gifted and top-ranked novelist with protean gifts — she dashes off columns for magazines and newspapers, is funny and appealing on TV shows, works diligently to help alcoholics, and has perception and style.

She has earned her fame and revels in it and will fight like the devil to retain it. She drinks only ginger ale these days and will not take even an aspirin if she has pain.

Joy, before her teens, was an entertainer — she took the floor for any occasion. She bridled quickly, fought for privacy, read avidly, struck out at any injustice, imagined or real, to herself or to others. After a dinner or a birthday party, Jill would come home as neat as she left — Joy would arrive disheveled. She would have had as good a time as Jill, but while Jill would be depressed that the party was over, Joy would be delighted with the experience.

Joy gravitated to the deprived, the put-upon, the poor, the orphaned, the unhappy — she was always hosting a member of the parade of her rather uncommunicative friends, and would pass out pieces of her wardrobe or her allowance.

She became more beautiful as years went by. When her own three children were grown enough for her to shed some of the daily responsibility for them, Joy went back to college and now is a trained and successful practicing psychologist. She, unlike Jill, is slow to lose her temper, but when she decides the time has come she awes her children and husband with mighty outbursts. An hour later the family has a good laugh, Joy leading the way.

Our son, Jeb, was sickly. He suffered from asthma, more than Jill did. He was thin and unable to compete in most sports. Since he and I were the youngest in our families, I understood Jeb's remoteness, but saw it disappear as he went into his teens. He began to circulate, developed friends (mostly macho types), learned how to drive and understand cars. He has a collection of trick information and lists, which he tosses at prospective "marks": "Who were the seven actors who played the Magnificent Seven?"; "Name the Seven Dwarfs"; "Name the actors who were the Twelve Angry Men."

Jeb, no longer thin or sickly, resembles the men in Miriam's mother's family. They were big, fair, balding, and strong. Jeb is six-one — keeps telling me he's down to two hundred and twenty pounds (he hasn't been in that neighborhood for years), sports a Viking's beard, is handsome and sassy. He looks like a linebacker for the Pittsburgh Steelers.

Jeb spent some years in the theater, but after his marriage to Anna Marie, an excellent dancer, Jeb determined to avoid the slings and arrows of openings and quick closings and decided to pursue a career in advertising, for which he has appropriate credentials: a good eye, wit, charm, poise, and talent. His success in commercial advertising has taken him from New York to Detroit, then Chicago, and now Saint Louis as a producer for D'Arcy, MacManus and Masius. He has won Clio Awards for his work and is extremely well liked. We exchange confidences like two old friends, and together we laugh a lot.

Both Miriam and I are relieved and proud that our children have forged their own patterns and succeeded. They went through the big years with levelheaded awareness and when scrimping time came they got along without groaning or mumbling. We've helped them, not with great amounts of money, but with enough to tide them over their tough times. Jeb keeps telling me that he had expected that all I would leave him would be the bound copies of my movie scripts, but when he learned I had given all of them to the University of Wisconsin he said, "How about a pair of socks?"

They have had their problems — some dangerous, others petty — but I believe they've learned what I learned from my mother — to endure, to "swim over."

Jill lives in Westport with her bright and blond children Johanna and Jeremy.

Joy lives in West Los Angeles with her husband, Arthur, and their outgoing kids, David, Saul, and Keren, in a home that has a strong Jewish identity and a marvelous, noisy, argumentative, and undisciplined atmosphere that Miriam and I find first funny, then after a few days almost unendurable. Joy's husband is an attorney. He's a good husband, a devoted father, and a decent and patient man.

Jeb has a home in Saint Louis with his wife, Anna Marie, two good-looking children, Gabrielle and Zachary (our seven grandchildren just happen to be special), and three cats — Starsky, Hutch, and Tondeleyo — also cute.

From the start Miriam insisted that the grandchildren call her "Grandmother" — she would have no part of Nanny, Granny, Mimi, or any other baby nonsense. (Our children never talked baby talk, and happily none of their kids did.) So Miriam is "Mom" and "Grandmother" except to Jeb's kids, who discovered that her middle name (honest) is Sunshine. I'm "Fox" to our kids and the grandchildren call me "Grandfox." Natch.

In 1975 we gathered all the family together for a Passover Seder. We haven't been together as a group since then. But the phone bills are staggering. (Letters to and from our three are unnecessary — the grandchildren, like most kids of their generation, don't write — as a matter of fact, most can't write — I mean actually write with a pen or pencil. The typewriter has destroyed the ability to write one's name on anything except a check or a credit card and that usually is an undecipherable scrawl unless we are obliged to do as directed, PLEASE PRINT.)

So our family is united by phones. I wish we knew our grandchildren better than we do, but time and circumstance keep us too much apart. (In March, 1977, Sam Raphaelson, the playwright, was given the prestigious Laurel Award of the Writers Guild for his lifetime body of work. On the occasion he commented, "I'm pleased, surprised, and honored that you know who I am. Now my grandchildren will also know.") While Miriam and I wish our grandchildren knew us more completely we wish, in turn, we knew them better.

What I know is that Miriam and I have given our children something of us, as our mothers and fathers gave us something of their experience and wisdom.

On a recent birthday, Jill sent flowers to Miriam and on the card wrote: "Dear Mommy, Happy Birthday. I am so grateful for the wit and art and love you taught me. All my love."

Miriam rated that.

In the years beginning with my stay at Metro I wanted to be as close to the children as possible but there were many times I had to leave for trips to New York and I was aware that the change in my position would affect them. But with time and some help they adjusted very well, as they did later on when the ax descended on my job.

We had built a new and spacious studio for Miriam and she worked six to seven hours a day. My schedule was a tough one, but at least I was able to run film at home and keep close to the kids.

Despite that, my mornings would begin with calls from or to New York, and by the time I got to the studio my energies and concentration were directed at my work.

Jill once wrote that as I prepared to leave for work she was aware that as I dressed and made ready to leave I put on my studio face. As I said good-bye to the children and Miriam, she wrote, "He was already at the studio." But then, when I arrived home, "the studio face was put back in the handkerchief drawer."

To that extent, I suppose I did have to lead a double life — but I tried to keep both parts of it full and true.

*M*y *first effort* at Metro was to try and find a routine that would keep me in touch with what was going on. I knew that any routine could become a rut, so I kept altering it, but essentially I kept my hand in by scheduling conferences with the executive staff; by visits to see directors and actors on starting dates of new films, followed up by periodic visits as the picture progressed; by viewing daily and nightly runnings of the film (dailies) shot each day, followed up with memos to the director and producer (ofttimes a face-to-face conference was indicated); and always by having conferences with writer and producer on scripts in work. The latter was a must because, before I checked in, producers would speak to their unit head and then relay what they wished to their writers, and writers were generally considered to be the most expendable of all the talents at Metro. I altered that condition.

It is true that in the years I was at Metro the chief architects of the film scripts we made were the writer and the producer. It was no studied attempt to denigrate the director but rather an effort to develop a closer relationship between the writer, the producer, and the director once he was assigned. Today's directors have more authority and control, but their average of success is no greater than when they worked as members of the team rather than as the sole keepers of the flame. We had neither the time nor the funds to hand over a script to a director who might then decide to junk it and invent a new one. The director would function closely with the writer, the producer, and me. Once a decision was made regarding the thrust and the form of the picture to be on our program, we shared a common image and goal.

We had not yet entered the period of the auteur theory, which designates the director as the picture maker. What has happened in recent years is a throwback to the early days of Rex Ingram, James Cruze,

D. W. Griffith, and others, who dominated their films from choice of story through every step of creation into the final cut, dubbing, and title cards. Big features of quality were rare — the executives were not yet schooled in the art and the directors were kings of the road. As talkies flourished and the number of pictures increased, the time pressure increased, and then heads of production took over — Irving Thalberg, Darryl Zanuck, David Selznick, Pandro Berman, Hal Wallis, and William Goetz. For some ten years at RKO and MGM I had their kind of responsibility — which is not in any way to suggest I was either like them or as good as they.

L. B. Mayer had, as indicated, built his Metro empire on the importance of the producer, and while my sympathies were with the writer, because I knew his frustrations, and the director, who I knew was the field commander on the set, I had to share production chores with, quite obviously, the producers. We had a good lineup.

The front-line producers at Metro included Sam Zimbalist, a brawny, dark-skinned man who walked with his head tilted back and his feet splayed. He was seldom without a panatela. His instinct for stories plus his knowledge of motion-picture techniques, a keen sense of cutting, and a broad range of good taste were evident in the pictures he made, which included *King Solomon's Mines, Mogambo,* and *Ben Hur.* He had a good sense of humor and was a murderous gin player.

I also discovered he was an unselfish picture maker a few years later when we got into trouble with the film *Across the Wide Missouri,* which was rich in detail poured into it by William Wellman, but despite the wonderful characterizations of Clark Gable, Adolph Menjou, the Indian actor Maria Elena Marques, Alan Napier, Jack Holt, and Ricardo Montalban, individual incidents that were exciting and funny, beautiful locations (it was all shot in country in and around Jackson Hole, Wyoming), it did not hang together. There was a lack of tension. The film sagged and stumbled. We previewed in front of an audience that greeted the cast and other title cards with a welcoming roar, but halfway through the picture the customers lost interest.

Seldom does a film baffle your judgment. When it is all over and you see it, you know if all concerned have reached a uniform image and have created a motion picture of quality. Whether it is going to be a highly commercial picture is always questionable. For instance, in the case of *Intruder in the Dust,* Clarence Brown's direction, Ben Maddow's script, the decision to film in Faulkner country, all contributed to the making of a masterpiece, viewed as such by critics and the scattered audiences that went to see it. But it was a dismal financial failure.

In the case of *Across the Wide Missouri* I knew, as in the old saw that in each fat man there is a thin man waiting to get out, there was in our flagging picture a damn good movie waiting to get out. The producer, Robert Sisk, Bill Wellman, and I shared this conviction but did not hit on a solution.

I called on Sam Zimbalist for his opinion. After watching the picture with me and puffing on his panatela in his rather regal manner for an hour, he perceived what all of us involved had missed — a focal idea expressed in personal terms. His solution was to frame the story of our chief mountain man, Gable, his Indian wife, his child, and his friends in the words of his son, who, now grown and also a man of the mountains his father loved, tells the story of his father and mother. Talbot Jennings, who had written the screenplay, wrote the narration. We rearranged the adventures and episodes in a straight narrative line, and presto — the good movie popped out and became a successful one thanks to Zimbalist.

In addition to Zimbalist there was Pandro Berman, once head of RKO, who was the producer at that studio of the first Astaire and Rogers films. At MGM he had produced *Sea of Grass* and *National Velvet*, and during my term at Metro *Ivanhoe*, *Blackboard Jungle* (under some trepidation to be reported on later), *Father of the Bride*, and *Father's Little Dividend*. He was vastly unheralded but in 1976 received the Thalberg Award, which he should have gotten at least twenty years sooner. Pan in those days was a roly-poly man with a boyish face, rosy cheeks, and seemed to be always tugging up his trousers. I never determined if his pants legs were too long or his waistband too loose.

Another bright star among the producers was John Houseman, producer for us of *Lust for Life*, *Executive Suite*, *The Bad and the Beautiful*, and *Julius Caesar*. John, with his impeccable taste, a tony accent, and handsome looks and bearing, fled the producing and directing reefs and settled down into a career as an actor, winning an Academy Award first crack out of the box, in *Paper Chase*. Now John, still acting in roles as sort of a latter-day Sydney Greenstreet, has resumed some of his duties at the Juilliard School as head of the acting company.

John, despite his imperious manner, was a joy to work with. *Executive Suite*, which I had read, bought, and was going to make as one of my own pictures, came to life when it did because my work load was very heavy. When John read it and was eager to take it over we worked together on casting and we agreed on Robert Wise to direct and Ernest Lehman to write the screenplay. When the picture was finished I proposed to John that instead of a musical score we use as "music" the sounds of the city — church bells, sirens, the roar of traffic, crowd noises, horns, the squeal of tires, faraway screams of brakes. He, as an old radio producer, bought the idea and shepherded the sounds through the hands of the sometimes reluctant sound-department chief, Douglas Shearer. It all worked far better than conventional music.

Lawrence Weingarten, a former executive of one of the units Mayer had set up, was now producing and he was good at it. Larry, as a long-time fixture at MGM and accustomed to wielding authority, appeared to shy away from me during my early days as head of production. (There was a rumor floating around that Mayer and I were doomed to find ourselves on a collision course and that if I lasted a year it would be a surprise.) But Larry relaxed as he learned I was trying to make everyone aware that I was sensitive to their prior relationships but that I also intended to do exactly what I had agreed to do — run production. Larry turned out some fine films, among them *Adam's Rib, I'll Cry Tomorrow, Pat and Mike,* and shortly after I left Metro, eight and a half years later, he finished production of *Cat on a Hot Tin Roof.*

Arthur Hornblow, Jr., was another experienced and capable producer. Arthur, a handsome man, had a curious tic that jerked his neck up and a bit to one side and that gave the impression he had a permanent haughty manner. Exceptionally well educated, unique in his manner of dress (he always wore short-length jackets), and gifted with a warm and cultivated manner of speech, Arthur lived a rich and full life. He was a wine connoisseur, which led someone to comment, "Arthur won't read a script unless it's at room temperature." But he produced some stylish and successful pictures, among them *Oklahoma!, Gaslight, The Hucksters, The Asphalt Jungle,* and *Witness for the Prosecution.* If some of his films failed (and all of us have had *that* happen) it never was because of vulgarity or cheapness. Arthur's manners were always courtly and proper.

Between the trio of musical makers — Freed, Pasternak, and Cummings — and Zimbalist, Berman, Houseman, Weingarten, Hornblow, and other producers on the staff, we had a reasonable chance of increasing both the quality and the number of pictures, which had fallen off in the four years between 1944 and 1948.

My schedule was demanding but still allowed me time with my family. Because RKO had built a projection room in my home, which MGM refurbished, I did a great deal of my screening at home with Margaret Booth, who became my film editorial assistant. Margaret, a birdlike lady with the hidden authority of a jackhammer, was never hesitant about her opinions, good or bad, thereby providing me with tough-minded aid that made me think a second time on many decisions. I had become a fairly good cutter under Selznick's tutelage and my work at RKO. I became a better one having Margaret as a proving ground.

During the early weeks I was not only activating production plans but I was continuing to see actors, producers, and directors. I had meetings with Mayer two or three times a week at which I reviewed decisions I had made, but if I felt he would prefer to be consulted on some of the larger and tougher ones I would lay them on the table.

Many times I found his judgments of great value. Some of his advice gave me an understanding of why Metro had prospered in better days. When I would suggest that I was interested in buying a story property but was stalling for a lower price, he would remind me that there was no sense in saving a few or even many thousands of dollars for a good story — "in trying to save some money you lose the story and lose something valuable for the studio."

The problem that was developing with Mayer was the desire of some of the producers and directors to keep up their connection with L.B. That led, in a few instances, to awkward situations, such as productions and scripts in the early stages being discussed with Mayer and then his giving me his opinions on material I had not yet read. I would often have a different appraisal, which would lead to a sticky hour of having to dissuade L.B. from his prior notions.

One of those early incidents involved Arthur Hornblow, who showed Weingarten his first batch of pages of the script of *Quo Vadis?* Weingarten didn't like the pages John Huston, who was also slated to direct, had written. Weingarten in turn went to Mayer, who called Nick Schenck to suggest that he hold up any commitments for construction in Rome of sets for the picture. Not having heard from me Schenck called, and I had to confess I had not seen the pages — indeed, I had not known they existed.

It was mandatory I see L.B. He said he had assumed I had read the material and expressed shock that I had not seen the pages. I knew that was nonsense but I didn't press the point. I told him delicately that I believed it was better for all concerned if the producers handed the pages to me, which might save L.B. the nuisance of reading inferior material. He then gave me the twenty or so pages and agreed to tell the producers to check with me before coming to him. I, in turn, observed that such an arrangement would prevent the growth of studio politics and any attempt to play our opinions against each other.

Then I was obliged to remind Weingarten that he was no longer a unit executive and that I did not expect him to go to Mayer with his opinions on scripts — particularly on other producer's scripts. Hornblow and I settled the matter quietly; Arthur told me that he had been importuned by Weingarten, who in turn had been asked by Mayer, to find out how the *Quo Vadis?* script was shaping up.

When Hornblow left my office I reviewed the series of talks and events and decided the hell with pursuing the matter any further. Each person concerned had heard from me and I had the feeling I had laid that type of trouble to rest.

Little did I know.

What became apparent as the weeks sped into months was that Mayer was eager to demonstrate to Schenck that he was still in charge. He had given his certain assay of *Battleground* as a picture designed for failure, forcing Schenck to ask me if I was sure of the project. Not wanting to have a continuation of debate on the subject, I told Schenck that if he wished me or ordered me to take the picture off the schedule I would immediately resign. That settled the issue.

As soon as possible I lined up the cast with Benny Thau. John Hodiak, Van Johnson, Ricardo Montalban, George Murphy, and James Whitmore, whom I had seen in *Command Decision* on stage and on screen, filled the starring roles. Enlisted in other parts were Jim Arness and Marshall Thompson, and thanks to General McAuliffe, we obtained the services of a platoon of veterans from the 101st Airborne, the "Screaming Eagles," who trained our actors and played themselves in the film. Bill Wellman and Robert Pirosh were ready for action and soon we were on the way.

Battleground had success written on it from the first dailies. Wellman zinged into the filming with the joy and enthusiasm of a young man. We had pruned, polished, and timed the script, and Bob Pirosh's experiences at Bastogne had given the scenario the ring of truth.

An added feature was the casting of Denise Darcel, a beautiful, youthful French actor. (Note: I don't know why women actors are called actresses; we don't say lawyeress, or doctoress, or writeress. I believe the "ess," as in Jewess or Negress, is a pejorative term having an almost animal connotation. End of note — beginning of argument.) Denise was interviewed by Wellman and me. She came in dressed for the part — a skirt tightly fitted, a sweater that clearly indicated there was no bra beneath it. When she moved, as Bill asked her to, everything jiggled — she was a movable feast.

There were no delays in the shooting — Bill came in twenty days under schedule and about a hundred thousand under budget — but what was important, he came in with a powerful, well-paced picture full of action and humor.

It made my first two years easier — much easier than if it had failed.

During 1948 I took on various chairmanships of charitable causes. These assignments were shifted from one studio head to another on the rather substantial theory that as boss of a studio you had clout — first, by the size of your own donation; second, by the fact that employees assumed if they didn't give they might be dubbed cheapskates or un-American, or, Heaven forbid, might get fired.

Among other responsibilities I headed a campaign for accelerating the sale of U.S. treasury bonds and held the chairmanships of the Motion Picture Permanent Charities Committee, the United Jewish Welfare Fund, and the University of Judaism. Also I found myself accepting awards, which were given with a measure of sincerity and a brimming beaker of hustle since a position as head of production makes one a hell of a shill.

There were also the previews and the openings. We had three for *Battleground* — in New York, Washington, and Hollywood.

Washington's was the fanciest. An honor guard, generals up to here, politicians and society. My favorite memory of the Washington splurge was a moment in the receiving line. Denise Darcel was present — all of her — in a strapless gown that made no great effort to conceal her very ample bust. I was standing next to her and next to me was a three-star general whose name I cannot remember. As guests walked by the general would introduce me and I in turn would introduce Miss Darcel.

I could not help noticing that the general was taking long glances in the direction of Denise's bosom each time she turned to acknowledge an introduction. I understood why. Each time she turned there was a fleeting but clear glimpse of her rather deep and generous cleavage.

During a lull in the introductions Denise excused herself for a few moments and the general, with a soft sigh as he watched Denise walk away, said in a warm Southern accent, "Mr. Schary, if we had had breastworks like that at Richmond, we never would have lost the Civil War."

While in Washington I had the pleasure of visiting President Truman, who was planning his vacation in Key West, Florida, and asked if I could arrange for him to see *Battleground* during his stay. I could, would, and did. He asked what other pictures we were making. I told him about our plans to make *The Outsiders*, dealing with a group of post–Civil War guerrillas. Truman was an excellent historian and went on at great length about the causes of that bloody war. He had an extraordinary memory for dates, names, and places, plus a catalogue of quotes from speeches delivered in the Senate during the great debates in the 1850s. "That's when the war began — in the Senate. After those decisions, war was inevitable — it just took a few years for the South to get enough arms to fire the first shot at Fort Sumter."

When I had returned to the studio on a happy note of triumph, film was flowing in from Rome, where *Quo Vadis?* was in production at Cinecittà studios. The schedule and cost of *Quo Vadis?* were ambitious. I've never been partial to big, heavy spectacles and have no real feel for them — they seem lumpy. During the early days of the shooting I noticed a number of "lumps." I wrote Eddie Mannix (who had gone to Rome to act as executive and help Sam Zimbalist to guide Mervyn Le Roy, who was the director) my observations about the static quality of the first days' shooting. Le Roy was overshooting and making too many setups. The film lacked mobility. We needed innovation in camera angles. Some of my suggestions were used, but the picture really came to life when Peter Ustinov came into the cast as Nero. As the shooting progressed I sensed that the film would be successful but that it would not be memorable. Years later I had a totally different appraisal of *Ben Hur* when we began to script it and do preproduction building in Italy.

Mayer was not displeased as the grosses began to come in and we were turning a good percentage of profit, but he was still unsure of my political position.

One day, after we had gone over some production reports, he referred to a memo I had written him regarding an editorial he had sent me by a writer named Rogge, who had deplored the entrapment of liberals into the Communist party. I had written Mayer that it was an interesting editorial, and had reminded him that to me the more pertinent paragraphs in Rogge's piece dealt with those 150-percent Americans such as those who condemned Helen Douglas and everyone who voted for her as being Communists.

I pointed out that in 1940 the America First party line — which stated that FDR was a warmonger, Hitler was not a monster, aid to England was not an American imperative — was exactly the Communist party line during the days of the German-Russian pact. Did that make the spokesmen for America First, Robert Taft, Charles Lindbergh, and Joe Kennedy, Communists?

Mr. Mayer dodged that by telling me that he had spoken to Westbrook Pegler, who viewed me as a spokesman for the Communist party line — if not actually a member of the party. "I told him," Mayer said, " 'You know me, Westbrook, to be a good American. Do you think I'd have a Communist work for me?' Westbrook, of course, said no. So I don't think he'll pick on you anymore."

I counted up to five very slowly before answering, "Well, L.B., thanks. But you know, people get strange ideas. About a month ago someone I know asked me, 'Dore, how is it you, a liberal, can work for a fascist?' I put him in his place by defending you and telling him, 'You know damn well I'd never work for a fascist.' "

The chances were, I thought, Mayer's attention span had snapped as I began my retort, because he didn't respond in any way to what I had said. But as I got up to leave I saw a glint in his eyes that told me he had heard the point and didn't like it.

Before I had arrived at the studio Schenck and Mayer had disbanded the unit system, which I had told them I would not use, and Sam Katz, Al Lichtman, and James McGuinness had resigned.

The dismemberment of the units placed more work on my calendar but it simplified getting things done. Decisions on stories formerly made by committee could now be made by me, or if I felt one was ticklish and might ruffle L.B.'s feathers, I'd take it up with him. Such a one was *The Red Badge of Courage.*

Gottfried Reinhardt, a son of Max Reinhardt, came to me with the notion of doing *Red Badge.* With him was John Huston, who wanted to direct and write the screenplay. John had one other idea . . . to star, as the coward who finally finds his courage, America's greatest World War II hero, Audie Murphy. I wasn't sure about the casting, but I knew and loved the book and I called Kenneth MacKenna, head of our story department, to clear any and all rights for the story.

Gottfried and John were delighted.

When I told Mayer about it he voiced some slight reservations but no serious objections.

The weekend after my talk with L.B. I played in a softball game — MGM versus Twentieth-Fox. At the time we had the highest-paid team in baseball — Gene Kelly, Stanley Donen, Mervyn Le Roy, Sam Zimbalist, and a group of other writers and directors none of whom got less than one hundred thousand a year. I think the boys let me play the first time because my salary raised the average. The second time was because I had gotten three hits in the first game, including the winning one. Anxious to keep my streak going I put on a pair of spike shoes, which Gene Kelly

The lion is real. I forced a smile and retreated.

The MGM baseball team "the Wolves." Among those present — kneeling: Henry Berman, Buster Keaton (with beard), George Wells, Gene Kelly, Bill Wright, Stanley Donen; standing: Sam Zimbalist, Pan Berman, Mervyn Le Roy, Roy Rowland, Richard Brooks, me, Gerald Mayer.

Monte Stratton, Jimmy Stewart, and Jane Wyman at the Photoplay *award dinner when Jimmy and* The Stratton Story *copped the gold medallions. The resemblance between Stratton and Stewart was so striking they could have been brothers.*

Veterans of Battleground, *Van Johnson and John Hodiak are saddened by casualties as reported by a weary medic*

George Burns rehearsed Lou Calhern and me in an act for the Studio Club at MGM. George kicked us if we forgot a move or sang a clinker.

cautioned me not to wear. He didn't expressly say it but intimated that at the age of forty-four, when I hadn't worn spikes for twenty-two years since my days as a camp counselor, it was a dangerous exercise. I waved his advice to one side. In the first inning we got the Twentieth team out, one, two, three. In our half two of our men got on base — the third and fourth were easy outs, and I batted fifth. George Seaton, an old and dear friend (we both arrived in Hollywood in 1932), was pitching and fed me an easy floater, chest high. I laid into it and it sailed far out — a cinch triple, but as I took off, my right foot turned. I fought off the pain that tore into my leg and I tried to run, further aggravating the hurt. When I reached first after stumbling, the two runs had scored — but while I was safe on first (barely) I was in agony and fell to the ground.

By the time I got home and received medical attention I realized that my budding career as an aged ball player was over. I had torn a thigh muscle, a calf muscle, twisted an ankle, pulled my back into spasm, and almost surely aggravated a pinched disk (later proved to be herniated). So I was put into a hospital bed brought into our home and placed into traction and told I'd be out of action for four weeks. *Then, perhaps*, I'd be able to be wheeled into the studio.

Miriam, my dear wife, had suggested before I went to the game that I should have my head examined. Lying in bed, I admitted she'd been right. But seeing no other signs of mental collapse, I kept on working.

A few days later Gottfried and John called and asked if they could see me. When they arrived they broke the news that Mayer had sent for them and convinced them not to do *Red Badge*, telling them that he had spoken to Mr. Schenck, who was also opposed to the enterprise. I told them they were cowards and that I intended to make the picture with or without them. That decision perked up their droopy spirits, recharged their batteries, and they left. I dictated a polite but firm memo to L.B. telling him why I wanted to go ahead with *Red Badge;* included were these paragraphs:

I cannot guarantee that *The Red Badge of Courage* will be a highly successful picture, or even a very good picture. I can only tell you that in my conscience I believe that it has a chance of becoming a highly important motion picture that will bring honor to the studio, plus every reasonable chance of ultimately making money. This is not a seasonal picture. If this picture is all I believe it can be, it is possible that it will be a classic picture — a perennial that will have a long life. In the hands of as brilliant a talent as Huston's, all these things are possible.

You know that I have not been indifferent to many of your warnings in the past, and quite recently in the case of *Europa* my second thoughts coincided with your own alarms. In this case I really have weighed carefully your own reservations, plus the fact that I know others in the studio dislike this project; but you told me that ultimately the decision to make this picture would have to be mine, and I have been thinking about it in exactly those terms, based on my own confidence and my own evaluation of the risks involved. I have Joe Cohn's latest figures in the matter, and I have John's assurances that he can do what is proposed to be done in terms of cost.

So, taking a very deep breath and hoping for the best, I would like to go ahead and get the picture started.

I got the following note from John Huston the next day.

June 9th

Dear Dore:

I felt like a complete shit yesterday busting in on you, but as things turned out I believe it was worth it. L.B. had Gottfried and me in to see him today and as a result of your letter, which he allowed me to read, he has withdrawn all pressures against the making of the film. More, if I am any judge, he is really rooting for us now. The honesty and courage of your letter hit him right where it should, and I feel that he is with us even if it doesn't turn out all that we hope it will be. I told L.B. that I was going to do everything in my power to prove him wrong, and he told me that he hoped I would succeed, and I tell you again, honey, I'm going to break my ass.

As ever,

Mayer called and said that he and Schenck were withdrawing their objections.

So that battle was won but my back and leg were flaming with pain.

However, I was alert enough to know that my memo to Mayer was not eloquent enough to have changed his mind. *Battleground* had been in wide release and was a smashing success. We had received excellent reviews and were on the way to bringing in a big profit to the company. The success had given me a credit card — a due bill — and in effect I had called on Mayer and Schenck to trust my judgment on *Red Badge* as they had on *Battleground*. I didn't mention the latter in my memo but the implication was there.

It would be dull to review each and every film that slipped through the studio during the time I was at Metro. (The entire list is in the back of this chronicle.) What may be of some interest is a record of those films that had a special significance during my stewardship at Metro.

The production schedule outlined for my first year, 1948–1949, included twenty-five films, thirteen of which had been completed or were in their last stages of production. Of those thirteen, *The Three Musketeers* with Gene Kelly, Lana Turner, and Van Heflin, a script by Bob Ardrey and a production by Pan Berman, was a rousing hit. The only other one of top quality was *Command Decision*, scripted by the original play's author, William Wister Haines, and directed by Sam Wood.

The twelve that came under my aegis, even though I contributed little except some degree of decision during their completion, contained the remake of *Little Women*, *Take Me Out to the Ball Game*, *The Barkleys of Broadway*, *The Stratton Story*, and *Madame Bovary*. The most encouraging fact was that eight of the twelve were profit making.

Hedda Hopper had greeted my appointment to MGM with the cheerful tidings that "now that Schary is going to Metro the studio will be known as Metro-Goldwyn-Moscow."

That seemed a bit more than a critical opinion so my lawyer had notified Mayer that he intended to advise Norman Chandler, then head of the Los Angeles *Times*, that we were going to sue Mrs. Hopper and the L.A. *Times* and its news associates for five million dollars. That information had brought Chandler, whom I liked, to Mayer's office for a conference. We learned that the item had been killed by Mr. Chandler after the first run and had not appeared in any of Mrs. Hopper's syndicated paper outlets. We were promised abject apologies by Mrs. Hopper and we dropped the threat of the suit.

This "Say 'boo' to you — 'pooh-pooh' to you" was a prelude to the praise Lady Hopper heaped upon me and my doings at Metro to an extent that at one of my sessions with L.B. he casually observed that too much publicity was of no value, in fact it might backfire. He said, "I don't give interviews — I don't want my name in the papers — Thalberg hated publicity — believe me, it would be better if you never put your name on anything."

Since he was in such a warm, confidential mood I could not resist saying, "L.B., I'll make a deal with you. Change the name of the studio to Metro-Goldwyn-Mayer-Schary and I'll never put my name anywhere else."

His answer? "Be serious. Take my advice."

He then repeated his avuncular statements about his modesty.

Most of the men of power I've known have been given to speak with immodesty of their modesty. What they really imply is that the publicity they *do* receive (and in most cases pursue) is due them. Harry Cohn used to speak of "publicity hounds"; Skouras was always criticizing Zanuck for "seeking" publicity while meanwhile Skouras was pumping away about his own activities. Joe Levine, an entrepreneur rather than a creative producer, is candid. He has items almost every day reporting on his travels, jokes, activities, acquisitions, and charities.

The fact is we are in an era of accentuated self-aggrandizement. Rock stars are covered in greater detail than Nobel Prize winners. Oscars, Emmys, Tonys, Obies, Grammys, Golden Globes are solicited by trade ads and ploys in favored columns. Bad taste in pursuit of glory awards is not only permissible, it is encouraged. Then the winners weep and thank everyone, beginning with their sister Kate and ending with the Almighty.

Ego-satisfaction is a necessity for each of us. The truck driver enjoys his reputation as a "heavy foot" who beats the schedule. Poor Tiny Tim may go on for years despite his rather ordinary voice and simple playing of a ukulele. (The "Tonight Show" gave him his share of celebrity.)

Flagpole sitters, goldfish swallowers, party crashers, Evel Knievel, center-fold beauties in girlie magazines, Warren Beatty's womanizing, panty raids . . . all the past and present absurdities often receive as much TV and newspaper coverage as an important scientific discovery. Celebrity is a big business. Fame is a custom-made reputation that wears better and longer.

In these times each of us who seeks ego-satisfaction can find it. A panting world seems to be waiting for us to be heard, or seen, or read about in all media. Celebrity and notoriety can often be confused but perhaps even Sirhan Sirhan satisfied his ego.

It is probable that J. D. Salinger, the literary recluse, draws his ego-fulfillment not only from his work but from the fact that his reclusion is so fully reported.

However, as I was saying before the above tangential comments, my first year set me up rather well. A studio loss had been turned into a profit and the production plans augured well for the future.

I had hoped to get forty films completed in my first year but missed by two. Of the thirty-eight, *Intruder in the Dust, On the Town, Battleground, Asphalt Jungle, Father of the Bride, King Solomon's Mines, Three Little Words, Annie Get Your Gun, Ambush, Border Incident,* and *Crisis* are worth remembering.

Crisis was a failure despite mixed notices and a cast starring Cary

Grant, José Ferrer, Signe Hasso and Gilbert Roland — all of whom were excellent.

When *Crisis* did not do big business in its opening engagements, the sales department labeled it stinko and argued that Cary Grant never would be accepted in dramatic roles. Coming to that conclusion they embarked on an advertising program, which completed the disaster, with a slogan, "See Carefree Cary in the Tropics." This come-on was tacked on to a sketch of a palm tree, a moon, and the silhouette of a native girl.

In those days the studio advertising department was a domain ruled by Howard Dietz in New York and by the sales department, also quartered in Manhattan, and headed by Joe Vogel and William Rodgers, who governed distribution.

Dietz was a clever man, sophisticated and sharp-witted, who was a marvel at selling a good movie for which he had enthusiasm and respect. But if he, Vogel, and Rodgers saw the first signs of resistance from exhibitors, they would give up the struggle and allow the film to slide into oblivion.

This division of responsibility was not unique to MGM. Each of the major studios was divided into two camps. There was a command post in New York that, in effect, became the strategic and tactical arms determining where the forces would be deployed. The California troops were considered to be behind the lines. We trained and formed the units (the films), and then sent them to New York for assignment. It never was a great trick to win with an obvious blockbuster. Only in unusual cases did a picture of high quality — ostensibly noncommercial — find sales and distribution willing to fight for an audience that some of us sensed was available if only it was sought out.

The New York offices were separated from the studio by three thousand miles and by a conviction that the picture makers were not as shrewd or as urbane or as businesslike as the New York executives. The Gothamites visited the West Coast for the viewing of rough assemblies of pictures in studio projection rooms or went to previews in neighboring towns in California. Unless the picture suited them in every detail and satisfied their individual tastes, our visitors would drag out arcane theories why the films would not work. Joe Vogel once went with us to a rousing, joyous preview of *Adam's Rib* and opined it was too smart for audiences outside of New York. The fact that we had previewed it in Santa Barbara did not alter his judgment.

The warlike relationship between Mayer and Schenck helped cement the hostility between N.Y. and L.A. and accounted for the continuing jaundiced and often hasty decisions made by the New Yorkers when they came west.

A case in point is *Lili*, a film we made some years later. We had trouble during the making of the picture. Mel Ferrer, ambitious to become a director, quarreled with Chuck Walters, who was directing. Helen Deutsch, the writer, found herself involved in the imbroglio and, not being a totally calm woman, she added to the rumpus. The producer, Edwin Knopf, his hands full with the fracas, came to me quite often and after a few visits to the set we were able to calm the troubled waters. Despite the turmoil going on Leslie Caron was giving a beautiful and touching performance and the theme song, composed by Bronislaw Kaper with lyrics by Miss Deutsch, was quite clearly a haunting and lovely asset.

Because of the bulletins that somehow reached New York, which indicated we were in a bind and behind schedule, the factotums came out for a look at the unfinished work. While I had resisted their intrusion, the question was whether or not they would place the picture into a release spot and date.

Before running the film I explained its unfinished state — no music track, color imbalance, sound not corrected, the picture still interspersed with blank film reading "Dissolve" — in short, those obvious shortcomings that we knew would probably affect their judgments. They said they understood. We ran the picture. At the conclusion there was a silence. Not a pregnant one. Just plain, rotten, quiet, chilly silence. Then Dietz said, "It's kinda cute." Rodgers said, "It's not ready." Vogel said, "An art-house picture."

They told me they could not set a release date.

"We'll look at it again when it's finished," Dietz said.

The group dispersed. Knopf was almost in tears. Helen Deutsch unleashed a string of salty curses. I began to look for a way out of the corner. Providence provided one.

Harry Brandt, owner of Brandt Theatres and a warm friend, was in California scouting around for pictures for his Trans-Lux Theatre in New York. He had seen a couple of our films but had not reached any deals with the New York group, who were reserving their choice product for the Capitol Theatre, the flagship theater of Loew's, Inc.

When Harry called me to say so-long I played a long shot and asked him to come over and see the unfinished *Lili*. He came, he saw, he loved it. He recognized the qualities we were sure the picture had. He gave me a happy hug and ran for the car that was waiting to take him to the airport.

In New York, Harry, aware that the mavens at Metro had put thumbs down at *Lili*, made a deal. He'd "take a chance" and play it at the Trans-Lux provided he would have an exclusive. No one else could play it until he was through with his run — no matter how long it would be. Agreed.

When *Lili* was cut, scored, dubbed, printed, we shipped it to New York. It opened at the Trans-Lux to rave reviews and excellent box-office returns. It settled into a run. Harry guessed it would run for a year. MGM finally paid a tidy sum to get Harry to allow them to run the film in Europe, then bring it into the States but not New York until Harry finished the run. The picture was an enormous success in Europe, grossing as much as if not more than it did in America.

The incident helped make Dietz, Rodgers, and Vogel a bit more cautious in their prophecies . . . for a short period of time. No one ever really changes. They try to or make believe they do, but under pressure the wax melts.

However, the *Lili* incident was still in the future.

Of the films that attracted attention during the 1949–1950 year, *Intruder in the Dust*, a screenplay by Ben Maddow adapted from William Faulkner's novel and produced and directed by Clarence Brown, remains a classic film in which Juano Hernandez gives a brilliant performance of a Negro gentleman with casual pride and easy courage. Clarence Brown, a Southerner, had approached Mayer to buy the book a short time before my arrival at the studio. When I checked in, Brown buttonholed me and I was able to persuade Mayer despite his reservations to go along with Brown's enthusiasm. We bought the book and Brown began preparing the script.

After our first preview, which was an excellent one (though some bigots wrote conventional racial slurs on the preview cards), Mayer complained that the Hernandez character was "too uppity. He ought to take off his hat when he talks to a white man — and he didn't even say thank you to the lawyer." L.B. predicted the film would be a dismal flop at the box office. I predicted it would be viewed in years to come as one of our best. We were both proven right.

Asphalt Jungle, directed by John Huston and written by Ben Maddow and Huston, was an enormous success but I was guilty of an egregious error. Despite Marilyn Monroe's small and yet startling role I did not recognize her star potential, particularly since we seemed to have a plethora of glamorous women stars. Darryl Zanuck signed Miss Monroe, she became an extraordinary figure in movie history, and for years I blushed with embarrassment each time her name was mentioned. I became the "Mr. Glogauer" figure from *Once in a Lifetime* who turned down the "Vitaphone."

The year's work contained a sad ending to Judy Garland's career at MGM. She had been ailing from the use of too many drugs and too much liquor. We had started *Annie Get Your Gun* starring Judy, with Howard Keel as her co-star. The first days of shooting were fragmented by Judy's late arrival on the set, then her complete absences, during which days we shot scenes with supporting players. Finally we viewed all of the film we had exposed and came to the reluctant conclusion that Judy neither looked nor sounded like her best self and that if we continued the picture with her we would wind up with an unreasonably expensive and ineffective movie. We replaced Judy with Betty Hutton, who gave one of her most outstanding performances and presented us with a highly profitable film.

Moving Judy out of *Annie* set up a controversy that we tried to ignore. We had gone through a previous episode during the making of *The Barkleys of Broadway* when Judy had been replaced by Ginger Rogers.

The studio financed a course of medical treatment for Judy in Boston. During the time she was there we completed *Annie*. Gene Kelly, having triumphed in *On the Town*, which he had directed with Stanley Donen, was ready for work, and Joe Pasternak had the script of a lightweight summer picture appropriately titled *Summer Stock*.

Judy had had months of treatment and we were told that she was ready to return to work and eager to do so. Since the medical judgment came from an outstanding physician, Judy was cast in *Summer Stock*.

During the preparatory steps of rehearsing, costuming, and recording and the early days of shooting, Judy appeared to be fulfilling her responsibilities. Despite some delay the picture was moving along even though Gene Kelly was finding it difficult to work with Judy. He explained that she was projecting a terrible odor whenever they had to play scenes face-to-face. The only clue, he told me, was that her breath smelled like formaldehyde. That sounded ridiculous. I checked out the symptoms with a doctor I respected, who told me it probably was paraldehyde, a drug used to bring drunkards out of their deep comas or delirium tremens. That appeared so farfetched I sent for Judy on the pretext of having a casual conversation about her state of well-being. We sat together on a couch in my office and I got Kelly's message — strong and overpowering.

Later that day I advised Gene of what I had learned. Trouper and loyal friend to Judy that Gene is and was, he kept the faith, working through the delays that became more frequent. Judy began to cancel appointments, became pettish, and we faced the possibility that we would not be able to finish the picture.

We called in the medical adviser who had been treating her in Boston. He advised a short break to refresh Judy. We did as he suggested. When Judy returned there was little left to do — except for a magnificent solo number for Judy, sung by her and danced by a group of male dancers. The number, "Get Happy," showed Judy in prime style. It was Judy in a time warp as good as she ever was — if not better.

When *Summer Stock* was in the cutting stages we were advised by the doctors in Boston that the wise prescription for Judy was to give her a long period of inactivity and a medical regimen to help her achieve a complete recovery from her catalogue of ills. We talked to her, offered her a full year off on salary and full payment of her medical bills.

Judy resisted the offer, dismissed the Boston advisers, and told us she was feeling fine and was ready for work anytime we had a script for her.

A short time later June Allyson, who was to appear in *Royal Wedding,* informed us she was pregnant. We spoke to Judy and asked if she was up to working again. She assured us she was in good condition and she looked it. She loved the script of *Royal Wedding* and we put the picture into the early-preparation routine.

Within a few days the cancellations began. Costume fittings, rehearsals for dancing and singing dropped like flies. We sent Judy a warning letter after she failed to respond to oral pleas. Costs were going up and when it became obvious that Judy was on a complete detour we stopped production and recast her part with Jane Powell.

Judy was finished at Metro.

I had first heard her at the Paramount Theatre in Los Angeles in 1936 singing "Stormy Weather." I remember that small girl singing in a voice that rocked the audience. In the early forties when Judy was twenty-one Joe Mankiewicz, Danny Kaye, June Havoc, Van Johnson, Keenan Wynn, and I prepared a surprise record for her. She was happy — blossoming into her magnificent years. Tragedy was a long way off.

It is ridiculous to believe that the studio ruined her — it didn't ruin other young stars such as Elizabeth Taylor, June Allyson, Jane Powell, Debbie Reynolds, Ava Gardner. L.B. adored Garland and it is nonsensical to think he would have recommended drugs or forced her to work. Heavens and hells on earth are personal accomplishments or punishments. The tides in Judy's life were not calm ones but others have swum over rougher waves — Judy was not a strong swimmer and she couldn't make it to the shore. She was Mrs. Norman Main in *A Star Is Born* who, in this scenario, like her husband, braved the sea to find peace.

Harold Arlen's music and E. Y. Harburg's lyrics for "Over the Rainbow" remain her epitaph.

Father of the Bride was first offered to Jack Benny, who had reservations about playing what he believed was too straight a part. Fredric March was eager to do the picture, but before setting it for March we offered the book to Spencer Tracy. What followed was a demonstration of two similar syndromes, one of which belonged to the gifted team of playwrights and screenwriters Frances Goodrich and Albert Hackett, the other to Tracy.

With Hackett and Goodrich the symptoms began with the team telling me they thought the book was "darling" but "we don't know what to do with it." I dosed them with my confidence that they could do anything, that the book was an easy one to adapt and they were an obvious choice to write it — "Please — for me." They agreed.

Two weeks later Albert and Frances reported they had no idea how to write the screenplay and to prove it they came in with a few pages to illustrate their inadequacy. The pages were good, we discussed the progression of the story, and after an hour they left, still in doubt, but — "We'll see if we can put it together." A few days later they called, excited and happy. "We've got it. It's going to be wonderful." Of course, they did have it and it was wonderful. The Hackett-Goodrich syndrome appeared each time they went to a new screenplay. All I needed for a cure was patience and a variety of soothing reassurances.

With Tracy the routine had a different mood but the same anxieties. First there would be reservations about the original material, followed by a crushing refusal; then a quiet talk with suggestions of how it could be fashioned to suit Spence. This heart-to-heart would be followed by a wave of enthusiasm, later dispelled when the first script was born. With doubts returned, another conference had to be called, suggestions of how to change and improve the script would be on the agenda, and finally we would have Tracy's approval. Sometimes Tracy would withhold his final and full ardor until the first day of shooting. However, once filming started, Tracy was a disciplined and cooperative performer in addition to being a brilliant actor.

With *Father of the Bride* both syndromes worked in their inexorable patterns. We finished up with a good movie that led in time to an equally successful sequel, *Father's Little Dividend*, with the same cast, writers, producer (Pan Berman), and director (Vincente Minnelli), along with the reappearance of the Hackett, Goodrich, and Tracy disquietudes. Amen.

While Sam Zimbalist's production of Rider Haggard's *She*, adapted by Helen Deutsch under the title *King Solomon's Mines*, was a rewarding film that brought us good reviews and much profit, my favorite recollection has to do with a semicrisis brought about by a few jackasses and two labor unions. These circumstances brought on the face-off: when the film was being edited after the return of the entire company's safari to Africa, we were aware that tension was missing in the sequence of the flight of the animals from the oncoming danger of a fast-moving grass fire. Our second unit had placed baggage and dummy figures in the distance over which the frightened herds leaped on their way to safety. What we lacked were close shots of our principal actors, who were not placed in jeopardy since we chose not to be guilty of manslaughter.

The answer to our problem of getting the close angles we needed appeared to be simple for the magicians on the back lot. They erected a huge screen painted with a startling reproduction of the African veld to match our camera shots. To reproduce the baggage and equipment of the safari party was a cinch. Our stars and doubles for the African bearers were no problem. But what about the zebras delegated to jump over the principals and their supplies? Easy. Get trained zebras. There weren't any. Easy. Then get trained jackasses and paint them with white and black stripes.

I assumed the matter was settled. Not at all. The painters refused to paint the beasts, arguing that the chore was for makeup men. Those worthies in turn said no. They did not make up asses. Such a job was for painters. When Zimbalist faced me with the dead-end situation, I reminded him that producers could do anything without infringing on union jurisdictions. "Sam," I said, "if I can't work out a solution, you go paint the jackasses." Sam said he'd paint elephants but not jackasses: "They're not kosher."

I called the two shop stewards of the unions involved and pointed out that unless they came to some sensible compromise I'd write a publicity release that would make both unions look like jackasses. I suggested we share friendly drinks while discussing the alternate compromises.

After an hour of talk, a couple of drinks, some laughter and dirty animal jokes, a meeting of minds was reached. The painters would do the painting but for the particular job they wanted to get makeup men's pay. The last laugh came when the painters learned they regularly got more than the makeup men.

Two days later we finished the sequence. When Charlie Lederer heard the entire yarn he said, "Ah, solved by a bunch of Jacks-in-the-bosk."

When Sam told Charlie his joke was feeble, Charlie, not one to be slighted, ran an ad one day after Christmas offering a dollar for each used Christmas tree to be delivered to an address (Sam Zimbalist's) anytime during the week after Christmas, preferably during the hours of 8:00 to 12:00 A.M.

The Beverly Hills police had to be called to shoo away the station wagons loaded with trees. Screams, yells, and curses filled the quiet streets of Beverly including those of Sam, who swore he would murder the person who pulled "that awful joke on me." Sam never found out. Both he and Charlie are dead.

In addition to the films in production I had to be involved to some degree in the preparation of at least forty scripts for the future. Not all of those made it to the sound stages but we were cutting down waste and reducing production costs by tighter script control and the elimination of contract people who were not being used effectively.

Also occupying my time was the disturbing business of clearances of men and women who were listed in infamous journals such as *Red Channels* and Jack Tenney's report of the California Un-American Activities Committee, which listed practically everyone in Hollywood. I suspected that Tenney might ask that the red stripes be removed from the American flag. Y. Frank Freeman, still retaining his post as president of the Hollywood branch of the Motion Picture Producers Association, was determined to institute a loyalty oath for all employees. Such an "oath" for state employees in California had been rejected by Governor Earl Warren. His action angered L. B. Mayer, Harry Cohn, Harry Warner, and Freeman (all of whom had always supported Warren), and they asked him to meet with the top studio executives to discuss the rise of communism in California. The meeting, which all studio heads attended, was held in Perino's, perhaps the classiest bistro in Los Angeles at that time.

Mayer, as former Republican California state committeeman, led the charge. Among other observations, he said that he did not want his children to be subjected to teachers who would "poison their minds." This seemed to be a peculiarly silly concern since his two daughters were married with children of their own.

Harry Warner, in his normal hysterical fashion, fulminated against the Red menace. Frank Freeman, in his Southern drawl, finished up the bill of indictment against Warren's decision to oppose the oath. Implicit in Freeman's talk was the possibility that Warren would not have the support of this august group if he didn't shape up.

Warren then took the floor. He spoke strongly. His pale complexion was highlighted by the red circle of anger on each of his cheeks. He tore the arguments presented to him into shreds. First he concentrated on Freeman's implication of possible nonsupport in the future. He said he could do without their votes or their financial allegiance. Then he turned on Mayer, pointing out that if Mayer's "children" were susceptible to being brainwashed by teachers, it was the fault of their upbringing at home. He said, "I have four daughters and if a teacher tried to convert them to communism, I feel certain they would succeed in converting him to democracy."

Warren fired a salvo at Warner, pointing out that the first people to sign a loyalty oath would be Communists, and ended by telling the group that they had reason to be ashamed for trying to pressure him on behalf of such a stupid cause and for embarrassing themselves.

He sat down to finish his coffee.

Bill Goetz, who was then head of production at Universal, Darryl Zanuck, and I applauded. Warren, rather startled, looked in our direction and smiled. Then he drained his cup, stood up, said good night, and walked out, giving our end of the table a farewell wave and grin.

Mayer and the others chatted among themselves for a minute or two. They didn't appear nonplussed or angry.

I had the feeling that they viewed Warren and us three — Goetz, Zanuck, and me — as unfortunate dimwits.

I expected that when next I saw Mayer he would refer to the Warren dinner. He never mentioned it. But he had called Bill Goetz and told him that his actions along with mine were inexcusable and that we both didn't understand what was going on in the world.

Determined to prove the advisability of combining low-budget pictures with expensive vehicles, I was attracted to a magazine story, "The Next Voice You Hear." Having prepared an outline for it, I turned the writing of the script over to Charles Schnee.

When Bill Wellman read the story and listened to what we had in mind he promptly agreed to direct, promising he'd make it below the proposed schedule of twenty-two days and a budget of $650,000. He delivered it in fourteen days for the startling price of $430,000.

The film received mixed notices but earned its keep. But since the staff of top producers was underwhelmed by the experiment, I assigned the smaller-budget pictures to new or less prominent producers, who brought in some respectable results.

When *Next Voice* was completed I visited New York to attend a sales conference and present a projection of fifty-five films to be made during the next sixteen months. As I was finishing my outline for a bigger and better MGM year, the injury to my back I had suffered some months before began to act up. As I continued to enumerate our scheduled pictures I could feel my muscles going into spasm. When I concluded my sales pitch I could not move my legs. I gripped the podium as if I were urging the salesmen to prolong their applause. Howard Dietz, who was chairing the conference, came toward me and in an aside whispered, "What are you waiting for — a bouquet of flowers?" When I told him I could not move, Howard suggested that the salesmen take a ten-minute break to enjoy the good news they had just heard. I raised a hand and waved the men farewell as Howard, aided by Si Seadler and others, lifted me and moved me behind the drape on the platform. Then I sat down. After a few minutes I said I wanted to go back to the hotel. Nick Schenck and Charles Moskowitz, the treasurer of Loew's, helped me to Schenck's car and took me to an orthopedist who had been told I was on my way to see him. He told me what I already knew, "You've got a severe spasm. I'll order a hospital bed sent to the hotel — stay there till I see you tomorrow — then we'll decide when you can go home."

By the time I got to the hotel and, helped by Miriam, managed to get into my pajamas, the hospital bed had arrived and with it a nurse to care for me. I accepted the bed but rejected the nurse until I discovered she used lovely perfume and had gentle hands. I was given some pills that eased the pain and put me to sleep.

Motion-picture trade papers, which tend to exaggerate what they consider bad news (and good news), reported my confinement. However, they also played up the pitch to the sales conference, and that was heartening news to the Metro employees. On the day following the appearance of these items I received a call from Howard Hughes.

He had read of my discomfort, wanted to know if I'd like to get back home, and volunteered to get me flown there. I told him I would have to ask the doctor if I could leave and added that I didn't fancy being part of a spectacle by being carried into a plane and becoming a sorry sight for other passengers. Hughes cut in with, "No, no — I'll send an empty plane with just a crew, a steward, a nurse, and I'll have a hospital bed riveted to the floor. I'll make all the arrangements — I'd like to do it for you. We'll land on my airfield and an ambulance will take you and Mrs. Schary to your home."

The offer flabbergasted me. I thanked him very much, told him I'd let him know, and hung up wondering if I were on the receiving end of a practical joke.

When the doctor told me I could not travel for a few days and that he'd rather I go home by train (that pleased me — I did not get over my fear of planes until the late fifties), I called Hughes, thanked him profusely, and explained I could not accept his generous offer. Miriam was disappointed. Even then, she liked the idea of flying — and flying under the dramatic circumstances offered by Hughes was something she had wanted to enjoy.

About a week later we went home via the 20th Century and the Super Chief. The men in the MGM production shop, having a knowledge of how uncomfortable a hospital bed can be, particularly if you're six foot one, had a surprise for me. When they had heard that I'd have to be in traction for a few weeks they had taken my large wooden bed and revamped it into a bed with machinery, switches, and buttons that could raise my head and body to any degree I wished and do the same thing with my legs. If one needed traction, this was the way to go. An added dividend was the fact that our children loved riding up and down. The bed remains in perfect condition after thirty years.

One afternoon while I was tied in bed with the traction weights pulling me in many direction, Howard Hughes, unannounced, came to call on me. Miriam, who had been on the way to her studio and was dressed in her artist's smock, answered the door. Hughes, not having met Miriam before and impressed by her very girlish look said, "I'm Howard Hughes. May I see your father?"

Not wishing to embarrass Hughes (and also delighted by the unintended compliment), Miriam escorted him to my room and left us, saying to me, "See you later, Daddy."

I was so surprised to see Hughes I didn't ask why she called me Daddy. Hughes pulled a chair near the bed and asked if there was anything I needed or wanted.

"No, thank you."

"Do you have much pain?"

"Not much, thank you."

He had come to see if there was anything he could do. For instance, he had had made for him during his recovery from his plane crash in Beverly Hills a bed that moved any part of the body — left side, right side, left foot, right foot. It also had a toilet built in with plumbing such as they use in planes. I said I could release myself from traction to use the conventional WC and that the bed the studio had made was very comfortable. There was a pause — a long one. I said, "How are you, Howard" — then I smiled. "That sounds funny — as if I said, 'Howard you Howard.'"

He nodded and replied, "Don't bother talking. I just came to see if you're getting better." Then he sat there. After a few minutes he reached out, touched my hand, stood up, and said, "If you need anything, let me know."

"Thanks, I will. Would you like a cold drink or something before you go?"

He shook his head no, hoped I would get better soon, and left the room.

For reasons I do not yet understand I felt extremely sorry for him. He seemed lonely — so anxious to make contact, and yet because he was unable to say much, I too had become tongue-tied and hardly had time to say, "Thanks for coming," before he was gone.

The visit was so unusual, I told some of my friends about it. Incidents become embroidered, become rumors, become obvious possibilities, and in a few days there were two or three items in the trades that speculated I might be leaving MGM for reasons unknown. I guessed it was because Hughes had paid me a visit.

When *The Next Voice You Hear* was reviewed favorably, I was pleasantly surprised to read Hedda Hopper's comments: "I've always been against messages in pictures but *The Next Voice You Hear* has one I love — spirituality and love. Dore Schary and Bill Wellman made this one for every member of the family. In fact, for America. It can't miss."

However, *sic transit gloria mundi*. After I was propelled out of Metro, in November, 1956, Mrs. Hopper decided to "make out my own list of best and worst [pictures] and let the chips fall where they may. Here we go."

1st Best picture of all time:
Birth of a Nation

1st Worst picture of all time:
Next Voice You Hear

Since then I've had to contend with the fact that columnists are human. They are liable to change their minds; however, Mrs. Hopper's estimate of me through the years behaved in yo-yo-like fashion. But I made her happy when I departed Metro — and I've always liked making people happy.

26

The year 1951 was crowded with work, events of some moment, climaxes, letdowns from a few films, controversy, and fortunately a highly rewarding run of films that brought us twenty-four Academy nominations and a bulging purse of profit.

The Red Badge of Courage was released in this year and became, and remains, a film surrounded by swirls of debate. Two facts are unassailable: it received wonderful reviews and was a mournful disappointment at the box office.

The early steps leading to its production were far more interesting than its actual production, which was not eventful except for the press it attracted to its location site, chiefly because of John Huston, who was coming off the rousing reception to *Asphalt Jungle*. The daily rushes were exciting. When John and his producer, Gottfried Reinhardt, assembled their final cut, I had misgivings regarding its length but none concerning its merits. I was convinced that everyone involved had done his best with *Red Badge*. We went to preview in a high state of exultation.

Sad to state, the preview was disastrous. The audience began to file out toward the end of the first hour, the pace of exodus increasing as the second hour wore on. At the conclusion, the approximately one-third of the audience remaining gave the screening a polite, short hand and slowly straggled out to write preview cards that were painful to read. "Slow" — "lousy" — "stinks" — "Audie Murphy was heroic to play it" — "burn it" — "dull" — "forget it" were some of the more respectable comments. Huston, Reinhardt, and I were stunned. As CO of the outfit, I had to cover up my feelings by suggesting that we meet next morning when our heads would be clear. (I prayed mine would.) One of the studio executives, who had gone to view the debacle, whispered to me mournfully, "I guess L.B. was right." Billy Grady almost cheerfully said, "*Comme çi — comme ça.*"

Huston said, "I'll talk tomorrow — I have to go somewhere and get a drink — get a lot of drinks." Al Lewin, director, producer, and screenwriter of *The Moon and Sixpence,* hung back and cheered Reinhardt and me by saying that all the picture needed was sharp cutting and clarification. I asked him to sit with us the next morning and help out.

My phone rang early that morning. It was John Huston. He said he had received a call from London offering him an important assignment, and he was on his way to the airport. He asked me to take over the film, assuring me that I could fix it. He was in a hurry. He wished me good luck, I wished him the same. I guessed he had found a usable raft but that we were to go down with the ship.

Lewin and Reinhardt, having met before the appointment in my office, appeared with an old but workable idea: why not clarify the progression of the story with Stephen Crane's words from the book? They had excerpted appropriate text, and after we consulted with the film editors to make sure there was film for the segues that would be needed, I told the editor to begin the job and suggested that Reinhardt use James Whitmore for the narrator. He had the mid-American voice we needed.

We were satisfied with the job, previewed a second time, and, quite obviously, had improved the vitality of the film, but it was clear that we were not going to have a box-office picture. It was too simple a story, and how could America's greatest war hero be a coward? The failure at theaters even upset some of the critics, who were unanimously favorable in their reviews.

Westward the Women, based on a story by Frank Capra, was directed by the ever-resourceful and skilled Bill Wellman from a screenplay by Charles Schnee. It did well, and following *Go for Broke!,* which was my other personal production for the year, helped stifle the gnawings from the disappointments we had with the pictures that shared the sad fate of *Red Badge.* Louis Calhern in *The Magnificent Yankee* and Paul Douglas in *Angels in the Outfield* gave two excellent performances in two exceptionally good films, and yet both pictures failed to capture the audiences they deserved.

I had thought that *Go for Broke!* might result in the same trip to the crying towel. It began with my suggesting to Bob Pirosh, who had written *Battleground,* for which he had picked up an Oscar, that we ought to go hunting for a story dealing with the Japanese detention centers that had come into being immediately after Pearl Harbor. The energy that

Earl Warren, then California's attorney general, applied to that woeful migration to those Midwest camps is the only ugly mark on that distinguished American's career.

To have rushed Japanese, who were American citizens, into those faraway areas — treeless, barren, lonely, surrounded by vistas of flat, scrubby plains — was unconscionable. The nisei were not guilty of anything but became victims of terror and panic, losing their homes, farms, equipment, and security. That crime against them we wished to report.

However, after we read material and talked about it and considered the tensions of the "cold war," we decided to latch onto a positive view of a negative fact. The accent on the affirmative was the story of the 442nd Infantry Battalion, the nisei combat unit that earned more medals and suffered more casualties than any other combat unit and proved more than any other factor the absurdity and shame of the detention camps. We designed a way of telling their story without omitting the truth of the nisei internment centers. In the main, our actors were veterans of the battalion, and many of the stories that Bob wrote were their stories.

The picture was a success; as an ironic lagniappe, it was a roaring hit in Japan.

Quo Vadis?, despite loud and mighty disapproval from critics, went its way to higher grosses than MGM had ever counted, except for David Selznick's *Gone with the Wind*.

In terms of today's merry-go-round, the $27 million *Quo Vadis?* grossed represents the proverbial peanuts. Despite overinflated reports of success, it is nonetheless true that films such as *Love Story*, *The Exorcist*, *Jaws*, *Jaws II*, *Star Wars*, and *The Godfather* have brought in individual revenues matching and often exceeding successful yearly grosses of major studios during the 1950s.

The three other pictures that produced handsome profits for us in 1951 were the musicals *Show Boat* (apparently it never stops being an attraction), *The Great Caruso*, which raised Mario Lanza to stardom and ultimately slid him to his downfall, and *An American in Paris*, produced by Arthur Freed, directed by Vincente Minnelli, choreographed by Gene Kelly, photographed by John Alton and Alfred Gilles. Gene was also responsible for discovering Leslie Caron. The one debate concerning the production was the cost of the ballet, which seemed to intimidate the New York executive squad. But Schenck did not stand in the way — rather he agreed that without the ballet (which was to cost $300,000) the picture would simply be a rather routine story of an American falling in

The King, Gable, greets Eddie Mannix, who is appropriately sloshed, as a Roman emperor at a party given to honor Eddie on his return from Italy after guiding Quo Vadis? *to completion*

A fake jam session by Celeste Holm, Dolores Grey, Anne Francis, and me. Johnny Green at the piano and the others are on the level.

Sukarno, aides, and Eric Johnston. I'm wearing my Stevenson shoe lapel button. Sukarno is loaded with medals.

James Mason and his former wife, Pamela, greet Queen Juliana of the Netherlands at a rather fancy luncheon at the studio. The queen became so interested in sets, actors, and studio activity that she kept ordering changes in her time schedule, thereby driving her staff into controlled frenzy.

Bob Walker's first film, Bataan, *moved him from "unknown" to "star." Lloyd Nolan, one of the stars, is shown listening to the young sailor's story of how he came to be stuck in the jungle.*

love with a Parisian girl. Alan Lerner's script was serviceable, but not up to any of his other successes. The music, dancing, singing, and imaginative projection of Toulouse-Lautrec's paintings in the ballet produced the classic.

While all the goodies were being shot, edited, and marketed, there were casualties, such as the two films starring Ezio Pinza. The opera star who became a sex figure in the Rodgers and Hammerstein musical *South Pacific* proved to be vulnerable to the huge close-ups of the camera. His *Mr. Imperium* and *Strictly Dishonorable* failed, not just because of him, but because they were not very good. After all, even Gable couldn't bring in the customers if the suit didn't fit.

By this time I needed a holiday. I wanted to take Miriam and the kids away for a breather, away from the studio and community activities that were wearing me down.

I was thinking of Sun Valley (too cold), Palm Springs (too near to the studio), a boat trip through the Panama Canal (no one liked the idea except me). While I was discussing my plans with Mayer, he told me that he and Schenck were delighted with the progress made at the studio and were going to offer me a new contract, extending its length and probably granting me stock options. He told me to call Schenck, who wished to discuss his ideas with me. "That's Nick," he said. "He always has to be the big I am, the big cheese. All he knows about movies you could stick in a cat's ass." It was the foregoing odd metaphor that made the moment memorable.

I called Schenck, who asked when I would be coming east. When I told him I planned a holiday but had not yet picked my spot, he suggested that I come to Florida — Boca Raton, to be exact. He was planning to be at his home in Miami for his extended winter vacation, and I could come visit him and discuss his plans for the future. He said that I was entitled to a good luxurious rest and offered to pay all expenses for the trip. Like the opportunities presented to the Godfather's friends, that was an offer I could not refuse.

So, we packed up — Miriam, Jill, Joy, Jeb, Walter Reilly (my executive assistant), and I — and off we went to Florida, joined by Leonard Spigelgass, who came along for the train ride.

At Boca Raton, then as now a hoity-toity rendezvous for golfers, dancers, and big spenders, we settled down to swim, boat, and enjoy. Jill, going on sixteen, fell in love with a dark-haired, brown-eyed pool attendant. Joy and Jeb entered the dance contests at night and won two bottles of champagne. All three of our kids went to a circus one afternoon and came home by cab a half hour later seething with indignation. They had learned (this *was* 1951) that the blacks were separated from the whites. When they insisted upon sitting with the blacks and were told that was impossible, they asked for a refund on their tickets, got it, and returned home. I kissed them.

Boca has always been a warm memory for us because it was there that we met Mel and Anita (Mofie) Bloch, who became our fast and dear friends. Much too soon, I had the sad assignment to read a eulogy at Mel's funeral.

Also at Boca, we were surprised to find that Ronald Reagan, a fellow liberal and FDR stalwart in the forties, was in residence with an attractive blond lady as an escort.

After a week's stay, I called Schenck, who sent a car for us, and Miriam and I spent the day with him and his very attractive, bright, and adored wife, Pansy. When lunch was done, Nick and I sat in the sun and he told me of his decision to grant me stock options and to extend my contract to December 31, 1957. He and Mayer had agreed to the broad outline, but he had asked for the right to tell me the details. He also said that if Mayer were to leave, I would take over the title of head of the studio in addition to my position as vice-president in charge of production.

He asked me about my relationship with L.B. I said it was an agreeable one, that Mayer, who at first had sometimes intruded, had now worked out a smooth modus operandi, and that I had learned from him. I also suggested that if Mayer were ever to retire, it would be advisable to keep him on in some advisory or consulting capacity. Schenck nodded and said that was a real possibility.

When our session concluded, Nick wished me luck, and agreed that I should call Mayer and thank him for his vote of confidence and the approval of the new deal. With a great sense of joy, Miriam and I returned to Boca.

I told Walter Reilly the good news and put in a call to Mayer. My thanks were profuse and sincere. I had a feeling that things were going to be all right.

But the mood changed two days later when the story of my new contract appeared in print with a bit of a splash. The announcement had been made by Nicholas Schenck and the omission of Mayer's name was a small flame that lingered and flickered in L.B.'s breast. I noticed the change when I called again from Florida. His manner was curt and he repeated his feelings regarding Schenck, accusing him of all sorts of things including vanity, arrogance, and ignorance. He also asked when I was coming back to the studio — "Not that I want to interrupt your *holiday*," he added sarcastically.

On my arrival back in Hollywood, the climate in Mayer's office was cool and remained that way, but dropped a couple of more degrees following a meeting I was asked by Howard Strickling to attend.

The meeting was in Mayer's office and included Tom Brady, a New York *Times* reporter. Some weeks before, during an interview with Brady at which I had been present, Mayer had been rather intemperate in some of his statements regarding New York, stockholders, and what he termed "dirty actors." Brady had quoted Mayer accurately and Mayer had called him in to lay him out and bar him from the lot.

Howard Strickling, the capable head of studio publicity and public relations, not wanting to midwife a rupture between MGM and the *Times,* had asked Mayer to have me sit in on this second meeting between Mayer and Brady. Mayer had simmered down and admitted he had said what Brady had quoted him as saying, but objected to the fact that Brady had picked criticisms rather than more positive items. After Brady left, without a reprimand but rather with a tacit apology, Mayer once again gave me the fifty-cent tour of why he never talked to the press.

Finished with that, Mayer seemed to relax. He appeared to be in a reflective mood. He reminded me that he had said that he would retire two or three years after I took charge of production, but now he said, "I've got second thoughts. What would I do with myself? I'm being honest. What would you do if you were me if you wanted or had to retire — be honest."

I said I didn't know because I wasn't him. I didn't have his personal history, his millions, his temperament. "It's impossible," I said, "for me to know or to guess what I would do if I were you."

He insisted — almost commandingly.

"Well," I volunteered, "I don't know how much you've got, but I assume it is in millions. I think, in your place, I'd travel, write, set up a foundation and administer it to provide ego-satisfaction, then I'd set up a fund for destitute people in the industry and do something on behalf of an industry that helped me become successful."

That set the alarm siren going.

"First," he said, "you say that because you're a *kobtzen* [Yiddish for pauper]. Second, don't spend my money. And I don't owe this industry or this company a goddamn cent. I got what I got because I deserve it.

Nobody gave me anything. Screw the company and screw the stockholders. Listen, why do you think I took a million a year — even if I got only ten cents for every extra dollar — that was so many ten-cent pieces and they added up. And, furthermore, I've been everywhere, so I don't want to travel."

By then, of course, he was not at all reflective. His voice was harsh and he hated the idea of my spending his money. Most of all, he hated me for not pleading with him to stay. But I had always assumed he would stay on as chief executive emeritus, or some such title, and his implication that he planned to remain neither surprised nor upset me.

Following that bizarre tête-à-tête my schedule continued in its rather orderly fashion. There were almost eighty previews during the year, and at home I viewed at least two pictures from other companies each week. Speeches, meetings, and dinners on the outside took up some sixty nights. On the free nights I was occupied with viewing the daily rushes from pictures in production. The chances of falling into a rut were few because of short holidays with the family and the shock of sad events that racked my emotions.

One such event was the end of the Robert Walker story. Bob had come to us when we signed him in 1942 for *Bataan*. His career had flowered at the same time as that of his wife, Jennifer Jones. But trouble tripped Bob. Jennifer's career passed his with her sure stardom in *The Song of Bernadette*, written and directed by George Seaton and produced by Bill Perlberg. His marriage broke up and Jennifer married David Selznick. Bob began drinking and asserting his vigor and masculinity by going into bars and brawling with men who were bigger and hit harder.

When the episodes could no longer be ignored by the authorities, I had a long talk with Bob in which I suggested he go to the Menninger Clinic in Topeka for treatment. He responded by yelling that he was not crazy, but when reassured that that was not my diagnosis, he listened as I explained that if he had TB he would be neither ashamed nor reluctant to try and cure himself.

His time in Topeka had helped him despite two instances when he had flown the coop and gone into bars to look for action and found it. But he had returned and made films, the last of which was *My Son John*, directed by Leo McCarey and co-starring Helen Hayes. Now he was receiving attention from a psychiatrist in Beverly Hills and appeared to be in control.

One rainy night on my immediate return from a preview, the phone rang and when I answered a voice shouted, "Dore — Bob's dead — Bob's dead." It was a new friend of Bob's, "Red" Henaghan, who through his tears and screams told me he was in Bob's house. I hung up, got into my car, and rushed to the Uplifter's Ranch, only about a mile away. The door to the house was open. Bob's doctor was standing there with his young assistant. They were both in shock. I pushed by them and went into Bob's bedroom, where Henaghan was sitting in a chair and sobbing. Bob was on the bed. He was wearing moccasins, slacks, a plaid woolen shirt with the left sleeve rolled up. There were bloodstains on his arm and the bed. Bob was dead.

The doctors gave me the story. Henaghan had called because Bob had been drinking and was getting violent. They had arrived and got Bob to lie down while they administered a shot of sodium pentothal. Some doctors choose not to run the risk of using such a drug in treating someone who has been drinking. It is not always a fatal risk, but according to some doctors, it is advisable to have oxygen handy when using the drug because of the danger that the depressive effect of the drug added to the depressive effect of a large amount of alcohol (which Bob had ingested) might cause a respiratory arrest.

Before long a fire respiratory unit arrived and with them Metro's police chief Whitey Hendry. He advised me to let them take over the rest of the unhappy details and to go home.

Bob's death was such a waste. He was a talented actor and a man who simply switched onto a siding and ran into a dead end.

One of the liabilities — and benefits — of a complicated job and attendant activities is that you get little time to savor the joys, or dwell on the morose events. You simply go on.

At the end of a story conference one morning, I asked to see Mayer regarding details of our production plans. I'd begun to go over some notes I had when his private phone rang. I asked if he wanted me to leave. He said, "It isn't necessary." Then into the phone, "Hello, yes, Bob. . . . No, I have no intention of talking to Nick Schenck. . . . Yes, of course, I have his letter, which I suppose you wrote for him." (By now it was clear to me that he was speaking to Robert Rubin, a co-founder of Metro and their chief counsel for as long as man remembered.) Mayer looked at me as he listened to Rubin and then retorted, "Never, Bob, never. You can tell Mr. Nicholas Schenck that he and Dore Schary can take the studio and choke on it." He hung up and stared at me, waiting for me to say something.

All I could think of was absurd: "What was that all about, L.B.?"

He answered, "I know how you and Nick schemed to kick me out, you son of a bitch."

I got up and started out of the office.

He barked, "Sit down and I'll tell you everything, you little kike."

By then I was out of range and out of his office. The first call I made was to my lawyer, David Tannenbaum. I said, "Get me out of here. There's a big quarrel between Schenck and Mayer and, lucky Pedro, I'm smack in the middle."

David said he'd follow up but added that I owed it to Schenck to be the first to tell him I wanted out.

Schenck asked me to return to Mayer's office and simply ask how L.B. wanted to work things out in the future. He urged me despite my misgivings by telling me that in the near future I would understand his reasons.

The next morning I drew a deep breath and walked into Mayer's lion's den, asked one question, and was bombarded with another barrage. I retreated, and called Schenck to renew my request to be released. Nick said, "Talk to me tomorrow morning after you've seen the papers."

When I had agreed and hung up, I was visited by Benny Thau, Louie Sidney, and Eddie Mannix, who urged me to return to Mayer's office and apologize. I asked, "What the hell for?" They explained that Mayer called everybody names. Thau said, "We never pay attention to it. He's called me every name you could think of — cursed me — but I went back and said I was sorry for making him angry."

I noticed that Mannix did little of the talking, and as the tawdry scene was played out, I remembered that Mannix was Schenck's man and probably had been cautioned not to press me too eagerly to return for another L.B. blast.

In any event, I had no intention of returning. Certainly I could not fathom why I had any obligation to apologize.

The next morning everything exploded. The papers heralded Mayer's statement of resignation. It was final and it contained veiled references to Schenck and to me.

I called Schenck and he informed me I was to take full responsibility until the entire executive staff would meet in Chicago to map plans for the future. The Windy City had been chosen as a halfway point for our rendezvous since Schenck was involved in some legal problem and was likely to be served with papers in California.

Thau, Mannix, Louis Sidney, Joe Cohn, Howard Strickling, and I headed east and Charles Moskowitz, Howard Dietz, William Rodgers, and Schenck flew west. We met for lunch at the Ambassador East Hotel and after the fancy meal Schenck outlined his plans to us, which called for Mannix, Thau, and me to take over the running of the studio in troikalike fashion with Mannix having the last word on decisions regarding retakes, added scenes, and assignments for directors. Thau was to be in charge of talent contracts and casting. Louis Sidney would guard the studio against infiltration of Reds, arrange the shooting schedules, and keep an eye on the money spent. Joe Cohn, as always, was to be in charge of physical production costs, building of sets, costumes, locations, and so on. The latter two men would be under command of Mannix, Thau or me . . . Tinkers to Evers to Chance.

Listening to the plan for the future, I heard the tolling of the bells. It was a plan that would bring on quick and complete disaster. I said I did not like the outline, and asked Schenck to adjourn the meeting so that I could speak to him alone without bruising feelings or agreeing to anything that I knew was not a practical solution to our new and urgent problem.

Alone with Schenck, I was much more definite: the plan would not work; each one of the men, except Joe Cohn, had his own ideas about his prerogatives. If they were given any authority over mine the studio would turn into a caldron of intrigues and ambitions and my position, which under optimum conditions would not be easy because of Mayer's sudden departure, would be untenable.

Therefore, I said, since my contract indicated clearly my own prerogatives, I would have to be in charge and have the final decisions, if I so chose, on all matters except those that were in the purview of Mr. Schenck. If he wished to abandon his own plan and my contract provisions, I would be ready to resign.

Schenck smiled and said, "No need for you to say that. I knew you would not agree, but I had to oblige the boys. I want you now to read the letter I received from L.B. two weeks ago." The letter, in brief, was a challenge. After Mayer excoriated me to Schenck for being incompetent, being unwilling to listen to anyone else, having a fondness for publicity and an interest in propaganda pictures, Mayer threw down the gauntlet to Schenck. It was either Mayer or I who had to go.

Schenck told me his response. He had written Mayer that, as the records showed, since I had taken over production there had been a sharp change for the better in production costs, profits, Academy nominations, and studio identification. Therefore, since Mayer had offered him no alternative, his choice was Schary.

Learning that Mayer was after my scalp eased my sympathy for him but did not divorce me from feeling that he was entitled to some courtesies. He had announced he was going to form his own company, and knowing his close relationship to many people at Metro whose careers he had sponsored and supported, I told Schenck that I intended to allow those people who asked to sign with Mayer to tear up their contracts.

Schenck gave me another of his enigmatic smiles and nodded his head. "Of course, if anyone wants to leave, it's okay. But please tell me who they are before you let them go."

Then he slapped me on the back and suggested we go back and tell the others.

The gentlemen did not like the news, but I promised we'd set up an executive committee. We'd meet each week, I'd listen to their questions, be guided by their suggestions, but, finally, the authority would be mine.

We had a farewell dinner that night and returned to our own fortresses in New York and Culver City. Howard Dietz and Howard Strickling were to coordinate the appropriate announcements and there I was, a new turn in the river was in front of me, and I had no idea what lay ahead.

The American Legion provided the first log in my way. They threatened that any or all films written by, produced by, or acted in by anyone on any Red list would be picketed. They also averred that Hollywood was still crawling with Communists and that they might create their own list of undesirables.

Bill Goetz and I met at a dinner party and talked about the legion's threat. I suggested that we reply with the best tool we had — movies. Why not make a film that would show Eisenhower and MacArthur making their statements that the training films made during the war had enabled soldiers to be prepared more quickly? Let's talk about the movie people who were in uniform and in action, the stars who traveled the world bringing entertainment to troops, the casualties among the soldiers from Hollywood and the entertainers. Tell the entire story of Hollywood at war.

Bill said he'd contribute the news clips from Universal. He suggested we also use film of legion conventions with shots of legionnaires using cattle prods to goose ladies and throwing bags of water down upon unsuspecting citizens. I got the editors working the next day and called Darryl Zanuck, who agreed to send over some Twentieth-Fox news clips for our use and concluded, "Count me in."

It was about a week later that Frank Freeman issued a clarion call for us (the studio production chiefs) to meet with Eric Johnston and Spyros Skouras at an emergency dinner session at the Beverly Hills Hotel.

Freeman, Goetz, Harry Cohn, Steve Broidy, head of Allied Pictures, and I showed up along with B. B. Kahane from Columbia. Zanuck had a preview and wasn't around for the display of fireworks that began with one of Spyros's favorite subjects: his arrival in America, his career as a shoeshine boy, and his meteoric rise because of opportunities offered him by America. Into his saga he introduced his brothers, his entire family, and his unflagging patriotism.

We had heard the same speech on many occasions: Bundles for Britain, Russian War Relief, United Jewish Appeal, Aid to Greece, and the Community Fund; so we waited, patient but bored, until the pitch, which was for us to be good Americans and support Eric Johnston's plan to stop the American Legion's attack on our industry.

Eric took the floor and informed us that the presidents of all the major motion-picture companies had agreed to the proposal that the legion submit names of persons who were supposed to be Communists and those who, by their actions and alliance with left-wing and liberal causes, could be assumed to be suspicious characters. These men and women would then write letters defending themselves to be channeled through the studios to the legion, who would rule thumbs down or thumbs up on the future of those whose letters were examined. The plan was worse than the original Waldorf policy. Everyone was under suspicion but Eric Johnston, Skouras, Cohn, Freeman, the notorious right-wingers, and the rest of the studio biggies — except me. It was open season for self-appointed guardians of Americanism.

Goetz and I protested vigorously. I outlined our personal plan. Fight the legion. Let us produce our picture, show it to our audiences, and let them judge whether or not we should be intimidated. "No — no — no," were the frantic cries of disapproval, and now we learned that Skouras had already accepted the plan and had received letters that "cleared" Elia Kazan, Marlon Brando, Anthony Quinn, and Katy Jurado, thereby avoiding the possibility that *Viva Zapata* would be picketed. I told Johnston that I would not be involved in any fashion. If Mr. Schenck wanted MGM to submit I would ask him to set up the clearance system, which I would do all in my power to circumvent.

"That," said Eric, "is between you and Mr. Schenck."

Goetz and I went to Chasen's after the meeting and agreed that the best procedure was to wait for the legion's list and then do everything possible to get some names eliminated. In some cases we'd have letters written so "Skouras-like" that there'd be no problem. In other cases we'd simply pay no attention to the list and allow the legion to cry havoc.

But it wasn't that easy. It was a damned nuisance. While it wasn't too long a time before the legion's scheme boomeranged, a number of actors and writers were left out of work. Some refused to write letters and had their contracts settled up in generous fashion, but in ignominious submission to the legion. However, Bill Goetz at Universal, Nate Springold and B. B. Kahane at Columbia, Zanuck at Twentieth-Fox, and I, along with some independents, succeeded in tamping down the fire.

The fuss quieted about two years later. A legion employee named Barslag wired an exhibitor that a documentary film I had made called *The Hoaxsters* was in itself a hoax. The theme of the picture dealt with the similarities of the Stalin and Hitler techniques in diminishing the independent power of the churches, schools, government, and army; further, it took a swing at those who not only labeled themselves 100 percent Americans, but 150 percent or 200 percent, and yet libeled blacks, Jews, nisei, and any minority that tried to raise its head above the crowd.

Mr. Barslag's wire, which in effect libeled me directly as a Communist, happened to have been sent to an exhibitor who was a member of B'nai B'rith and a staunch guardian of the Anti-Defamation League. He called me, and when I asked if he'd send me a copy of the wire, he said he'd do better. He sent his son by plane to give me the original. When the wire was in my hand, I instructed Tannenbaum to wire James O'Neill, the head of the Americanism Division of the legion, and inform him that we were entering suit for libel in the sum of five million dollars and investigating whether or not I could press criminal charges against Barslag.

O'Neill called me and asked me to hold my fire. His men had viewed *The Hoaxsters*, were impressed with everything it had to say, and Barslag was no longer with the legion.

"When did that happen?" I asked.

"When I heard from your lawyer," said O'Neill.

The last step took place when O'Neill came to California accompanied by the former Gauleiter of the Parnell Thomas Un-American Activities Committee, Prosecutor Robert E. Stripling. O'Neill had asked to see me alone. I said, "You're bringing a guest — I'll have one, Eddie Mannix."

During our lunch meeting I paid no attention to Stripling but I liked O'Neill, who asked me directly, "Were you actually planning to fight the legion with a picture kicking hell out of us?" I admitted I had had such a project in mind. O'Neill then admitted it would have been a sad blow. By now the legion realized they had that well-known bear by the tail and were eager to let go.

The remainder of the lunch was pleasant. I did advise O'Neill that a legion post in Saugus stank with the odor of anti-Semitism and refused nisei veterans' entrance into their rolls. He said he knew about the situation and if the post didn't change their tune they'd lose their charter. I don't know if they ever did — but after a while the legion accepted nisei veterans.

The legion's quest was abandoned. The lists finally disappeared and people returned to work in films and TV, but a heavy cost in courage was paid by the industry and a dreadful price was paid by those we could not protect. I never did learn who had told O'Neill about the plan for our film.

When the legion began its rather short reign of troublemaking, Y. Frank Freeman, Harry Warner, and C. B. DeMille chose that time to revive the question of the loyalty oaths. But this time the Motion Picture Industry Council had been in existence for a few years and had acquired status and stamina. The debate on the institution of a loyalty oath was a humdinger. Frank Freeman stated he would sign a loyalty oath presented to him by anyone. I asked, "Even the Ku Klux Klan?" He granted there would be exceptions. Harry Warner proclaimed that while he loved his brother Jack, he'd put a rope around his neck and drag him to the nearest police station if he learned he was a Communist. Jack got the only laugh of the evening when he said, "Harry, that would be very uncomfortable."

I had been asked by the anti-oath side to make our first statement of opposition. As I did, DeMille, sitting next to Joe Mankiewicz, began scribbling notes. Later Joe told me that DeMille had informed him he planned to send all my remarks to Joe McCarthy, who was now considered by Hollywood to be the doyen to whom we should all pay obeisance.

Bill Holden followed me and blistered the producers and the other naysayers, and when he finished there was nothing to be said except to call for a vote. We won in a landslide with some of the opposition ambling over to our side.

It is my belief that the rejection of the loyalty oath was the beginning of the end of the overt right wing that had dominated studio policy. I was convinced that the power of the guilds never again would permit an industry as powerful as the motion-picture business to bow to the intrusive whinings of any so-called Americanism quasi-investigative body.

As proof of my optimism I predicted that motion pictures were safe from television competition for another four years at least. To show my confidence, I announced a program of forty films for 1952, half of them to be in color. (How strange it must seem to the reader that in 1951 color was not yet a staple in picture production.)

Regarding TV: In October I had asked Nick Schenck if he had ever considered a merger with a TV company such as RCA as a hedge against the possible clout of TV.

Schenck recounted a meeting with General David Sarnoff in 1948. (Sarnoff had received his title in the army. Schenck was called "General" instead of "Chief" or "Boss." I speculated that they might have called each other "General," but Schenck disabused me of that.) Sarnoff, according to Schenck, had come to discuss a possible alliance between NBC and MGM. Schenck had discounted the feasibility of such a move. "I said, 'David,'" Schenck told me, "'what have you got to offer? We've got the pictures.' So," Schenck continued directly to me, "the same thing goes today. What have they got to offer?"

Years later I remembered that conversation and in a talk I had with Sarnoff one evening before we began a group study of passages in the Talmud, I asked if that had been the substance of his meeting with Schenck.

Sarnoff laughed, said it was so, and commented, "Nick was getting old. He didn't want any more problems. If Nick had been fifteen years younger, I never would have gotten out of his office without a deal." Sarnoff had to be right, but I wondered, if a deal had been made, how much Sarnoff might have regretted ceding away part of NBC's fortune.

27

The war with the radical right and left never ends. You may win battles but other forays begin unexpectedly. This time it was the heroic brigade of witch-hunters.

A radical right group, inspired by Jack Tenney, California's self-appointed chief magistrate in tracking down Reds, went after me by picketing all MGM films. They had assumed a title, aimed at gaining support from blue-collar workers, the Wage Earners Committee. They also decided to attack Stanley Kramer, accusing him and his films of being Red oriented. My suit against them was for $2,304,531.65, a figure I viewed as comic. I told Tannenbaum, "We'll probably get the sixty-five cents." But our claim was valid, and early court hearings leaned heavily in our favor. Members of the Wage Earners Committee, terrified at the possible claims against them, began to send in letters of resignation with copies to us to clear them of any liability. The pickets disappeared and for a time so did Jack Tenney. We didn't even get sixty-five cents, but the committee ceased to exist and that was a good enough victory.

The studio, by early 1952, had recovered in part from the trauma of Mayer's farewell, but during the remaining years of my term at Metro, I never had the friendship of Ben Thau. To some degree it was my fault. I had warm associations with Joe Cohn, Eddie Mannix, Louis Sidney; but I did not receive what we now call "vibes" of friendliness from Thau. As a result, I stood away from him. I did not quarrel with him but I seldom laughed with him. He was a naysayer. During a year when studios were making a large number of pictures, more pictures failed than succeeded. In some cases, the failures served a purpose in eating up overhead and in a way added to the profits of the successes. But a naysayer had a field day. By acting as Cassandra, he could in time be known as the guy who predicted all of the flops.

If one he had counted on to fail turned up a natural eleven, he could say like a gentleman, "Well, I guess I was wrong on that *one*."

The political games played in studios are no different from those in the realm of big business, the halls of academe, or government. Being involved in all three areas I got to know that the game plans are the same, only the vocabulary differs. And let us not forget the grim aspects of the games as they are played in television companies. The power games and hustles are played as aggressively even in community-affairs organizations.

A few months had passed since Mayer had gone when, during a phone call one morning, Nick Schenck asked me, "By the way — how many people have asked to be released from the contracts?" He knew damn well there had been none. I could see his catbird-seat smile right through the phone.

Mayer had announced two or three productions on his independent schedule, but he didn't get to do any of them. The fact is that Mayer was an entrepreneur; bold, reckless, tough, rough, and mean as a polecat, but he had never made a film nor could he have. However, he did draw the basic pattern for a big studio, and all those that followed were imitations of MGM. Mayer's unique gifts were his vision and the verve to bring his dreams into reality. I understood and respected that — it reminded me of my father's extravagant reveries, which he had never realized.

When the industry suffered serious wounds from TV exhibition, MGM became a conglomerate, surviving in the main because of its extraordinary real estate enterprises.

United Artists, Warners, Paramount, and Columbia are hostages to big outside interests. Universal is a country all its own, ruled by Lew Wasserman with Jules Stein as emperor emeritus. Twentieth-Fox has come to life with *Star Wars* but has already lost the leadership of Alan Ladd, Jr., who led them to the gold mine. The Hollywood world has changed, but the games go on and the warfare is more serious and bloody because the rewards are so great.

But the rules are still identical. Give the guy a chance at bat — if he gets a hit or two, fine, but when he misses, go in and tell him how to start hitting again. If he makes trouble, sing out, "Anything you can do, I can do better," just like Irving Berlin said in the song. If he doesn't listen, give him a "Go-man-go," meaning go someplace else.

My stint running MGM lasted eight and a half years. In the twenty-plus years since I left, there have been more than two dozen chief executives in New York and Hollywood, all of whom have bitten the dust except a few of the most recent ones who have been there over a year as of this writing.

What's true of Metro is true of other studios, except the empire of Universal. But if Wasserman should ever resign (which is as doubtful as Reagan giving up dreams of being President), the games would surface. You can bet they are presently being played in the lowlands of Universal's fiefdoms.

Games? Take a glance at the baseball world. Baseball managers are always under the gun. If they lose they are fired and ofttimes they talk too much. But then they shift to other teams and win. The fact is, owners never went to bat and got a hit and don't know it's very hard to win a pennant.

Each executive in a movie company believes he has the formula, the mystic alchemy that would make him better than the current behind that's sitting in the top chair. So it was at MGM. Thau, I know, resented me. Mannix wanted the job, but didn't ache for it. Louis Sidney would have loved the assignment. Joe Cohn wouldn't have taken it if it had been tossed at him — he had other interests: wineries in Napa Valley, tennis, bridge, and antiques.

The minor satraps play safe with the top dogs. They pledge allegiance to the flag and to the republic for which it stands, and they call themselves "company men" whose secret slogan is "Screw you, Charlie, I'm staying on no matter who moves in."

But the producers, directors, writers, and actors with whom I worked closely were warm, were more aware of what I was trying to do and helped me get it done.

As time went on, I again felt a twinge of sympathy for Mayer. He had been abandoned by those he had aided, but I knew that when my turn came to exit through the doorway, no one could come along with me. Why should they? Why should they have followed Mayer? They had their own fish to fry. Mayer was making announcements but not activating anything, and soon he became involved in a move to take over MGM and get rid of the "scoundrels" who had sacked him. Yet, I had sympathy for him. He could have stayed on as a consultant, done little or no work, yet retained standing and reputation in the community. But he had no inner life to sustain him. All he had was bitterness and a burning yen for revenge.

We released or made forty films in 1951–1952. The standout was *Singin' in the Rain,* the perennial classic by Comden and Green, Gene Kelly, and Stanley Donen. Arthur Freed was the producer, but essentially went along with the tide on this one. Debbie Reynolds popped up as an ebullient and talented star.

Another profitable and well-made movie was *Scaramouche*, a fast-moving adaptation of Rafael Sabatini's swashbuckling novel in which Stewart Granger skewered a few dozen rascals.

Above and Beyond, the story of the *Enola Gay*, the plane that dropped the A-bomb on Hiroshima, and its pilot, Colonel Tibbetts, was scripted by Bernie Ley, Norman Panama, and Melvin Frank, and directed by the latter. It was played effectively by Robert Taylor and Eleanor Parker.

Then there was the nationwide release of *Lili*, previously noted. *The Bad and the Beautiful* gave Lana Turner her best role since *The Postman Always Rings Twice* and Kirk Douglas played a combination of David Selznick and as yet unknown David Merrick. The film was produced by John Houseman, directed by Vincente Minnelli, and written by Charles Schnee. It picked up five Academy Awards.

But the biggest profit maker of the year was *Ivanhoe*. Years before at RKO, I had swapped Theodore Dreiser's *Sister Carrie* for Paramount's priority rights to *Ivanhoe*. Aeneas MacKenzie, who was signed to write the screenplay, backed away for a time since he had an emotional grudge toward Sir Walter Scott for not having had the moral courage to write the "appropriate" ending for *Ivanhoe* by having Ivanhoe discard Rowena and marry Rachel, the daughter of Isaac of York, both of them responsible for saving Ivanhoe's life and arranging for the ransom of King Richard. Scott had been the subject of attacks by his contemporaries for what they charged was submission to anti-Semitism by leaving poor Rachel out in the cold. Most prominent were the charges leveled by Thackeray in a blistering monograph.

MacKenzie wanted to rectify the wrong in his screenplay and though I argued that it was sacrilege to rewrite a classic, MacKenzie refused to touch the script. We then had made the deal to co-produce with Arthur Rank's company, but those plans had been aborted in toto when I left RKO.

Hughes had no interest in doing *Ivanhoe* and released the rights to us. I handed the production to Pan Berman along with a cast of Elizabeth Taylor, Joan Fontaine, Robert Taylor, and George Sanders. Richard Thorpe enlisted a magnificent English supporting cast and we gambled for "baccarat."

Before starting production, I had a call from Barney Balaban, then president of Paramount, asking me to reconsider making *Ivanhoe*, expressing qualms that the character of Isaac of York, the Jewish moneylender, would activate stereotypic concepts and lead to more anti-Semitism. An anti-Semite needs no reason to activate his bigotry and I reminded Balaban that the only profession open to Jews in the days of King Richard's reign was moneylending. As a matter of fact, they were encouraged to become moneylenders because they were trusted. Balaban, after he struck out with me, went to Schenck, who spoke to me about the issue but did not press it. I went ahead with the project.

After we viewed the rough cut of the finished film in Hollywood, I was convinced we had an important box-office attraction, and I invited the New York ad and publicity contingent to come out and look at it.

Despite my normal reservations about letting them see unfinished work, my enthusiasm signaled them in. They shared our estimates and Dietz hurried back, brought the good word to Schenck, Rodgers, and Vogel, and to Arthur Loew, who was in charge of European distribution.

In rather a short time, Dietz sent me a layout of the main advertisement for *Ivanhoe*. It featured Eliazbeth Taylor and Joan Fontaine looking at Robert Taylor. Each of the ladies was pictured copiously endowed with breasts that were more than suggested — they were practically revealed. I argued against Dietz's layout on the telephone and then in a letter in April, 1952:

I feel that the 24 sheet on *Ivanhoe* is an ordinary 24 sheet and will not sell tickets. I think *Ivanhoe* will be a successful picture, because I think it is moving and good — and I think its values are sound motion picture values. Certainly the presence of Elizabeth Taylor and Joan Fontaine, two beautiful women, helped the picture, but certainly the 24 sheet is a dishonest exaggeration — not of their womanly charms, but rather of the content of the picture. It is my hunch that many people will assume from the 24 sheet that Hollywood has done it again by taking a great classic and cheapening it with what is usually referred to as "the Hollywood glamour."

My final argument is: (1) Those people who have never heard of *Ivanhoe* will not come in as a result of the 24 sheet, any more than they came in to *His Kind of Woman* or *The Wild North;* (2) Those people who are very interested in seeing *Ivanhoe* will be discouraged by the 24 sheet; and (3) Those people who may want to encourage school children or more discriminating customers into the theatre will automatically view our production in a distorted fashion.

During these days when we are gambling time and effort in *trying* to make good pictures, and when we are gambling sums of money on subject material, it seems to me short sighted to lump every picture we make into the same "bosom school" of salesmanship.

My final protest is that you sell yourself short. If after the years of devotion and skill you have brought into this industry you cannot sell *Ivanhoe* except by four attractive organs plastered on a 24 sheet, I think we all ought to pick up our tents and say "The jig is up" and go into some respectable business like running a string of whore houses in Calcutta.

My fondest always, even though I have probably irritated you beyond all measure.

Dietz, in good humor, agreed to make the changes I suggested and the ad campaign was more than satisfactory as were the grosses that flowed in. Considering what has occurred to today's films, maybe I should have gone to Calcutta.

Looking back, it was a good year with the exception of one acute disappointment — my misadventure with *The Plymouth Adventure*, the story of the voyage of the *Mayflower* to America and the founding of the first colony at Plymouth. Schenck, Mannix, Joe Cohn had pleaded with me to cancel the expensive picture. Ben Thau's dire prediction I discounted. He also had had reservations about *Ivanhoe*. But my instinct told me the naysayers were wrong and I bulled my way into production with a script by Helen Deutsch and direction by Clarence Brown.

Perhaps I was working against a jinx. In the early years of silent pictures Charles Ray, a gifted comedian (I remember with boyish affection one of his films, *The Egg-Crate Wallop*), risked his own fortune and career on a serious film titled *The Mayflower*. It sank with all hands and literally ruined Charles Ray. Darryl Zanuck, a long time later, produced *Noah's Ark* and that one never got to Mount Ararat. John Huston defied the jinx and foundered with *The Bible*. In any event, some people liked *Plymouth Adventure* but there weren't enough direct descendants of the original *Mayflower* passengers to help it cross over to success. The picture proved to be a bummer, and I could feel the hot breath of the board directors.

However, Schenck seemed unperturbed, because we had cut the average cost of a film from about $2,200,000 to $1,400,000 and were averaging forty films a year. But there were things blowing in the wind. They didn't reach us until 1953. They were CinemaScope, 3-D, and television.

Unaware of the havoc they would wreak, we went about our business and our diversions.

Mario Lanza had, through the efforts of Joe Pasternak, appeared in a number of trifling but rather successful films. He was working as a piano mover when it was discovered that he had a remarkable tenor voice, which he himself identified as Caruso's sent to Lanza by the Almighty in a heavenly transplant.

Lanza was a crude and arrogant young man given to temper tirades, heavy eating, and beer drinking, and as his career generated into stardom, he became ungovernable. *The Great Caruso* showed Lanza at his best — his voice was brilliant, his performance more polished — but even before that triumph he had presented us with a host of problems, which I faced with him at my home. He had given me his list of grievances, all on the grounds that *Caruso* would make him a great star, and he now insisted he was to be treated as one. Far from incidentally, the man who had the first dream to film Caruso's story was Jesse Lasky, who had pursued me from Selznick's studio to RKO, but finally got to me and Pasternak at MGM when he argued that Lanza was ideal for the role and we agreed.

It seemed politic to remind Mario that MGM had a long list of stars who had preceded him. I told him that the studio through all its years had had to survive, despite the loss of Jean Harlow, Wallace Beery, Marie Dressler, John Gilbert, Edward Arnold, Bob Walker, Lionel Barrymore, and a host of others, and if it came down to it, Metro would have to get along without him. That sobered him up and we sailed through the making of *Caruso* with little or no trouble.

We ran into gale winds with *Because You're Mine*. Mario's co-star was Doretta Morrow, fresh from her success on Broadway in *The King and I*. Mario had now developed into an undisciplined and unguided talent. His weight went up and down like a carousel horse. His costumes were altered and re-altered each week. Weight settled on him quickly and he would diet it off as quickly. John Carroll, who was his friend, worked out with Mario, sparring, running, dieting, but finally had to give up the task when Lanza continued to break training.

A climax occurred the first day Mario and Doretta were to record their songs in the music stage accompanied by an orchestra of some seventy-five men and women conducted by John Green. Following a short rehearsal period they started to record their first duet. Suddenly, Mario, with a vivid curse, stopped and turned to Doretta and said, "You've got to be more sexy. Push up to me, let me feel your pussy next to my cock."

Doretta ran out of the stage and up to my office. By the time she got there I had heard the lurid story from John Green and Joe Pasternak. When Doretta appeared I expressed our outrage. I assured her it would not happen again. I would talk to Mario. Forget today's session. We would try again tomorrow.

After sobs, tears, and threats to walk out of the film and sue somebody, anybody, Doretta agreed to try the next day.

When Mario and she faced each other the following morning nothing was said. I had sent for Mario, warned him that his behavior was unforgivable and would not be tolerated. He said Doretta was not sexy enough for the part, that the role should be recast. Having been told casting was none of his business and ordered, on threat of being suspended, to be on the music stage the following morning, Mario had politely said, "Okay, but shit on all of you."

As Mario and Doretta finished their first few bars, Mario again yelled, "Stop," and addressed himself to Doretta in the same fashion as the day before, being even more precise and more obscene. This time Doretta went to her dressing room, called her agent, and refused to talk to Pasternak or to me.

Joe and I had a session to consider what could be done. Joe had an idea how to threaten Mario psychologically yet ostensibly physically. The notion became a one-act play.

We would hire a stunt man who, the next morning, would pose as a marine veteran stationed at Camp Pendleton, only a couple of hours from Hollywood. He would appear at nine o'clock the following morning at Mario's dressing room, identify himself as Doretta's brother, and would announce that he had rushed up to break Mario's jaw. The stunt man we picked was twice as broad as Mario and had the look of a guy who could make mincemeat of the average man. But he would be instructed not to hit Mario — it would not be necessary. Mario would quail. Joe left to get things in order: hire the stunt man, get his uniform, rehearse his lines, get ready for the show.

Within the hour Doretta, with her agent shepherding her, arrived at my office. They wanted a release and proper compensation. I agreed, but pointed out there was a great deal we would lose. I suggested one more attempt to save all of us. Instead of recording the songs at this time, I would schedule scenes to be shot on one of the sound stages. If anything went wrong — anything — I would give Doretta the salary due her for the entire picture and allow her to leave with no hard feelings but rather with sympathy and my apologies.

The agent convinced Doretta to accept the deal.

The stunt man, dressed in a marine sergeant's uniform with campaign ribbons and medals covering his chest, arrived next day at 9:00 A.M. as scheduled, pushed open Lanza's dressing-room door, introduced himself in a loud voice, and threatened to beat Lanza if he said anything except, "I'm sorry. Forgive me. I'll never do it again."

Mario did as "Doretta's brother" suggested. For three days the menacing marine sat on the stage and before "going back to Camp Pendleton" warned Lanza that if he heard even one complaint from "my sister, I'll come and you'll sing soprano for the rest of your life."

There was not a single nasty word said by Mario. He was honey, ice cream, and butter, and we went through the picture with no more upheavals except for the continued re-altering of his clothes.

When the picture was wrapped up, Doretta came to say good-bye and asked us to give her regards to her "brother."

My life by this time was divided into three unequal parts: the major segment was MGM; the second, my family and community and charitable work; and the third, my interest in politics. Having heard Adlai Stevenson welcome the delegates to Chicago for the 1952 convention, I had been drawn to his style, eloquence, and good humor. Once he was nominated, I headed Stevenson's campaign in Hollywood but rejected Steve Mitchell's offer to act as national committeeman for California. Mitchell was national chairman of the Democratic party and I suggested that Paul Ziffren, a prominent attorney and loyal Democrat, was better qualified and could lend more time to the effort throughout the state.

In a speech to a convocation of exhibitors, I had, after conferring with Schenck, announced a program of eighty-three pictures to be dished out in the next nineteen months. The announcement had come shortly after we again led in the Academy nominations by gathering up twenty-nine. As a result it came as a shock to learn that despite the bountiful grosses coming in from our successful films, we were facing diminishing returns from our so-so program fill-ins.

Schenck proposed that I cut down our year's program to thirty-eight productions and not announce 1953's slate until we had a better view of what was happening to us and to other companies in the industry. In an effort to stave off rumors of layoffs and panic-making shutdowns, Schenck proposed, and I agreed, that the executives who could easily endure reductions in their salaries take a cut of one thousand to fifteen hundred dollars in their weekly pay as an indication that we were the first to accommodate to the changing economy.

Schenck, past his legal difficulties, came to Hollywood and attended a mass rally of our four thousand employees. He asked me to act as spokesman. Instead of giving grim tidings, I kept the meeting business-like but good humored, and the message that, for the first time, the royal court would be the first to take a cut to prevent the lower-salaried folk from being penalized drew a loud and enthusiastic response. Rather than a mood of discouragement we were able to project encouragement and a determination to adjust and bend with the wind rather than break.

Because grosses were up but profits were down, we reasoned that by reducing the number of releases and being more selective in the number remaining on our schedule, we could keep our grosses up and increase our profit. In 1952–1953 we released a total of forty-four pictures and after determining policy, we decided that in the 1953–1954 schedule we would list only twenty-eight.

TV was beginning to demonstrate its punching power and we were beginning to hurt. One of my friends, Ed Lasker, said to me toward the end of the year, "I believe you've been appointed captain of the *Titanic*." That crack drew more blood than he knew, for I've been bothered by one nightmare all my life since the day in 1912 when I saw the headlines and the ink drawings showing the *Titanic* sinking. My nightmare places me in the ship, alive, as it sinks to the bottom of the sea.

But I had been fighting off the shrinking profits by cutting out the fat from the payroll. There was not too much extra weight in the ranks of producers and directors, which were down to twenty-three and seventeen respectively. Contract writers had been sliced from fifty-four when I took over production in 1948 to twenty-two, and contract actors were pared from ninety-nine to sixty-six. I thought that perhaps more would have to be chopped by the following year. Not all of the contract people had been lost by studio fiat. Independent production was taking hold. Actors were leaving to form companies in which they shared profits or to make deals with our competitors who were willing to pay a percentage of profits or 5 to 10 percent of the gross. Many actors, such as James Stewart and Clark Gable, came back from the war and, aware that taxes took 60 to 70 percent of their salaries, said, "To hell with that," and went off to greener pastures where they would own a piece of the action.

Using the time between my duties and eliminating sessions on the tennis court, I worked with Adlai Stevenson and Bill Blair, Stevenson's chief adviser, on Stevenson's commercials. Stevenson had a tic that on screen was easily spotted and worked against him — he tended to make a tiny smile after each point, even when he voiced a searching or serious statement. We worked to cure him of that and succeeded.

When the first convention of the California Democratic Council (an organization brought to maturity and strength by Alan Cranston) was held in Sacramento in 1952, I was asked to give the keynote speech. In it I spoke of Senator Windrip, a character created by Sinclair Lewis in *It Can't Happen Here*. It was clear I was talking about Joe McCarthy. At a meeting in Santa Barbara in 1950, Steve Mitchell, Ed Pauley, Paul Ziffren, Pat Brown, and two or three others had suggested I run for governor. The idea was preposterous. I knew enough about politics in California in 1950 to be sure you could not defeat Earl Warren, who had been defeated in the 1948 election as a candidate for vice-president running with Tom Dewey, but had resumed his seat as governor. Not only that, I was not equipped to hold an elective public office. I was too stubborn, rebelled at red tape of any kind, and, while I am an amiable man, I do not take peremptory orders with good grace.

However, it was because of my continuing interest in the political scene that I had been asked to do the job at Sacramento. I had a fine time doing it, but Schenck didn't approve of my assignment. Once again, there were mumblings and inquiries as to whether I'd be willing to run for governor of California. I said I had enough problems trying to run MGM.

During the presidential campaign, I traveled to New York to see Schenck and bring him up to date on what was going on in the studio. Schenck, as were every one of the studio presidents and production heads, was in Eisenhower's camp. Each time I saw Schenck he asked me to be careful about Stevenson. There was the nasty and untrue rumor about his sexuality and Schenck confided to me that some unnamed professor at Princeton had told him Stevenson was a Communist. That too was, of course, nonsense. Part of Joe McCarthy's crusade was to name everybody a Communist including Eisenhower, General Marshall, and Truman.

While I was visiting New York, Leonard Lyons, the happy host of the column "The Lyon's Den," snared an invitation for me to ride on Truman's train from Buffalo to New York City, campaigning for Stevenson. Lenny was a cheery man who looked for the bright side of the moon on all occasions. He had few enemies and armies of friends. He enjoyed his work more than anyone else I ever knew. He loved the prowls about town. He loved celebrity but never abused it. Famous people came to his sons' Bar Mitzvahs, not because they wanted or needed their names in Lenny's columns, but because they loved Lenny and his charming wife, Sylvia.

Lenny, as fond as I of Truman and his daughter Margaret, hustled me to Buffalo to join the President's entourage. When I packed for the trip, I put a gray shirt in my bag, planning to wear it for the train trip the next day instead of donning a white shirt, which might look quite gray after a dozen whistle-stops, getting off to watch Truman handle the crowds. So I took a gray shirt, and also a white one. However, when I dressed that morning in Buffalo it occurred to me that gray was simply too informal. Perhaps it would be more correct to wear a white shirt; and to complete my look as a Yankee Doodle Dandy, I put on a red, white, and blue tie.

The day with the President was a gala one. He signed menus for his guests, who were Lenny, Abe Feinberg, and me. He talked easily and candidly. On MacArthur: "I should have fired the son of a bitch a year before I did." The atom bomb: "There was no other choice. The generals said an invasion of Japan would cost us a quarter of a million lives." Toughest decision: "Going into Turkey and Greece. It could have meant war with Russia." Eisenhower: "He didn't have enough guts to stand up to McCarthy and defend George Marshall." Stevenson: "He's a decent man but I find him wishy-washy." Nixon: "He's a liar and he'll always be one." Churchill: "A snob but a very nice man."

It was such a comfortable day that we forgot we were spending it with the man who could gather about him the greatest power in the world. Each time before we stopped at one of a dozen stations crowded with folks eager to see him, Matt Connolly, his secretary, handed him a sheet of information, including football games and other data of local interest. Truman would glance at the material, then step out for a homey chat in his flat, matter-of-fact, crisp Missouri voice.

Each time he left the crowd yelling, "Give 'em hell, Harry."

I remember fragments of talks:

"Listen, now, your football team is playing Batavia and you gotta go get them."

"Now, there's one Democrat running and one Republican, and if you don't elect that Democrat you'd ought to be ashamed of yourselves."

"Don't worry about that fellow Stevenson. He's got brains and gumption and he'll make you a hell of a President."

"Now you just listen, I like Ike too. I made him a five-star general — but I wouldn't vote for him as mayor of Peoria no less vote for him for President."

"You just remember, comes rain, snow, sleet, or hail, you get out on Election Day and make Stevenson your President."

When lunchtime came, HST said he wanted to nap. We left his car and checked into the press and Secret Service Pullman next in line. We sat and talked to Matt Connolly and I remarked on the casual mood of the President, his friendliness, and his utter lack of pomp and circumstance.

Connolly told us that Truman was the same at all times; ornery and tough when angry and a warm cracker-barrel storyteller when relaxed.

Truman, Matt said, had a fearsome respect for the office of the presidency but never let it affect his own personality. "God knows," said Matt, "Truman isn't humble but he doesn't say, 'I am the President,' a hundred times a day."

As we click-clacked along Matt said, "There's one odd thing he's a stickler on. Maybe it's due to his haberdashery days, but if someone comes to call on the President, it is expected that he will wear a white shirt. Truman believes the office of the presidency should be respected by a proper mode of dress. White shirts, yes — colored shirts, no."

I clapped a hand to my head and then reported my silent debate about my shirt. Lenny was wearing white. Abe had on a striped shirt, but the stripes were blue on a clear white background.

"Well," said Matt, "maybe there's something to what he feels. You guys all did wear white."

In later years I saw President Truman, then former President (he hated the term ex-President) many times. I always wore a white shirt.

The election polls in 1952 showed Eisenhower leading, but hope springs eternal, particularly among poltical partisans, and we were buttressed by the private opinions of newsmen who were, in the main, supporters of Stevenson. Adlai had won most of them over by his reason, his bold and eloquent campaign speeches, and his quick and sharp humor. Being an admirer of Lincoln, Stevenson peppered his ad-libs and prepared talks with references to Old Abe.

Perhaps the objective, in addition to Adlai's obvious interest in Lincoln, was to take the subject of Lincoln away from Eisenhower. Eisenhower had his special armament — he sounded just like Clark Gable. In addition, there were the rumors concerning extramarital affairs. Sex — that is, heterosexual sex gossip — never hurt a candidate. When Jimmy Roosevelt, during a congressional campaign, was blasted with a scandal involving five women, Jimmy did not deny the charges — he confirmed them and was reelected to Congress with the biggest majority he had ever polled. We kept hoping that someone would blurt out a story that Stevenson was shacking up with four or three, two or even one married lady. There were whispers about him and Marietta Tree, but no one took them seriously. There was a rumor that one of his admirers had said, "I'd gladly lay Adlai any day." We never got that into print — darn it.

In order to hype up Stevenson's campaign in California, Paul Ziffren asked if I would stage an outdoor party for AES. Of course, I agreed, and asked Bill Goetz if he would co-host the shindig. He was delighted and volunteered the booze. I opened up my home and grounds and supplied the tidbits, barkeeps, and chairs.

The party was a smash; no one turned down the invitation and once word got around Bill and I kept adding to the list. The guests endured the required frisking by Secret Service men of ladies' purses and the checking of any small package or briefcase for hidden weapons. The day was a dream — sunny, mild, California without smog. More than five hundred guests swarmed in to greet the man from Libertyville and there were the obligatory handshakes, photographs, and smiles. It was a good, warm, and successful party. Bill and I overlooked the fact that five hundred votes do not an election win.

Stevenson lost the campaign. Bill Goetz and his wife, Edie, Mayer's daughter, lost their inheritance. Mayer, in furious rebuttal for having his son-in-law support and even sponsor a party for a Democrat *and* in concert with me, rewrote his will. As Bill said, "That was the biggest contribution anyone made to the Stevenson campaign."

As 1952 drew to a close and we gained some satisfaction from film grosses, there were signs of new events that would throw the industry into turmoil.

To bring in money to cover losses, some studios had already sold their film backlog to TV or to promoters who planned to sell to TV. Warners was the first and sold for what was supposed to be a staggering sum, $18 million. It was a bargain for the buyers, controlled by Eliott Hyman, Ray Stark, and Lou Chesler. They waited a short time and in turn sold their rights to United Artists for a huge profit, and United Artists turned their investment into gold when movies became a staple for telecasting. The big winner was Ray Stark, who began his extraordinary metamorphosis from agent into a fabulously rich and talented producer.

Twentieth-Fox also sold their old inventory, at a better price than Warners, but they too sold cheaply considering what they might have realized if they had hung on to their films.

Paramount made a better deal. MCA bought their package of more than two thousand films for $35 million plus a rider that if things went well with MCA's sales to TV, Paramount would be entitled to a bonus of another $15 million. MCA did so well that in a comparatively short time Paramount got their total price of $50 million. MCA parlayed their investment, which in rather a short span of time led to the extraordinary development of the present Universal City studio and many ancillary enterprises. In view of what MCA picked up, Paramount lost uncounted millions by not holding back their product.

Forces were being brought into play to combat the drain of movie grosses because of TV. The industry challenged television with Cinerama, 3-D, CinemaScope, a lessening of motion-picture code restrictions, and a drift toward multistar pictures with higher risks.

In some ways the year ahead, 1953, was going to be the year that marked the beginning of the end of the big studio system: the size of the studios would diminish; deals with independents would proliferate; TV productions would occupy stages once forbidden to them; the rating symbols with their meaningless identifications would be born; and stars like Bogart, Gable, Cooper, Tracy, Marilyn Monroe, Robert Taylor, Joan Crawford, Robert Ryan, Susan Hayward, Tyrone Power, and Leslie Howard would be reincarnated years after their death by the "Movie of the Week," the "Late Movie," and all the other movie programs on TV.

What would also be born would be a new form of extravagant picture making with greater rewards, greater losses, greater risks — and with that new industry would come a new pantheon of stars. However, the labor contractions to bring forth the baby would be painful.

28

*T*he Metro production highs during 1953 were *Julius Caesar, The Band Wagon, Mogambo, The Long, Long Trailer, Kiss Me Kate,* and *Knights of the Round Table.*

Before dealing with some of these I must report on three of the lows. The first of them was *Bright Road,* a lovely, warm story of a black boy, J.T. Starred in the picture were two newcomers, Harry Belafonte and Dorothy Dandridge. Emmett Lavery wrote the script and Gerald Mayer, one of our new young directors, did an inspired job; but we couldn't get anyone in to see the picture. It was honest and appealing and will always be a favorite of mine and a puzzle as to why it could not even return its original low cost of $490,000.

The second disappointment was *The Actress,* written by Ruth Gordon, directed by the redoubtable George Cukor, produced by Larry Weingarten, and played by Jean Simmons and Spencer Tracy in another of his interesting and unusual performances.

Failure is a more common occurrence than success, and most times, the reasons for failure are apparent — so you swallow and go on to the next effort. But *The Actress* was beautifully played, written, and directed, and was one of those failures that depress you. It's like pitching a no-hitter but losing one to zero.

The last of the three lows was my own production, *Dream Wife,* starring Cary Grant and Deborah Kerr. It was written by Sidney Sheldon, who had written *The Bachelor and the Bobby-Soxer* for me some years before. He had directorial ambitions, and since Cary was willing to go along with the gamble, I assigned Sidney to do the job. It would be an easy out for me to blame Sidney for the leaden failure. The fact is I liked the script. I thought Cary was delightful and Deborah first-rate. One fatal flaw was that the picture was in black and white and screamed for the richness of color. Sidney Sheldon's job as director was not a Mike Nichols first time at bat, but it was workmanlike. The plain and unalterable truth is that the picture didn't work because the central core of the plot was phony. Perhaps if played for farce it might have worked, but it was my fault for not recognizing that possibility long before we put the film in the camera.

The high moments, of course, are like meals at the best restaurants with you as a guest. *The Band Wagon* was essentially a thin but funny script by Comden and Green, not up to their topflight scripts of *On the Town* or *Singin' in the Rain;* but it did provide a proper background for the Arthur Schwartz–Howard Dietz score from their Broadway revue of the same name. The numbers performed by Fred Astaire, Cyd Charisse, Jack Buchanan, Nanette Fabray, and Oscar Levant were absolutely enchanting. The entire production was a triumph for all concerned, including, of course, Vincente Minnelli and Arthur Freed. It was one of those films during which, as an executive, you simply sit, enjoy the rushes each night, and then congratulate everyone concerned with the production for not having given you a moment's unrest. There are not many like that.

When John Houseman and Joe Mankiewicz came to see me about the casting of *Julius Caesar,* they brought with them a tape recording they asked me to play of an actor they thought might be able to do Marc Antony. I listened, liked it, and asked, "Who is it?" They answered, "Marlon Brando."

For a moment I thought they were putting me on, and then I played it again and this time I recognized certain sounds that told me it was Brando. They had learned Brando wanted to play it, for a salary, no percentage, and that he'd be pleased to tell me so in person. That meeting was arranged and I was captivated by him. Brando has the aura — a special corona that rests around him — as it did around Charles Laughton, or Gable or Tracy. As it does around Olivier.

Because of the subject, we were able to assemble a magnificent cast, the likes of which would be almost impossible to find today. John Gielgud, James Mason, Greer Garson, Deborah Kerr, Lou Calhern, Edmond O'Brien joined Brando. The film was made for two million dollars and served to move Brando into another echelon; the word was out — Brando could play anything. There was no trouble— no acting up — no delays. The picture was a success.

I have always had a fear of remakes. From the time I arrived at Metro I had been importuned to allow remakes of *Mutiny on the Bounty, The*

Four Horsemen of the Apocalypse, Tale of Two Cities, and *Red Dust.*
I had turned them all down. What was lacking in each of them was the
core, the casting of the main character — there was no Charles Laughton
or Rudolph Valentino or Ronald Colman, and while Gable was still around,
there was no Jean Harlow. Therefore, when Sam Zimbalist came to me
with his desire to do a remake of *Red Dust,* I said no. But Sam argued
that Gable was still vigorous, some years older but still a male sex figure.
And Ava Gardner was available and a close match in sex appeal for
Harlow and actually more striking. Certainly someone could be found
to play the English lady. Sam had already interested John Ford in directing — that was a plus. We began our search for the leading English lady.
John Ford wasn't pleased with the idea of Deborah Kerr. Greer Garson
was too mannered to suit Sam Zimbalist. Ben Thau rightly argued that
we might find someone new. The quest led us through all our voluminous
racks of tests — we found nothing. Then we began to look at the re-
jects that other studios made available to us. While I could not take the
time to view all of the film, I told the searching detail to yell if they
sighted the promised land.

One afternoon they yelled. I joined Ford, Zimbalist, and Thau in the
projection room and we viewed a test that Twentieth-Fox had made for
a film called *Taxi* to have co-starred Dan Dailey and a yet unknown female actor. The test was of a pretty girl who had a rather ordinary Irish
accent and who looked drab and uninteresting — but not to John Ford,
who reminded us she was the lady who had played Gary Cooper's new
wife in *High Noon.* My memories of *High Noon* were of the principled
and unconquerable Cooper, the men who stalked him, and that tough,
bitter, and honest ending. The wife, an unsympathetic role, was over-
shadowed by Katy Jurado, the once and now past mistress.

Ford had his reasons for liking Grace Kelly, for that's who the
woman was: "To begin with, for Chrissakes, all she did in *High Noon* was
shoot a guy in the back. Cooper should'a given her a boot in the pants and
sent her back east. Now, then, as far as this test — Darryl miscast her. But
this dame has breeding, quality, class. I want to make a test of her — in
color — I'll bet she'll knock us on our ass."

John's argument won the day. He made the test. It and Grace Kelly
were stunning. We signed her to a long-term contract. John Ford enabled me to even the score with Zanuck. He got Monroe — we got Grace
Kelly.

Mogambo was the new title for *Red Dust* and we avoided mention-
ing that it was a remake. Some reviewers never had seen the first version,

others had forgotten it, and still others gave it passing mention by noting that *Mogambo* was better than the picture upon which it was based.

However, many of our producers wanted proven women stars and we had a host of them (Gardner, Lana Turner, Elizabeth Taylor, Kerr, Garson, Eleanor Parker, June Allyson); though we showed our staff the Kelly test for their interest in using her in future films, we didn't find takers. That is, not until *Mogambo* hit the *Variety* "boffo" category. But by that time, Hitchcock had used Grace Kelly in *Dial M for Murder* and *Rear Window*, then in *To Catch a Thief*. Finally, we got her back for *High Society* and *The Swan*, but then Prince Rainier got her for a longer and more holy contract and she became Princess Grace.

There was a good-natured debate after her enormous success as to "Who Made Grace Kelly?" Stanley Kramer claimed her because of *High Noon*, an invalid claim because he never followed up. Hitchcock had a good case. He'd given her good roles but she had been around and Hitchcock had not done anything about her until our film *Mogambo*. John Ford deserves the big hand of applause because he spotted something all the others had missed. I take a small bow for signing her up on contract, a rare stunt in 1953.

But as I wrote in the *Saturday Review* in answer to that question, "Who Made Grace Kelly?," I summed up the inevitable and incontrovertible truth — God made Grace.

The production of *Kiss Me, Kate* came during the climax attendant to the introduction of 3-D. Years before Pete Smith had narrated an MGM release of an independently made series of comedy shorts that introduced the red and green plastic glasses to audiences who would soon find themselves feeling walleyed from their use. The experiment died. However, because of the looming and ever-growing might of television, the picture business was grasping at any device that appeared to be the white knight who would slay the dragon. When *Bwana Devil* revived 3-D in its old form and was a hit, the stampede was on.

We made one picture, *Arena*, which I loathed watching with the glasses. The damn things gave me a frightful eye ache and headache. When I went to my eye doctor, he said, "If you people keep up that 3-D menace you will be sued for millions. It is a device of the devil to give eyestrain, pain, and upset stomachs. What I'm saying, Dore, is you are all crazy." While I had not yet reached all of those conclusions posed by Dr. Robert Hare, I had determined that 3-D was a freak entertainment, that it was no white knight, and that it was marked for extinction.

On May 1, 1953, there was a meeting in Hollywood of the entire

The big laugh came as I announced it was time the executives took the first cut in salary — adding, "That is the kindest cut of all as far as you're concerned"

Ava Gardner, Clark Gable, and the apotheosis of the auld sod, John Ford, during the making of Mogambo

In Dream Wife, *Cary Grant, baffled by a flood of Oriental crates, asks Deborah Kerr for an explanation*

Richard Widmark, a fine man and a hell of an actor, faces an AWOL *in* Take the High Ground

executive staff of Hollywood and New York. I asked that the meeting be held on the West Coast so that we could show the New Yorkers some of our work in progress and have a long session without being dragged away from our first priority — making films and keeping an eye on the cost.

Since I was the host, Schenck had asked me to prepare an agenda and make an opening statement. The agenda had four items:

1. The number of films to be made
2. The camera and screen devices to be used
3. The question of use of stereophonic sound
4. The use of color and black and white photography

My statement at the meeting went on to present the conclusions that I had reached with my staff. Referring to Mr. Schenck's objective of reducing our inventory, I said we were cutting down our grandiose promise of eighty-three films in eighteen months, putting our finished product into earlier release, and planning to make a lesser number of films in the fiscal year ending June 30, 1954.

I outlined our disappointments but argued that we could not avoid taking risks on a few films of size and scope. Such films, if successful, could help us through this bad time. I also pointed out that despite the cuts in contract personnel, we still had enough talent to make eighteen to twenty-two large-budget films and four to eight small-budget pictures. During our sessions, I would review our screenplays and stories.

Next I dealt with 3-D, which they knew I loathed. Joe Vogel, head of sales, had invested $500,000 in the purchase of the plastic eyeglasses. In summing up my arguments against 3-D, I said, "We are opposed to 3-D except for a very special, a unique or freaky film."

(During a rather heated discussion following my presentation, I foolhardily predicted that before long we would be advertising pictures "You Can See Without Glasses." Lucky me. That's exactly what we did after first exhibiting *Kiss Me, Kate* in 3-D, which succeeded in keeping audiences away in angry droves. We got them to come in by plugging the fact that the picture was *not* in 3-D. We had prepared for the contingency by making two screen dimensions during production. We were stuck with a massive load of red and green eyeglasses but we made up for it in final grosses.)

Then I went into my doubts regarding CinemaScope, which involved a lens that enlarged a squeezed film image into a wide, eye-stretching picture on an outsized screen. I ventured that some of the men had changed their opinions radically. In my own case I had changed it three or four times. At first I liked it, then I didn't like it, then I liked it pretty well, and then I rebelled against it. I believed that if presented under the best circumstances, on a huge screen placed at a proper distance from the viewer, it was certainly effective, but my lack of faith in it as a method was predicated on my information that it was not practical for general exhibition. Anyone sitting in a forward seat in the theater was doomed to get a headache or a queasy stomach or grow dizzy. I said that it was restrictive and that while it had been beautifully exploited, we had as yet no solid demonstration that it would work successfully for a major studio's full program of pictures. To me it was a special kind of image that required a special kind of selling, and I thought it would be a mistake for Metro to devote itself to a program of films that provided no retreat into more standard exhibition.

I won that argument in the long run, but had some disagreements with Darryl Zanuck, who quite naturally wanted everyone to follow his lead into total CinemaScope production. I had to write to Zanuck and point out to him that if we abandoned all our standard production plans, we would, in effect, be jeopardizing our entire inventory of films awaiting release with a price tag of $50 million pinned onto them.

We could not inferentially deprecate the potential value of such non-CinemaScope films as *Julius Caesar, Mogambo, The Band Wagon, All the Brothers Were Valiant, Knights of the Round Table, The Long, Long Trailer,* and *Take the High Ground,* all of which were successful when they reached their release dates and played into 1954.

When we came to discuss the advent of new sound devices, there was solid agreement that we use stereophonic sound.

Our last agenda item concerned color. I argued that color was a necessity and had added millions in revenue to *Ivanhoe* and *Quo Vadis?,* but that Sam Goldwyn had achieved a kind of screen immortality with *The Best Years of Our Lives,* which was in black and white; and I volunteered that *Battleground* wouldn't have made any more if it had been in color. What I was suggesting was that we not rush into full color production but reserve black and white for films admirably suited for the old standby.

For a few years my position held water with films such as *Blackboard Jungle, Trial, Ransom,* and others; but when it came to *Bad Day at Black Rock* the setting and the script called for color, and I perceived that the story also lent itself to wide screen to accent the vast and lonely locale.

To some degree color television helped bring on the death of black and white film.

The conference we had was of value. There appeared to be a better understanding of common problems and for the first time we appeared to be having some mutual respect.

Later in the year we had another acute talent crisis. Lanza was to make *The Student Prince*. He had recorded all the songs. There was no argument in that department; he sang beautifully. The problems began with our shooting schedule. Mario checked in overweight. He was told he needed to reduce. John Carroll continued to try and help him. Lanza became meaner. His language was pure gutter speech and lacked the saving grace of even a spot of humor. He was also eating caldrons of pasta and drinking flagons of beer and wine.

He skipped starting dates, reported in late for wardrobe fittings, and made an utter nuisance of himself. When speaking to Mannix and me he called us and the other executives a stream of obscenities. He was fortunate Mannix was in a judicious mood. Mannix was still ironfisted and could have coldcocked Mario if he had decided to.

We warned Mario and pleaded for him to reorganize his life. He was flirting with oblivion for himself and we told him so. He was too far gone to listen. He left after telling us we could go fuck ourselves.

Mannix and I agreed that Lanza was off the rails. I called Schenck and suggested we had no alternative. We had to fire Lanza and sue him for damages incurred by his not doing his job, and we should make sure we had the rights to his recordings.

Schenck believed we were being hasty. He was planning to come out to see his brother, Joe, who was ill, and he would talk to Lanza.

Mannix and I were present when in a few days Schenck arrived for his meeting with Mario, who showed up almost on time. Schenck, in his warmest and most persuasive manner, told Lanza how much Mario was admired, that he owed his life to his fans, and that we were willing to help him regain his disciplines.

Mario responded by saying that Schenck didn't know what the hell he was talking about. He went into high gear from there, telling Schenck that everyone at the studio was an idiot. He said he himself was a genius with the God-given gift of Caruso's "pipes." He rambled on, not permitting Schenck to interrupt him, and referred to Mannix and me as stooges. By then I knew Schenck had heard enough. I said to Mario, "We've heard this before, Mario, you can go home." He invited us to go to hell and left. Schenck shook his head, put a finger to his temple and twirled it, and said only one word, "Crazy."

Lanza was given notice of his discharge. He sued MGM for his records. We sued for damages and ownership of his records. The judge read Lanza's deposition, threw up his hands at the incoherent flood of obscenities and non sequiturs, and threw Lanza's case out of court.

In a short few years after he left MGM, Lanza made some unimportant pictures, destroyed his body by his routine of gaining then losing fat. He ate too much, drank too much, and died suddenly of a massive heart attack.

He was still in his thirties.

We went ahead with Edmund Purdom as the Student Prince and he did a superb job of synchronizing his lip movements to Lanza's voice. The picture returned our investment and a fair to middling profit. Lanza's recordings were the prime ingredient for the picture's success, and that success went to Purdom's head. He believed he was responsible for the happy result. He asked for a new contract. We denied it. He asked for a release. We granted it.

The early autumn brought the pleasure of Jeb's Bar Mitzvah, for which he was prepared by Rabbi Jack Pressman, a young and deeply committed teacher who also gave me my first lessons in conversational Hebrew as it is spoken in Israel. (The language is a difficult one. I've retained a rather sizable vocabulary and have added to it through the years, but my grammar is shockingly bad — I speak a pidgin Hebrew.) Jeb's introduction into manhood was properly conducted in Pressman's Conservative synagogue, and the service was in Hebrew — at least 90 percent of it. The friends who attended prior to the lunch we served at home included Jews whose only contact with the Holy Tongue was *shalom, kosher,* and *mazel tov,* a number of non-Jews who suffered through the rather long service in a devoted act of friendship, and a few friends who knew the service and enjoyed it. I was my usual reserved self — I wept with happiness. Jill and Joy were bored stiff. Miriam went through all of it with her hankerchief at her eyes.

The lunch was super. The weather was magnificent, the food ample, and the drinks relaxing. Jeb's speech to the guests avoided the clichés. He started by saying, "Today I am supposed to be a man, but if that's so, why do I want to go upstairs and read my comic books?"

He had some other one-liners and then grew serious about his future ambitions. He said he would like to grow up to be a good Jew. Also a good American like "Franklin Roosevelt, Harry Truman, Adlai Stevenson, and Woodrow Wilson." The Republicans asked for equal time. Jeb ad-libbed a tribute to Abraham Lincoln but said, "That's as far as I go."

During the remaining months of the year, I was asked to do a great deal of public-relations work on behalf of the industry and the studio. I gave a lecture on NBC radio regarding the changes in motion-picture technique, wrote articles on the same subject, wrote pieces for *Variety*, orated against "gloom in Hollywood," and upheld the star system, meanwhile working like hell to decide where to land us in 1954 and to select a program of eighteen new stories that would stave off panic.

We were losing stars. Clark Gable was preparing to leave for independent deals, Red Skelton walked into TV for fame and fortune, Garland and Lanza were gone, but we had pared our heavy overhead down to a workable and profitable level, and were confident about the picture releases for 1954, which included continued distribution of our heavy grosses from 1953.

However, rumors drifted like slow-moving wisps of cloud that finally evaporate; I was leaving MGM, I was going to be fired, I was ill (well, I did get ulcer symptoms and Sam Goldwyn called to say, "Don't get them — *give* them!"). Where these rumors started I could only guess, but to pay strict attention to them was a waste of time and energy. Once during the war when Joe Mankiewicz, Edwin Knopf, Bob Vogel, and I were car pooling our way to the studio, we passed a new, large structure that was just completed, but no one knew what it was or was intended to be.

We decided to start a rumor. It was, we plotted, a secret factory for making a plane with seven engines, equipped to carry a crew of forty men and protected by armor heavy enough to cause bullets to drop away like dead flies. It could fly high enough to avoid any known antiaircraft. It had a name — the *Avenger*. That was our creation and we agreed to drop the information casually, as if it had been told to me by a serviceman, to Joe by his houseman, to Bob — head of our foreign censorship — by an opposite number at Paramount. Knopf was to have been told by his brother Alfred.

Within a few days the story of the plane came back to all of us in many guises: its name had changed to *Atlas* or *Victory*. It was the result of the achievement of a spy who had stolen German plans for such a plane. Finally the rumors stopped. It turned out to be, for a short time, an assembly plant for jeeps or something like that. The truth is, that was a rumor — I lost all interest in the building and never gave a thought as to what it really was. I still don't know.

So rumors about my soon-to-be relinquishment of command might have been started by someone's wishful thinking — or a secret plan of Schenck — or a vow by Mayer that I would soon be "included out." Perhaps it was a demonstration of an observation made by Napoleon: "What is history but a fable agreed upon?" It could be I was being told a fable that would turn out to be history.

But now it was New Year's Eve. We celebrated the apparent fading away of Joe McCarthy but worried about the arrival of Richard Nixon, who had been a fellow we had tangled with years before in the campaigns of Jerry Voorhis and Helen Gahagan Douglas.

But we drank to everyone's good health and a good year, and made resolutions that none of us ever kept.

29

*M*GM's *thirtieth anniversary* was celebrated in 1954. By year's end it seemed it had run on forever. My notes on the happenings include happy and sad events, moments of success and failure, satisfactions and frustrations, and, of course, the round-robin schedule of production, speeches, Jewish study and activity, and my family concerns.

Jill, now eighteen, was admitted to Stanford. Miriam and I shall never forget watching her walk into her dormitory carrying her large panda toy, an assortment of dolls, and a sheaf of long dresses. She refused our wish to help her unpack because it would make her "seem childish." However, there were some things she could not carry and once it became clear that other fathers and mothers had to help install the freshmen (freshladies? freshpersons?), Jill ceased protesting. We left her after a while with a checking account, a comparatively clean room, and a roommate whom Jill was certain she would not like, and we headed back to our home. Miriam cried — the first bird had left the nest.

But long before, as the months of winter, spring, and summer had sped their way, a few contingencies reared up.

The first was Howard Hughes's confrontation with the Motion Picture Producers Association over the advertisements for the film *Stromboli*, directed by Roberto Rossellini. The picture had received startling press coverage because of the overt love affair between Rossellini and Ingrid Bergman, who was the star of the film. Hughes took advantage of all the clamor and clanging of the publicity by producing a series of ads picturing Stromboli, the volcano that gave the picture its name, as a rather obvious phallic symbol. The lava and fire spurting from the cone contributed to Eric Johnston's ire. He fined Hughes and demanded he withdraw the ads or face dismissal from the club.

Hughes never responded well to threats and there were angry statements, talk of lawsuits, and lurid press coverage, all of which did not do much to help the box office because, the truth is, the film was a minor endeavor. As the tempo of activity increased, I was surprised to receive a call from Hughes, who asked to see me. I knew he would not wish to leave his own compound so I volunteered to go to his offices at Hughes Aircraft. Hughes said he'd send a car for me and suggested we have lunch in his quarters.

The following morning a car (a limousine) picked me up and drove me to the factory gates, which were guarded by competent-looking men wearing side arms. I was led to a large room, half the size of a tennis court, in which there was nothing but a bridge table, four folding chairs, a bare blackboard, and a large picture of the *Spruce Goose*, Hughes's wooden flying boat and a notorious failure. He had designed and constructed it to carry 750 men, with all their needed equipment, into action. Its total time aloft had been a few minutes about forty feet off the ground.

After a short wait, during which I felt as though I was in a scene written by Kafka, Hughes entered wearing his sneakers, rumpled slacks, and a white shirt with the sleeves rolled up above his wrists. He said, "Hello," and "Thanks for coming."

Then we walked out of the room and into a vast shop in his plant where there was a bank of machines turning out bombsights for the air force. Hughes spoke to me about metal fatigue and told me that each of the machines in the line had moments of resistance to being worked too hard. It sounded like Kafka but Hughes assured me it was true. That tour of perhaps ten minutes was followed by a trip in Hughes's private car, a beat-up Chevrolet. He wanted me to see his plant, his private airport, and the huge helicopter he was developing that was planned to lift a freight car. When I asked if that was possible, he said, "Yes, it will fly." It did.

That concluded the two-dollar tour and I was wondering why he had asked me to come. Certainly he hadn't asked me merely to show his wares and certainly he couldn't have been interested in demonstrating his cuisine, which was served in a small private room and consisted of a glass of tomato juice, a steak, sliced red tomatoes, and tea.

When we finished our food, I glanced at my watch, saw that the better part of an hour had passed, and said, "Howard, my desk is loaded. Was there anything in particular you — "

He cut in, "I want to ask you one question. Am I right or wrong about those ads for *Stromboli?*"

Hughes was not a man you fenced with. I said, "You're wrong, Howard, the ads are obscene."

He asked me to tell Johnston that he would withdraw the ads. I said he ought to give the word directly to Johnston.

Hughes said, "I won't call the son of a bitch. Would you at least tell him to call me?"

That I would.

As Hughes was driving me to the limo that was waiting for me I asked, why me, why had he asked me?

Hughes said, "I trust you. You didn't rub my nose in the dirt after *Battleground* was a hit. I don't trust any of the others to tell me the truth."

Of course, I was complimented. I hoped he was giving me the right reason.

At the studio I called Johnston and said that Hughes wished to speak to him. I wouldn't tell him why except to say that the call would be worth the price.

That was the last time I saw Hughes, but I did speak to him twice on business regarding the loan-out of Janet Leigh to his picture *Jet Pilot*, on which Hughes wasted a bundle and part of four years' time.

In 1947 at RKO, as I mentioned, Joe Losey had suggested Stephen Vincent Benét's story "The Sobbin' Women" as a good yarn for a musical. It was tied up by Josh Logan, who was planning to do it as a stage vehicle. When I went to Metro I told Ken MacKenna to call the agent, Harold Friedman, and ask what he wanted if Josh, who still had his option, would drop his interest. Ken reported that Friedman would insist on $35,000. "Tell Friedman that the day he hears Logan has dropped it we will pay the price," I advised Ken.

Finally, after a wait of six years, we got the property, changed the title to *Seven Brides for Seven Brothers*, assigned Stanley Donen to direct, Michael Kidd to do the choreography, Albert Hackett, Frances Goodrich, and Dorothy Kingsley to do the script, and away we went with Jack Cummings as the producer.

There had been a plethora of ballets in musical films and I asked Michael Kidd to try and avoid balletics on this rather rugged outline. He nodded. Some weeks later, Mike asked me if I'd like to see a rehearsal of the big barn-raising number — with the entire cast involved. When? "As soon as you get here," Mike answered. Five minutes later I was seated next to Mike and the number started. It was athletic, acrobatic, funny, full of marvelous muscular dancing and absolutely wonderful. Everyone was breathless as it ended — including me. The crew joined in the applause.

Mike turned to me with a mischievous grin and asked, "Is it too balletic?"

Still brimming with joy and surprise I could only shake my head and give Mike a bear hug.

Everything worked. Howard Keel and Jane Powell were supported by five magnificent dancers, Marc Platt, Matt Maddox, Jacques d'Amboise, Tommy Rall, and Russ Tamblyn. They, with Keel and Jeff Richards (neither of whom could do a soft shoe), were the seven brothers. The dancing and the score by Johnny Mercer and Gene DePaul brought us an outstanding thirtieth-anniversary hit. We also received the tidings that Metro led the Academy nominations' roll call with thirty-two.

To pay tribute to MGM's history, Ed Sullivan set aside one of his Sunday night shows in which I was to narrate the MGM story. The day before the show I was on the run from Miriam's studio to rehearse, but as I avoided tripping on one of our dogs, I landed heavily on my chest against a brick facing. I fell and could not breathe without piercing pain. Obviously, I had cracked some ribs. I was helped into a chair and waited for our doctor, Bob Portis, an orthopedist who picked the right profession — he was not only good for his patients, but because he was always skiing and breaking various bones in his own body, he saved a fortune by the reciprocity doctors offer each other.

"That's what you did all right," Bob said. "I think maybe two or three ribs. No, they didn't puncture your lung." He taped me up, told me to take pills he'd send over to me, and rest for a few days. That was not possible since I was due at rehearsal and was slated to go on the air the next day. I was excused from rehearsal and told I could go over my lines before the telecast on Sunday.

The next afternoon, Sunday, I arrived at the TV studio neat in my black-tie outfit. I was taped as tight as a drum — if I dared draw a deep breath someone was obviously driving a knife in my chest. Portis, my genial orthopedist, had furnished me with pain pills that gave me, despite my physical discomfort, a mental euphoria that kept a silly smile on my face.

Ed Sullivan, a onetime softball player who played on the MGM team one Saturday and hit a home run for us, tried to make me as comfortable as possible. A big armchair was provided and we picked our way through the show. The script had been prepared by Sullivan's writers and read by Howard Strickling. I had read it between gasps of pain and waves of happy illusion that I was feeling fine.

The show went on the air and I have little or no memory of it. I've never seen a tape of it ("kinescope" was the term at that time). But two dreadful oversights were recorded. One, Mayer's name was hardly mentioned, his efforts and record slighted. Two, and more serious, when *Gone with the Wind* was recalled, the name of David O. Selznick wasn't heard or seen. Mayer used the occasion to level another attack on me. David joined in and did himself no great service by declaring that I had implied that I had produced his epic film. After a few days when the fire had abated and it became clear that no one but Mrs. Hopper had angrily reported the inadvertent omission, I called David and explained the circumstances. He granted his reaction had been a case of overkill and happily our friendship continued.

The weakness most people of celebrity live with is that they take press clippings too seriously. We are inclined to believe all the laudatory comments laid on our brows and scream bloody murder if we are panned or criticized. The reactions come with the territory. On two occasions I have objected to what I still believe were unjust and harmful reviews. In both instances I should have kept my mouth shut.

In the first case, a reviewer in a national magazine referred to *Battle-ground,* a favorite of mine, as a rather vapid and inaccurate film, aiming his best shots at the ending of the film when the C-47s fill the sky, as the fog clears and the sun bites through, and bring relief to the besieged GI's at Bastogne. He charged that such an ending was like the conventional U.S. cavalry rescue in too many trite movies. But the fact was that the sky *did* clear as the C-47s rendezvoused above Bastogne and the siege *was* lifted. General McAuliffe and the "Screaming Eagles" who were with him said that's the way it happened, and so did the press corps that reported the event.

By voicing my complaint in person to editors of the magazine, I alienated a friend, and despite the one bad notice the picture had been a smash. So nothing was gained by my righteous indignation and nothing had been lost by the review that had angered me.

The second time had to do with a play I had recently written with Amos Elon, based on his biography of Theodor Herzl, the founder of political Zionism who first generated the thrust that created Israel. The play opened on Broadway in November, 1976, and with no exception was panned. But one reviewer, in addition to panning it, degraded it and me. Since the TV station that employed the critic had notified all producers and writers that they were invited to use the network to rebut any review, I jumped at the chance. What I didn't reckon with was the fact that the critic, after my remarks, could take a second crack at me — which he did. So once again, I had gained nothing and lost more than I would have lost anyway by bearing it — not necessarily grinning, but simply bearing it.

In both cases, I had forgotten my rule, which was to avoid swinging back unless a deep principle was involved — an attack on friends, an injustice, a political rumble, bigotry — something that involved a point or a person other than myself.

This rule came into being in 1951 when I was in Florida on that fateful vacation when Schenck gave me a new contract. One morning when I was on the way to a cabana to prepare for a swim, a guest whom I had not yet met stopped me and asked if I had read Westbrook Pegler's column that morning. Learning that I had not, he said, "I read him every morning and today he talks about you, and it's the first time I ever heard him say anything nice about anybody. He thinks you're great."

That news alarmed me. Pegler didn't dislike me, he hated me. I thanked my informant for his pleasant report, went to the cabana, got the column, and read it. It was a highly sardonic, sarcastic piece, in which he accused me of predicting that "Reds" would be able to return and continue their work in poisoning Hollywood movies. To prove his point, he talked of one Twentieth-Fox picture directed and written by people Pegler suspected were part of the "Red front." In writing about me, Pegler used capital letters to stress his sarcasm — "NEW HOLLYWOOD GENIUS," "GREAT NEW PRODUCER," "BIG MAN," "SMARTEST MAN," "HOLLYWOOD LEADER." All his references were opprobrious. I came to the conclusion that the guest who had greeted me was putting me on. When he reappeared in his cabana, a few canvas swags away from me, I asked him why he was so impressed with Pegler's comments. Earnestly he said, "Why, he names you the biggest man in Hollywood and the smartest. He really admires you."

When my neighbor dove into the sea, I smiled at a thought — what if Pegler were inundated with a flood of letters congratulating him on his paean of praise to me — it would be a delicious kick in the nose. Then I concluded that few people read carefully and there was no point in pursuing a lie — unless it's a damn big one — and certainly no point in preening over every item that contains a word of praise.

So the Selznick-Mayer fire burned out, but once in a while in a book or an article, there is a notation about that Sullivan show and my "deliberate" attempt to take credit for MGM's thirty years of triumph, which would have meant that I began my affinity with the Lion when I was nineteen.

At about this time MGM, which had been the last of the Mohicans, ran out of legal devices, deterrents, and dodges, and were compelled to divorce the ownership of their theaters, leaving them with their distribution operations and film production activity. This divorcement procedure (largely cosmetic) was designed to prevent production companies that owed theaters from freezing out pictures made by competitors. (Time has knocked the entire problem into obsolescence: during the thirties, forties, and fifties Hollywood produced some four hundred pictures a year. That number, diminished to perhaps eighty in 1976, is now climbing to one hundred. However, TV subsidiaries of the picture companies make many hour-and-a-half films that become two-hour specials once the commercials are added.)

The new arrangement renamed Schenck as president and retained me as a vice-president and head of the studio for MGM. Loew's, Inc., became the distribution arm, no longer allied with production. The new alignment brought a flurry of activity in Metro's stock, which led the exchange for a day for reasons that still remain obscure to me.

Gable left the studio for the pursuit of happiness and a better share of the take in independent setups. Schenck was still opposed to giving stars a piece of the action even though Thau, Mannix, and I were persuaded that the time was due for us to bite the bullet.

But then we put into production *Executive Suite*, a John Houseman production, directed by Robert Wise and written by Ernest Lehman. We assembled a cast of stars, most of them under contract, whom most likely we could never have corraled on the open market for the price we charged to our production: Fredric March, Paul Douglas, William Holden, Louis Calhern, Barbara Stanwyck, Walter Pidgeon, June Allyson, Shelley Winters, Nina Foch, and Dean Jagger. The roles they played were not cameos — they were rich parts. The picture cost $1,383,000. To assemble the equal of such a cast today and enlist a director, writer, and producer such as Wise, Lehman, and Houseman would cost in the classy neighborhood of eight to nine million dollars. We grossed four million — today's gross could zoom up to twenty-four million. The success of *Executive Suite* strengthened Schenck's resolve not to bow to the agents who were yelling, "Let my people go!"

Other films going through the mill were *Men of the Fighting Lady* (a small-budget picture that did big-budget business), *The Last Time I Saw Paris, Betrayed,* and *Brigadoon.*

The most controversial of the new films was my own production, *Bad Day at Black Rock.* Nick Schenck was annoyed that I had co-hosted a rally with Bill Goetz for Adlai Stevenson at the Hollywood Bowl and had been told by directors of the company, he said, to ask me to cut down on my support of Stevenson. Again he reminded me that Stevenson was controversial and repeated the lies that AES was a former Communist and a homosexual. Schenck asked me to hold off producing *Bad Day at Black Rock* until he came to California within a week or two.

The McCarthy-Army hearings were in session during the spring and early summer, and we were not able because of our work to view any of the proceedings until nighttime. After eating a hasty dinner, looking at the rushes, and spending a little time with the kids, I would watch the excerpts of the hearings on TV. The strain of work, the intense aggravation with the hearings (I called Steve Mitchell, Democratic party chairman, each morning and asked him to make suggestions to Senator Symington to hit back at McCarthy, who was threatening him) were wearing me down. I also was annoyed at some of my friends who were nervous about attacking McCarthy. When I tried to raise some funds to help finance the publication of a book titled *McCarthy and the Communists,* written by Moshe Decter and James Rorty, I received "I'm sorry" — "I can't" — "Please don't ask" from worried friends, but Armand Deutsch, a former aide and then a producer (he worked on *Ambush* and *The Magnificent Yankee*), did pony up a cash contribution. The book when published was a valuable aid to Senator Aiken of Vermont when he led the successful move in the United States Senate to censure McCarthy.

All this, plus a sudden growing tension with Schenck, which I could not understand, made me ill. One night I kicked the TV set, pulled out the plug, and realized I better go see my doctor. His diagnosis, shared by a specialist, indicated ulcer symptoms.

The fact is I didn't have ulcers. Rest, medication, and diet, including a lot of milk (those were the days of the "sippy" diet) drove the pain away and the X rays showed the slight "shadow" had disappeared, which also meant I didn't have cancer. But what I did get from all the milk was a kidney stone, and I learned the meaning of "climbing up a wall." I was taken to a hospital, where I spent three lost days under morphine sedation. The morning they decided to operate, I passed the arrow-shaped calcium stone and my body jerked for two more days until the morphine wore out.

Then Schenck appeared and we had our first rowdydow and it was a beaut. Schenck had come prepared to order me to cancel *Bad Day at Black Rock.* Still feeling the effects of my battle with the kidney stone, I was less than patient and certainly I had no intention of abandoning *Black Rock.* We argued this out in the garden of my home. Schenck raised his voice and, in response, mine went up a decibel or two. Finally, I refused to take the picture off the schedule and told Schenck he could fire me or I would quit if he went over my head and ordered the studio not to do the picture. We both quieted down. Our voices relaxed. He said he didn't wish to make a final issue on the question. I apologized for yelling. He asked for a glass of milk. Then we talked about the studio. We avoided politics. We went into see Miriam in her studio. The sun came out. Peace.

I had offered the finished script of *Bad Day at Black Rock*, which had been adapted from an original story by Don Maguire titled "Hondo," to a few producers. Pan Berman and Sam Zimbalist said no. John Houseman was busy with *Executive Suite* and so I decided to do this one as my own act of faith. One or two directors turned it down, so I went off the lot, captured the imagination of director John Sturges, and assigned Millard Kaufman, a former marine officer with a combination of toughness and hard intellectuality, to write the screenplay. Having offered it to Spencer Tracy, I was prepared to wrestle with the Tracy syndrome of off again, on again. It came on schedule.

Tracy said he liked it but the guy who came to Black Rock had no real character.

Listening to Tracy was always a pleasure. This time I learned something about the script. He was right — the character of McCreedy needed a personal story, an inside problem, a subtext. I promised we would find one. Millard and I spent a night wrestling for something that would fill out the space. I remembered that years before, when I was with Selznick, I had worked on a story for Joe Cotten, Ingrid Bergman, and Eric von Stroheim that fell apart before it went into screenplay. But the character that Joe was to have played was a war veteran who had had a crippling injury to one hand. I tried that notion on Millard. It pulled things together. It made Tracy's reluctance to fight more credible, his desire to bring the medal to the father of the nisei who had saved his life in combat more understandable, and when there was no way out except to resist and strike back, it gave Tracy's character a new confidence that he could prevail even without the use of one hand. Millard and I worked it all out in that one night and Millard rushed home and went to work on rewriting the screenplay.

The next morning I called Tracy, told him I had good news. He came in a few hours later. I laid out the new character line and he smiled and said, "That's it," and wanted to know when we'd get started.

Everything worked. Our location people found an abandoned railroad track stretching for miles in the heart of the Mojave Desert. It ran flat and straight as far as the eye could see. Ideal. Our art department and architects designed a tiny, dusty, woebegone town and built it next to the track smack in the middle of the length of the rail line.

Then we put together a dream cast. Robert Ryan, Lee Marvin, in the role that I believe made him an important actor, Ernest Borgnine, tremendously mean and menacing, Walter Brennan, droll and unexpectedly heroic, Dean Jagger as the weak-livered sheriff, Russell Collins as the jackrabbit telegraph operator, and Anne Francis as the misguided young woman.

Next, I decided not to have any music. Only sounds. First the quiet of the speck of a station in the heart of desolation. A wind blowing, a yowl of a coyote, the far-off horn of a diesel engine, then the roar of the train. The music department hated me. *Executive Suite* did not have a score and once again I was dishing them out of the deal.

Millard finished the script, we sent it to Tracy, he loved it. Everything was coming up roses. We scheduled our first day of shooting — a Monday in early summer. On the Friday before that Tracy sauntered into the office, sat down, and said, "Kid, you got to get yourself a new boy. I'm not going to do the movie."

During the years I had tried many ploys to get rid of the Tracy syndrome. I had tried flattery, pleading, anger, reason, humor, but as we sat facing each other I had the feeling none of those previous tactics would work. I tried something new — apparent acceptance — with a kicker.

I said, "Okay."

That surprised Tracy, who said, "You mean it's okay — really?"

"Sure," I said. "I was supposed to make only twenty or twenty-two pictures this year. It won't make a fuss if I lose one."

Tracy bit. "Well, great, then there's no problem."

The kicker came into play. "None for me, maybe for you, Spence."

"Like what?"

"Well," I said quietly, "you see, Spence, we've built the sets, signed the cast, done the whole works; and while it's no skin off my nose, I'm sure Schenck will ask the price and — well —" I paused as if calculating — "well, about four hundred and eighty thousand — and I'm sure Schenck will make me sue you for the whole ball of wax."

Tracy took a long beat. "You would do that to me, you son of a bitch?"

I nodded. "I'd have to."

Tracy got up. "Well, I'm goddamned. There you are sitting in that goddamned chair in the middle of summer in your air-conditioned office, and I'll be in the stinking hot summer sweating my balls off. Some deal!"

I took my cue. "Spence, if it will make you feel better, I'll go to the Mojave with you. We'll sweat together."

"You better be there Monday morning." He went to the door, then turned and faced me. "You really would have sued me, wouldn't you?"

I smiled. "If you really would have walked out of a picture two days before shooting — yes."

Tracy said, "See you in Black Rock, Monday."

Monday, my son, Jeb, and I were there. We stayed three days.

When I told Tracy I had to go back to work in the studio he shook my hand, waved so-long to Jeb. The company went through all the location work in less time than scheduled.

The film, as I cut the first rough version, discussing it each day with John Sturges, came to exciting life. In a short time, with no music but with my "creative" sounds, we went to preview. We died for the first ten minutes because the picture fought like the devil to capture the audience, who were, because of the opening silence, puzzled as to what kind of film they were watching. Once they found out, the picture moved, but then faded out, again without music.

John Green, convinced I was wrong, had come to the preview and had brought André Previn, who was under contract to us, along for the trip.

The verdict was clear. The opening needed music. John Sturges said so, Green, Previn, Herman Hoffman (my production aide on this picture), Millard all agreed. The fact is, I, too, knew I was wrong after those first ten minutes.

I asked Previn to give us something loud, throbbing, martial in undertone. Sturges and Hoffman also suggested putting long helicopter shots under the titles and hammering the music over them. Agreed.

Hoffman went up as a second-unit director and did the shots, which were wonderful. André's score was perfect. Schenck, after he saw the film, told me he was glad I made it.

Everything considered, it was a good year and I knew we had some special ones lined up for next year.

Because of the reduction in number of new films and the distribution of films made in 1954, there was an overlap of releases during the years 1955 and 1956; films finished in 1954 were still running in 1955 and those made in the latter year were given full release in 1956. The same delays took place with pictures made or prepared under my aegis in 1956 that did not get to theaters until 1957 and, in a few instances, not till 1958.

My final two years at MGM, 1955 and 1956, were productive ones, but buzzing overhead during my working days were the persistent rumors that I was doomed to walk the plank. There were quarrels within the board of directors, who were deeply concerned with the opening moves being made by a group of businesses to obtain control of MGM; and the talk at cocktail parties centered on L. B. Mayer's ambition to regain his former eminence and rid the studio of Schenck and me.

The fencing and fighting between Schenck and Mayer had a long history. Mayer justifiably took credit for creating the size and tone of Metro, which was one of power based on the style and talents of Thalberg, who set the pattern for MGM production until his early death in 1936. But assembled in the studio were talented men and women who had continued the Metro mode — directors such as Sidney Franklin, Victor Fleming, Mervyn Le Roy, Fred Zinneman, Woody Van Dyke, and Robert Z. Leonard; producers Hunt Stromberg, Bernard Hyman, Lawrence Weingarten, Sam Zimbalist, John Considine, Jr., Arthur Freed; designers Adrian, Irene Sharaff, Helen Rose, and the extraordinary Cedric Gibbons; plus an army of distinguished writers who shuttled in and out under Thalberg's insatiable search for literary excellence; and finally the fabled "more stars than in Heaven," which was L. B. Mayer's main thrust for MGM primacy, achieved with the contract list headed by Gable, Tracy, Norma Shearer, Wallace Beery, Marie Dressler, Myrna Loy, William Powell, Lana Turner, Robert Taylor, and the incomparable Greta Garbo.

Schenck, however, had euchred his way into his position of power in New York by amassing a personal fortune estimated to be in the area of forty million dollars, which is an extremely nice area. Schenck and his brother Joe were Russian emigrants who had struck a mother lode in the establishment of the Palisades Amusement Park. Joe eventually became a founder with Darryl Zanuck and Spyros Skouras of Twentieth Century–Fox. Nick Schenck in a stock deal acquired control of Metro-Goldwyn-Mayer, which had previously been acquired by a triumvirate of Louis Mayer, Robert Rubin, and Harry Rapf, with Mayer the guiding force.

Mayer was a Canadian. He had come to the North Country from Russia with his parents and settled into New Brunswick. Mayer had been in the junk business, had seen the opportunities in the budding exhibition of motion pictures, and had, as had other pioneers such as Adolph Zukor and the Warner brothers, reasoned that the big bucks were in the production of the films. Consequently Mayer came to California, aggressively joined in the early biting competition, and emerged as the toughest, most skilled infighter of the pack. He had successfully wooed Thalberg away from Carl Laemmle and built MGM into the top *rancho* in the Hollywood plains.

Certainly Schenck had business acumen and a style that Mayer lacked. He also criticized Mayer's manner of speech and even his eating habits. He knew everything about Mayer's romantic interludes with some of the Metro stars and he deplored Mayer's extravagance, such as chartering a plane to travel to Mexico with a covey of stars to dress up the occasion of his getting a Mexican medal. When the studio was returning big profits and winning Oscars, Schenck closeted his irritations; but as soon as the profits sagged for a short time after World War II, Schenck's criticisms were brought into the open.

Mayer's answer in opposition to Schenck's observations was to speak of Schenck's "two faces — the smiler and the killer," to resent Schenck's power and constantly talk of his own glowing achievements. Mayer also threw out gossip anent Schenck's family being put into positions with high salaries. (This didn't swing much weight what with L.B.'s own display of nepotism.) Nepotism is resented only by folks who do not benefit from it. The fact is, it always goes with the master suite; in big business — the Fords; with the Rockefellers it is obvious; in politics, FDR all the way up to Carter. Show business is loaded with sons, daughters, cousins, and a variety of other relatives. What Mayer concentrated on was Schenck's ownership of businesses and concessions run by or dummy-controlled by some of his kinfolk.

With this going on and the pressure getting strong and Schenck beginning to to grow weak, the board was able to "elevate" Schenck to chairman of the board and move Arthur M. Loew, a son of Marcus Loew, into the presidency of Loew's, Inc. That suited me fine. Arthur was an unusual man. He was cultivated, had a continental flair achieved during his years as international president of distribution. He was no schemer, and finally he had respect for and understanding of talent combined with an excellent sense of good business.

Physically, Loew had a touch of elegance and he did many things well. He was a top bridge and excellent tennis player, a first-class yachtsman, bowler, and billiard player.

His appointment as president put a brake on the adversary forces that were moving into battle positions, and consequently seemed to quiet the whispers re my departure. Arthur did tell me that since my contract was at an end the thirty-first of December, 1957, it might be sensible, since my job inevitably was going to be more administrative than creative because of Arthur's determination to make independent deals in tune with the changing times, for me to consider forming an independent setup to become effective the end of 1957 and turn over the administration of the studio to someone who enjoyed making deals rather than making films. He and I agreed that for the benefit of the present operation it would be wise if neither of us said anything concerning the future arrangement.

So I dug into my work with a freer mind and much enthusiasm. We had our full share of failures but quite a parade of distinguished films.

The biggest and most embarrassing failure was *The Prodigal*. Charlie Schnee wrote and produced it and Richard Thorpe directed. In all candor, I hustled Lana Turner into playing it opposite Edmund Purdom, who had not yet made his move for the big money he claimed to deserve. The sorry fact is I liked the script. I thought it would draw an audience. What I forgot was that C. B. DeMille had an exclusive on the Bible. Poor Lana swayed her way through the film, but it was a hopeless task. The script was lifeless. After two weeks' shooting I saw we were in quicksand. I had the production office calculate the cost if we stopped the picture dead in its tracks. When I heard that the sets were already built, that the costumes were tailored and the contracts for outside talent were signed and sealed, I guessed our loss would be well over a million. My guess came close — it would amount to $1,200,000.

I decided it would be less costly to finish the picture on an accelerated schedule and hoped that we wouldn't fare too badly. Except that when Lana left Metro she retained an unremitting dislike for me. But despite what I believe is the worst film I ever supported, we only lost a bit more than half a million. Despite the agony without any ecstasy, I did save the company $700,000 by finishing the zinger. That year Wade Nichols, the editor of *Redbook*, awarded us a large silver cup as the studio of the year for *Bad Day at Black Rock*, *Blackboard Jungle*, *Trial*, *Love Me or Leave Me*, and *Interrupted Melody*. In his presentation, he admitted he was tempted to fill the prize with manure in tribute to *The Prodigal*.

Bad Day at Black Rock had been released with a shower of wonderful reviews and good business. There was a smidgen of controversy because of the karate shots that Tracy gave Borgnine, but happily those countries in the Far East viewed the final fights as justifiable, and when I received the following memo from Bob Vogel, head of our censorship bureau, I sent Millard Kaufman and John Sturges a note:

Dear Fellas:
Cut yourself a piece of cake and enjoy it with me. Thanks and fondest.

DS

[*283*]

Bob's memo dated February 9, 1955, read:

Dear Dore:
I know of no precedent to the censor action referred to in letter from MGM Australia, (and I've fought with Australian censors during the making of 1,000 MGM pictures):
"Jack Alexander, the Commonwealth Film Censor, viewed *Bad Day at Black Rock* last evening in our theatrette.
"He was so engrossed with the sincerity of the portrayals, the moral of the story and the excellence of the production, that he considered it would be sacrilege to make any deletions, which normally have been made. So the picture was passed intact, without any cuts, with an 'A' Certificate."

Unless you remain objective that kind of news can make you forget a picture like *The Prodigal.* Too many people are eternally embarrassed by their mistakes in judgment and try to forget the nails of failure by sitting only on the soft cushions of success — which can harden one's arteries.

30

The Donnybrook Fair of my years at Metro was because of *Black-board Jungle*, the controversial and two-fisted Evan Hunter book. Richard Brooks had read it and was very excited about it, as was I once I went through it. Without a second thought I decided to buy it and in quick order we made a deal and announced the fact with pride. Then the slugging began. Frank Freeman, head of Paramount, called to suggest I not make the picture. I told Frank, in his Southern accent, that it really was our business, not his. He claimed it was his because he was head of the local office of the Motion Picture Producers Association. I said, "It still goes, podner, it's really just our business." Richard Brooks was assigned to write and direct and I asked Pan Berman to produce. When those items hit the press, I got a call from Eric Johnston, who, as president of the above MPPA, asked me not to go ahead with the production. He and I exchanged pleasant differences of opinion, but he warned me that the government might try and stop me because of the nasty look at our school system it would give foreign countries. I told Eric to catch up on his reading — magazines and newspapers had carried stories of juvenile delinquency in Italy, France, Germany, and, of all places, Russia.

Obviously, Johnston called Schenck, who suggested that perhaps I should reconsider. I had only one argument for Schenck. "Nick, you're suggesting I give up on a film that might earn us nine or ten million dollars." Nick asked me how much it would cost. I had a rough estimate of $1,200,000. He said go ahead.

Then Pan came to see me and said he had heard from Freeman and Johnston and from some friends who were nervous about his doing the job. I promised Pan that I would take take full responsibility when the sky fell. I said, "Pan, live dangerously." Dick Brooks did his best job up to that time. (He is sometimes forgetful. In a recent interview he said that he made the picture for $380,000. The final cost was $1,160,000. He also said that Mayer pleaded with him not to take the assignment. Mayer had been gone for two years.) However, it was Dick's idea to grab "Rock Around the Clock" for the main title and a new sound and volume was born — rock. It helped make the picture by starting it off on a high, wild, and modern note. The preview told everyone we had a smash hit. (The last gross I saw was over eight million. I'm quite sure it has reached ten million or more by now.)

Then a new opponent appeared — Clare Boothe Luce, the ambassador to Italy. She refused to go to a showing in Venice, the picture was withdrawn, and she urged that it be barred from exhibition in Europe.

When the picture hit New York there was another cloudburst of diatribe. The city school board said that the picture was untrue — as they were avowing that, teachers were being walloped black and blue and students were being raped and knifed. Fortunately, there were teachers who were willing to speak up with evidence as to why *Blackboard* was true. As a matter of fact, some months later a committee was finally appointed by the school board to investigate what was going on in the schools and their report verified the horrors.

As a cap to the fracas, Senator Kefauver came to Hollywood to investigate movies — he meant *one* movie, *Blackboard Jungle*. I knew the senator casually and was not overly fond of him. He called me as his first witness. He explained that he was in Hollywood to learn whether we acted responsibly when making a film such as *Blackboard Jungle*, which was stirring up such a great deal of negative comment. He asked for our bona fides and I presented two huge volumes of news clippings reporting crimes committed by juveniles in school long before the writing, making, and releasing of *Blackboard*. I then asked the senator what he found so forbidding in the picture. He admitted he had not yet seen it. I suggested that there seemed to be a lack of responsibility in his investigation. In a few days the senator, having had enough of "bourbon and branch," adjourned the session and returned to Washington.

We followed up Glenn Ford's return to stardom in *Blackboard Jungle* with *Trial*, written by Don Mankiewicz and produced by Charles Schnee (it cleared him of malicious mischief for *Prodigal*), and co-starred Arthur Kennedy and Katy Jurado with Ford. It was a rouser but was abused by the right wing and ignored by the far left because it dared to show that their motives were not always honorable. Mrs. Hopper missed the point of the picture and laid another blast at me. Sam Goldwyn called me to say, "Don't read Hopper. Just keep making pictures like *Trial*."

My first business conversation with Sam Goldwyn took place a few weeks after I had gone to Metro in 1948. He had called me to suggest he had a marvelous dancer, Virginia Mayo, who would be available for an MGM picture for a consideration.

"What consideration, Sam?" I asked.

Sam replied, "You have a girl there, I always forget her name, something like Liney Tinley or Lawry Turley — something like that."

"I believe you're thinking of Lana Turner, Sam."

"Yes, that's the one. I could use her."

"Sam, why would you want her if you can't remember her name?"

He laughed. "I'll make her a star."

His laugh gave him away. He knew her name but he was simply trying to pull a cute little flimflam.

From then on I'd occasionally lunch with Sam in his private little dining room in the natty Goldwyn studio. His company was engaging and the food was superb. He was a wise and an independent man. Almost every Hollywood malaprop is put in his mouth and every funny story about a hapless, angry, reckless producer is told about him.

I was not an intimate of his, but I spent time in his home and at his studio and I was first witness to two Goldwynisms. They came almost in one breath. They came because of his intensity, and you were so caught up you didn't laugh, but you said to yourself, "Don't forget that one."

The two I remember stumbled out as he was speaking of the superiority over the years of American films and their popularity with mass audiences all over the world. Then he went on:

"Let me tell you something — there's a lot of talk about this new English picture — about the nuns — *The Black Neuroses* [I wouldn't dare tell him, "You mean, *Narcissus*"] — it's not doing such good business — Americans don't like those English pictures — most Americans — believe me — you go out on the street and ask everybody and you'll find ten out of a hundred agree with me."

When Sam came to Metro to make a deal for Metro to release *Guys and Dolls*, the men in New York found they were no match for his business knowledge. Metro's distribution charge at that time was 35 percent of the take for domestic bookings and 40 percent for foreign. They didn't dare suggest that, but did suggest they'd take it on for 27½ domestic and 32½ foreign. Sam offered them 20 percent. They finally settled for 22 percent, and 30 percent overseas.

One day Sam Goldwyn suggested that I was wasting my time and energy running a studio. He offered to set me up as an independent producer, "the same thing you did with Selznick." I answered truthfully, "Sam, I love you too much to work for you. Anyway, you need me like you need another arm."

Sam had a high-pitched giggle, part snort. He said, "You're right."

Sometime before the tenth anniversary of the United Nations, I was asked by the San Francisco committee in charge of the social functions to stage a show for the occasion. Some of the actors and entertainers were still shell-shocked from the McCarthy, American Legion, and Un-American Activities committees but Frank Sinatra was the first to say, "Sure, buddy. I'll bring my own boys." That meant musicians. Then George Murphy volunteered to act as MC, telling me, "You need at least one Republican in the act." The dinner before the show was hosted by Mayor Christopher of San Francisco, who didn't guess right on even one name — as he read the list of dignitaries on the dais he and the audience gave up at the same time and we waited for what Christopher would do with the next name and then joined in the good-natured laugh. There were, among others, "Dog Hammerscold," "Moulatav," "Anthony Bunsh," "Carl Romewli." I became "Door Scary." As a matter of fact, there was one name he did get right, Frank Sinatra's — but not "Everall Harrymen." It was a marvelous introduction to the show.

As an honorarium for having put together our small revue, I was given a front seat for the following night to hear former President Truman make the celebratory address. The San Francisco Opera House is redolent with memories and beautiful to look at, and when I presented my VIP ticket, two handsomely uniformed officers began to escort me to my front seat. I confess I preened and if the song had been written at that time, I might have burst into "If My Friends Could See Me Now." I granted that some people in the audience were probably looking at me and wondering, "Who's that?," but I was quite sure by now my name was flying across and up and down the aisles. As we were about to reach my row, a group of ladies were looking at me and pointing — obviously I was famous. Then one lady quite audibly spoke up: "I told you, didn't I? There is only one man in Hollywood with enough guts to come to the United Nations and there he is — Darryl Zanuck!"

I did have some shred of dignity left — I merely said as I passed by the lady, "Thank you, madam, for those kind words."

Harry Truman was wonderful that night. He talked in lofty terms and yet was hard and firm when he spoke of the obligations of members of the United Nations. He made us think of what had gone on in

Korea. He evoked the memory and the dreams of Wilson and Franklin Roosevelt. When he finished, he deserved and got a standing ovation.

Shortly after that festive evening, the industry ran a dinner on behalf of the Truman Library Fund. As chairman of the Motion Picture Industry Council, I was responsible for the program.

The evening ceremonies began with the singing of "The Star Spangled Banner," followed by my introduction of Conrad Hilton, who was to lead us in the Pledge of Allegiance to the Flag. When I introduced the estimable gentleman, he stepped to the podium, reached into a coat pocket, and drew forth a typewritten copy of the pledge.

As he started and then proceeded haltingly with glances at his small manuscript, the audience boomed ahead of him and Mr. Hilton's was the lone voice at the end murmuring, ". . . and justice for all."

After dinner there was an obligatory speech by Y. Frank Freeman, a short tribute by Ed Pauley, and a few words from Governor Edmund Brown, followed by entertainment paced by "Old Blue Eyes" Sinatra, José Iturbi, and Sammy Davis, Jr. Then President Truman was introduced and made a gritty, warm, and amusing speech of appreciation.

We raised a sizable sum for the library.

During the dinner I had time to talk with President Truman. I'm aware that I was not the only person, and certainly not the first person, whom Truman told of his exchange with General Eisenhower, then President, as they were riding together to Eisenhower's inauguration. "Eisenhower made a late apology to me," he said, "that he was sorry he couldn't get to my inauguration in 1948 but he was tied up in Europe with his military duties. Well, I said, 'General,' " Truman took a beat, then went on, "after all, he still wasn't Mr. President until he took the oath. So I said, 'General, if I had wanted you there, I would have *ordered* you to be there.' "

No wonder Merle Miller's book of Truman's reminiscences was called *Plain Speaking*.

A month or two later I was visiting in Washington, and after a meeting with Eric Johnston in which we talked about Kefauver's Humpty-Dumpty appearance in Hollywood, I decided to visit Gettysburg, partly because Jeb had come east with me and wanted to take a look. We traveled there and were received by Walter Coleman, the historian and a genial man, who gave us a step-by-step tour, larding in anecdotes and historical details as we moved on. At one point, as we marched, as Pickett's men had marched, toward the high-water mark at Cemetery Ridge directly into General Mead's cannons, Jeb said, "Dad, can't you put this down on film — all of it, the statues, the guns . . . ?" He trailed off, thinking I was brushing off the idea. But I wasn't. I told him it was a wonderful idea. By the time we finished the tour and stood at the cyclorama, I had formed a pattern of how to do it. I asked Mr. Coleman if he would come to California and do a chronological step-by-step outline for me, in just the way he had done — "Put in everything — then I'll do a script and send it on for your corrections."

We made all our arrangements. He cleared the red tape out of the way, and within two months our crew, headed by Herman Hoffman, were in Gettysburg getting the film we needed for our editing. We combined motion pictures, still shots (hundreds of them), sound, music, and narration and came up with a half-hour documentary that is shown at Gettysburg to this day. So Jeb — take a bow.

Dwight Whitney in writing a profile of me referred to my desire to listen to as many people and their ideas as possible, as the Open Dore policy. Often it proved to be a burden. But just as often I struck gold. A case in point began when Miriam and I were in New York in 1954 to attend the opening of a gallery show of Miriam's paintings. As I was standing in a recess of the room I was approached by a young man and an equally young woman, both of whom reminded me of a description once applied to Heywood Broun's appearance, "He always looks like an unmade bed." However, they were both eager eyed and intense and asked if I would make myself available to listen to their demonstration of electronic music which was so novel and —. I told them that we were returning to California the next morning and that I had no time to oblige them. To assuage their obvious disappointment, though, I promised that if they ever came to California I'd be pleased to listen with an open ear and mind. I was sure that was the end of our association.

But a few weeks later these two young people were announced by the receptionist at the desk in the Thalberg Building. When they arrived in my office they were better groomed, and having gained entrance they were more assertive and articulate. They had a recording and played it for me. I was captivated by the sounds and fascinated by their account of how those sounds were produced.

As we talked it occurred to me that their "music" was ideal for the score of our first science-fiction film, which was presently in production. I had little interest in "sci-fi" pictures, as they are now dubbed. But the story of *Forbidden Planet*, scripted by Cyril Hume, was different. It had a different slant and a different villain — not a creature or a humanoid with an odd look but rather a psychological villain, the beastly id of a rational man that ultimately destroys him.

I called Johnny Green, head of our music department, and Nicholas Nayfack, the producer of the film, and their reaction to the music was identical to mine. We made a deal with the young couple, Louis and Bebe Barron, and their contribution to *Forbidden Planet* has helped keep it as a film that is studied and examined by film buffs and students. It was the first sci-fi picture in color, had a marvelous robot called Robby who was blessed with a sense of humor, and had imaginative sets, special effects, and miniatures that acted as prototypes for films that followed of the same genre. Candidly, I did not expect it would have the interest it has maintained, which has in fact increased in the years since it was made. But if nothing else, it proved to be a plus for the "Open Dore" policy.

My long and productive years in film inevitably result in the fact that some of the films I worked on as writer or producer or executive in charge of production fade in memory — some I choose to forget, others I wish I could remember. But one that remains indelibly for me is *Raintree County*.

Kenneth MacKenna, the head of our story department, asked me if I had ever read the book. I had not. Ken said he doubted that anyone at MGM but the original reader and he himself had ever read it. The story had been told to Mayer and his executives before I came back to MGM. It had been bought. It was still lingering on the shelf.

I read the book, loved it, and assigned Millard Kaufman to write it, David Lewis to produce it, and Eddie Dymytryk to direct. Our cast included Elizabeth Taylor, Montgomery Clift, Rod Taylor, Eva Marie Saint. We were going to introduce our own wide-screen device, which was really a matter of using lenses much like those for VistaVision or CinemaScope. We sent location crews to spot interesting and unusual locales as we began shooting some scenes in the studio. The details of Clift's subsequent horrendous automobile accident have been tellingly described in the books about Clift. What has not been told is the concern I felt about sending this large-budget film on location without some measure of insurance in the event something went amiss.

Normally, studios carried "self insurance," an invented term that indicated that insuring thirty to fifty pictures a year would be very expensive and over a period of years would total up in cost way beyond the probable cost of a random accident or two.

But in the case of *Raintree*, I convinced Mannix to take out a policy.

The random accident did not occur on location, but one night after a party in Hollywood when Monty slammed into a tree and almost killed himself.

After we learned the extent of Monty's injuries there was some talk suggesting that we recast his role, take our insurance funds and redo what had already been photographed. My own views were that we were rushing a decision prematurely; that if Monty recovered and had been summarily booted out of the picture we would have done him an injustice, and I felt sure that Elizabeth Taylor, who adored Monty, would refuse to do the film and be willing to face suspension. I talked to her and she confirmed my opinion. We closed down the company and waited for Monty to recover.

When he checked back in after a long, painful healing process that included plastic surgery, we had to face the sad fact that Monty was hooked on drugs and liquor that eased his pain and drove the demons of his accident from his mind.

Elizabeth was totally supportive. She nursed him, aided and covered for him. On the very bad days she called me for help, and during the time we continued our production I became fond of Monty. There was a little-boy vulnerability about him; beneath the pain, drugs, and liquor there was a generous and dear young man who had not matured emotionally. It was as if a fourteen-year-old had been suddenly moved into a thirty-year-old time frame and that, coupled with his accident, seemed to doom him. He exaggerated the extent of his disfigurement and rushed into the comforting arms of pills and alcohol.

Finally, *Raintree County* was finished but by the time it was placed in the docks for dubbing and scoring I was gone from the studio. I was asked to go to a preview, and despite what everyone had gone through — the delays, the scenes with Monty, the added expense — the picture was good. The New York contingent and some of the crew in the studio were convinced they had an expensive failure. Happily it was a success — not a very distinguished one, but Elizabeth won an Academy Award nomination for her wonderful performance. She deserved one for her loyalty to and care of Monty Clift.

I had maintained my relationship with Governor Stevenson and accepted, as did so many others, the fact that he'd be the 1956 candidate against the Eisenhower-Nixon ticket. A story in one of the national magazines drew my attention and I wrote Stevenson a letter, excerpts of which follow:

. . . certainly it must be clear that the opposition views you as the toughest candidate they have to deal with and the strategy is to make you look "aloof" in contrast to Eisenhower's and Dickie's "charm." You are to appear "erudite" (egghead in full dress) and intellectual in contrast to the "simple" and "direct" and "cracker barrel" administration that we are just finishing.

Despite the fact that big business has been running the show, the publicity boys have done a good job of selling the public on a "simple" fellow and have even made capital of the extraordinary preoccupation with golf, fishing and holidays all over the country. Further, if the charge is made that Eisenhower has lacked decision and straight line handling of issues (i.e., McCarthyism), then they're out to make you look more indecisive — more indirect — more evasive. In contrast to Ike's grin, upon which so many voters have relied to solve our ills — you will be pictured as dour. But, of course, when you are witty, you are going to be blasted for making light of grim circumstances. For you and those around you to know all this — as you do — is to be forewarned — but to attempt to circumvent all these techniques is almost impossible. What you say and what you do in direct appeal to the voter has to be your concern and not how the opposition will distort your conduct or inveigh against your actions. F.D.R. and H.S.T. faced hostile press and bigoted and senseless abuse. They won because what they did and what they were and what they stood for reached the voters over all the barrancas that the opposition placed in their paths.

For some time I've been working on a theme . . . the "Personality of Power." In it I quote the psychological observation that a man is in fact three men — what *he* thinks he is — what *others* think he is — and what he *really* is. There is, I think, still a fourth identity — what he *tries* to be. My hunch is that what he tries to be fuses all the others and brings the true portrait of the man into focus. But certainly there are areas that the best biographers and historians can only explore without ever learning the truth. These are the areas of a man's mind and thoughts that he leaves to himself — we can get hints and clues by judging only what the man says and does. What I'm getting at, albeit laboriously, is to urge you, despite all else, to be yourself. . . . What I'd like to suggest is that in some of your early talks — you talk a little of yourself — what you are and what you believe — a sort of location trip inside the heart of A.E.S. The glimpse you gave in that dark November hour of 1952 by using the Lincoln quote is what I mean. Why can't a candidate reveal some of his yearning and some of his dreams? Intimacy with a good man brings friendship. It works between two; it also works with millions.

I wonder if one part of one talk couldn't tell the voters that you know the nature of attacks that will be made upon you — tell how you are going to be blasted and why — how you will be damned if you do and damned if you don't — but that nevertheless you're going to be exactly what you are — give or take a pronoun.

I'd love to have the voters hear you on that subject — my hunch is that they would love you for it. Lincoln's debates with Douglas gave people such revealing glimpses into his heart and his mind. Some of it has to be sharp and witty — some of it serious — some of it colloquial — some of it learned — but perhaps if you decided to do it — it would be *you* — all of you — that they would see and hear. . . .

On November 23, I received his note of acknowledgment:

November 23, 1955

Dear Dore:

I am sorry I have neglected your letter — your most excellent and helpful letter. I have marked well what you have said; indeed, I have put it away to read and reread several times.

Thank you, my dear friend.

Yours,
Adlai

Whether his candidacy and campaign would be influenced by what I wrote I had no way of knowing, but I felt it had to be said.

In New York Arthur Loew had taken firm control of the company while *Raintree* was still in production and he was a stabilizing force, a fact that eased my burdens. Since he did not object to my continued interest in political or community affairs, I accepted the job as chairman for the 1956 Stevenson campaign in southern California.

We were into final editing and scoring of *The Swan* with Grace Kelly, Alec Guinness, and Louis Jourdan, directed by Charles Vidor, and we were delighted by the Pasternak film *Love Me or Leave Me*, written by David Fuchs and Isobel Lennart and also directed by Charles Vidor. James Cagney was brilliant and Doris Day came out of her pasteurized identity and delivered a hell of an exciting performance.

Also of note was *High Society*, a musical version of the Philip Barry play *Philadelphia Story*, adapted by John Patrick, directed by Chuck Walters, and produced by Sol Siegel. It had a marvelous cast of Bing Crosby, Frank Sinatra, Grace Kelly, and Celeste Holm.

I mention these along with three others because they were all made during my last year at Metro and, summing up, I believe it was a hell of a year to go out on. The three others — *Somebody Up There Likes Me*, *Teahouse of the August Moon*, and *Designing Woman*.

James Dean was slated to play Rocky Graziano in *Somebody Up There Likes Me*. When we had lent Elizabeth Taylor to Warners for

Rocky Marciano said, "Hey, you got a good-size fist — I think mine is harder." I assured him it was.

Grace Kelly on the set of The Swan *was doing handiwork in between takes. Obviously she was born to be a princess.*

Tracy and Ryan are amused that I'm complaining about the heat in the Mojave Desert. Jeb, on the right, is pleased he's out of school.

An amused Lauren Bacall and a short-panted Gregory Peck face a puzzled doorman in De-signing Woman

Giant we had obtained the services of James Dean for one picture and had elected *Somebody* for that one.

Dean had read the book and came to see me on a Friday afternoon to discuss the project and his possible participation in it. We had never met. He entered my office wearing large, dark sunglasses, moccasins, a short brass-buttoned denim jacket, a dark blue shirt, and clean light-blue jeans.

He waved a hand at me, said nothing, and peered intently at an old Italian puppet given me by my sister, Lillian. After eyeing it, he said, "Old." I nodded. He proceeded from the puppet to other things in the office: some pictures painted by Miriam, a few odd ashtrays, an antique typewriter, an embossed copy of Satchel Paige's *Rules for a Good Life* (including one I've never forgotten, "Don't look back, something might be gaining on you"), and a lovely kaleidoscope Miriam had given me.

During this survey, he'd slide his glasses up to his forehead to closely examine each item, nod his head in a pleased manner, and yet say not a word except, "Old."

I broke the silence.

"I wish you'd tell me what role I should play. Should I be in back of the desk with a fat cigar — or should I swing a golf club or polo mallet —?"

Dean looked at me and smiled, walked over, thrust out his hand to me, and over our handshake sat down and said, "How are you?" Apparently I'd passed a test of sorts.

We spent an hour together. He had liked the book but had worries. What about the makeup? Could he learn to box well enough? Could he get the "dese, dem, and dose" accent so it wouldn't appear phony?

The makeup was a cinch. Johnny Indrisano would teach him the boxing and make him look good. The accent was easy. I demonstrated and said, "If I can do it, you can." But best of all, Graziano would be around — all Dean would have to do would be to listen to Rocky.

We agreed that he would come in Monday morning to meet the makeup people and make some tests. He'd meet the writer, Ernie Lehman; Charlie Schnee, the producer; and Robert Wise, the director. We talked about movies and plays and careers. Before leaving he said, as he pointed to the puppet, "I love that." I told him if he was good as Rocky I'd give it to him as a present.

Then he was gone.

The next day, Saturday afternoon, he was killed in his Porsche while driving to see some auto races.

"The show must go on" is a cliché and thousands of people have asked, "Why?" Why the devil must it go on? Tradition — duty — the audience — all those are quick answers. The fact is, after the sentimentality and the hundreds of stirring anecdotes, the show must go on because the customers are out there, have paid their money to get in, and it's a bleeding loss if you have to pay it back.

But with our picture there was something else. We had a good script and commitments. It would have been a foolish beau geste to abandon them. We drew deep, hard breaths. I tried to forget the finely chiseled face and warm eyes of Dean and murmured the other cliché, "Let's get the show on the road."

Paul Newman had made a picture for us, still unreleased, *The Rack*, a tense and tough story of a Korean War veteran accused of breaking under the strictures of a prison camp.

We liked Paul very much. Though he had not yet punched his way into real stardom, I felt he needed only one big juicy part to get there. We cast him as Rocky and he was absolutely marvelous. For us it was a success. For Paul it was the rocket that sent his career into orbit. *The Hustler* and *Hud* kept him there permanently.

Regarding *Teahouse of the August Moon:* the producers of the stage play had had a problem raising funds for its production on Broadway. We bought the play in 1952 at a bargain price of $175,000 and it turned into a solid hit. We had agreed to hold off movie production for a period of time, and in 1955 when that time had passed I was approached by Marlon Brando, who wanted to play the role of Sakini, the interpreter. He was willing to work at a reduced salary and without a share of the profits.

What he did want was to test makeup, have a say in costuming and some consultation on the script before we went into production. Considering our happy experience with *Julius Caesar* I agreed to his requests, and once again we had no problems with Marlon. Our troubles began in Japan with spells of heavy rain that stopped our shooting. But the real shock came with the news that Louis Calhern, who was cast in the film, had suddenly died of a heart attack.

We ordered the company back to the studio. The technical crews went to work on the back lot and with their magical skills reproduced our location sites in Japan. Beyond minor differences between Brando and Glenn Ford, which provided some bad moments for director Daniel Mann, everything went smoothly and the film proved that Brando was easy to work with if the path was marked clearly and no booby traps were placed on the road.

Designing Woman was my last personal production for MGM. It was an enjoyable experience and became an enjoyable film, and I remember it with a touch of irony because it was a comedy. I left MGM, after all, with a laugh.

While these productions were being outlined and scripted and cast, and the final screenplay for *Ben Hur* was being prepared by Karl Tunberg, I was told by Les Petersen, our contact man with radio and TV companies, that CBS was eager to make a deal for four showings (one a year for four years) of *The Wizard of Oz*. Les was certain we could get a million dollars for the deal and of course we would retain all our rights. We okayed the deal.

Within a week, before there was any news release of our first tie-up with TV, I got a call from Arthur Loew, who informed me that the New York board had received and were considering an offer of $50 million for a backlog of 726 films made before 1948. Loew was opposed to the deal and was asking for my opinion. It was clear that it was a ridiculous offer. It would have been a simple task to list at least twenty-five pictures that in a short time we could rent for a million under the same terms as those of the CBS deal. Loew asked me to make such a list and hurry to New York to face the board of directors.

By the time I arrived, the sales department had stripped *Gone with the Wind* from the list of 726 and Lou Chesler, a financier, had cut his price to $35 million. That news made my presentation easier and Arthur Loew as president made our position a persuasive one. Mr. Chesler's offer was rejected.

By retaining all our rights to our product and by setting up a leasing arrangement we had, in the long run, increased our potential revenue to at least $200 million. The most recent proof of that was MGM's outright sale of *Gone with the Wind* to CBS in early 1978 for $35 million.

31

While I was in New York I heard from Paul Butler, the national chairman of the Democratic party, who asked me to consider making a film for the convention to be held in Chicago beginning August 13. I arranged to meet Paul in Chicago on my trip back to California, at which time he outlined his notion for me to make an hour-long documentary of the history of the Democratic party during the FDR and Truman administrations and their accomplishments in ridding the country of the massive and corrosive effects of the 1929 crash and resultant depression. Following the film we would reveal the keynote speaker, who would relate his remarks to what had happened since the days when Eisenhower and Nixon had taken over.

It was an innovative idea.

Paul did not know who the narrator would be or who would keynote the convention, since he had political hassles to settle, but would advise me as quickly as possible.

Having taken on the job I enlisted the help of Allen Rivkin for his political savvy, Norman Corwin for his eloquence, and Bill Gordon, who knew everybody, for his fund of information and superfine memory. I set up some rules to insure myself against using any of Metro's funds or resources. Norman, Allen, and Bill were not presently employed by MGM. Each telephone call, long distance or local, was charged to the Democratic party. We were to assemble and screen the film at California Studios, controlled by Jack Gross, who once worked with me at RKO.

Norman, Allen, and I worked at night or on weekends. We knew our subject; we were veterans of the depression and had been active during the FDR and Truman years, so the work went well. What stock newsreel film was owned by MGM we paid for as we did for all the prints we were assembling at Jack Gross's studio, where he had hired film editors. My executive assistant, Walter Reilly, followed all the details in hawklike fashion.

When we were almost ready I called Butler and reported that we were in need of the party's decision. Who was to narrate and who was to keynote? Paul had worked out his problems and told me that Senator John F. Kennedy of Massachusetts was to narrate and Governor Frank Clement of Tennessee was to be keynoter. I knew of Senator Kennedy but had no notion about Clement except that he had succeeded Kefauver as governor of Tennessee.

Butler said, "It's a good balance, North and South." I suggested that Paul come to California as soon as possible to view what we had so that we would not have to face a committee later on to explain why we goofed.

Paul arrived, looked, and left pleased, had no complaints or suggestions, told us that he was sure the large networks would carry the film as part of the convention program. At our signal he'd send Kennedy and Clement to screen the film, and arrange for Kennedy to be photographed and to narrate. He asked us to order at least two dozen prints of the finished product. We told Paul we'd be ready for Kennedy and Clement in ten days — on a Sunday. Norman Corwin would do a temporary narration track that Kennedy would hear and see how it matched the film.

Our schedule didn't change and on the appointed Sunday I called at Peter Lawford's home (he was then Kennedy's brother-in-law) to meet the senator and bring him to my home.

Hundreds of millions of people all over the world saw Kennedy and it is difficult to add anything to what they saw. He was handsome, lean, with a New England sea complexion, a smile that won your heart. His quick wit and keen intelligence were icing on the cake. After ten minutes you were compelled to say, "He's a candidate."

Norman Corwin, Allen Rivkin, Reilly, and I sat with the senator in my library and we went over the script. He had a few minor corrections, words to sound more like his own. After two hours I drove him back to Peter's home so he could take a swim and return at six for a drink, dinner, and the running of the film now titled *The Pursuit of Happiness*.

At six, the group assembled. Paul and Mickey (Mrs.) Ziffren, Allen Rivkin, Bill Gordon, Norman Corwin and his wife Kate, Lenny Spigelgass, Reilly, Miriam, Jill, Joy, Jeb, and I, Kennedy and Pat Lawford. The only absent guest was Governor Clement. I had received a call at five-thirty notifying me the governor would be a few minutes late.

At six-ten, another call; the governor was on the way.

At six-thirty, there was another message; the governor was on his way. Estimated arrival time, six-forty-five.

At six-fifty the phone rang. Wrong number.

At seven-ten the governor arrived.

It was a startling entrance. He was a handsome man with a tasteless choice of clothes.

He wore a rather broad-brimmed black hat, a blue suit with a broad white chalk stripe. His tie bore a large appliquéd donkey. The tie carried a chain tie swag with his initials, also a tie clip. After profuse apologies delivered in his deep-down Tennessee accent, he asked for bourbon and water and sat down, revealing his socks, which boasted appliquéd donkeys on both sides.

After a few pleasantries we sat down to dinner. There were sixteen of us including my family. By then Jill, who had been married to Jon Zimmer, who was on duty in the navy, was looking at Kennedy with what I was sure was love at first sight. Joy, I think, had the same idea. Jeb was looking at Clement as if the governor were someone from outer space. The governor was sitting at Miriam's right and Paul Ziffren at her left. Kennedy was at my right and his sister Pat on my left. The dinner was informal, relaxed, and the talk easy and void of political chatter.

I had toasted the senator and governor before dinner and since there were no other amenities to be observed, after the meal, I started to push back my chair to suggest we move into the projection room. But the governor beat me to the punch. He rose and asked if he could say a few words and proceeded to do so, except that the words were not few. He began by thanking "our hostess, the charmin' lady of the house, Mrs. Schary, the genial host, Door Schary, the senator from the great state of Massachusetts, John Kennedy, the Democratic National Committee chairman of California, Paul Ziffren" — everyone at the table was named, which spoke volumes for the governor's memory but little for his judgment. He followed up the roll call by speaking of how honored he felt, how delicious the food had been, how good the wine, how eager he was to see the film, and finally, how welcome we'd be as guests of "my dear wife Ceil and myself at the governor's mansion in Tennessee"; then he finished up with thanks and sat down.

Normally, a word of thanks from a guest at dinner rates a thank-you but this after all was more — an after-dinner speech. Politely, we applauded. Kennedy said, "I say ditto. Let's see the movie," and we left the table. As I escorted Kennedy upstairs to my bathroom he said, "I'll bet his keynote speech is going to be a long one."

Minutes later we were all in place and I rolled the film. When it was over, everyone was delighted. I then was aware that Clement had not said anything.

Above: This Jackson Day dinner in early *1948 that I MC'd included Melvyn Douglas, Mrs. R., Danny Kaye, Frank Sinatra, and Jimmy Roosevelt*

Center: Marlon Brando on the set of Teahouse of the August Moon *said something funny to Stevenson but I can't remember what it was. Adlai seems uncertain. Director Danny Mann doesn't care.*

Below: President Truman came backstage, advised us to cross hands: "That way they can't crop either one of you out of the picture — not me either"

Above: Party hosted by Oscar Chapman after the opening of Campobello, January 30, 1958. The then Senator John Kennedy is on Marietta Tree's right — the fellow perched behind me, I don't know.

Below: Moss Hart and his beloved Kitty are eyeing John Roosevelt as if to say, "How could you have become a Republican with a dad like FDR and a ma like Eleanor Roosevelt?" And that's exactly what they did say, whereupon John and I overdid our laugh.

I asked for Clement's reaction. He sat up straight and spoke sharply, telling the group that it was impossible for any speaker to follow the emotional tug of the picture. His remedy was for him to speak first and screen the film after his speech. I explained that it wasn't chronologically or dramatically consistent to have him speak of the lack of passion, compassion, and liberalism in the four years of the Eisenhower administration and then tell the story of the progressive (though controversial) twelve FDR and eight Truman years.

He said, "There's no speaker could follow that movie, except William Jennings Bryan."

That provided a fortuitous cue. "That's exactly why Paul and the others picked you," I said.

There was a count of one-two-three, then, "Well," said the governor, "then I've got to do it and say it my way. I mean, your outline of what I'm supposed to say won't work. I plan to bring that convention to its feet. And you can't tell me all I've got is twenty-five minutes — once those people start cheering, you can't stop 'em."

I ventured that FDR could stop a crowd by raising his hands. That cue line laid an egg.

Clement went on, "Now understand, that's a beautiful picture and I'm sure you," pointing to Kennedy, "will be great. But Mr. Schary, you're a picture maker and I'm a speechmaker — so it's got to be me who writes and makes the speech."

I got rid of the immediate problem by telling Clement that his plan would have to be discussed by Paul Butler and him directly. Clement nodded his head. Kennedy broke the leaden pause by asking what time we wanted him at the studio the next morning.

Clement's car arrived to fetch him to his hotel. Walter Reilly volunteered to drive Kennedy and Pat to her home. Jill, Joy, and Jeb retired. The Ziffrens checked out after Paul remarked that he was going to talk to Butler and suggest another speaker.

Seven of us remained, Allen, Norman and Kate, Bill Gordon, Lenny, Miriam, and I. Allen said, "We're screwed." I didn't think so. Perhaps we could get Paul to make a different choice of keynoter. I suggested it was late, and we had to work with Kennedy the next day and night and try to finish up his narration.

As we were saying good night Norman ventured, "Why not suggest that Kennedy do the picture and then let him do the keynote? One idea — one guy."

I promised I'd ask Butler.

But the idea fell on the floor. Paul told me his Southern contact, Sam Rayburn, chairman of the convention, had agreed on Clement, wanted him and no one else, and since he had agreed, reluctantly, to Kennedy as narrator, there was nothing to do except move ahead.

Kennedy was easy to work with, responsive and quick. We explained that narration, if delivered at the same pitch and pace, could be monotonous, and Norman and I, particularly Norman because of his experience, showed Kennedy how to alter some of his readings. Everything was *kol b'seder*, all in order.

Before going to Chicago for the Democratic convention in August, I received an interesting letter from Winston Churchill that ended the possibility of our doing a film I had been anxious for us to have on our schedule. In reading about the prime minister I had sensed there was an exciting story to be told of his early years. I wrote Mr. Churchill expressing my interest, and was happily surprised to be told by him to contact his "Solicitor, Mr. Anthony Moir." Within a few days another letter arrived, informing me that Mr. Moir was going to "be absent from London for a further fortnight" and "that it would be useful if" I would send a representative to meet with Churchill's "Private Secretary, Mr. Anthony Montague Browne and let him know further details."

We followed up and after some weeks of protracted negotiations were on the verge of a deal when Miss Marge Thorson, representing us, was told that Mr. Churchill had to call off further talks because of prior verbal commitment he had made during the war with Jack LeVien.

Within a few days I received the following letter of explanation:

16 August, 1956.

My dear Mr. Schary,

I am indeed sorry for what has occurred, and the trouble and expense to which you have been put. I liked your original proposal and gave it to my lawyers to clear. In the seventeen years that have passed, I have changed my lawyers, and when we applied for information the ones concerned, a most respectable firm, overlooked altogether the transactions of 1941. In the war time I was absorbed in public affairs and left to others many matters of personal interest, giving my authority where it was needed. From my memory, which does not get better as the years go by, I accepted without making any personal investigation what was told me by trusted advisers about these complex matters.

It was a lucky thing that the vigilance of your company put me on the track before we became more deeply involved. I have now today for the first time seen all the documents, which are conclusive.

[*307*]

I shall be quite willing to make a contribution to the expenses to which you have been put.

Let me assure you that, if I should be successful in arranging for the rights to be re-vested in me, I shall be happy to re-open with you the negotiations which had reached an advanced stage with Miss Thorson.

I have written similarly to Mr. Loew.

Yours sincerely,
Winston S. Churchill

I thanked Mr. Churchill for his courtesy, but declined his generous offer to share expenses incurred, by writing him that any negotiation has a risk quotient.

When I was ready to go to Chicago for the convention I told Mannix to take me off the payroll for the week I'd be away and in contact only by phone. Mannix said I was foolish, "call it a vacation." By then we had sent Paul Butler prints of *The Pursuit of Happiness,* and he had asked me to see him as soon as I got to Chicago. His urgency was based on his uneasiness with Governor Clement's keynote speech, which he asked me to read. I went into an adjoining office, read it, thought it was corn pone, grits, and molasses but that if the last ten pages were excised it would serve. Butler had told Clement his similar reaction but had been rather sternly rejected. Would I see Clement and try to get him to cut?

The governor greeted me with a warm handshake, listened to what I had to say, smiled, and gave me the velvet finger. "Dore, my friend," he purred. "You made a beautiful picture and I respect you, but I've got a hell-raiser of a speech and you got to respect my feelings — so does Butler — so you tell him that's the speech I'm gonna make. No cuts — and I may even add a couple of ad-libs."

I smiled back, finished my drink, went back to Paul, told him he was on a sticky wicket, then went to the Convention Center to check the movie on the big screen. The sound needed adjusting but the projection was good. Following the checkup I went to Stevenson's home for a late meeting — mostly party bigwigs who had gathered for drinks and gossip.

Normally I'm not a drinking man but the 1956 convention was divided into cocktail parties, meetings in my hotel suite, sessions with Stevenson, Butler, newsmen at the Pump Room after convention programs, and frantic rides from the Ambassador East to the convention site in the stockyards, accompanied by siren-screaming police escorts. The escorts were cut down after a few pedestrians and police officers were injured in accidents but the drinking continued. The way to keep the energy going was by drinking Scotch and water. In any other week I'd have been dead drunk during those few days but I remained cold sober. However, I've not drunk hard liquor since that time. I wouldn't dare. Not with my hypertension.

With the work and the gossip and the whispered lowdowns, most of which were proven wrong, there was fun. Also a sad moment.

Butler asked me to take President Truman a print of the film. At the Congress Hotel I was ushered into his suite late one afternoon. Truman was alone. I presented the print as a gift of affection from the party. During that one visit I found Truman depressed and rather remote from interest in the party affairs. He was convinced that Stevenson would lose, that he was the candidate at the wrong time, and that he might make a good secretary of state but never a good President. What struck me forcibly was a tacit revelation of his bitterness, along with the fact that there were no visitors waiting for him. My feeling was that he was attending the convention as a matter of party allegiance rather than as a matter of interest. After a few minutes he changed the subject, asked about Miriam, thanked me for coming, and told me he'd be at the opening session for the running of the film.

The picture was telecast directly from the convention by NBC and ABC but rejected by CBS. That rejection brought the party a windfall of publicity and Butler used it carefully and wisely, threatening to bring complaints to the FCC; to sue CBS, accusing them of bias; to order them to run the film as a courtesy to the American public; et cetera, et cetera. All of the jabber gathered coverage but truly signified nothing except to give those people who saw the picture the feeling that they had been in on a historic event.

And in a way they had, because John Kennedy became a national political celebrity. As a result of his performance and his personal appearance on the convention platform he became the favorite for the vice-presidential candidacy.

When Clement followed Kennedy to the platform it became clear that Butler's idea had not worked out. Clement was right — no one could follow the movie. Clement tried — and in trying went astray by adding the ad-libs he had threatened, by stressing his words, by using carnival tricks like peeling off his coat to demonstrate his enthusiasm, and by developing what performers call "flop sweat," a condition that appears when you become aware your act is dying.

The crowd began that inevitable walking jag peculiar to convention delegates, and newsmen with cameras, mikes, and tape recorders swept into the void. I slipped off the platform and waited below, not wanting to see the obvious failure of the keynoter.

After an hour he came down, sweating, coatless, and stunned. He looked at me, wiped his brow, stepped toward me with an embarrassed grin, and said, "You were right — twenty minutes too long." The grin disappeared into a grim look of defeat and he quickly walked away.

Kennedy and Clement.

Triumph and defeat.

Cheers and tears.

Politics.

The following day I met with Stevenson to discuss the vice-presidential candidacy. Stevenson had already determined that Hubert Humphrey would not match up on the ticket since both of the candidates would be from the Middle West. By that morning pressure was mounting for John Kennedy, and Bob Kennedy was already at work mobilizing a campaign directed at the delegates. Estes Kefauver had the South fairly well under control for his run at the vice-presidency, but no candidate can win anything with just the South on his side — he needs help from the North. Stevenson was halfhearted about the 1956 stab at the presidency and, not inclined to stir up a battle on the floor, he decided to allow the delegates to nominate a man of their choice — to declare an open convention.

Despite my affection for Humphrey I felt, in opposition to others, that Kennedy would be a stronger candidate because of the very fact that he was a Catholic, which some advisers felt was a debit rather an asset, and that his strength in the East would be of value.

The fight on the floor of the convention for the vice-presidency was a rouser. The contest, first a three-way struggle between Humphrey, Kennedy, and Kefauver, settled into a two-man race between the latter two, and as the voting on the final ballot began Kennedy appeared to be the winner. But at a crucial moment when the California delegation was clamoring to be heard to announce their entire delegate support for Kennedy, which would have served up the nomination, Sam Rayburn deliberately ignored Pat Brown and stalled all the other state chairmen until he was informed by phone that Tennessee had completed its caucus on the floor, at which time Rayburn recognized Senator Gore, who announced that the entire delegation had shifted to Kefauver, giving him the nod. The race was over.

Both Humphrey and Kennedy were better men. Perhaps neither would have helped defeat Eisenhower, but certainly Estes was no great help in the campaign.

On my return to the studio I discovered that a new crisis was developing with our finished version of *Tea and Sympathy*. I had met with officials of the Legion of Decency and had satisfied them and Robert Anderson, the playwright, with the few and inconsequential changes suggested. But the Legion had reconsidered and now had taken the position that the Deborah Kerr character had to die after being divorced. (This was, in effect, her punishment for having given the young student a healthy sex experience.)

My debate with Loew was fruitless. He did not want the picture to be deprived of the seal of approval from the Legion of Decency, and therefore he agreed to use their suggested narration in the form of a letter the schoolmaster's wife had written before her death.

It was compulsory for me to put my feelings on the record and I did so in a letter to Loew on September 7, 1956.

Dear Arthur:

I didn't talk to you yesterday, nor did I write you, because I've learned that when anyone is angry his thinking can get a little muddled and his words rather harsh. However, I do want you to know what is on my mind and in my heart.

As I write this, I have not heard how the recording on TEA AND SYMPATHY went, and of course I haven't received it, naturally, and I do not know whether it will or will not eventually hurt the picture. But I do know at this point that we have made a number of sacrifices. To begin with, we have abandoned a principle. Secondly, we have, I think, alienated a good and valuable writer. And, thirdly, though of course this is too early to tell, we have hurt a valuable picture.

This isn't just another picture to me. You know how hard I worked for it and on it, because I believed deeply that it was a story well worth telling and that it could make a contribution not only to our company, but to the art of motion picture making. In good conscience and with a full measure of responsibility, we hammered out a story that not only fulfilled the obligations to the Code, but finally emerged as a picture of which the Code office was proud. While all those who worked on it were paid and paid well for their services, I think they brought something above and beyond the nominal effort. They approached it as a labor of love.

And now two or three people sitting in a room have insisted on words that are trite and self-righteous. We had a good battleground on which to wage a fight. . . . I think we could have gone into battle with flags flying and with good ammunition. But we have retreated and run away. Our forces are divided and I wonder what will happen to us when we approach a property such as CAT ON A HOT TIN ROOF.

I am heartsick about the decision — heartsick about the ads — which I believe look like ads on a cheap exploitation picture, and I feel it is my duty to put all of this in a letter to you. . . .

Loew responded to my letter by phone with understanding and yet he felt we had to offer no more resistance.

I did win a battle with the Legion on *Cat on a Hot Tin Roof* with a suggested outline. I went to Geoff Sherlock, who was running the Motion Picture Code office. Once that was done I assigned Larry Weingarten to produce and Richard Brooks to write and direct.

Much to everyone's amazement Arthur Loew resigned as president of Loew's, Inc., and to everyone's stunned surprise Joe Vogel was elected president. I called Arthur but he was closemouthed regarding his reasons for stepping away from his job. He merely said, "One day you'll find out why. Good luck and thanks for calling."

Certainly the response was enigmatic and I suspected it was meant to be.

The presidential campaign had come to full bloom and withered away with a resounding defeat for Stevenson, a landslide victory for Eisenhower. This anticipated disappointment was followed by a story in *Time* titled "Somebody Up There Doesn't Like Him," which predicted I would soon walk the plank.

That led to my call to our new president, Joe Vogel, and my trip to New York for the Monday morning meeting with Vogel and his presentation to me of the anonymous letter that was the suggested reason for my dismissal and that finished my emotional and official tie to MGM.

However, there were legal steps to be taken, and when I awoke Tuesday morning for my meeting with Bill Fitelson I was prepared for what was to follow during the next few days. Or I thought I was.

32

That Tuesday morning I met with Bill Fitelson. The first thing he asked was if I had notified Tannenbaum that he was no longer representing me. Assured that I had, Bill suggested we get to work. I gave him a review of my meeting with Vogel and handed Bill a copy of my contract. As he glanced at it I thought back to my prior meetings with him. He had been at my home in California on two occasions and I had been impressed with his candor, his political opinions, and his acid humor.

We had also spoken on the phone a few times regarding some of his clients (he had an impressive list of stage personalities, including Mary Martin, Elia Kazan, Josh Logan, Alan Jay Lerner, Comden and Green, Jerome Robbins, and Harold Rome) and it was he who had first solicited my help in getting funds for Moshe Decter's devastating exposé of Joe McCarthy.

Bill is rather short, has a finely chiseled face with a thatch of shiny black hair and eyes that always seem to be asking questions. He resembles a beardless miniature Lincoln.

While he was examining the papers I had given him, Morgan Maree called to confirm he would arrive that night and would check with me regarding the time of a meeting with Vogel on Wednesday.

After his hurried look at my papers Fitelson expressed some problems we might face regarding deferred payments that were due me but said he wished to discuss that concern with his partner Bert Mayers, whom I had not met, and with Morgan Maree.

Bill then advised me that Arthur Loew's resignation as president had followed after Schenck had told him he was in contact with Sol Siegel to replace me. Loew, who had resumed his position as head of the International Division of Loew's, was also preparing to abandon that post and hand it over to Maurice "Red" Silverstein. Loew had plans to brush off all the convolutions of the executive contingent at MGM and retire to a quieter and more restful life at his home in Sand's Point.

Fitelson reported his own opinion that the men in New York had gathered round to protect Schenck and had treated Loew shamefully.

Bill concluded by telling me it was a good thing I was through with Metro and that he was happy for me. At that time I did not share his enthusiasm. I was merely anxious to be rid of the negotiations and the flurry that would follow the announcement that I had been dismissed.

The following morning Morgan, Fitelson, and I joined forces. Morgan had brought additional papers and records. Bill was still alarmed at the possibility that the contracts did not guarantee the deferred payments to my estate in the event I died during the period of time the payments were due; moreover, he had reservations about whether or not MGM could devise a way of negating the payments due me. But that was a problem to be met after the meeting with Vogel, which was scheduled for three o'clock that afternoon. Bill suggested I leave once I had informed Vogel that Morgan and he were my accredited representatives and introductory amenities were concluded.

When we got to Vogel's office he was surprised to see Fitelson, whom he knew, and professed to be happy to meet Maree.

We in turn were surprised to see Vogel flanked by Ben Melniker, Irving Greenfield, and Charles Moskowitz — lawyer, accountant, and treasurer, respectively. After the polite hellos I made the statement regarding Bill and Morgan and prepared to make my exit.

Vogel asked me to stay for a few minutes. He then repeated that he wished everything to "be handled nicely, decently. Dore rates that and I'm sure there'll be no problem." We quickly skimmed over easy details. I could retain prints of my personal productions (I only had a few), the projection-room equipment would be mine, my staff would be retained until I left (my plan was to move into an office of my own and bring Lucy Ballentine, my executive secretary, and her assistant, Betty Arrighi, along with Walter Reilly, my assistant, into my quarters as loyal and talented friends who would help me in whatever tasks I might undertake).

Vogel then made an uncalculated error. He wanted Fitelson to see the anonymous letter with the list of my imagined indiscretions he had shown me. Fitelson looked at it, showed it to Maree without a word, and then asked me if this was the same letter I had seen. When I nodded he dropped it on Vogel's desk and said, "Stick it." He then added, "That could be the kind of letter they might be writing about you, Joe, a few years from now." Bill then asked me to excuse myself. Joe had one more sentence to say to me: "We'll get up a statement, a nice one, saying you resigned."

I said, "No. No statements. I did not resign. Let's wait until everything is settled." As I started to leave Bill asked me to wait in the conference room.

The secretary in the outer office gave me the message that Howard Dietz had called and asked if I would see him in his office. Dietz made no reference to what was happening but wished to discuss ad campaigns for *Raintree County* and *Teahouse of the August Moon.* I examined the ads, had some arid comments about them, and was taken aback when Mr. Schenck called me while I was with Dietz. After hellos, Schenck said, "I just want you to know, Dore, I had nothing to do with this." I said, "I'm so glad to hear that." We said good-byes.

That call was immediately followed by one from Vogel's conference room. Morgan and Bill were waiting to see me. Apparently decisions had been reached very quickly. I was to get $150,000 in settlement of the $300,000 due on the remainder of the employment contract. I also was to get the deferred payment of $850,000 over a period of eight and a half years but with no guarantee of those funds to my estate. It was Morgan who proposed that we take out an insurance policy to cover the payments due me. We all returned to Vogel's office with the proposal but Moskowitz insisted there never had been any agreement, written or otherwise, that I get the deferred payments.

I reminded Moskowitz of a conversation in Schenck's office in which Schenck had deliberately asked Moskowitz to remember that he was now telling me that those payments were due to me or to my family, in the event of my death, and that he would leave a note to that effect in his desk for Moskowitz as testimony to the conversation.

Moskowitz said he vaguely remembered some talk to that effect but could not remember a single detail.

Fitelson suggested that Schenck might remember all the details, particularly if the matter came to court and he was placed under cross-examination.

Vogel doubted if things would ever reach such a state. He was willing to accept the insurance plan and that would obviate any further trouble on that score.

Again the false, warm, polite good-byes and exits.

As Morgan, Bill, and I were walking across Forty-fifth Street, Fitelson explained he had made the rather veiled threat regarding Schenck being cross-examined because once before he had had Schenck on the stand and had gotten what he wanted as Schenck folded under the pressure of severe questioning.

At my hotel we were joined by Bert Mayers, Bill's partner. He was very unlike Bill. He had heavily hooded eyes, very large capped teeth, and a portly build. When listening he watched me intently, and before he answered he closed his eyes; when he opened them he rolled them heavenward and finally spoke his piece with incisive and decisive clauses. He would take over the final stages of the contract negotiations, watch for the "little things" that often pass unnoticed. Finally he asked that if, during the final stages, I had anything to say, I would ask him rather than direct my questions to the other parties "whosoever they may be."

Despite his rather dictatorial approach he was a reassuring advocate and I sensed that as a team Bill and Bert were probably invincible once they joined hands.

Now the hour was late, the next day was Thanksgiving, and Bill, Bert, and Morgan retired to their holiday appointments and Miriam and I spent the evening with my sister, Lillian, and a few of her friends. The Thanksgiving Day dinner was with my dear cousins Saul and Hope. The weather was beautiful, the dinner lavish, but my spirits were drained, I had a period of depression, and Miriam and I went back to the Sherry-Netherland. Miriam watched television and I began to think of what I might be doing in the years to come.

I had spent twenty-seven years in Hollywood as a screenwriter, a producer, an executive, and had been chief executive of two studios. I realized I wanted to be free to do my own work. Why not change course? Perhaps I could avoid hitting the shoals that often entered the lives of former studio heads who fretted and fussed their time away thinking of their past reputations. I was in New York — had money in the bank — an assured income for almost ten years. Why not head for a goal I had never reached — a success on Broadway?

There had been a production in Hollywood of a comedy I had written, but that had stumbled. *Too Many Heroes* in 1937 had not startled anyone except Kelcey Allen. Euphoria hit me like a refreshing shower. Suddenly I felt relieved and confident. My reactions were emotional and physical. I knew precisely what I wanted to do and would do. My eyes teared with joy. I walked into our bedroom, took Miriam in my arms and hugged her, and said, "I'm going to write a play."

At that time I was free of doubts, of fears, and irresolution; all those came later.

The next morning I received a call from a friend of mine, a reporter on the *Wall Street Journal,* who told me that the story headed "Somebody Up There Doesn't Like Him" had been planted by Ben Sonnenberg, who had been retained by Ed Weisel on behalf of Lehman Brothers, a member of which was on the Metro board. Apparently, when an organization wants to shed you they employ the best talent to do the job. They can get someone to arrange the contract, hire the hit man, and presto — the job is done.

All I had to do for the rest of the day was to be examined for my life-insurance policy. I passed the test.

Also, I had an idea for a play.

I called Eleanor Roosevelt at Hyde Park and she invited Miriam and me to visit her at Val Kill the following day. We had seen her many times during the years and had developed a pleasant relationship.

We lunched with Mrs. R. on a cold and brisk day. Val Kill was her retreat from the busy, complex life she led. Her meals were never Cordon Bleu cuisine, but they were served family style and were filling and, most important, they were with her. She was interested in what was going on with me and I sketched some of the background. I then told her I had a tentative notion for a play dealing solely with FDR's illness, his partial recovery, and finally his dramatic entry into active politics when he nominated Al Smith in 1924 at the Democratic party convention at Madison Square Garden.

She liked the bare sketch and suggested I contact FDR, Jr., for further discussions and asked that I write her a more detailed outline once I had thought it through.

It was a significant day. Miriam and I drove home happy.

The rest of our weekend was a joyous one. On Monday I called Franklin, Jr., and we set a date for Friday the thirtieth. Later that day I heard that the MGM contract negotiations were moving slowly and might be delayed longer than I had hoped; but Tuesday I was called to meet in Melniker's offices, where some problems immediately surfaced. I was asked to sign a letter resigning as of that date, November 27. I asked Melniker to allow Mayers, Maree, and me to discuss it by ourselves. To my counselors I explained I had two reasons for refusing to sign the letter. One: since my official tenure according to the final contract was dated December 31, a letter indicating I resigned as of November 27 could possibly nullify the first contract if future circumstances tempted MGM to try to do so. Two: I did not wish to resign, since my deferred payments were based on the termination of my employment and it was specifically stated that if I resigned the payments would not be made. So the letter must avoid "resign" and use "termination of employment." Finally, but this was simply personal, I was tired of what Tennessee Williams termed "the odor of mendacity" and I wanted it to be clear that I was fired.

Mayers lifted his eyes under his lids, meditated for a moment or two, then agreed to my two points but felt that my personal point "seems to be a case of self-flagellation."

When Melniker rejoined us a noisy conference ensued; he could not understand why the points were raised. Mayers skillfully convinced him by pointing out that if for any reason in the future Melniker should not be employed any longer by MGM someone else might take advantage of the discrepancy in dates and that while we were willing to trust Melniker, we might not wish to trust a new man. Melniker gave in. A new letter was written, we signed it and the contracts, and were then invited into Vogel's office to watch as he completed the signing.

Bert Mayers took leave of us after appropriate congratulations and thanks and Vogel asked Morgan and me to stay for a few minutes.

He wished to tell us that he was pleased all was settled with no nastiness. Was I as pleased?

I told him I was reminded of a story my mother once told me of a groom on a Russian farm who had been instructed by the landowner to go to the stables and shoot a horse that had broken its leg. A few minutes later, there was the sound of a shot and the groom reappeared to say he had done the job as quickly, efficiently, and mercifully as possible. Would the landowner take a look? Yes, he would. The landowner went to the stables, surveyed the work, and said, "Yes, you did it quickly, efficiently, and mercifully — however, you shot the wrong horse."

Vogel smiled vaguely and said he wanted to part as good friends. I responded by asking, "Now that it's all over — one question, Joe. Why? Why so fast — right now?"

He explained that it was due to stockholder pressure plus his desire to get his new organization of the company under way. For Morgan's benefit I asked what pressures had been brought to get rid of me. He responded, "You see, Dore, you're strange. You're — an egghead. People don't understand that. Those guys on the Coast, they cut you up, Dore — cut you up terribly. And then there are people here in New York — stockholders — some of the board of directors — who are your enemies."

Vogel went on as I glanced at Morgan, who was eyeing Joe intently. "You see, they don't understand a man like you — all those speeches and that committee work and then this business with the election and Stevenson. And like I said, you're an egghead as far as they're concerned."

I interrupted. "Joe, there's something else you might add, which makes their case even better. I'm also taking lessons in conversational Hebrew." Joe waved his hand and said, "That's what I mean."

"Perhaps," I said, "it would have been better if I had been a golfer, played the horses, had a good-looking chick on the side, and played in the heavy gin and poker games." Joe smiled and nodded. "Actually, that seems more normal. You don't get complaints about things like that."

That ended all I wished Morgan to hear. We said good-bye and left.

When we reached a cab, Morgan gripped my arm and said, "I'll be a son of a bitch. I never heard anything like that." Morgan dropped me at the hotel and we said farewell. Morgan, sun bronzed, handsome as a Marlboro cigarette cowboy, lover of hunting and owner of horses and dogs, was going home. He told me he'd tell Selznick the entire tawdry story. "What are your plans? Got any?" he asked.

"Yes," I said, "I'm going away — for a long time — maybe a year. I'll tell you more when I get back to California."

We shook hands and Morgan was on his way back to Marlboro country.

Now that the contracts were signed it was time to telephone the news to the family. They reacted with no outward signs of alarm. Jill and Jon were staying at the house to keep control while we were away and she said, "Don't worry, Fox." Joy said, "We love you." Jeb was out with some of his friends but I knew he'd be understanding. We told Jill to talk to the staff at the house and tell them not to start looking for jobs — our plans were still not clear. Then I called Walter and Lucy at the studio — told them to start packing and to look for temporary offices as soon as possible.

The next few days were spent tidying things up in New York. Howard Dietz released a statement announcing my departure without letting me see it but he at least did not say I had resigned. I had the feeling he enjoyed indicating I had been asked to go.

But the calls from California began. Friends checked in for words of encouragement and good cheer: Cary Grant, "Come back and let's go to work"; Spencer Tracy with a crisp "Fuck 'em"; Monty Clift, "Whenever you need me, just say show up. On any stage — I'll be there"; Myrna Loy, "I love you"; George Seaton, "Believe me, they'll miss you"; Ed Lasker, "Now you got time to improve your backhand"; Van Johnson, "When do I go to work?"

When Friday came I met with FDR, Jr., who represented the family. He told me that Stanley Kramer had offered $250,000 for the rights to a film on FDR. What did I have in mind? I asked, did Kramer have a story? Not yet. I had one and it was to be a play, and while I could not offer the money Kramer was willing to put up, I had a hunch that if my play worked the family would get more than a quarter of a million. To prove my devotion to the idea I had, I was willing to offer 50 percent of all my royalties from the play and from the movie rights. Franklin agreed that that was generous. He would sign a deal provided Mrs. R. had approval of script. I could not grant that. If after some time she changed her mind about being portrayed, I would have lost all the time I had invested. The family would have to rely on my affection, my talent, and my commitment. I did promise that once the play was completed I would read it first to Mrs. Roosevelt, and if there were items that she strongly objected to I would make an effort to correct or alter them — but she had to believe in me rather than have approvals. Franklin felt that that was reasonable since they knew of my work on behalf of FDR and my warm friendship with Mrs. R. I said that when I had written a synopsis of what I had in mind I would send Mrs. R. a copy so that she would know I had no idea of transgressing on the years of their lives following the 1924 convention.

Franklin asked who would be representing me, and I told him Lew Wasserman and Bill Fitelson.

Franklin smiled. "That's a capable couple."

We chinned for a while and I walked over to MCA and briefed Lew, who thought I had been too generous but did understand that what was at stake was not some extra money but the chance I was taking of going back to the theater after years of identification as a studio head.

Once other announcements of my leaving MGM appeared the number of telephone calls increased. They were heartwarming and reassuring. We kept quiet regarding the FDR play.

A finished cut of my film *Designing Woman* was being shipped into New York for me to make my final cuts and changes, but since the print wasn't due for a few days Miriam and I went to dinner parties hosted by Lillian and by Martha and Cecil Brown, chatted with Leo Rosten, the Lou Cowans, Danny Kaye (when he signed with Sam Goldwyn it had been suggested he alter his nose — he was grateful I had talked him out of that), and spent time with Saul and Hope and Miriam's family.

I was tentatively approached by Robert Weitman about doing some television work, but Miriam and I were already making plans that would rule out TV or movies for at least a year; when the deal with the Roosevelts was signed we would go home, then take a rest in La Quinta, that lovely resort in Palm Springs, before going to Europe for our first grand tour, which would include England, France, Italy, Greece, and Israel. Joy and Jeb would come along. Jill I think had her first regrets about being married and missing the trip.

The night before going to the MGM screening to view *Designing Woman* we made a nostalgic trip to Newark where I was feted at the YMHA. I rambled on about Moss, the Y Players, the Shapiros, and my old friends who came out by the dozens made me feel contented and comforted.

At 10:30 the next morning I met Adrian Fazan, the film editor who had come east with the print of the film, which looked surprisingly good. There were a few cuts to be made, some film to be recut, and music to be excised that had impaired some laughs rather than improving upon them. As I was concluding my notes to Adrian, Mr. Schenck appeared (in order to reach the private executive dining room one had to pass through the projection room). When he saw me, he stopped and insisted that when my work was finished I join him in his exclusive private room in the dining area. Later I thanked Adrian for her work, asked her to give my fondest to Vincente Minnelli and other friends at the studio, and made my way into the dining room, where Melniker, Vogel, Greenfield, and others were finishing up. They greeted me as if nothing had changed. The only embarrassment was mine.

In Schenck's cozy nook were Charlie Moskowitz and Schenck. After I ordered my food, Schenck, with his usual polite and careful good manners, asked Charlie to excuse himself. When we were alone Schenck abandoned his story of a few days back, when he had said he had nothing to do with my being ousted.

Now he sat back and unburdened himself. He had determined a year ago that I would have to get out. He had confided that to Loew, who had disagreed, which Schenck thought proved a defect in Loew's executive discernment. All this plus what followed was delivered in a soft narrative way as if he were telling why he preferred shad roe to trout. "I didn't want Arthur Loew to be president — the man I groomed for the job was Charlie Moskowitz — but," he shrugged, "nobody wanted him except me." When Schenck had accepted that plus the fact that Loew would not fire me, he decided to find someone as president who could also take on my responsibilities at the studio. He sent for Sol Siegel (that's when Loew quit) and suggested that he and Moskowitz would run sales and distribution and Siegel as president would run the studio. Siegel, accompanied by David Tannenbaum, had submitted his terms for a deal.

However, the board of directors wished to give Siegel only a one-year contract.

Schenck frowned. "Now you know that's ridiculous, Dore, to offer a head of production only a year's contract as head of production." I nodded agreement as he continued, "You can imagine how embarrassing that was for me." I again nodded. Schenck had resubmitted Moskowitz's name for president, but he was turned down and Vogel was selected as the compromise candidate — "though," Schenck said, "he's not the best man for the job at all."

I then ventured to ask why he was so anxious to get rid of me. He said it was because I never made any of the pictures he wanted me to make. When I asked which ones, he couldn't remember. I said I couldn't either but I did remember some he didn't want me to make, *Red Badge of Courage, Ivanhoe, The Great Caruso, Blackboard Jungle, Bad Day at Black Rock, Battleground, Prisoner of Zenda.* He responded by repeating that if I had listened to him things would have been better.

I said, "It's possible, Nick, that you were wrong with some of your suggestions." He answered with firmness, "I have never been wrong — except once, when I gave you authority to run the studio."

After that thrust he said he had no hostility toward me and that he was my friend. I smiled and said, "Why are my wrists bleeding?" He chuckled and I concluded, "Well, Nick, I have no hostility toward you and thanks for the lunch."

The very next day I had breakfast with Adlai Stevenson. After some talk of the election, during which he mentioned he had been hurt to a degree by Harriman and Kefauver during the primaries, he commented as he had in a letter to me shortly after the convention that the figure who would undoubtedly be the strongest personality of all in the future would be John Kennedy.

He then said, "No more about all that. Tell me about your troubles." I gave him a short synopsis including details of my settlement. His eyes widened and he wondered, "My God, why don't they work something like that out for defeated presidential candidates?"

The next day Miriam and I left for home. When we got on the 20th Century I laughed and Miriam asked why. I observed, "There's no caviar from Nick Schenck. It's all over. Nick has slipped me a mickey."

33

*P*roperly, *our family absorbed* most of our time the first days we were home. Despite their cheery behavior we detected signs of their concern. Were we planning to move? Were we broke? Was I disheartened and dispirited? We also saw signs of restiveness from those who worked in the house. But it became clear as the holidays came along and as the bonuses were delivered that there was no sign of panic. Miriam and I entertained friends for dinner and viewed movies (Zanuck, Bill Goetz, and the other studio heads were generous and behaved as though we were still on the job).

As I had anticipated, no one volunteered to join me in any enterprise I might devise. But friends like Lenny Spigelgass, Allen and Laura Rivkin, Sylvia and Danny Kaye, Chick and Don Hartman, Hy Engelberg, Romy and Hildi Greenson, Millard and Lori Kaufman hung in there with affection but with some alarm when I advised them I was going to try writing a play. When I told them it was to be about FDR they spoke up. "It's too early." "For the love of Pete, why a political play?" "They'll kill you in New York." "Oh, no!" So I stopped talking about it and spoke instead of our proposed trip to Europe and Israel. When I mentioned I had begun Hebrew lessons, the general reaction was laughter — "It will be *so* valuable in Paris and Rome."

The trade papers announced my return home and the opening of my office. There were no ripples. No paper was foolish enough to comment affirmatively on my behalf because MGM might not furnish as many ads, but my friends on the papers told me privately that I had been given the knife.

I believe that what saved me from a depression was the decision to go to work immediately on something of my own. Even though I was aware that I'd be gambling at least a year of my time and probably most of the cash I had in the bank, I knew too that if I failed I'd be getting $100,000 (minus the insurance premium of $12,000) on each January 1 for nine years and that if necessary I could probably get a job producing pictures. If the play succeeded — well — I made no plans for that because that would set me dreaming, not working.

Miriam and I went to La Quinta for a rest, some sun, tennis, and work. Lew Wasserman had advised me that the deal with the Roosevelts was set and he was sending the papers to Bill Fitelson for his okay. So I had to write the outline for the play I had in mind. I had not even thought of a title. In my early notes I had merely written "The Roosevelt Story." After a few days in La Quinta, I sat down and determined that I needed a definite identification at least for my own use. I held a pen in my hand and looked down at the paper and what Thornton Wilder once described happened to me — the words came down my arm and onto the paper and I wrote, *Sunrise at Campobello*. It was exactly like that — no thought — no design — it just took place.

The outline, filling a few pages, took no more than a couple of hours. I knew from the first that the play would end as FDR walked those ten steps to the rostrum on his crutches. It wasn't invention. It is there in the published record of the proceedings of the 1924 Democratic convention at Madison Square Garden.

I sent the pages on to Lucy Ballentine, who typed them up and sent me copies. I sent Mrs. R. the original.

Roger Stevens was visiting Mary Lasker, who was also at La Quinta, and dropped in to tell me he was interested in the rumor that I was planning to write a play about FDR. If it was true, he would like to produce it. I thought it was premature to speak of production when all I had was an outline, but I thanked him.

In a few days I heard from Franklin, Jr., who sent me a Xerox copy of the outline I had sent Mrs. R. She had read it on a plane heading for Morocco, had scribbled her approval on the first page, and mailed it back. Now all I had to do was write the play.

First I wrote a piece for Max Ascoli's magazine *The Reporter* (Paul Jacobs aided me as editor) on Hollywood and the mythic figures it produced. Finished with that I began to sketch out act structures and a cast of characters for *Campobello*.

One night just as we were preparing for bed Joy called us — her voice was two octaves up — she had met a man and she was in love — his name was Arthur — "the last name is funny, Stashower — but I'm in love." When had they met? A few days before. Where's he from? Cleveland.

What's he do? He's a lawyer — just out of the Coast Guard. We said it sounded awfully quick. She had a good answer: "Quick? You and Mommy met one night and decided to get married a week later. Jill and Jon met and two weeks later she was flying high and you said, 'All right.'"

That was true. Miriam spoke to Joy and kept saying, "What kind of a name is Crashover?" Then it became "Smashcower." Finally she said, "Oh, well, we'll be home in two days and we'll meet him." We did, we liked him and, as Joy said, "It's going to be wonderful. He's a lawyer, he's Jewish, and he's a Democrat." I agreed that was fine except he was a Cleveland Indian fan and the only good things I'd heard about Cleveland was that there was a President by that name and Paul Newman was born there.

However, before taking off on our trip to Europe the family agreed to go to Cleveland and meet the Stashower family, which was a numerous clan and a devoted one. I began to like them and Cleveland. The date for the wedding was set for September the first. *Mazel tov.*

Finally, we were ready for our trip, which had been arranged with the help of the MGM travel bureau, which was accommodating and capable. We were taking our station wagon, a Mercury, loading it inside and out with so much luggage there was barely room for Joy, Jeb, Miriam, and me. Jill and Jon were going to come east in five or six weeks to to meet us in New York, where we would be ensconced for about a month before heading bag, baggage, and wagon for Europe on the U.S.S. *United States.*

Off we went via Gallup, Oklahoma City, and points east with a groaning load, a dolorous Joy, who was expressing her regrets at leaving Arthur, and Jeb, who wanted to drive.

Before we had embarked on this long trek our friends had chipped in and given us a splendid twenty-fifth anniversary party. They had written special material, rehearsed and staged it elegantly. For a response I had written a long review of our twenty-five years of marriage and I'm afraid I wore out my beloved friends, but I figured if we all sank in the briny at least I would have left a record of what our twenty-five years of love and life had been like. I've reread it recently and my objective opinion is that it does not stand the test of time.

In eight days our caravan pulled up in front of New York's Ritz to the dismay of the doorman, who must have felt that gypsies had descended on the posh hostelry. But we had arrived and there was much to be done.

Carl Haverlin, president of BMI and a Civil War buff who describes himself as looking like a renegade Confederate colonel who stepped into the wrong century, is a constant friend, and he had arranged for me to meet Carl Sandburg to discuss with him the possibility of doing a TV documentary. Sandburg arrived on a cold, rainy afternoon and asked for some port wine and a cookie. As we talked he wrapped himself in an afghan provided by Miriam. We talked about the last chapters of his final volume of the life of Lincoln — the ones titled "Blood on the Moon." I had tried to get it made as a film but had failed, as had Sidney Franklin and others who had tackled it for me at Metro. Sandburg related his feelings at the time he was typing out the death of Lincoln. "I believe I knew Lincoln better, deeper than anyone who ever lived in his time or since — he was my friend — and he was dead — and as I wrote I started to cry and even as my tears fell and moisture dropped from my nostrils — I kept writing — I couldn't stop crying or writing."

By now Miriam and I were in tears and so was Sandburg as he lived that scene once again. Finally he stopped, dug into his pocket for a large handkerchief to dry his eyes, and said he had talked too much. I protested that he had not. We agreed that when I returned from Europe we'd meet again and talk about the documentary. He patted Miriam's cheek, shook hands, and went away.

Bill Fitelson had spoken to me about the Theatre Guild, whose interests he handled, and he had in turn spoken to the Guild about the play. As yet there had been no public word about what I was doing except planning to go on a sabbatical.

Now I had my first meeting with Theresa Helburn, who was sweet enough or smart enough to say she remembered *Too Many Heroes* and had liked it. Terry was a gray-haired, handsome woman whose reputation, like Cyrano's nose, preceded her everywhere she went. She was loved, respected, feared, disliked, appreciated; all in all, a complex, talented, and tough-minded lady. Lawrence Langner, whose magnificent head was his glory, also had a complicated but large reputation. His wife, Armina Marshall, a good actor and a playwright who had became one of the reigning triumvirate of the Guild, had not yet achieved the eminence of the first two members. But it was the Guild that had given a sheen and style to the American theater. They had brought quality. They had aimed high and seldom had missed, but even the misses had had taste and merit.

At the time I met with them in March, 1957, some of the gloss had gone. A few failures in the theater always demean a reputation. Deference does not last long on Broadway. It was lost to O'Neill in his lifetime;

it has been recently denied to the work of Tennessee Williams and Arthur Miller; Sidney Kingsley has been reluctant to take another chance at the wheel of fortune. Years later a reputation may be reborn but by then its owner is usually dead and buried.

But now I was with the Guild hierarchy and they wanted to hear the kind of play I had in mind. I had added to my outline, I had scenes, some dialogue, and effective curtains. I told my story. At the end Terry and Armina were in tears and Lawrence put out his hand and said, "We'll do it." Bill said to Langner, "You and Dore will do it — as co-producers." There was no disagreement. I then sprang my surprise. "I will finish the play by August. I want it to open on Broadway on FDR's birthday, January thirtieth, next year. That's a must."

Langner calculated, "Rehearsals begin in early November. Open in New Haven — then two weeks in Boston — two weeks in Philadelphia. We can do it." They thought the play could be staged for $120,000. I would have to raise my half. There was chortling and delight. Langner opened a bottle of sherry and we drank to "luck."

They wanted to announce the news. I said I was planning a press conference at the hotel within a week. Would they come? We could make it a combined news story.

It went well. There was a large turnout of reporters and columnists. When I announced that my first work after leaving Metro was to write a play about the years of FDR's illness and recovery and co-produce it with the Guild, we got a buzz of interest that was not only encouraging but exciting. After questions and comments the writers left and Terry, Lawrence, and Armina, pleased and exuberant, joined in the celebration.

Lawrence brought us down to earth by reminding us that the play was to open January 30, 1958 — just about nine months away. He suggested the Guild executives go "and let Dore start writing."

Bill began framing the production contracts, the news got wonderful coverage, and suddenly I realized I had committed an act of outrageous chutzpah. I was going on a long trip, had to come back in July with a first draft of a play that was to open on FDR's next birthday date — and had also accepted a commission from the Los Angeles *Times* to write a series of letters from some of our stops along the way. I could, I thought, turn out to be the most loudmouthed jackass in show business.

Fighting off my fears, I called Mrs. R. and she consented to give me two days at Val Kill so that I could ask her a flood of questions to help me establish the ambience of Campobello in 1921 and to acquire some details that might have eluded me in the biographies I had read. By the time I reached Val Kill a few days later I had a list of about a hundred questions — some picayune, such as the children's clothes and picnic food, others as intimate as details of her nursing of FDR during the early days of his almost total disability and paralysis.

Mrs. R. was candid about everything. When she talked of having to catheterize FDR a few times each day and night she was explicit, telling me that though it was a difficult job that might have led to infection, she handled it with skill and delicacy. With a smile she said, "When Dr. Draper visited us from Boston the first time he complimented me by saying that a professional nurse could not have done better. In a way, that was the most rewarding thing anyone has ever said to me."

During the first afternoon and night we worked steadily except for breaks for tea and dinner and a cup of cocoa and an apple before bedtime. Age had molded Mrs. R's features into a softer and warmer appearance. Her hair, now gray, and her eyes, where the pain of the past still lurked, were beautiful. However, her energy had not flagged during the years. Each time the fire burned low she would insist on heaving logs into the fireplace herself. She said she enjoyed doing it. She moved gracefully and quickly. I remembered how she had almost worn me out some years before when I visited her at Lake Success, the site of the first United Nations headquarters, and she had walked from building to building with long strides at a pace that rivaled that of a long-distance walker.

She showed me to my bedroom and told me she'd wake me for breakfast. I spent some time reviewing my notes, prepared for the next day's session, and fell asleep as if drugged. The wake-up knock on the door was at seven o'clock. Not a long sleep, considering I'd turned in at twelve-thirty. A hearty breakfast of juice, hot cereal, muffins, toast, eggs, jam, and tea restored my energy, and after a short walk in the chilly morning we returned to the living room and the warmth of the fireplace. We finished up the questioning a short time after lunch.

Mrs. R. wished me a pleasant trip and as she walked me to the station wagon she said, "Don't make any of us too goody-goody."

Departure day for our hegira rolled up and we packed our gear, arranged for the car to be placed in the hold of the ship, and waved our good-byes to Lil and others who came to see us off. Jill and Jon were almost too late but did make it to our suite to hug and kiss us bon voyage. It was obvious she wished she was going with us but I told her she was for the time being the keeper of the gate. We promised her letters and cards and lots of presents.

We pulled away for the long trip. Joy and Jeb went exploring. I organized my books and papers, then Miriam and I also went on an exploration of the huge ship and ran into Cornelius Ryan, who was on his way to gather material for a new book. (Which he later titled *The Longest Day*.) He also introduced us to the secretary of the Duke and Duchess of Windsor, who had arrived on board with a pair of dogs, a hundred pieces of luggage, a maid and valet *and* the secretary.

She said she could arrange for us to meet the royal couple but, remembering his sympathies toward Germany before the war and his disinterest regarding what was happening in the world, I begged off. Miriam felt a bit cheated but I told her, "You know Mrs. Roosevelt — a duke and duchess next to her is peanuts compared to a hot chocolate sundae with whipped cream."

Marc Connelly was also on board and he loved to play backgammon. I played bridge with some of the travelers and Miriam trimmed Marc, much to his disgust.

Later, after Joy and Jeb went to their room, Miriam turned in and I went to work at the desk and began to sort out all my notes and place them in sequence — Act I, Scene 1, and so forth, up to Act III, Scene 3. I did not like the sound of the foghorn. I wanted to feel sure the captain could see where the hell he was going. This was my first trip on a large ship and I kept thinking of my nightmare — the *Titanic* lying some thirteen thousand feet down. I took a Dramamine and fell asleep, and woke up to discover we were still afloat and the day was sunny.

The voyage went quickly and my work went well. We enjoyed ourselves. (Long arm of coincidence department — a steward on board whom we came to know and like was named Jerry. Fourteen years later when we moved to our present apartment the doorman was our old friend Jerry, still bemoaning his lost job on the *United States*.)

We landed at Le Havre, then trained to Paris where we switched to the Simplon express heading for Venice. It was nothing like the movies. The cars were crowded, the diner was on a two-serving table d'hote routine. Our staterooms were devoid of toilet facilities except for two urinals, convenient for Jeb and me but a delicate contrivance for Joy and Miriam.

Jeb and I crowded our way into the second serving in the diner and found ourselves surrounded by Italians. They spotted us as Americans. *Dové?* I understood that word and gathered from the rest of the question they wanted to know where we were from. America. Hooray. Again, "*Dové?*" Hollywood. Ah! Hollywood! Applause. Jimmy Cagney! Yes. Bogart! Yes. Monroe! Yes. They helped us get extra rolls and slices of ham, cheese, and turkey, which we smuggled out in napkins. As we left, one of our rooters passed us a bottle of wine. As I tried to pay, he waved no. I said "*Grazie.*" One thing about working in motion pictures, you learn to say hello, good-bye, please, thank you in a large number of languages. We waved our thanks and *buona notte.*

By noon we had arrived in Venice, checked into the Gritti Palace, and for a few days we reveled in the wonders and beauties of this fabulous city and were captivated by the polite pigeons. But each night before going to bed I wrote. Whether it was just one or two pages or five or six, I wrote. Fun was fun, traveling was fun, but I had a deadline — each night moved me a day closer to January 30, 1958.

We rode the gondolas and motorboats, bought presents for Jill and Jon, wandered the streets for bargains (always got stuck — we are poor shoppers), and almost each day parked ourselves at the Piazza San Marco to drink white wine and listen to music. We gaped in wonder at this miraculous city in the water, which brought to mind Romeo and Juliet, even though this was Venice and not Verona.

The boat we took to Israel was a small Italian liner named *Messapia.* It was a trim white vessel, our suite was luxurious, and the food was fine. The roster of passengers was fascinating, comprising Spanish and Italian pilgrims on the way to the Holy Land, young Israelis returning home from furloughs gained after fighting in the Sinai battles during the early part of 1957, English tourists on their way to Israel, Greeks returning to their homes after visits to France, and a few Germans, heavily booted and loaded with cameras, binoculars, and walking costumes. I sensed this latter group was not popular with the other passengers — certainly not with me; the death camps were only twelve years behind us.

But as the voyage took hold of us we ignored the Germans and enjoyed the boat, the Spaniards, Italians, and Israelis.

Athens and the remains of Grecian glory were sights we would never forget.

The weather on the sea-lane to Haifa was superb but our stop at Cyprus was aborted because of minor uprisings that were feared lest they grow into a major conflict. Then the open sea to Haifa, and we arrived just an hour after another ship had docked with immigrants from Slavic countries who were shouting, singing, and crying as they viewed the Promised Land and the end of their flight from country to country.

This was Israel, a homeland for Jews whose restoration my Zayde and all devout Jews had prayed for three times a day during their entire lives.

We were greeted by Meyer Weisgal, the head of the Weizmann

Institute — a man who looked like Ben-Gurion and talked English, Yiddish, and Hebrew, all with a New York accent, his speech flowing from one tongue to another. He radiated joy, authority, and energy. He and his dear wife were our hosts during our stay in Israel; first for a few days in Jerusalem, then the rest of our time in Rehovoth with the institute as our base. When we stepped on Israeli soil for the first time I realized what it meant and would mean to me the rest of my life.

My roots are in American history, culture, and mores. And yet my religion, which is Jewish, is not simply a ritualistic faith. It also has a national history. Our faith is bound up into our heritage, written in the Bible and in the annals of Roman, Turkish, Assyrian, and English history. The fact of our national primacy in Israel is recorded in Jewish, Christian, and Moslem theology. This I knew before I came to Israel.

I could never leave America and live in Israel. I am too old and not hardy enough, but most important, as Saul Bellow observed about himself, my life as an American is not dispensable; I could never abandon it as I could never abandon my faith and my emotional and religious ties to Israel now that I have been there a number of times and have drunk the nectar of its spirits and dash, its courage and its resourcefulness.

When on this first visit I went to the museum of the Warsaw Ghetto Fighters, I was faced with the shock of the photographs taken by the Germans of the humiliation and destruction of Jews — of the way SS troopers shot and butchered Jews — men, women, and children. I saw the soap made from Jewish bodies, mattresses from hair on Jewish heads. We were there on a Friday and as we left, in order to be back at the hotel before the Sabbath, we exited the dark tunnels of the museum (it has since been replaced by a larger and better one) and, after blinking at the bright sunlight, we saw on a flagpole the blue stripes and blue Star of David on a field of white. The flag belonged there. It deserved to be there.

Israelis are avid movie fans and Weisgal had arranged for me to give a talk on the history of American movies. I prefaced it with a few short opening paragraphs in Hebrew — the listeners accepted my movie remarks with much more respect but they liked the fact that I had the nerve to try out my Hebrew. Weisgal said, "Your Hebrew after ten more visits will be also as good as mine — which is not saying much."

One evening we were invited to the home of Mrs. Chaim Weizmann, the widow of Israeli's brilliant first president. After dinner there was to be a bridge game. As we walked from the dining room into the living room to play, Meyer whispered a caution: "Listen to me — make some mistakes — she likes to win."

Mrs. Weizmann reminded both Miriam and me of Miriam's mother. She was a woman who kept her chin up to erase any sign of a wattle. She wore gloves to keep her hands pure white. Her wardrobe and the former president's house in which she lived were kept immaculate. She was Israel's first "first lady" and behaved in the manner she thought was appropriate. I liked her because she was neither embarrassed nor self-conscious about those perquisites she simply accepted as rightfully due her.

We had arrived in Israel in time for the first Israeli Independence Day celebration since the Sinai war in early 1957. The victory parade was held in Tel Aviv, where a million people congregated, coming by bus, car, train, wagon, donkey, motorcycle, bicycle, and foot. There is a standard wisecrack referring to times set for Jewish celebrations of all kinds. It runs, "The dinner begins at 6:30 JT." J.T. — Jewish time. We were driven to Tel Aviv to make certain we would arrive before the start of ceremonies that would begin (they said) at 10:00 A.M. in front of the canopy and stands where the dignitaries were seated along with some designated VIPs. We were on time and found ourselves seated next to Hubert Humphrey and a few American army officers who had come to consult with Israeli army officials as to the recent campaign and its extraordinary victory for the Israelis as compared to the halfhearted campaign waged by the French and English.

At exactly 10:000 A.M. — exactly — a flight of Mystères swept above the crowded streets and as the sound of their jets was swallowed by distance an army band led by a former British drum major, who had remained in Israel, marched to the front of the canopy. The march-step tempo of the drums stopped and the band came to a halt. There was silence. Then a million people took a deep breath as the drum major lifted his heavy baton, and as the downbeat fell the band began the Israeli national anthem, "Ha'Tikvah," "The Hope."

Having been raised in the catering business and having been involved in Jewish community affairs for all my years, I have heard "Ha'Tikvah" played hundreds of times. But I never had heard it played by an Israeli army band in Israel. The times before it had seemed a dirge, a sad, plaintive song of despair and plea. Now it was a triumphant statement, a thrilling, rousing paean, and as tears came streaming down I saw that they were on Humphrey's cheeks, Miriam's, Joy's, and everyone's around us. When the band finished there was a roar of cheers and applause that thundered its path through the city. The band broke into a military march and strode away and the parade groups, which had been marshaled near them, stepped behind them as the marching proper began at precisely five minutes after ten. The army does not follow JT.

That parade and the celebrations that followed at the Weizmann Institute and in the streets of Rehovoth were stirring events. We cancelled our boat reservations to Rome, deciding that five more days in Israel was worth more than another return trip by sea. We made plans to fly to Rome.

In the next few days I was stymied by the dates, ceremonies, dinners, and Passover observances (which occurred during our stay) that kept me from working on the play. We saw almost all of Israel; it is not difficult to do so in a short time since it is a country about the size of Massachusetts.

Before leaving for Rome, where our station wagon was lodged (we hoped) having been driven there from Paris by one of David Lewis's staff (he was the MGM representative in France), Meyer asked me to write of my impressions, which he wanted me to express at a dinner in New York sometime in November. I promised I would, and the night before I left I made a few notes for a playlet to be called *Sentimental Journey*. I put my scattered observations on paper and then put them on the back burner in the briefcase. I said to Miriam, "Let them cook, I'll get to them, but *Campobello* comes first."

Israeli drivers are notoriously fast and reckless and the trip from Rehovoth to the Lod airport was so frantic that it almost cured me of my fear of flying. Miriam used to drive me mad with her delight of air travel; she would keep up a running commentary (she always sat at the window seat). "Dore, look down at those clouds"; "Look at those boats, they look like toys we used to buy the kids"; "There's a plane out there going the other way." She still chatters whenever we fly but now that I'm a confirmed plane passenger I don't mind it — as a matter of fact, I even bother her with some of my observations.

The air trip to Rome in those days included a stop in Athens for lunch. After reaching our destination, we went off to the Seven Hills of antiquity. The wagon was there with the baggage we had left inside intact. We spent a few nights in Rome. One evening while walking on the Via Veneto we met Nunnally and Dorris Johnson. Nunnally, the gifted writer and producer, was blessed with a pixie face and humor to match, coupled with a warm Southern accent. Dorris, his wife, remains as beautiful and as dear as she was twenty years ago. They were in Rome before going to Montecatini, where they were going to take the baths and the waters. Before that, they were going to visit the Vatican the very next morning. Nunnally asked if we'd like to go along. "I got a friend in court — he'll get you in with us to watch the Pope greet a couple of hundred of the faithful."

He asked where we were staying and said he'd let us know before bedtime. Now they were on their way to dinner. Two hours later, after having run into a half dozen other Americans we knew and having had our dinner, we returned to our hotel and found a note from Nunnally that carried a series of instructions including what time we would meet — 7:00 A.M. in front of Saint Peter's. Miriam was to wear black, have a shawl over her head, wear gloves, cut down on jewelry; he recommended that I wear a dark suit and white shirt, told us the name of the monsignor who was to escort us, and after the long, explicit list he added a PS: "If you are captured — swallow this."

The performance by Pope Pius XII, who had just recovered from a rather long illness, was quite extraordinary. While we were in a special visitors' box that accommodated perhaps forty of us, at least five hundred pilgrims from different countries were there to see the Pope and when he arrived, carried on an uncovered palanquin, he was greeted by loud shots of "Papa! Po-pe!" He exchanged his white skullcap with the cap of one of the pilgrims and in an instant had exchanged that for another pilgrim's and kept up the exchange as he was slowly carried along — scores of pilgrims went away with skullcaps that had rested on the Pope's pate.

The cheers and boisterous reception rang through the large room. The Pope smiled. He was lowered in front of a flight of about fourteen steps leading to a platform, rapidly bounced up the steps, and when he reached the platform turned and greeted the pilgrims with a grin and a wide gesture of welcome. Nunnally whispered, "He's great — all he needed to say was 'Ta-ra!'" It was a spectacular entrance and was followed by a short speech in English, Spanish, Italian, French, and German, undoubtedly the same speech, but certainly an impressive display.

Before we parted from Dorris and Nunnally he said, "Since you didn't kiss the Pope's ring, you may kiss Dorris's ring." I said I'd rather kiss Dorris, which I did and we went our way.

We wended our way through the mountains north into Tuscany, stayed over in Florence to see the overwhelming art collections, and took advantage of the opportunity to meet Bernard Berenson, a friend of Max Ascoli — the owner and editor of *The Reporter* — who had arranged for our visit to Mr. Berenson.

Miriam and I left Joy and Jeb to their own resources. Joy was now mooning. Had she made up her mind too soon? Was Arthur *really* in love with her? She with him? Should she buy all the laces, gowns, lingerie that Miriam was planning to shop for in Florence? Jeb, beyond recording our trip with his camera, had only one chief concern: how to meet an accommodating lady who would invite him into her apartment or even just a room to rid him of his virginity.

At I Tatti, Berenson's home in Fiesoli, we were pleased to meet Mary McCarthy, who was a guest using the magnificent resources of Berenson's art library for a book she was writing.

Berenson was a wisp of a man, short and very thin, his hands porcelain delicate, his Vandyke and mustache the color of his face — he brought to mind that long ago memory of Ben Yehudah, the compiler of the first working Hebrew dictionary whom I had seen when I was a young boy. Perhaps it was that memory that led to the exchange I had after lunch with Mr. Berenson.

He was a pleasant host, articulate and warm, pleased to show us some of his paintings. He told us he favored Giotto and the Sienese school of painting. He seemed to hold modern painters in disfavor, saying they were imitators. His taste, he said, ran to those who were originals and not those who followed.

After the tour of his quite exquisite home and library we gathered for lunch. He had a hearty appetite. Over the dessert of wine, fruit, and cheese he asked where we had been and I gave him a quick rundown. He asked for my impressions of Israel. He listened and expressed reservations. He told me he had been born a Jew but had rejected the faith because it was no longer valid and had become a Catholic. I commented that during his courteous tour he had told us that he liked the original and did not favor the followers, and I suggested that his views on religion were inconsistent with his views on art — since Judaism was the original and Catholicism had come along quite a bit later. Miss McCarthy laughed; Mr. Berenson pointed a finger at me, smiled, and said, "You're a provocateur." We dropped the matter but later, before he excused himself to take his nap, he asked me to send him a copy of *Life Is with People*, a book that deals with the history of Jewish life in the *shtetls* (villages) in Russia and Poland. When I got back to California I kept my promise to send it. I never heard if he received it.

We traveled from Florence to Pisa with a stop at Montecatini to see Nunnally and Dorris, who had met Lenny and Sylvia Lyons for their health stay. Nunnally showed up with a glass of water in his hand and said, "If I should suddenly leave you — please understand — these waters take a man's underwear unaware."

Finishing our short visit with the Johnsons and Lyonses we hied to Pisa and Jeb and I ascended the Leaning Tower, which compels you to hug the inner wall of the spiral walk. Joy and Miriam, as do most of the spectators, watched our progress from the long view — just in case the tower decided to fall.

Our destination for a long stay was the Splendido in Portofino. We settled in and each night, since there was little to do and we chose not to do it, I used the time to finish the first act of the play. What concerned me most was, what did FDR sound like in the early twenties? His memos, letters, and references seemed to indicate he was rather stiff and formal — a quality that sloughed off after his illness and his subjection to his wheelchair. He had become more colloquial, sharper, and tougher, and had lost some of the looking-down-his-nose tone. I wanted to catch that change as the play progressed. By the time the first act was finished I had confidence that I'd be able to do it. We loved Portofino and Rapallo and hoped that one day we could return for a very long stay.

From Portofino we drove to Cannes. Jeb's single memory of that port of call was the sight of a few topless sunbathers, gender — female. We visited Monte Carlo and were invited to have tea with Princess Grace and her new baby daughter. Grace is a thoughtful hostess; for her wedding Miriam and I had sent her a silver wedding bowl engraved with the seal and the initials of the royal couple. It was prominently displayed on a table in the room where we had afternoon tea and cookies. I have no way of knowing if it was a gesture of thanks but I guessed it was.

Princess Grace told us she was still taking French lessons, that her life was a totally happy one, and why shouldn't it be? — it was a fairy tale come true. She said that the arrival of her daughter, Princess Caroline, finally had made everything seem real.

There was little work I could do as we traveled toward Paris, visiting Arles, Les Baux, Vichy, Avignon, the châteaus of the Loire Valley, and Tours. Ultimately we arrived in Paris on a Sunday in early June. It was ghastly hot and the city was quite empty. We had trouble finding our way to the Ritz Hotel since Parisians are not exactly cordial unless you can communicate in perfect French, a language for which I have a tin ear. Miriam has a fairly good reading vocabulary but cannot speak it. Joy had taken high school courses, which proved inadequate. A policeman, when I stopped to ask where I was, merely yelled at me in French and gestured for going the wrong way around a circle. I smiled at him as he was screaming and muttered, "You're a rude son of a bitch and I do not like you or your city."

We got to the hotel through the kind auspices of a young Frenchman who signaled us the path to Le Ritz with elaborate directions: three squares to *droit* (that we knew was right); four squares to *gauche* — left; a circular motion — circle; he stood erect, one hand stuck in his shirt, the other behind his back — ah! Napoleon. *Oui!* — he pointed — Le Ritz. We all shouted, "*Merci.*" Our young friend nodded and waved to us, and following his directions, we drove up to the Ritz in our dirty station wagon, which needed a bath, oil, and a checkup. The doorman knew of a garage but did not speak good enough English to direct me to it, or, more truthfully, I did not understand enough of his combined French and English to trust myself to try to make it unescorted. He called to a taxi driver and explained in French that I was willing to have a driver escort me to the garage, then I would return him to the hotel in a cab and pay him generously for his time. At least I hoped he had understood what I had asked him to say.

The driver was a chunky man with a leather cap, a stereotypic movie French taxi hackie; a cigarette drooped from his lip getting stained with saliva; he kept saying, "*Oui, oui.*" When he settled in our car he began to indicate the road to the garage. As we drove he examined the wagon, said, "*Le grand auto.*" I said, "*Oui.*" He looked at city stickers plastered to our side windows by Joy and Jeb. "Ah," he said, "Firenze." "*Oui.*" "Roma." "*Oui.*" "Vichy," he pointed thumbs down. "*Oui.*" Then he saw a sticker from Israel that Jeb had bought in Tel Aviv and had placed in the car when we got to Rome. He said, "Yisrael." No one, unless he speaks Hebrew, says Yisrael. I answered, "*Ken*" — yes. The gates opened; he was a Jew, born in Turkey, had gone to Israel, lived there for fourteen years, his family was still there — he suggested that when we got to the garage I should let him talk, otherwise the attendants would cheat me — "They dislike Americans." All this in Hebrew.

He took over, made himself available for tours during our stay in Paris, and I had the satisfaction of writing to my friends that Hebrew, as a matter of fact, had been of great value to me in Paris.

We met Grace and Abel Green of *Variety*, in the obvious place, on the rue de la Paix. They invited us in for drinks at their hotel to greet fellow Americans who gravitated toward each other as if in refuge from the French. David Lewis took the family to the Café de Paree. Jeb beamed at the naked ladies, who seemed laminated with too much powder and makeup. Las Vegas, these days, seems fleshier and much sexier but I assume so do the chorus ladies in Paris.

Miriam and I spent one evening visiting the Irwin Shaws at their home in Neuilly and again found ourselves with a group of Americans. While they were expatriates, spoke good French, and liked the tax-shelter aspects of living abroad, I sensed that they ached for America. A number of them have returned. That evening when we got back to the hotel Jeb and Joy were waiting for us. Joy expressed mild disgust that Jeb was waiting to tell us what he considered his good news. He had gone into the night and met a lovely lady, who had invited him to a nearby apartment and had initiated him into one of life's great pleasures — sex. I told Jeb he seemed happier than when he had been at his Bar Mitzvah. He said, "Why not? I didn't have to make a speech."

From Paris to Deauville, out of season, happily — because I made up for lost time. I rewrote some of Act I and began Act II. Then to London via Boulogne and the English Channel ferry. We checked in at Claridge's for a marvelous stay. Wolf Mankowitz, then writing for a newspaper, headed a group of journalists for a press conference and they were unusually kind to me. They asked if I was going to meet my schedule of opening the FDR play in January. With a hidden doubt in my mind, I assured them I would. When they left I resumed, rather furiously, my work on the script and I kept it up during the days in London and the trip home on the *United States*. We landed on July 5.

In New York I read the two completed acts to Lawrence, Armina, and Theresa — they were more than pleased. What about the third act? In a few weeks. They were having trouble raising their sixty thousand dollars. I had not yet made a move toward getting mine. There was a lot to do. They had booked the Shubert Theatre in New Haven, the Colonial in Boston, the Walnut in Philadelphia, and the Cort in New York. But we had to decide on a director, a cast and, of all things, get the money. Lawrence arranged for me to meet Tyrone Guthrie, who expressed little interest in the project; not wishing to be upmanshipped, I expressed little interest in him. Bill Fitelson became angry with me when I expressed my willingness to gamble my own money for my share of the capital. He argued that I had gambled enough. I had used up, from January 1 until that day in July, over a hundred thousand dollars for the office and staff, the house and staff, and the trip — plus sixty thousand for taxes. "What if the play fails — it could, you know — most do — what if you lost sixty thousand — what then?" Bill asked. The answer was I'd be broke.

Donovan, our butler, came east to pick up our wagon and drive it and most of our luggage home. We left for home two days later by train. Donovan had already arrived when we checked in.

Miriam and I had a heavy agenda. The first item was simple — the distribution of gifts. Item two, Joy's wedding: catering by Chasen's, invitations, hotel reservations for the out-of-towners, music — I was back to Schary Manor. The other important item was to raise the money for my share of the production. I called friends — got some turndowns, but others chipped in without a murmur. Bill Fitelson was also making approaches in New York but the going wasn't easy. Billy Rose told him that the play was a disastrous idea — doomed to ignominious failure. But Ardie Deutsch came in, and so did Ed Lasker, Fred Gash, Lenny Spigelgass, Arthur Loew, Mel Bloch. I received a letter from a Leonard Goldwater who wrote that he wished to invest five hundred dollars, that he was a paraplegic, a victim of multiple sclerosis, that he wanted to be part of the project. I thanked him but explained that plays were a risky investment and I urged him to invest only his good wishes and said that I would like him and his wife to be my guests at the opening. His return letter advised me not to be concerned; he had made investments in other shows, had done extremely well, had a green thumb for picking winners, and asked me to accept his participation. I accepted.

While the activities recited were bubbling along, I secreted myself each night in my quarters, a large sprawling arrangement that contained a dressing alcove, library, a working area for files and desk, and my bed all in one room. I re-edited the first two acts and wrote the third act, which was the easiest to do since I had piled up copious notes and had already written the very last scene that comprised the last five minutes of the show. Once everything was typed I decided to give my sister, Lil, her second husband, Paul Small, and my close friends the first peek at the finished script.

We gathered for a buffet. The doctors present told their offices to hold all calls; Donovan and Andy, our chauffeur and extra butler for large dinners, were to take our calls and not disturb us unless the roof fell in. We settled down in the projection room, and with a quickening pulse and a flush of apprehension that my friends would hate the play, I opened the script and began to read. Anyone who has addressed an audience, a large or small one, knows very quickly if he's holding his listeners, losing them, or droning them to sleep. I began to list the cast of characters: Anna Roosevelt, Eleanor Roosevelt, Elliott Roosevelt, Franklin Roosevelt, Jr., James Roosevelt, John Roosevelt, Franklin Delano Roosevelt, Louis Howe, Sara Delano Roosevelt, Governor Alfred E. Smith, and the rest of the twenty-two characters. I could sense my friends reacted as an audience would as they looked at a program. It was an exciting group of names and the flush of apprehension left me. I read the play. After Act I we stopped for a short break. There was applause. After Act II they said, "No intermission." At the end of the play they were sobbing and laughing — they came to me with hugs and handshakes and the wagging of heads and with words of happy talk. They were confident the play would be a success.

When the evening was over Lil stayed behind with Paul to talk; she had a family failing — we all cry easily. She was still red-eyed. Paul, her husband, a cigar smoker, an agent, and a Broadway character out of Damon Runyon, was willing to bet a fortune on the play. Lil just wanted to be alone with Miriam and me to tell us how deeply she felt — how much the play would mean for me and for those who would see it.

Miriam and I went upstairs after everyone had gone. The house was quiet. I held her and thanked her for the hours she had spent typing up those pages in staterooms and hotels across the Atlantic and in England, Italy, France, and Israel. I told her that as I read the play I had mentally marked lines that were false, speeches that had to be cut, scenes that needed sparking up, but that I had the warm feeling we had a very good chance at the brass ring.

The next morning my euphoria diminished. Lawrence Langner called to tell me they were having great trouble getting investors, and when could they have a finished script? He seemed troubled and indicated that we might not be able to meet our rehearsal date — after all, no director, no cast, no complete financing, and no finished script.

I responded by telling him I had the script, it would be mimeographed and I'd be on my way to New York with the copies within three days; that I'd be meeting with Vincent Donehue, recommended by Bill Fitelson and the Guild, to get his reaction to the script, the third act of which I had sent to him the day before — he had received the first two acts from Fitelson. Re cast, I reported that Van Heflin, Joe Cotten, and Charlton Heston's agent had turned down the project; I agreed that they should send the play on to Anthony Quayle. As to money — I had my share either in hand or promised. Finally, as to not meeting our rehearsal date, it was still more than two months away — *coraggio!*

The meeting with Donehue restored my spirits. He was a lean, enthusiastic young Irish-American with a liberal background in politics and religion. His eyes were a pale blue, his hair crew-cut, and his emotions on the surface. As he talked of the play he teared up — he had casting ideas for every part except FDR — but he thought Quayle would be excellent, with the reservation that it would be unfortunate if our great American President were played by an Englishman. Although Vincent's credits on major TV shows were important, his credits on Broadway were limited. Still, his direction of *A Trip to Bountiful* starring Lillian

Gish had received excellent notices. But in any event, I've always responded to young directors in film and saw no reason why I should not use the same yardstick of choice in the theater — enthusiasm, taste, a devotion to the theme, knowledge of the medium, and the breath of authority. Vincent passed all the tests.

34

Lucy Ballentine and Betty Arrighi were running herd on Joy's wedding preparations, Walter Reilly was holding a tight grip on the office and editing the final letters I had written regarding my trip abroad. I had written letters, published in the Los Angeles *Times*, to Humphrey, Stevenson, Eddie Cantor, and Eric Johnston while en route. On my return I had scribbled outlines of letters to President Truman and to the Douglas Fairbankses, who had been particularly hospitable to us when we were in England.

The letters comprise a journal of our voyage. Beyond my first impressions the only prediction that seems to have stood up is that Italy was inexorably heading toward Communism. My hunch that French, Italian, and English films would rival the success of American pictures was half right — many of them have matched Hollywood products, if not exceeded them, in imagination, art, style, and subject, but while none have been able to reap the enormous returns of the American disaster, sci-fi, or horror entries, directors such as Ingmar Bergman, François Truffaut, Vittorio De Sica, Federico Fellini, Carol Reed, Bernardo Bertolucci, Akira Kurosawa have influenced our native film creators.

Since the Hollywood house staff led by Miriam had everything in hand and since time was moving up fast it was necessary for me to travel to New York and see the Langners and Theresa Helburn. Our friend Claire Krumgold was apartment hunting for us in New York, searching for a pied-à-terre where we could bivouac for a while until we either failed (in which event we would retreat to Hollywood) or succeeded (if so, we'd settle down in the East).

The toughest test for the play was to read it to Mrs. Roosevelt. I called her to set a date. She asked if she could have a few others listen to it. I agreed but asked her to please limit the number.

We set a time for me to come to her home two nights after my proposed arrival in New York.

Shortly after my return to New York I learned that the Guild was offering a package deal to their list of investors, who were turning up their chins at the prospect of putting money in *Campobello*. But they were lining up to buy shares in the Guild presentation of an English production of an Australian play, *Summer of the Seventeenth Doll*, which was a big success in London. The Guild was denying their backers a piece of *Doll* unless they made a similar investment in *Campobello*. That scheme was working so well Lawrence was no longer concerned about raising his 50 percent of the production cost.

But they were concerned by the time lock. It was nearly the end of August when I met with Lawrence, Theresa, and Armina. Bill Fitelson sat in to hear that the Guild wished to cancel out their bookings and put the play off until later in the season or, if necessary, the following season. After listening to the reasons for their forebodings I said that if they were afraid to go ahead I would take over the production as a solo enterprise, that I would get the money or put up my own and I would not abide any more delays. They would have to let me know by that evening if they were to go ahead or give up their interest. No later than that evening. I'd wait at the hotel. Then I got up and went back to my rooms and began to figure out how I could possibly realize my radical ultimatum. I had demonstrated bravado but now, alone in the hotel, I trembled. What the hell would I do if the Guild pulled out?

Within the hour Bill called and said, "You did the right thing. The Guild will go ahead. They want to meet with you tomorrow morning." I heaved a very deep sigh. Almost immediately I felt fatigued, and fell asleep.

The following day I talked to Langner on the phone but said I wanted to take the day off and prepare for the reading to Mrs. Roosevelt. I went over the playscript, made some cuts, added a few clarifications, called Moss Hart, *kibitzed* with him and set a dinner date.

I rested, then called Miriam, who wished me luck, and at eight o'clock promptly I stood alone in front of Mrs. R's town house in the east seventies, adjusted my tie, took a deep breath, and pushed the bell button. Typically, Mrs. R. herself opened the door, welcomed me, and moved me into the living room, where were gathered Lady Reading, a cherished friend of Mrs. R., Henry Morgenthau, Jr., Jimmy and Franklin Roosevelt, Jr., Trudi Lash, and Mrs. R., which made an audience of six. Mrs. R. seated herself facing me only three feet away to accommodate her bad hearing. My chief concern was one that had troubled me during the writing — had I written FDR in the mood and tone of his conversation in the years 1920 to 1924? I outlined the scope of the play, read the cast of characters, asked if everyone could hear me, then took an anxious breath and began.

As the first act went along, my tiny audience laughed, nodded, and were quiet at the right moments. At the curtain of the act, Lady Reading and Trudi pressed handkerchiefs to their eyes. I suggested an intermission but Mrs. R. asked if I could go on without one. I went into Act II. It was clear everyone was enjoying it. They gave me courage to play it more strongly, and as the act ended Mrs. R.'s head was lowered. The others were obviously moved and stirred.

Act III got the reactions I had hoped for. When I finished reading there was a pause. No one said anything. I surmised they were waiting for Mrs. R. to have the first word. I saw that she had wiped her eyes — then she gently raised her head. Her eyes were red. She said, "It sounds exactly like Franklin." That opening broke the ice. The others chipped in with words that rang in my ears. After a cold drink and amid the glorious relief I was feeling, Mrs. R. said there were four items she wished to discuss. The first was that I was too kind to her. I said I truly didn't think so. Second, while she thought I had handled her mother-in-law quite accurately, there might be some who would think I had treated Sara rather harshly. Lady Reading didn't think so, neither did Trudi nor young Morgenthau. Jimmy and Franklin, who had always been cosseted by their grandmother, thought I might have been a little rough on her, but they agreed she had been a tough old bird.

Point three was that Campobello at that time did not have electricity — oil lamps were *de rigueur*. That was a help in the rewrite since it added a good piece of business for Louis Howe and gave Ralph Alswang opportunity for interesting lighting.

The final point was, "Dore, I know that it is more theatrical to have Franklin on crutches but actually he was on his canes by then." Jimmy chimed in, "Ma's right about that. I walked with him to the podium and he handed me his canes."

I knew they were both wrong, and as tactfully as possible I explained that they were substituting the 1928 convention for the 1924 convention. Both times FDR had nominated Al Smith but in 1924 he was still on crutches — by 1928 he had been able to use the canes. Mrs. R. protested and so did Jimmy. Fortunately I had brought along pictures, which I had planned to use to prove how carefully we were reproducing the walk to the podium. Apologizing for proving my point, I showed them pictures of FDR with his crutches just before he had handed them to Jimmy.

Jimmy said, "My God, I forgot. Of course, now I remember."

Mrs. R. studied the picture and said, "I suppose I didn't want to remember." She handed me the picture. "Dore, you've written a beautiful play — even though you've been much too generous to me."

The others reassured her I had not been. What I didn't know at the time, nor did most people, was the truth of the story of FDR and his affair with Lucy Mercer and the biting hurt it had brought to Eleanor. But what pleased her, Franklin, Jr., told me later, was that I had handled the illness and her valiant response to FDR's travail with truth and compassion. "Most of all," Franklin said, "it really sounded like Dad. You made some of us boys look like the Katzenjammer Kids, but maybe we were."

I laughed. "No maybe. You were."

As I left, I kissed Mrs. R.'s cheek. I returned to the hotel and called Miriam, then the Langners, then Vinnie Donehue. Miriam was ecstatic, as was Vinnie, and indeed so were the Langners, although Lawrence could not restrain a zinger: "Remember, *you* can't play FDR. We need an actor."

"See you tomorrow," I said to Langner. To myself I said, "Why the hell doesn't he shut up?" But it was good he did not. Lawrence had persistence, intelligence, and a sharp, sound sense of drama.

Now things moved along. A casting session produced many decisions. During the next few days I met brigades of actors. The Guild had by now read the complete script and Helburn, the most critical of the three, merely said, "Go into rehearsal — anything that's wrong, you'll see." We agreed on Vincent Donehue to direct. Ralph Alswang was signed to do the sets and lighting, Virginia Volland for wardrobe, and we were on the toboggan — without an FDR, with Lawrence still holding out for Quayle.

I had to return to California for Joy's wedding. Claire had found an ideal, small, and comfortable apartment at the Alwyn Court on Seventh Avenue and Fifty-eighth Street and I spent some time with our decorator, Fred Von Aw, who took over the job. I left it all in his capable hands.

Joy and Arthur's wedding was held in our garden. It was a happy and beautiful occasion. The sky was blue with a proper dotting of fleecy clouds. Rabbi Pressman performed his usual warm wedding ceremony and we laughed, kissed, cried, danced, and ate until Joy and Arthur scurried away for their honeymoon. Miriam said, "Now the second bird has left the nest." She said only Jeb was left to us and that he in time would also take off. I observed, since in those days I always called Jeb "Horse," that his leaving might not be likened to that of a bird taking flight. For some years Jeb would still be home, wherever that would be.

In a short time Miriam and I took off for New York for the long pull leading to January 30, 1958. The family stayed behind to await the verdict.

Walter was coming in to New York to aid me. Armina had set up an office for us in their town house on West Fifty-third Street and each day brought on a quickening of the pulse. Before we left California I had interviewed and read a young actor recommended to me by Garson Kanin for the role of FDR. His name was Arthur Hill. He looked the role, if somewhat thin, had the right voice and accent, but was simply too young. Walter and I had gone over lists — talked of many actors — but had not yet felt that odd but definite click that tells you, "That's the one."

During our casting sessions we would take time out to discuss random notions as to actors who could play FDR. Our notions were often repetitious, or absurd, impractical — once I suggested, "John Barrymore would be ideal, if he weren't dead."

But we were agreed on the casting of Eleanor (Mary Fickett), Al Smith (Alan Bunce), Sara Delano Roosevelt (Anne Seymour), Missy Le Hand (Mary Welch), and Louis Howe (Henry Jones). Smaller roles were filled in — the Roosevelt butler was assigned to a newcomer, James Earl Jones, and the youngest son, John Roosevelt, was to be played by a youngster, Jeffrey Rowland, who was to achieve TV stardom in "The Waltons."

Alswang's set designs and lighting patterns were exactly right — particularly the way he mastered the problems involved in staging the last scene, simulating a platform that projected from upstage toward downstage and that gave the audience a clear and unobstructed view of FDR walking on his crutches toward the podium.

Virginia Volland's costumes were perfect; a few minor corrections from Vinnie Donehue were necessary for his staging, but the colors, styles, and designs were absolutely right.

As everything progressed toward the rehearsal schedule I felt the hot breath of Lawrence Langner's warnings that the time was getting short and we still didn't have our FDR. I avoided contention by talking of ads, of a logo, and of the proper publicity for the production. Lawrence was not put off. Finally I had to face the truth. If we delayed any longer, we might lose Quayle — that would mean the entire structure would fall apart. It was on a Friday that I bellied up to the facts and told Lawrence that on Monday, if I couldn't think of anyone other than Quayle, I would swallow my resistance and we would go with Quayle.

That night Reilly ate with Miriam and me. We had assembled all our notes on casting, casting books from the East and West coasts, Burns Mantle "best plays" volumes of the last few years, and after dinner we sat down and began our search. Miriam seated herself in a corner and took up some intricate crocheting. Reilly urged me not to hurry past names — "Let's discuss each one as if it were new to us." We began but it was impossible to be totally objective. As the hours went by I became more impatient. Reilly pointed out that though he had had a first nega- tive reaction to Quayle, it was only based on his being English, and was not because he was lacking in talent for the part. Then I recollected that Quayle had played one or two American roles in films. Walter observed that they were Irish parts and said he was once again negative. Back we went to the books. The rest of this is the way Reilly and I remember it — and Miriam agrees . . . why not? She plays the leading role.

Miriam suddenly chimed in, "There's one name you're forgetting."
I asked, "Who?"
She said, "You know."

Miriam, who can remember the names of her grammar-school teach- ers and the name of a woman sheriff in Bradley Beach in 1920, cannot remember the names of people we had dinner with a few nights ago. She also cannot remember names of pictures (unless they were exhibited thirty years ago) and she is absolutely awful about names of actors except Cary Grant, Spencer Tracy, and Robert Ryan.

So when she popped that "You know" at me I tried to be patient.
"What was he in?" I asked.
"Lots of pictures."
"What pictures? Name one."
She said, "Westerns, costumes, kings — like that."
My patience wavered. "What the hell is 'like that'?"
She had her answer: "Beards and history parts. He's tall."
"Miriam, let us alone."
She went on, "You had him in many pictures at MGM."
Walter cut in, "Miriam, lots of actors were in pictures at MGM — when Dore was there we made almost three hundred."
There was a pause and I suggested that Miriam not bother us.
She did. "He was a President."

Walter said, "A President, let's see, a President — Washington? FDR? Jackson? — Lincoln, maybe?"

Miriam said, "Yes."

I said, "Henry Fonda?"

Miriam said, "No."

Reilly broke in, "I know — you're thinking of Massey. Raymond Massey."

Miriam nodded. "Yes."

I said, "He can't play FDR."

Miriam said, "You're right. He'd be awful."

Politely I said, "Miriam, shut up."

We returned to our lists. About twenty minutes later, when we were at the edge of desperation, I was about to call Langner and tell him to get Quayle. Miriam, who hadn't said a word for those twenty minutes, now cut in.

"I've got the man," she said.

Walter sighed. "Oh, no. Not again. Who this time? Wallace Beery?"

"No, really," Miriam said, "I know this one is right — and you know him very well."

I said, "Miriam, for Chrissakes!"

"Listen to me." Miriam was intense. "He's perfect — he's got light eyes, he's tall, good looking, light hair —"

"Miriam, *what the hell* is his *name?*"

"I don't know."

"You're driving us crazy."

"You had him in a picture —"

"What picture?"

"Don't be silly," Walter volunteered. "Miriam doesn't remember."

"That's right," Miriam agreed.

I asked loudly, "What was it about? Can you remember what it was about?"

"A kidnapping."

"A kidnapping?"

"A *kidnapping?*" Walter repeated as dumbly as I.

"What picture did we make about a kidnapping?" I asked Walter.

"The only one I can think of is *Ransom*."

"Miriam, that one was with Glenn Ford."

"No, it wasn't."

"Wasn't what?"

"That was the picture. But not the actor."

[*348*]

"Please, Miriam, don't argue with me. Glenn Ford was in the picture. We bought it from a television show — in the TV version he was played by —"

"Ralph Bellamy!" Walter shouted.

"I told you! That's the man," Miriam proclaimed.

"Ralph Bellamy! Ralph! Miriam, you're a doll! A genius! Of course, where the hell have we been? Why didn't I think of him? Why didn't Lawrence? Or Armina? Or you, Walter? Why — he'd be perfect!"

Miriam beamed and said, "Next time, listen."

I kissed her.

I reached for the phone and called Lawrence. When I told Lawrence we had the man — Bellamy — he quickly agreed, gave me his number (he must have kept a phone book the size of a standard one issued by the telephone company), and I called, kicking myself again and again for not having remembered Ralph in his stage hits *State of the Nation* and *Detective Story*, and wondering if his damned phone was out of order — or if he was out — or in Europe — or — or — then he answered.

Many, many years before I had written some personal-appearance bon mots for Ralph and I had played tennis at a club he had owned with Charles Farrell in Palm Springs. So I greeted him with, "Hello, Ralph, how's your backhand? This is Dore." His greeting was hearty. I asked him about Alice, his wife, and after a few more nonessential Q's and A's I ventured, "Would you like to read a play?"

His answer had a smile in it. "The one about FDR? I wondered when you'd get around to me."

He told me that he and Alice had come from the theater and were heading to their country place for the weekend. He'd be glad to read the play if I could get it over to him within a half hour. When I asked where he lived he said, "The Osborne. Fifty-seventh and Seventh Avenue."

"God is good," I said. "I'm across the street at the Alwyn. You'll have the script in one minute."

"I'll call you Monday morning," Ralph promised.

Walter delivered the script in less than a minute, returned to the apartment, and said, "He looks sensational. Let's start praying."

We talked and talked some more, going around in nervous circles. I had the feeling I would not sleep until Monday morning came around. Then we wanted sandwiches and a bottle of beer and we munched and quaffed for over an hour. The ring of the phone at twelve-fifteen was a sharp alarm. I picked it up.

"Yes?"

"Dore, this is Ralph. While I was packing, Alice read the first two scenes in Act I, handed me the script, and said, 'Read it now — it's for you.' Well," Ralph continued, "I've just finished the first two acts. I stopped crying a few minutes ago. When do we start rehearsals?"

Then he told me he'd finish reading the play and see me next morning — "the hell with the weekend." I hung up, grabbed Miriam, and hugged, apologized, thanked her, and kept saying like an idiot, "He loves it — he loves it — he loves it." Walter said, "Now, I think I shall have some Scotch." He did.

The next morning when the doorbell rang I opened the door and there stood Ralph, a cigarette holder clenched perkily in his mouth, a fedora perched on his head with the front brim turned up, and a broad smile on his face.

I grabbed his hand and said, "Mr. President, welcome." Then we embraced.

Before Ralph's arrival I had called Lawrence and given him the good news and we had an appointment for Monday morning. Ralph had spoken to his agent, Howard Hausman, and was ready to go to work. Vinnie also was to meet us Monday and there was a hurry-up schedule of labors for Ralph. He had to spend time at the rehabilitation hospital to learn how to manage the braces, the wheelchair, the crutches, how to crawl as FDR had crawled. I didn't know then, and neither did Vinnie, but later Dr. McIntyre, FDR's doctor, came to New York and showed Ralph, Vinnie, and me how FDR had managed whatever movement he was capable of — how to shift from the wheelchair to another chair and back, how to stand up after he had locked his braces and been handed his crutches, how to crawl on his haunches by placing his hands behind his back and pulling his body toward them, and how after crawling he had figured out a way of getting back into his wheelchair by the use of his powerful arms, hands, and shoulders. Ralph was a good student. More important, he was in superb physical condition.

Everything was coming up roses — then I took a tumble.

35

During the months when the production schedule for *Campobello* was enduring and surviving the shoals, storms, calms, embargoes, contentions, strains, and fears that seemed to beset us, I had, with some regret but because I had pledged myself to Meyer Weisgal, applied my free hours, of which there were mighty few, to the writing of *Sentimental Journey*, a dramatic journal of my impressions of Israel, which was to be presented at the Weizmann Institute dinner at the Waldorf-Astoria main ballroom on the evening of November 26, 1957.

Having completed the script I prevailed on Lawrence Langner, who granted me the enlistment of their casting wizard at the Theatre Guild, a lady who bore the first name of Ruth coupled with the unfortunate second name of Frankenstein (in later years she married a gentleman named Kramer and she now spends her life boating and flying all over the West Indies and the Netherlands Antilles).

Ruth had the capacity to find the best and most appropriate people to bring a script to life. In order to give *Sentimental Journey* clear verisimilitude I decided to play the narrator, who was obviously me, the author. All things considered, I reckoned I was ideal for playing myself.

I would have drafted Vinnie Donehue to direct but he was, of course, too occupied with preparing *Campobello*. Vinnie was a tireless worker and we had established a comfortable and productive working arrangement. As he read and reread the script and plotted his moves and attitudes toward the characters, he made copious notes, and when he had enough of them, we would meet at my apartment and go over the list. Many of the items were minor — most of them I agreed with and made changes to accommodate Vinnie's perspectives. Some of his notes were questions, answers to which I had available either in my own concepts of what I wanted the play to be or in books I had read; other questions were tabled for me to look up in pages of the bibliography I had brought to New York with me.

Therefore, since Vinnie was so gainfully employed I opted to direct the Israeli play myself. That meant finding time to talk with the conductor of the orchestra, to ensure his meeting the cues on time, and ultimately rehearsing the band for its rendition of "Ha'Tikvah" in as close a copy as possible of how that military band had sounded in Tel Aviv. Also, the cast had to be rehearsed, costumed, and directed on a two-level platform on the Waldorf stage.

The afternoon of our performance everything and everyone was ready — actors, orchestra, light men, costumes, platform — and as we began to set the lights, I stepped back on the platform to be sure the actors in the rear would be properly lighted. I forgot there was a three-foot drop from the platform to the stage. I stumbled and tumbled and landed on my back. There were cries of alarm, everything from the reverent "Oh, my God!" to the hasty "Oh, shit!" But, helped by a few of the cast and two stagehands, I got to my feet, insisted I was feeling fine (once again — that old standby — "The show must go on"), and proceeded with the rehearsal. I felt a dull ache but since I could move my legs, arms, and neck I properly concluded I had not broken my spine. We finished two run-throughs and dispersed to our homes. "See you at seven" constituted my so-long to the troops.

When I arrived at our apartment I was limping and my back was beginning to feel sore and stiff.

I called my friendly orthopedic surgeon, Dr. Fred Marek, with the news of my acrobatic turn, and once he knew of my needs he said, "Lie down, I'll be there in twenty minutes."

Maybe it was really forty minutes. When he had completed his examination he agreed there were no signs of a fracture, but said he would take X rays in the morning — "Be in my office at nine." He gave me a shot to carry me through the performance, presented me with two pills in the event I had any sudden pain, and called the drugstore to send up a heavy surgical belt — actually a jockstrap with a wide belt. He suggested that as soon as the play was over I come back, "get into bed, and take those two capsules." After all that he reminded me to be in his office at nine and concluded by saying, "You're going to be laid up for at least a week."

Miriam ordered a car to pilot us to the Waldorf and to wait for us at 10:00 P.M., our estimated departure time.

Everyone told me the play was good, that I was very effective, that they laughed and thrilled at the right places. I listened to part of what

Abba Eban had to say, then I thanked my cast, and Miriam and I ducked out.

I gingerly worked my way into bed, stretched out, and took the pills Marek had suggested. They must have been powerful. Miriam insists and I agree that when I take a strong drug, before slipping into unconsciousness I go into a long speech on any subject that may trip into my mind. That night, Miriam said I gave a long disquisition on death, which disturbed her until I began to feel sorry for little birds who drowned in the sea — then she patted my head and I was out until eight in the morning.

My visit to Dr. Marek reaffirmed that I had no fracture, but I had belabored my disk. He ordered me to go to bed. He would send someone to measure me for a brace for my back, and told me to use a stout cane whenever I got out of bed. But first, "Stay in bed. Whatever has to be done — get people to come to you." He insisted that if I didn't do as he said I'd have big trouble — but if I obeyed his orders I'd be able to attend rehearsals, "*if* they get a reclining chair or a hospital bed for you to rest in while you watch."

For the next few days Vinnie paid his visits and we went over each cut and each additional word that Vinnie felt would clarify a thought. We discussed every reading and every move. He reported that Ralph was working at the rehab hospital and amazing everyone with his dedication and quick responses.

Vinnie wanted a cast reading before he went into rehearsal — wanted me to hear the entire script and check all the actors — changes could be made within five days if someone seemed not to fit in. Since I couldn't go to the theater for the first few days, the company came to me. On cue I shuffled out, on my stout cane, a sad and helpless picture, took my place on the couch, and listened as the cast read the play to me. They all sounded first-rate. I had a feeling that something should be added but I didn't know what or where.

Lawrence, Armina, and Terry were at hand and they were delighted. They stayed on after Vinnie and the cast departed for the theater, and reported there were good advance sales at the box offices in New Haven, Boston, and Philadelphia.

Lawrence had some reservations and concerns about the ads. He felt there might be resistance to the play because people might think it political. He wanted to add a line, "Not a political play." I thought that was a silly idea. I had drawn the first sketch for the *Campobello* ad of FDR in white slacks, a cardigan, and a white canvas hat, standing with a cigarette in his mouth and Fala crouched at his feet. An artist developed

Nunnally Johnson at Montecatini, holding his mug of mineral water and poised as if to run for cover

The pose that landed Ralph on the cover of Life

THE THEATRE GUILD and DORE SCHARY
PRESENT

RALPH BELLAMY
IN

SUNRISE AT CAMPOBELLO
BY **DORE SCHARY**

MARY FICKETT   HENRY JONES
ANNE SEYMOUR
AND
ALAN BUNCE

Directed by **VINCENT J. DONEHUE**

Settings & Lighting by **RALPH ALSWANG** · Costumes by **VIRGINIA VOLLAND**

Well, our names didn't get up in lights, but Vincent Donehue and I were more than satisfied with the billing

Vinnie giving the cast of Campobello *the final words for the "gallop" on opening night in New York . . . a break for food, then "Curtain going up"*

Mrs. R. chose to sit in the second row from the back on opening night. She said, "I want them to look at the play and not at me."

In Ralph's dressing room he and I enjoyed that embrace after the final curtain. We both knew we had a hit.

the sketch into an effective ad that became the play's logo and gave a sense of the time before FDR's presidency. I argued against Lawrence's notion and suggested instead the line, which we used, "The story of FDR during the years 1920 to 1924."

When everyone had gone, I tried to concentrate and learn what I felt was missing in the play. Instead of discovering it, I returned to bed and fell asleep . . . but awoke within the hour with severe pain. Dr. Marek sent over some additional painkillers, which dulled my aching back but made me feel punchy. I decided to cut down on the pills and keep my head on straight. In the late afternoon, trying to visualize what might have gone on at rehearsal, I thought I discovered what was missing in the play. It needed an introductory scene in the first act that would show FDR in action as a vigorous Washington politician, finishing up his chores as assistant secretary of the navy, packing up his bags for his vacation at Campobello. Quickly I mapped out a scene; it was ready to sketch out for Vinnie when he came to the apartment after rehearsals to report that all was well. He had a few more suggestions for cuts and felt that the first scene at Campobello was a bit of a problem, but he'd rather discuss that once I came to the theater and saw it in motion. He also reported that Bellamy would likely know his entire part, line perfect, within another day or two. "He's fabulous," Vinnie said, "absolutely fabulous."

When we finished fixing up the few holes that needed darning, I sprang my idea for the new added scene. Vinnie liked it very much, I believed it would start the play on a more active note. I promised he'd have it in hand within a couple of days.

One Saturday evening cousins Saul and Hope showed up with a complete hot dinner. I had to eat lying almost supine. The food was good but I couldn't get much of it down where it belonged. However, it was good of them to show up with a CARE package and typically thoughtful.

Vinnie came to the apartment each day after rehearsals with his clear, precise observations. Within an hour I'd make notes on what had to be altered — often I completed some of them while Vinnie was still at hand so that he could put them into work the following day.

Before the first week of rehearsals ended Dr. Marek came to visit in answer to my ultimatum that I would no longer stay in bed and that I was going to get to the rehearsals if I had to travel by ambulance. After his examination he surrendered, provided I'd wear the brace, use the cane, get a Barcalounger chair in the theater, and go to and come from the theater in a limousine. That was an expensive routine but certainly a nice way to work. The experience gave me a permanent daydream — to travel around New York, uptown-downtown-crosstown, in a limo — never to depend on dirty cabs or buses or steamy subways.

My colleagues at the Theatre Guild rented a Barcalounger, which was set up in an aisle, and on the last day of the first week I hobbled into the theater and received a rousing welcome. I accepted with grace by saying, "I've come here to see just exactly how you have loused up my play."

Stretched out in the lounge chair, I had the wondrous experience shared by every playwright — a first complete run-through. At the end I greeted the players with my usual stoicism — tears and thanks.

The day before I had sent typewritten copies of the new opening scene to Lawrence, Armina, and Terry Helburn. Lawrence, after the run-through, said he'd like to ride home with me, and on the way he told me that he did not believe it was necessary to add anything to the play. I disagreed and asked to have Alswang design the setting — a room in a Washington hotel — and said that I was going to have Vinnie put the first scene into rehearsal.

"You're making a mistake," Lawrence warned me.

But we went ahead and at the end of the second week the scene was in and our run-throughs were looking tighter and sharper.

At the end of the third week, with Lawrence still muttering and carping about the scene in question, I asked Moss to come take a look at the play. He had not read the script, had not asked to; as a matter of fact he had said he could judge better once he saw the play on its feet.

So here it was — on its feet.

At the end, the few people, guests of the management, applauded. Moss and I walked to the rear of the theater.

Moss said, "I've only three things to say. One, it is absolutely wonderful. Two, the opening scene is a waste of time — I urge you to cut it. Three, isn't it possible for the audience to hear FDR speak at the end of the play? I think they will be disappointed if they don't."

I thanked Moss for his opinion. By now Lawrence had joined us and was eager to know Moss's reaction. Moss told him. Lawrence was delighted that Moss shared his judgment of the scene, which by now was also losing my own enthusiasm. "Okay, Lawrence, the scene goes. I'll tell Vinnie to consign it to the deep six." (The scene disappeared with no regrets from Vinnie or Ralph, who admitted they had never truly liked it but had assumed I'd reach the decision on the road.)

However, I disagreed with Moss about the ending, which showed what actually had happened in 1924 at the convention: the delegates, having heard of FDR's paralysis and his long recovery spell, had expected to see a withered, helpless cripple; instead they saw a big, strong man lift himself out of his wheelchair, take his crutches, and with a tight grin walk to the rostrum, quickly hand his crutches to his son Jimmy, and stand erect, a bronzed, handsome figure with an infectious, proud, warm smile and his right hand raised on high in triumphant wave as he accepted an astounding ten-minute ovation from the delegates, who had stood up in tribute to the phoenix that had risen from the ashes.

I added, "FDR was not able to quiet them during those ten minutes. If this play works I believe the audience will react almost as the delegates did to FDR in 1924. If they don't — I believe the play is flat and will be a failure."

This time Lawrence sided with me.

Moss said, "I can't get to New Haven for the opening but call me and tell me how it went. I pray I'll be wrong."

The last run-throughs went well and the costumes properly looked like the 1920s, but when I saw the sets being put up in New Haven, the lights being hung, I got a sinking feeling they'd never be ready for the opening performance.

But they were ready. I limped to the rear of the theater and stood there braced by my cane as the show sped along with only a few fluffs and a dull spot in Act II, Scene 2, when FDR tells his daughter a story with a moral that lacked clarity, spice, and lay like a lump of clay. As Act III raced along I waited with hurried pulse for the end and for the audience reaction. Moss's prayer was answered — he was wrong. The audience cheered — there were bravos and tears and yells.

I went backstage to talk to the cast and crew. It became a custom each night during the tryouts. I thanked them — they thanked me. Kisses, hugs, embraces, handshakes were expressions of joy along with watery eyes and trembling chins.

Later, Vinnie, Lawrence, Armina (Terry was ill and couldn't attend), Walter, Warren Caro (than an executive with the Guild, now an executive with the Shubert organization, always a good friend) and I gathered in one of the suites at the old Taft Hotel — a wretched hostelry once well described as looking like "a discarded set from a flop that never made it past New Haven." We exchanged notes. There was general agreement that the show was going to be successful, but I knew I had to get a better story for Ralph in the second scene of Act II. There was some criticism that Anne Seymour was a little too sharp and angry as Sara

Delano, but Vinnie and I both felt she could be brought into harmony with the others after a few performances. No, I told Lawrence, I would not approve of replacing her.

The meeting broke up and I called Moss. When he answered the phone he knew it was me. "Well, Butch," he said, "tell me." I told him. He was delighted. I assured him he'd have tickets for opening night in New York. I called Lil in California and gave her the happy words. Called the kids and promised they'd have enough to eat for the next year or two. Called Lenny and Allen and asked them to pass the word around.

The first newspaper review in the morning appeared in the Hartford *Courant*. In essence its reviewer said, "Mr. Schary should go back to writing 'B' pictures in California. The play is dreadful, devoid of drama, wit and talent." The notice went downhill from there.

My joy crumbled like a jigsaw puzzle falling off a table. I was distraught.

Though others told me not to pay attention to the review, I could do nothing but pay attention.

My back hurt, my spirits flagged, I couldn't eat, and I felt too embarrassed to walk into the theater. But Lawrence, with his jaunty fedora, his confident air, sauntered into my room and announced that the *Variety* notice was going to be excellent, calling it a hit. He reassured me that very few people in New York read the Hartford *Courant*. I wondered how many people in Hartford read *Variety*.

But, cheered up, I thanked Lawrence, told him I was going to rest and try to cook up a better yarn for Bellamy. I stretched out in bed next to Miriam, who, after the usual Taft Hotel breakfast of soggy toast, tepid strong coffee, stiff fried eggs, and dried grapefruit, had gone back to sleep.

I went over old stories, Aesop's fables, dirty jokes that could be cleaned up, folktales, I thought of punch lines — nothing happened. I went to old Jewish fables — the man who took his horse to Minsk, the wise men (fools) of Chelm, and then I remembered — happily I remembered — the story of the rabbi who was visited by one of his congregation who told him she was going crazy — her children, her husband, his mother, his father, her brother were driving her mad with the loud continual noise in their little house. The rabbi suggested she take her chickens and geese into the house. When she did that with no relief, he told her to take her lambs in; then when that didn't work, told her to take ducks into the house; and when that failed, he told her take her horse into the house. When she returned, frantic with unhappiness, he then said, "Now, go home and take your horse, the ducks, the lambs, and your chickens and your geese and run them all out of the house and come back and tell me what happened." The lady returned, grateful. "Thank you, Rabbi, now it's so wonderfully quiet in the house."

I changed the locale from Russia to upstate New York, the rabbi became a wise old farmer, the lady a farmer's wife. The Jewish intonations became upstate farm idiom.

When I handed it to Ralph later that day he loved it. He said he'd have it ready for the opening in Boston. I said I'd need another day to polish and get it right. Ralph merely said, "We'll open with it in Boston." Vinnie nodded his head, "Yes."

(Later on, after the opening, whenever I watched from the rear of the house I could always tell who the Jews in the audience were; as the story would be half over they would turn to each other and smile, recognizing the migration from Russia to the Adirondacks.)

In Boston Vinnie rehearsed in a hired hall while the Colonial Theatre was being hung with the lights and scenery. Ralph had the story down cold. The cast were loose and happy — like a champion baseball team.

When opening night came our audience, mostly black-tied and beautifully gowned, swept in, and the house manager whispered to me, "Most of these opening-nighters are hard-nosed Republicans. Don't let them get you down."

I was determined this night to see the show from an audience perspective. Miriam and I sat in the fifth row on the aisle. No one in the vicinity knew me. The curtain rose, the audience pit-pattered their hands for a fraction of a second. The play began.

The first scene ambled on its way interrupted only by a mild reception as Bellamy made his entrance. Some laughs came from the balcony but seemed to fade away as most of the audience showed no jubilation. Indifference or disinterest is contagious in the theater and it was crystal clear that the main body of the orchestra was spreading its disinterest with the effectiveness of Typhoid Mary.

At the end of the scene there was a polite acknowledgment or a grateful hand that *that* was over — I couldn't tell which. Scene 2 breezed along, the company behaving as if the audience were loving them instead of sending up frostbite. Very little applause greeted the end of the scene. The third scene went its merry way, the company still doing their job as if they had made up their minds that Vinnie, Lawrence, Armina, and I were the only ones in the audience and they knew *we* loved it. Act I ended — there was a good hand from the balcony and some scattered enthusiasm in the orchestra. A couple next to Miriam and me stood up and a man, in a loud voice, called to others who had come with them — "Let's get out of here — I had enough of that son of a bitch when he was alive." As he walked out Miriam put one foot in his path and he stumbled but did say, "Excuse me." I did nothing — said nothing. I was an icicle. The play was a frost. We were dead.

Posting Miriam in the front lobby to catch snatches of comment, I went backstage to buoy up the cast, but instead they greeted me with words of encouragement. Ralph said, "Cheer up, m'boy. We'll get them in the second act."

The second act began minus some twelve couples in seats down front who had departed with complaints to the theater management ranging from "extremely dull" to "outrageous lies." My stomach was somewhere in my lower bowel, my heart was in my mouth, and I was zero cold. However, the laughs seemed sturdier; and when the moment came when FDR demonstrated how he had learned to crawl and made his exit with only the bottoms of his shoes showing, not even scuffed as they would have been had he ever walked in them, the audience, moved by the helplessness and yet simple courage of the man, suddenly broke into a loud roar of applause. I looked around and noticed women reaching for handkerchiefs and men wiping their eyes. The idea of the untouched soles of the shoes was Ralph's. He was right too about the second act; from that moment on the audience was on our side, rooting for us, enjoying the play, expressing their feelings with bursts of appreciation. It was as if the departure of those twelve couples had released the pent-up emotions of the rest of the audience. As the curtain descended on FDR trying to stand on his crutches, there was a storm of an ovation. I kissed Miriam and rushed backstage. My temperature went to normal. I hustled into Ralph's room, and as I entered he said, "I told you we'd get them."

The third act played like firecrackers and Roman candles and as the play ended the theater was a sea of emotion. People got to their feet applauding, calling "Bravo," crying and smiling at the same time, and then — then I knew — unless the scenery collapsed, the cast went berserk, or Ralph lost his voice — we'd be going into New York as an odds-on favorite.

The audience hung around — a good sign. Armina and Lawrence were circulating in the lobby, listening for comments. Vinnie was backstage. Miriam and I joined him. There was a pandemonium of delight.

The pre- and postperformance routines took form during the two weeks in Boston. Ralph had his "family" join him onstage each performance five minutes before curtain time. They would ad-lib as a family.

It brought a consistency to the performances and a relationship between them that was close and affectionate. After each show Vinnie and I would join the company onstage while the curtain remained down and simply burble some notes of praise or criticism, make slight cuts or add a few extra words. There was nothing else to do except to keep the performance at what Vinnie called "a warm pace."

The notices in Boston were wonderful. Elliot Norton, the respected dean of the New England critics and most appreciated by New York theater people, loaded us with praise, identifying the play in his first paragraph:

In the long range of the American drama, there have been few really great plays. "Sunrise at Campobello," by Dore Schary, is one of the few great ones. Simple, unpretentious, warm, good-humored and heroic it is touched with grandeur and even magnificence and it makes the theatre once again a place of glory.

He closed his review with these words:

. . . and there is a scene of final glory, in which the acting, the staging and all the elements of the theatre are so magically and perfectly fused that it will likely remain forever fixed in the minds of the opening night audience. Not once in a decade does the theatre reach such a moment of glory as this climax of this great play.

We sold out in Boston and as word filtered down to New York and Philadelphia, lines formed at the box office. When we got to Philly, the performances had moved from "a warm pace" to Vinnie's "fast trot" — he was reserving "the gallop" until the preview shows in New York. Philadelphia was like Boston. But there was one sad note. I called my sister, Lil, who was to have come to New York for the opening, and learned that she had fallen and broken her hip. That fall, unknown to us, was the first of a series of illnesses that weakened her and altered her joyous personality. My friends in California were reading the news in the trade papers and Walter Reilly was sending them the out-of-town notices. I kept the nasty one from the Hartford *Courant* in my wallet just to keep my ego on an even keel.

When we arrived in New York we had to wait until the sets and lights were brought in. Rehearsals — easy ones because Vinnie was not ready for the full gallop — were held in the lounges below the orchestra. There was the exchange of gifts, and being so near to opening night I wanted to tell everyone what I felt. Having written it out, I read it to the company. Some of it dealt with what I had learned from Vinnie, the Langners and Terry, the cast, the crew, and my own reactions. After the opening paragraphs, which described our fears and responsibilities to each other and to our audiences, I spoke of the challenge facing us:

Less than a week from now we face the opening night crowd in New York. We have had our skirmishes in New Haven, Boston and Philadelphia — we have other skirmishes ahead on previews Tuesday and Wednesday — but Thursday is the payoff. That's when all of us put everything on the table and roll for the big seven.

There isn't one of us, young or seamy, veteran or novice, who isn't touched by the excitement ahead of us (as I write this, my pulse is quicker and my hand faster as I think of that night) — and because of it, all of you will have to work that much harder and truer. And then, if the ball bounces our way, you must work even harder. Plays have opened big and skidded downhill because of an indifference and complacency that stalked the stage after opening night. An actor should give as much as he can at each show and if he doesn't, he is shortchanging the customers as surely as if he were picking their pockets.

Then I went into detail, complimenting each performer, star or bit player or understudy, and adding a word of observation regarding their characterizations. I concluded with a prayer:

In my religion there are prayers of thanks for all things — when we see a sunset or a rain, or a beautiful tree, or when we drink water, eat food, or awake, or go to sleep, or when we meet a good man or woman. Prayers for everything. And there is a prayer — a catch-all prayer of thanks for anything we may miss. In Hebrew it is "Baruch Atah Adonai Elohainu Melech H'Olam, Ha 'Tov Ha' Ma' Teev" — which means: "Blessed be the Lord our God, King of the Universe, He Who is good and brings goodness."
We have shared good so far.
For that let us be thankful.
Let us all do what we can to help make the future good.
With love and appreciation. Thank you.

In New York there was a preview on Tuesday, January 28, and a benefit show for the Nassau County Democratic party on Wednesday the twenty-ninth. Rockets and machine-gun fire. This was FDR country and the politicos had a ball. After the third-act curtain, Governor Harriman held up his hands to halt the applause and asked me to come to his box.

Another wave. I got there, my cane keeping me from running but helping me from falling. I had to say something — and fortunately remembered what Eddie Lasker had wired me. I rewrote it a tiny bit: "Well, all I can say is that you are much easier to please than a board of directors." That "in" audience got the point and greeted it with pleasure.

The opening-night party was to be hosted by Oscar Chapman, former secretary of the interior, who had taken the top floor of the Sherry-Netherland for an elegant postperformance to-do. As I dressed for the trip to the theater, I thanked the Lord. Nine months before I had told the press I planned to open the play on the next anniversary of FDR's birth. I had made it. It was January 30, 1958 — the seventy-sixth year of his birth — not quite thirteen years after his death — long before the revisionists launched their attacks and some twenty-one years before other historians would revise the revisionist literature.

The audience included Mrs. Roosevelt and all the Roosevelt children and their families, Adlai Stevenson, Margaret Truman Daniels and Clifton Daniels, John F. Kennedy, Isadore Lubin, Sam and Mrs. Roseman, Mayor and Mrs. Wagner, Congressman Sam Rayburn, Billy Rose, Moss and Kitty, Ben Cohen, Senator and Mrs. Lehman, Lew and Edie Wasserman, the Fitelsons and the Altmans and the Mayers. And naturally, Fred Marek — just in case I fell on my back.

Everything came together — weather, performance, traffic, publicity, notices — it was a jamboree. The notices ranged from great to good. Perhaps the one I enjoyed the most was John Chapman's, in the New York *Daily News*. He concluded his rave review by writing, " 'Sunrise at Campobello' is an altogether lovely work for the theatre — and this notice has been written by a black Republican who has hated much of what FDR did and tried to do."

Miriam and I had gambled a year of our lives and a large bowl of cash. Lucky seven. It was strawberries and cream, chocolate sundaes, banana splits, American Beauty roses, bright sun, full moon.

It took time to absorb all the good things that tumbled into my arms — time to think things out.

But — I came to understand.

My life had till then been full of events — sad and glad, rich and poor — success and failure, love and dislike, births and deaths. Soon Jill, in April, was to present us with our first grandchild.

The years in Hollywood had, in Samuel Johnson's words, been a "heyday: an expression of frolick and exultation, and sometimes of wonder." I had, I believed, seen the best of the heyday — the laughs, the art,

[*366*]

the motivation, position, honors, satisfactions. It had been right for me to turn a corner and head away from Hollywood. I had seen it all.

Now, in New York, I had another time of frolick, exultation, and certainly of wonder. We would move to New York, to a new time, a new life; there would be high tides and shallows, blue days and heydays for Miriam, the children and their families, and for me. It was all waiting — all yet unknown — all the good — all the bad. Everything was in the hands of the Lord. That was all right with me.

Waldorf Conference Statement

Members of the Association of Motion Picture Producers deplore the action of the ten Hollywood men who have been cited for contempt of the House of Representatives. We do not desire to pre-judge their legal rights, but their actions have been a disservice to their employers and have impaired their usefulness to the industry.

We will forthwith discharge or suspend without compensation those in our employ and we will not re-employ any of the ten until such time as he is acquitted or has purged himself of contempt and declares under oath that he is not a Communist.

On the broader issue of alleged subversive and disloyal elements in Hollywood, our members are likewise prepared to take positive action.

We will not knowingly employ a Communist or a member of any party or group which advocates the overthrow of the Government of the United States by force or by any illegal or unconstitutional methods.

In pursuing this policy, we are not going to be swayed by hysteria or intimidation from any source. We are frank to recognize that such a policy involves dangers and risks. There is the danger of hurting innocent people. There is the risk of creating an atmosphere of fear. Creative work at its best cannot be carried on in an atmosphere of fear. We will guard against this danger, this risk, this fear.

To this end we will invite the Hollywood talent guilds to work with us to eliminate any subversives; to protect the innocent; and to safeguard free speech and a free screen wherever threatened.

The absence of a national policy, established by Congress with respect to the employment of Communists in private industry, makes our task difficult. Ours is a nation of laws. We request Congress to enact legislation to assist American industry to rid itself of subversive, disloyal elements.

Nothing subversive or un-American has appeared on the screen. Nor can any number of Hollywood investigations obscure the patriotic services of the 30,000 Americans employed in Hollywood who have given our Government invaluable aid in war and peace.

Filmography

To include the names of all the writers, producers, directors, cameramen, actors, editors, designers who worked on the films listed would be to fill a small book. However, I have already mentioned many men and women involved in the making of the films listed. Complete lists of everyone concerned are available in scores of reference books.

Some of the pictures were dismal failures, others quite forgettable, some were good or very good. A respectable number were exceptional, and a few were quite brilliant and are not only remembered by many observers who saw them when they were first released but have been subsequently embraced by new viewers who first see them as they appear in theatrical revivals or on TV.

My contributions to the films enumerated were in many cases maximal, other times minimal; for some I provided a guiding hand or appropriate criticism, to others I contributed misguided advice. I believed many of them were doomed to failure. I balanced sorry appraisal by believing that many of them were slated for shining success. I was, in some instances, wrong on both counts.

Perhaps a goodly number of them would have been made without my being there; however, I am satisfied that many of them would not have been made if I had not been there to plead, push, and convince others that they had to be made. Wrong I was — and right I was. I am not embarrassed by the record.

Noted are films I wrote, or produced, or supervised as executive in charge of production or as head of a studio. The letters are keys to my relationship to each film: (SP) screenplay, (OS) original story, (PRO) production, (EX) executive in supervisory capacity, (DIR) director.

Berlin Express
I Remember Mama
Sister Kenny
Lady Luck
Nocturne
The Locket
Code of the West
They Won't Believe Me
Desperate
Thunder Mountain
Riff Raff
Nightsong
Return of the Badmen
Race Street
Mystery in Mexico
Tycoon
Fort Apache
Rachel and the Stranger
Station West
Bodyguard
Design for Death
Every Girl Should Be Married
A Woman's Secret
Mourning Becomes Electra
Clay Pigeon
Adventure in Baltimore
The Rustlers
Roughshod
Tall in the Saddle
The Velvet Touch
Easy Living
Dangerous Profession
Out of the Past

AUGUST 1948 TO DECEMBER 1956 —
MGM
(THOSE PICTURES WHICH WERE PER-
SONAL PRODUCTIONS ARE INDICATED BY
PRO. ALL OTHERS WERE UNDER MY
EXECUTIVE SUPERVISION.)

Act of Violence
The Three Musketeers
Easter Parade

Edward, My Son
Black Hand
Caught
The Stratton Story
The Barkleys of Broadway
The Secret Garden
Big Jack
The Great Sinner
That Forsyte Woman
In the Good Old Summertime
Neptune's Daughter
Scene of the Crime
Border Incident
The Red Danube
Malaya
Battleground   PRO
Tension
Challenge to Lassie
Take Me Out to the Ball Game
On the Town
The Yellow Cab Man
The Doctor and the Girl
Side Street
East Side, West Side
Conspirator
Shadow on the Wall
Any Number Can Play
Intruder in the Dust
Madame Bovary
Adam's Rib
Key to the City
That Midnight Kiss
Nancy Goes to Rio
Ambush
Please Believe Me
Stars in My Crown
Watch the Birdie
The Big Hangover
The Skipper Surprised His Wife
The Magnificent Yankee
Crisis
Father of the Bride
The Reformer and the Redhead
Annie Get Your Gun

The Toast of New Orleans
Three Little Words
Grounds for Marriage
Two Weeks with Love
Duchess of Idaho
Kim
Cause for Alarm
Teresa
Devil's Doorway
The Outriders
King Solomon's Mines
Dial 1119
Right Cross
Mrs. O'Malley and Mr. Malone
Vengeance Valley
Mystery Street
The Happy Years
To Please a Lady
The Next Voice You Hear   PRO
The Miniver Story
A Life of Her Own
Pagan Love Song
Three Guys Named Mike
Summer Stock
Royal Wedding
The Asphalt Jungle
A Lady Without a Passport
Father's Little Dividend
Lone Star
Westward the Women   PRO
Soldiers Three
The Wild North
Home Town Story
The Red Badge of Courage
Callaway Went Thataway
It's a Big Country
The Light Touch
Go for Broke!   PRO
Invitation
Shadow in the Sky
Just This Once
Too Young to Kiss
The Painted Hills

No Questions Asked
Night into Morning
Mr. Imperium
Strictly Dishonorable
Across the Wide Missouri
Texas Carnival
Angels in the Outfield
The Tall Target
Inside Straight
Bannerline
Rich, Young and Pretty
The Man with a Cloak
Calling Bulldog Drummond
The People Against O'Hara
The Law and the Lady
Kind Lady
The Strip
Quo Vadis?
The Belle of New York
The Great Caruso
Love Is Better Than Ever
An American in Paris
Show Boat
Excuse My Dust
The Sellout
The Unknown Man
Singin' in the Rain
I Love Melvin
The Merry Widow
Skirts Ahoy!
Lovely to Look At
Everything I Have Is Yours
Small Town Girl
Plymouth Adventure   PRO
Battle Circus
Scaramouche
Pat and Mike
Sombrero
Glory Alley
Holiday for Sinners
Young Man with Ideas
Talk about a Stranger
Carbine Williams

Above and Beyond
Because You're Mine
Million Dollar Mermaid
The Prisoner of Zenda
The Girl in White
The Clown
Lili
Washington Story   PRO
Sky Full of Moon
You for Me
Desperate Search
The Bad and the Beautiful
The Hour of 13
Jeopardy
Time Bomb
Rogues March
Ivanhoe
When in Rome
Confidentially Connie
Fearless Fagan
My Man and I
The Naked Spur
The Devil Makes Three
Apache War Smoke
Julius Caesar
The Band Wagon
The Story of Three Loves
Never Let Me Go
Mogambo
The Girl Who Had Everything
The Long, Long Trailer
Give a Girl a Break
Bright Road
Easy to Love
Take the High Ground   PRO
Young Bess
The Affairs of Dobie Gillis
Main Street to Broadway
All the Brothers Were Valiant
The Actress
Fast Company
Big Leaguer
Kiss Me, Kate

Knights of the Round Table
Half a Hero
Code Two
Arena
Cry of the Hunted
Ride, Vaquero
Torch Song
Remains to Be Seen
Saadia
Dangerous When Wet
Escape from Fort Bravo
Latin Lovers
Scandal at Scourie
A Slight Case of Larceny
Dream Wife   PRO
The Great Diamond Robbery
Tennessee Champ
Gypsy Colt
Seven Brides for Seven Brothers
Prisoner of War
Men of the Fighting Lady
Flame and the Flesh
Seagulls over Sorrento
Betrayed
Her Twelve Men
Valley of the Kings
Rogue Cop
Jupiter's Darling
The Glass Slipper
Many Rivers to Cross
The Last Time I Saw Paris
Rhapsody
Bad Day at Black Rock   PRO
Green Fire
Rose Marie
The Student Prince
Beau Brummel
Executive Suite
Brigadoon
Athena
Deep in My Heart
Blackboard Jungle
The Prodigal

Moonfleet Trial
Hit the Deck
It's Always Fair Weather
Love Me or Leave Me
Quentin Durward
Guys and Dolls
Meet Me in Las Vegas
The Tender Trap
Forever Darling
Bedevilled
Interrupted Melody
Kismet
I'll Cry Tomorrow
Diane
The Cobweb
The Last Hunt   PRO
The King's Thief
The Scarlet Coat
The Marauders
It's a Dog's Life
Ransom
The Swan   PRO
Tribute to a Badman
Lust for Life
The Rack
The Catered Affair
Slander
The Barretts of Wimpole Street
Invitation to the Dance
Gaby
These Wilder Years

The Great American Pastime
Hot Summer Night
Julie
Tea and Sympathy
The Opposite Sex
The Power and the Prize
The Wings of Eagles
Forbidden Planet
Bhowani Junction
The Fastest Gun Alive
Somebody Up There Likes Me
Edge of the City
The Happy Road
High Society
The Teahouse of the August Moon
The Man in the Sky
Ten Thousand Bedrooms
Raintree County
Designing Woman   PRO
I Accuse!
The Vintage
Something of Value
Les Girls

1958—POST MGM

Lonelyhearts   PRO/SP
Sunrise at Campobello   PRO/OS/SP
Act One   SP/PRO/DIR
Israel: The Right to Be (Documentary)   PRO/SP

Index

Page numbers in italics indicate photographs.

[*379*]

[*381*]